W0263074

Informatik – Fachberichte

Band 5: GI – 6. Jahrestagung. Proceedings 1976. Herausgegeben von
E. J. Neuhold. X, 474 Seiten. 1976.

Band 6: B. Schmidt, GPSS-FORTRAN, Version II. Einführung in die Simulation
diskreter Systeme mit Hilfe eines FORTRAN-Programmpaketes, 2. Auflage. XIII,
535 Seiten. 1978.

Band 7: GMR–GI–GfK. Fachtagung Prozessrechner 1977. Herausgegeben von
G. Schmidt. XIII, 524 Seiten. 1977.

Band 8: Digitale Bildverarbeitung/Digital Image Processing. GI/NTG Fachtagung,
München, März 1977. Herausgegeben von H.-H. Nagel. XI, 328 Seiten. 1977.

Band 9: Modelle für Rechensysteme. Workshop 1977. Herausgegeben von
P. P. Spies. VI, 297 Seiten. 1977.

Band 10: GI – 7. Jahrestagung. Proceedings 1977. Herausgegeben von H. J. Schneider.
IX, 214 Seiten. 1977.

Band 11: Methoden der Informatik für Rechnerunterstütztes Entwerfen und
Konstruieren, GI-Fachtagung, München, 1977. Herausgegeben von R. Gnatz und
K. Samelson. VIII, 327 Seiten. 1977.

Band 12: Programmiersprachen. 5. Fachtagung der GI, Braunschweig, 1978.
Herausgegeben von Klaus Alber. VI, 179 Seiten. 1978.

Band 13: W. Steinmüller, L. Ermer, W. Schimmel: Datenschutz bei riskanten Systemen.
X, 244 Seiten. 1978.

Band 14: Datenbanken in Rechnernetzen mit Kleinrechnern. Fachtagung der GI,
Karlsruhe, 1978. Herausgegeben von W. Stucky und E. Holler. X, 198 Seiten. 1978.

Band 15: Organisation von Rechenzentren. Workshop der Gesellschaft für
Informatik, Göttingen, 1977. Herausgegeben von D. Wall. X, 310 Seiten. 1978.

Band 16: GI-8. Jahrestagung, Proceedings 1978. Herausgegeben von S. Schindler
und W. K. Giloi. VI, 394 Seiten. 1978.

Band 17: Bildverarbeitung und Mustererkennung. DAGM Symposium, Oberpfaffen-
hofen, 1978. Herausgegeben von E. Triendl. XIII, 385 Seiten. 1978.

Band 18: Virtuelle Maschinen. Nachbildung und Vervielfachung maschinenorientierter
Schnittstellen. GI-Arbeitsseminar, München 1979. Herausgegeben von H. J. Siegert.
X, 231 Seiten. 1979.

Band 19: GI - 9. Jahrestagung. Herausgegeben von K. H. Böhling und P. P. Spies.
XIII, 690 Seiten. 1979.

Band 20: Angewandte Szenenanalyse. DAGM Symposium, Karlsruhe 1979. Herausgegeben von J. Foith. XIII, 362 Seiten. 1979.

Band 21: Formale Modelle für Informationssysteme. Fachtagung der GI, Tutzing 1979.
Herausgegeben von H. C. Mayr und B. E. Meyer. VI, 265 Seiten. 1979.

Band 22: Kommunikation in verteilten Systemen. Workshop der Gesellschaft für
Informatik e. V.. Herausgegeben von S. Schindler und J. Schröder. VIII, 338 Seiten. 1979.

Informatik-Fachberichte

Herausgegeben von W. Brauer
im Auftrag der Gesellschaft für Informatik (GI)

22

Kommunikation in verteilten Systemen

Workshop der Gesellschaft
für Informatik e. V.

3.-4. Dezember 1979, Berlin

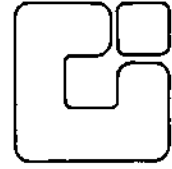

Herausgegeben von
Sigram Schindler und Jürgen C.W. Schröder

Springer-Verlag Berlin Heidelberg GmbH

Herausgeber

Prof. Dr. S. Schindler
Technische Universität Berlin
Fachbereich Informatik (20)
Ernst-Reuter-Platz 7, 19. Etage
1000 Berlin 10

Dipl.-Ing. J. C. W. Schröder
DATEL GmbH
Geschäftsbereich Danet
Bartningstr. 55
6100 Darmstadt-Kranichstein

AMS Subject Classifications (1970): 68–02
CR Subject Classifications (1974): 2.4, 3.8, 3.9, 4.3, 4.9

ISBN 978-3-540-09865-2   ISBN 978-3-642-67553-9 (eBook)
DOI 10.1007/978-3-642-67553-9

This work is subject to copyright. All rights are reserved, whether the whole or part of the
material is concerned, specifically those of translation, reprinting, re-use of illustrations,
broadcasting, reproduction by photocopying machine or similar means, and storage in
data banks.

Further, storage or utilization of the described programms on date processing installations is
forbidden without the written permission of the author.

Under § 54 of the German Copyright Law where copies are made for other than private use,
a fee is payable to the publisher, the amount of the fee to be determined by agreement
with the publisher.

© by Springer-Verlag Berlin Heidelberg 1979
Originally published by Springer-Verlag Berlin Heidelberg New York in 1979

2145/3140 - 5 4 3 2 1 0

PROGRAMMAUSSCHUSS

J.C.W. Schröder, DATEL/Danet

H. Fetzer, Nixdorf

H.G. Hegering, LRZ München

E. Holler, GfK Karlsruhe

E. Jessen, U Hamburg

P. Jilek, Siemens

J. Kanzow, BPM Bonn

E. Raubold, GMD Darmstadt

S. Schindler, TU Berlin

P. Schnupp, Softlab

C. Schünemann, IBM

O. Spaniol, U Bonn

LEITUNG DES PROGRAMMAUSSCHUSSES

Dipl.-Ing. J.C.W. Schröder, DATEL/Danet

TAGUNGSLEITUNG

Prof. Dr. S. Schindler
Technische Universität Berlin
Fachbereich Informatik (20)
Ernst-Reuter-Platz 7, 19. Etage
1000 Berlin 10

VORWORT DER HERAUSGEBER

Veranstalter des Workshops "Kommunikation in Verteilten Systemen" ist
der Fachausschuß 3/4 "Rechnerorganisation und Betriebssysteme" der Gesellschaft für Informatik e.V.

Der Workshop ist auf die derzeit dominierenden Aktivitäten im Rechner-
netzbereich hin orientiert, nämlich auf die starken Standardisierungs-
trends und die Dienste der Deutschen Bundespost im Bereich Datenfernverarbeitung. Wir haben damit die gegenwärtig zentralen Anwenderan-
liegen in den Vordergrund gestellt.

Aufgrund des starken Interesses an dem Workshop erschien es sinnvoll,
diesen Tagungsband mit allen Beiträgen herauszugeben. Wir möchten
allen Referenten dafür danken, daß sie ihren Beitrag in eine veröffent-
lichungsfähige Form gebracht haben.

Darüber hinaus möchten wir auch allen denjenigen danken, die auf andere
Weise am erfolgreichen Zustandekommen des Workshops mitgewirkt haben,
insbesondere

- dem Sprecher des Fachausschusses 3/4, Herrn E. Jessen
- den Mitgliedern des Programmausschusses
- den in der Organisation tätigen Mitarbeitern
- dem Springer-Verlag für die Bemühungen um diesen Tagungsband.

Unser ganz besondere Dank gilt Frau Mahler, Herrn Reible, Frau Shoemaker
und Frau Ruhlmann für die vielfältigen Hilfen bei der Vorbereitung der
Tagung.

Berlin, Oktober 1979

Sigram Schindler

Jürgen C.W. Schröder

INHALTSVERZEICHNIS

Der Datex-Dienst mit Paketvermittlung (DATEX-P)

Der Datenpaketvermittlungsdienst der DBP

Friedhelm Hillebrand

Bundesministerium für das Post- und Fernmeldewesen

Stand: 04.06.79

<u>Inhalt</u>

1 Bisherige Aktivitäten der DBP im Bereich Datenpaketvermittlung

1.1 Allgemeines
- Mitarbeit in Normungsgremien

- Pilotprojekte für begrenzte Anwendungen und
  Anwendergruppen
  - Zugang zu US-Datennetzen Telenet und Tymnet
  - EURONET
  - BERNET/BERPEX

1.2 Vorbereitungen für ein öffentliches Netz

- DBP-interne Untersuchungen zu Einzelfragen (Topo-
  logien und Kosten, Dienstleistungsangebot, Bedarf)
- Konsultationsrunde mit Anwendern und EDV- und
  Fernmeldeherstellern im Ausschuß/Arbeitsgruppe für
  Fragen der Datenfernverarbeitung beim Fernmelde-
  technischen Zentralamt
- Einzelgespräche/beratungen mit ernsthaft interessierten
  Anwendern
- Einzelgespräche mit Herstellern von Fernmeldeeinrichtungen

- Grundsatzentscheidung der DBP über Erweiterung des
  Datexnetzes um Datenpaketvermittlungsleistungsmerk-
  male (Datex-P)
- 2. Änderungsverordnung zur Verordnung für den Fern-
  schreib- und Datexdienst (01.01.79 in Kraft getreten)

2 Zum heutigen Dienstleistungsangebot der DBP

2.1 Heutiges Dienstleistungsangebot der DBP

2.2 Analyse des heutigen DBP-Dienstleistungsangebotes

2.1 Heutiges Dienstleistungsangebot der DBP

1 Öffentliche Wählnetze

Datex 200	842
Datex 2400	821
Datex 300, 4800, 9600	83
Öffentliches Fernsprech-Netz	26 413
Öffentliches Telex-Netz	423

2 Öffentliches Direktrufnetz

HfD	36 216

3 Posteigene Stromwege   2 938

4 Internationale Mietleitungen   378

5 Andere   625

6 Summe   68 739

Stand 01.05.79

2.2 Analyse des heutigen DBP-Dienstleistungsangebotes

2.2.1 Allgemeines
- Dienstleistungsangebot beschränkt sich grundsätzlich
  auf bit-transparente feste oder "geschaltete"
  Leitungen
- Kompatibilität zwischen verschiedenartigen DEE
  nur auf physikalischer Ebene gewährleistet

2.2.2 Zum Direktruf-Netz

- Ziele
  - Liberalisierung der Benutzungsbedingungen
    zur Förderung der Datenfernverarbeitung
    Verschiedene Benutzer an beiden Leitungs-
    enden
  - Verbindung einer HfD-DEE mit anderen öffent-
    lichen Netzen
  - Zulassung einer begrenzten Vermittlung in der
    DEE

- Offene Probleme
  - Nur relativ großer Benutzer kann aus
    Roh-Dienstleistungen der DBP und privaten
    "value added"-Funktionen vermitteltes Netz
    bauen
  - Inkompatibilität der so entstandenen Netze
  - Wünsche der Anwender nach unbegrenzten
    Verkehrsmöglichkeiten.

3 Der Datex-P-Dienst als Erweiterung des DBP-Angebotes im Bereich der Dateldienste

3.1 Allgemeines zur Datenpaketvermittlung

3.2 Zusammenarbeit mit anderen öffentlichen Netzen

3.3 Ziele zum Datex-P-Dienstleistungsangebot

3.4 Überblick über Dienstleistungsangebot

3.5 Gebühren

3.6 Weiteres Vorgehen

3.1 Allgemeines zur Datenpaketvermittlung

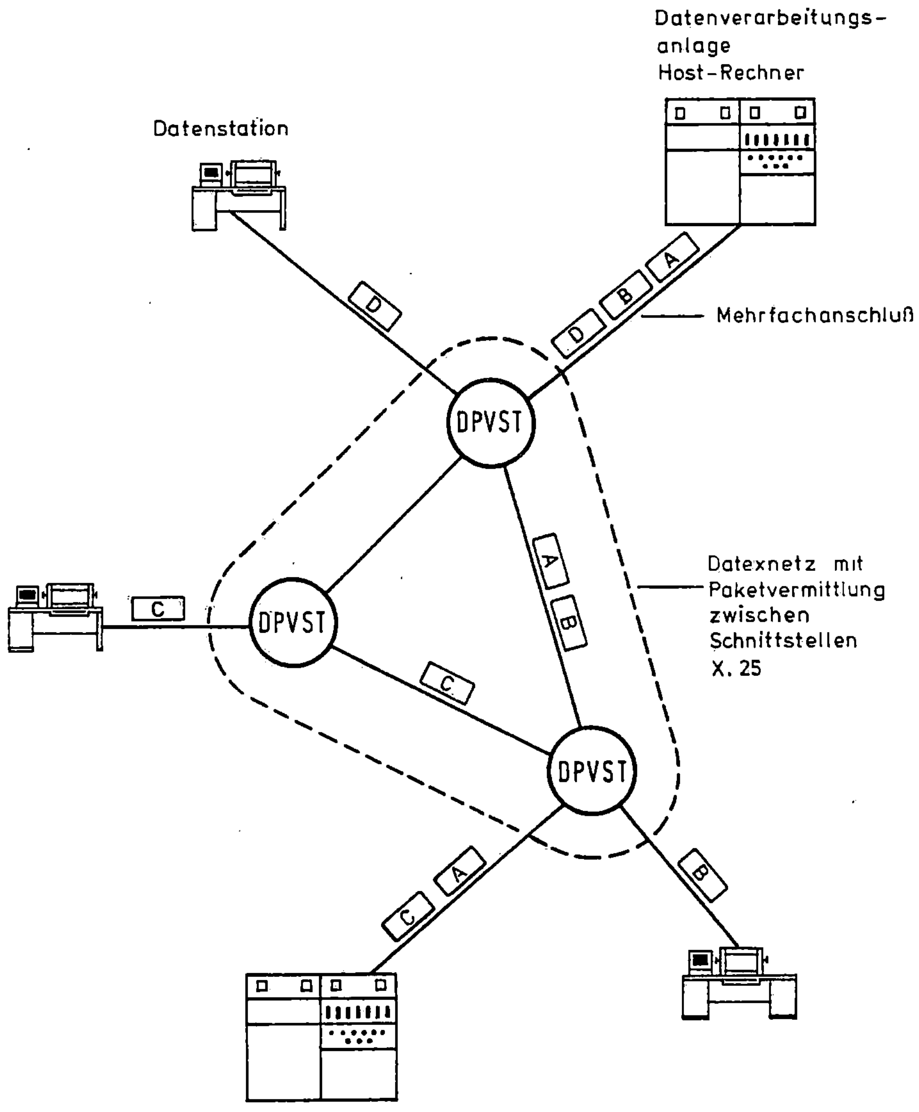

X Paket der virtuellen Verbindung
DPVST Paketvermittelte Datexvermittlungsstelle

Haupteigenschaften Datenpaketvermittlungstechnik

- Basissystem
  - Speichervermittlung
  - Integration Vermittlungs- und Übertragungstechnik
  - Integriertes statistisches Multiplexverfahren auf Anschluß- und Verbindungsleitungen
  - Dynamische Betriebsmittelzuteilung
  - Geschwindigkeitswandlung auf Anschluß- und Verbindungsleitungen
  - Verbesserte Nutzung von Netzressourcen

- Ergänzungsmöglichkeiten
  - Codewandlung
  - Prozedurwandlung
  - Nachrichtenvermittlung

Datenübermittlungsprotokolle

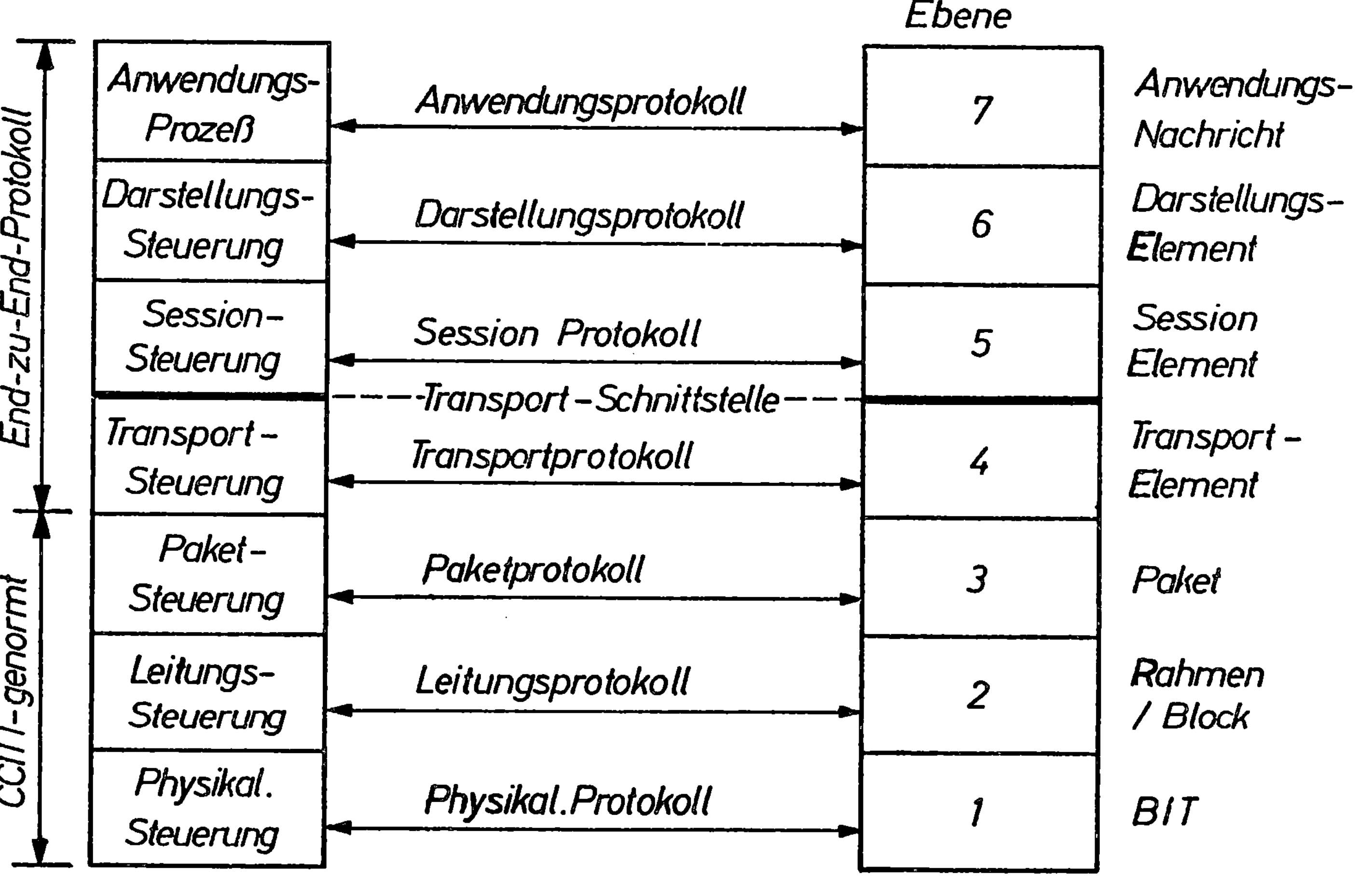

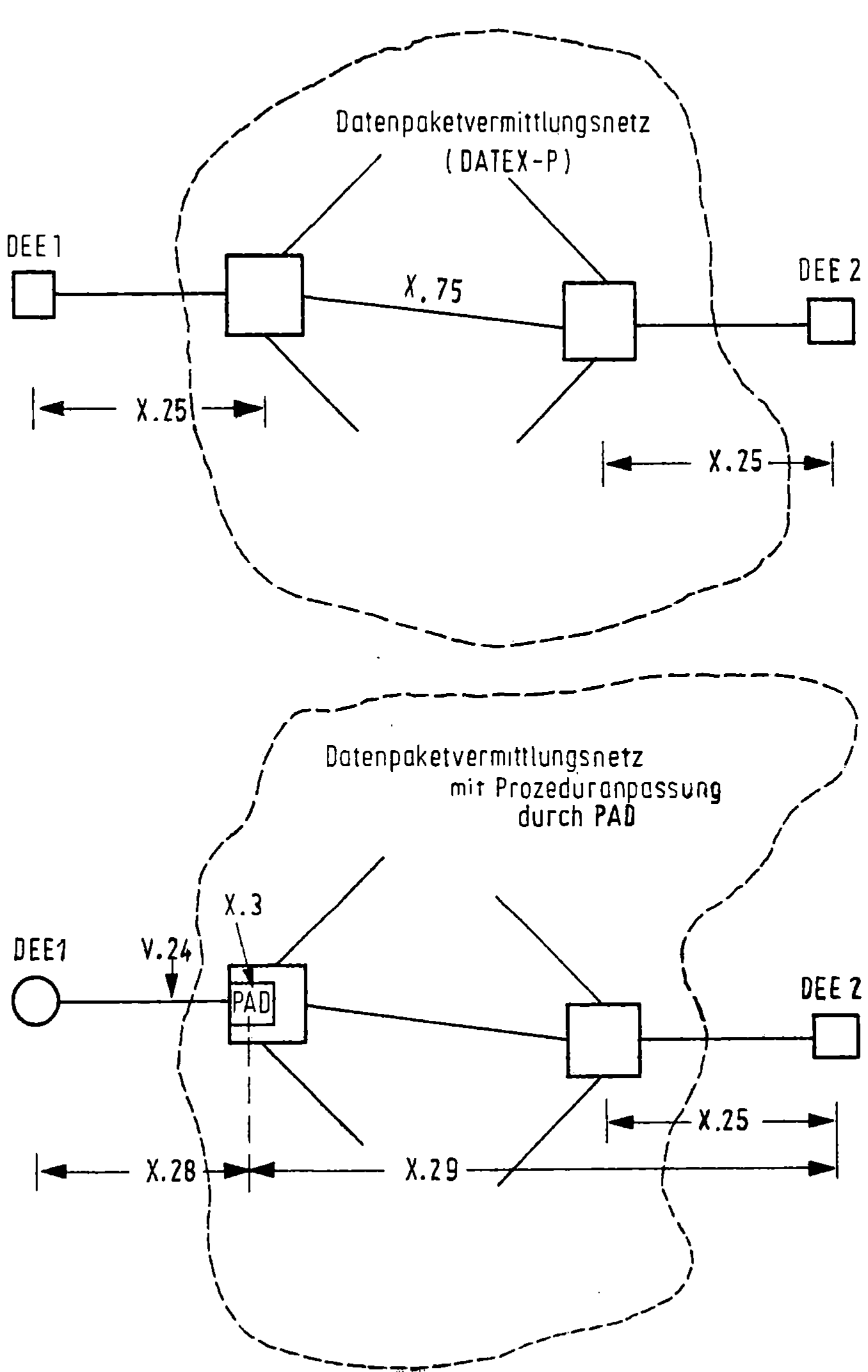

DEE   Datenendeinrichtung

PAD   Anpassungseinrichtung zur Anordnung und Zusammenfügung
von Paketen (Paket Assembly / Disassembly Facility)

3.2 Zusammenarbeit mit anderen öffentlichen Netzen

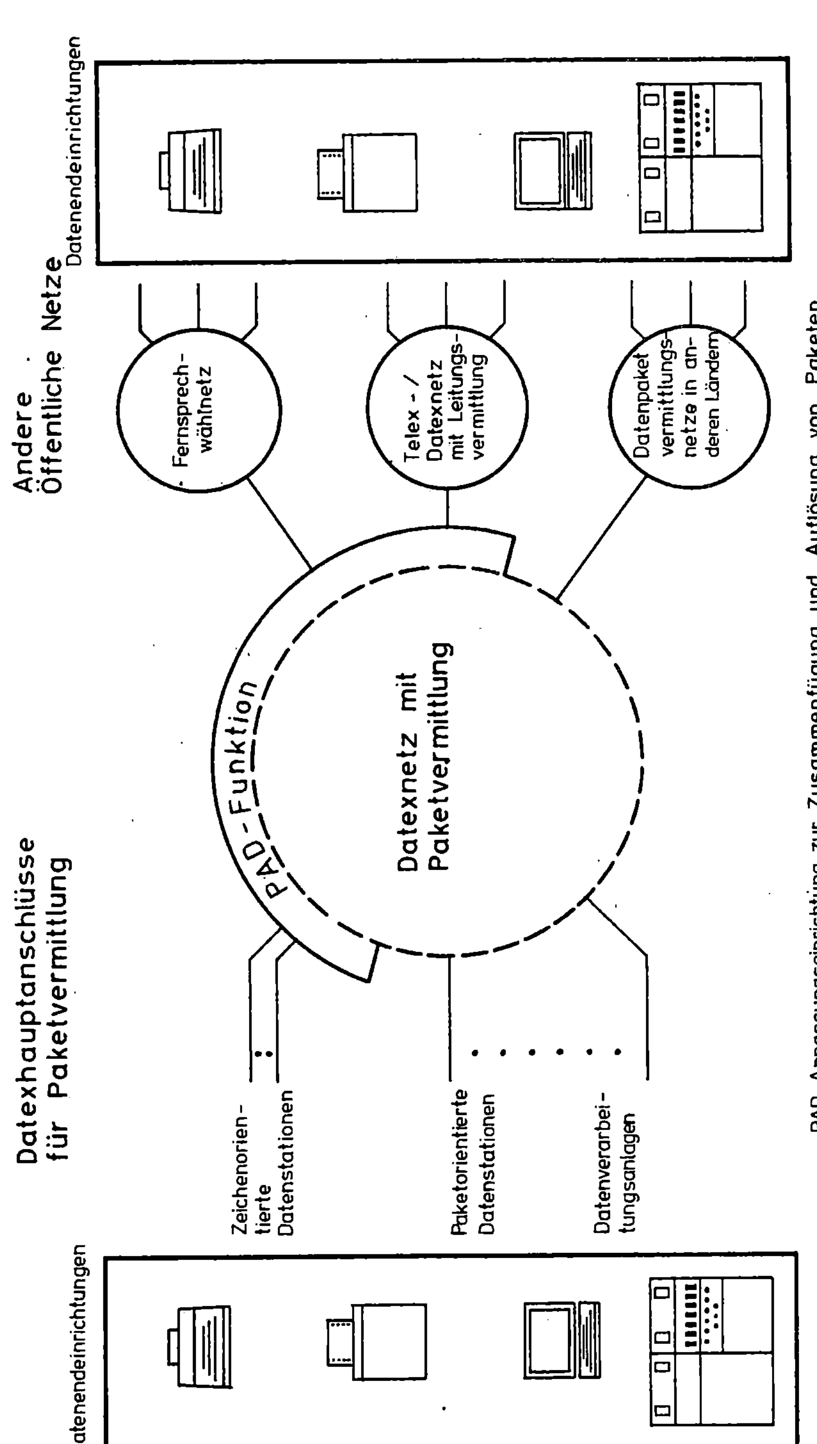

PAD Anpassungseinrichtung zur Zusammenfügung und Auflösung von Paketen (Packet Assembly / Disassembly Facility)

Zusammenhang zwischen dem paketvermittelten Datexnetz anderen öffentlichen Netzen

3.3 Ziele zum Datex-P-Dienstleistungsangebot

3.3.1 Einordnung des Angebotes in das allgemeine Datenübermittlungs-Dienstleistungsangebot der DBP

- Der paketvermittelte Datexdienst zielt vornehmlich auf Rechnerverbundnetze sowie auf Dialoganwendungen insbesondere auch solche mit Kompatibilitätsdienstleistungen.

- Soweit jedoch Konkurrenzsituationen zu bestehenden Dienstleistungen entstehen, soll dem Teilnehmer die freie Wahlmöglichkeit erhalten bleiben.

3.3.2 Hauptziele des Datex-P-Dienstes aus DBP-Sicht

- Grundstein zur freien Kommunikation in einem offenen System
  (Datentransportsystem für das offene System)·

- Marktgerechtes Dienstleistungs- und Schnittstellen-Angebot

- Für Anwender, die Rechnerverbundnetze aus HfD und privaten
  Knoteneinrichtungen zusammenschalten wollen, soll der
  Datex-P-Dienst ein leistungsfähiges und kostengünstiges
  Datentransportsystem mit umfassenden Funktionen bereitstellen.

- EDV-Service-Unternehmen und ihren Kunden soll insbesondere
  für Dialoganwendungen ein Datentransportsystem angeboten
  werden, das verschiedenartigen Terminals den Zugriff zu
  verschiedenartigen Rechnern freizügig, dialoggerecht und
  kostengünstig ermöglicht.

- Der Datex-P-Dienst soll in dafür geeigneten Fällen das
  Datentransportsystem neuer Fernmeldedienste bereitstellen
  (z. B. Bildschirmtext - Verbundnetz).

- Der nationale Datex-P-Dienst soll internationalen Verkehr
  zu/aus ausländischen oder internationalen DPV-Netzen wei-
  terleiten.

3.3.3 Haupteigenschaften des Datex-P-Dienstes für Anwender

3.3.3.1 Basisdienst

- Funktionen
  - . Optimierung für Dialogverkehr
  - . Eignung für Stapelverkehr
  - . Verkehr zwischen Datenendeinrichtungen mit verschiedenen Geschwindigkeiten
  - . Herstellerneutral
  - . Anwendungsneutral

- Wirtschaftlichkeit
  - . Mehrfachnutzung Hauptanschlüsse
  - . Benutzungsabhängige Gebühren
  - . Entfernungsunabhängige Gebühren

3.3.3.2 Zusätzliche Dienste

- Anpassungsdienstleistungen vom Netz her
- Übergänge zu anderen öffentlichen Wählnetzen
- Erweiterung um Nachrichtenvermittlung

3.4 Überblick über Dienstleistungsangebot

	Merkmale Datenend-einrichtung für	Übertragungs-geschwindigkeit bit/s	Gleichlauf-verfahren	Protokoll	Code im Datenfeld	Bemerkungen
	1	2	3	4	5	6
Basisdienst	Hauptanschluß mit X.25	2400	synchron	X.25 mit LAPB (X.29)*	Codetransparenz; Version von DIN 66003/ IA Nr. 5 empfolen	
		4800	synchron			
		9600	synchron			
		48000	synchron			In der Einführungsphase mit gewissen geografischen Einschränkungen
Zusätzliche Dienste	Hauptanschluß mit anderen Schnittstellen über PAD	110 bis 300	asynchron	X.28 (X.29)*	Codeumsetzung gewisser Codevarianten vorgesehen**	
		1200	asynchron	analog X.28 (X.29)*		
	Zugang über PAD aus öffentlichen Wählnetzen	50	asynchron	noch festzulegen	ITA Nr. 2	Zugang über das Telexnetz
		110–300	asynchron	X.28 (X.29)*	Version von DIN 66003/ IA Nr. 5 empfohlen	Zugang über das öffentliche Fernsprechnetz und das leitungsvermittelte Datexnetz
		1200	asynchron	analog X.28 (X.29)*		Zugang über das öffentliche Fernsprechnetz
		(höhere Geschwindigkeiten)	synchron	noch festzulegen, Berücksichtigung von DIN 66019	Codeumsetzung gewisser Codevarianten ist vorgesehen**	Zugang über das öffentliche Fernsprechnetz und das leitungsvermittelte Datexnetz

* nur für paketorientierte DEE, die über PAD erreicht werden sollen
** werden noch im Benehmen mit Anwendern festgelegt

3.5 Gebühren

3.5.1 Grund- bzw. Zugangsgebühr

- Hauptanschluß für DÜE bei Teilnehmer, Anschlußleitung, DÜE
  in Netzknoten, Leitungsabschluß: Fester Monatsbetrag, ent-
  fernungsunabhängig, Funktion von der Datenrate
- Einwählen aus anderen öffentlichen Wahlnetzen
  . Übliche Gebühren des anderen Netzes
  . Zugangsgebühr (für DÜE und Leitungsabschluß im
    Datex-P-Netzknoten):
    Funktion von Verbindungsdauer (Minuten) und Datenrate

3.5.2 Anpassungsgebühr

Gebühr für PAD-Benutzung für Netzstandardterminals (Start Stop
und weitverbreitete Datensichtgeräte)
. Funktion der Verbindungsdauer (Minuten)
. Maximaler Monatsbetrag bei Zugang über HAs (entspricht
  3 000 Minuten = 50 Stunden)

3.5.3 Verbindungsgebühren

3.5.3.1 Allgemeines

- Entfernungsunabhängig im Bundesgebiet und Westberlin
- Auswahl der Gebührenbelastung für Rufenden oder Gerufenen
  möglich (Bei Zugang aus anderem Wählnetz vorerst nur Be-
  lastung des Gerufenen)

3.5.3.2 Zeitgebühr

Gebühr für fest für die Verbindung reservierte Betriebsmittel
des Netzes
- Bei virtueller Wählverbindung:
  Funktion von Dauer (Minuten) und Geschwindigkeitsklasse
- Bei virtueller fester Verbindung:
  Fester Monatsbetrag, Funktion der Geschwindigkeitsklasse
- Bei Zweipunktverbindungen ist gewählte Verbindung bei 150h/Monat
  billiger als feste Verbindung, darüber die feste Verbindung

3.5.3.3 Volumengebühr

- Einheit Segmente (= 64 Oktetts)
- Segmentberechnung je Verbindung
  . Berechnung von Paketen die Benutzerdaten tragen
  . Messen der Benutzerdaten jedes Paketes in Segmenten
  . Mindestzahl, von 50 Segmenten je Verbindung (Abdeckung
    des Aufwandes des Verbindungsaufbaus)
- Degression der Gebühr als Funktion des Volumens, für das
  ein Hauptanschluß gebührenpflichtig ist (vgl. 3.5.3.1, zweiter
  Spiegelstrich)
- Nachtreduktionen

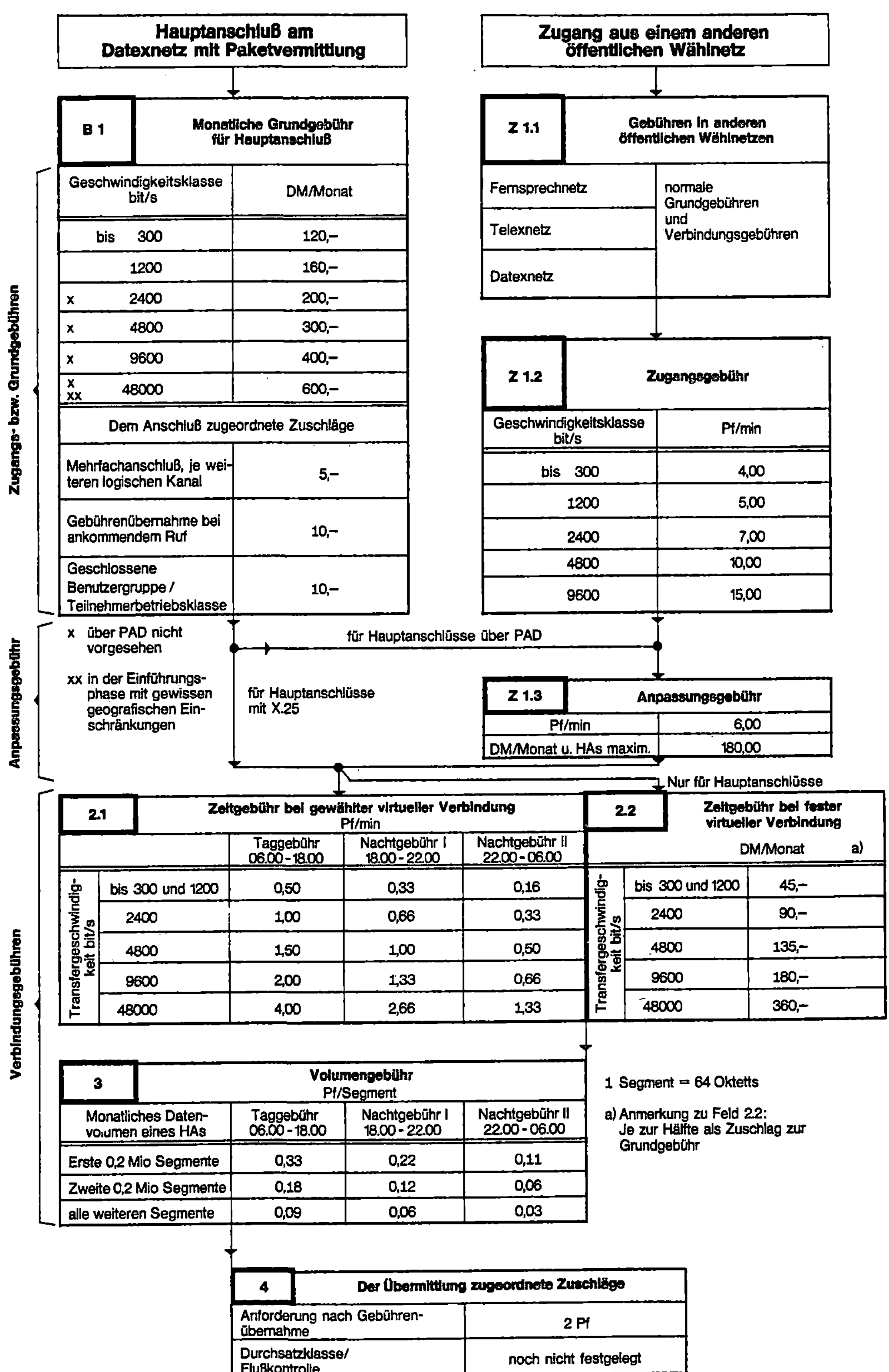

Bild: Hauptgebührenpositionen

3.6 Weiteres Vorgehen

	Soll-Termin	Ist-Termin
Ausschreibung der technischen Einrichtungen für die Datenpaketvermittlung	Frühjahr 1979	06.04.79
Bekanntgabe der Grunddokumentation für die Schnittstelle X.25	01.03.79	01.03.79
Bildung eines Teilnehmer-Arbeitskreises	Mai 1979	29.05.79
Auftragsvergabe	Mitte 1979	
Bekanntgabe der gesamten Schnittstellendokumentation	Mitte 1979 (nach Auftragsvergabe)	
Ergänzung der Verordnung, Verwaltungsanweisungen	im Laufe des Jahres 1979	
Einführung des Dienstes	Mitte 1980	
Teilnehmer-Probebetrieb	12 Monate	

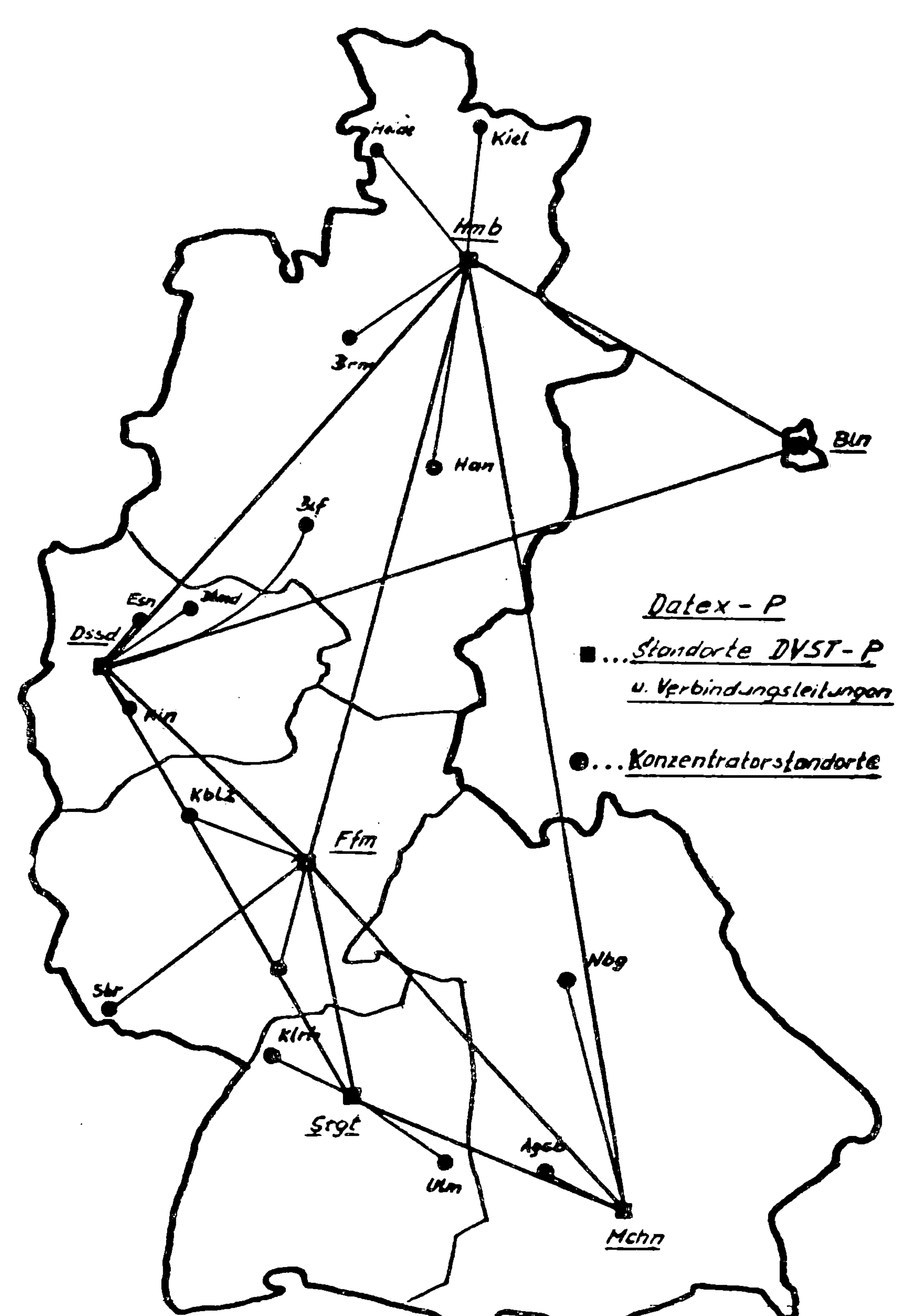
Haide
Kiel
Hmb
Brm
Han
Bln
Dsf
Esn
Wend
Dssd
Kln
Koblz
Ffm
Sbr
Nbg
Klrh
Srgt
Agsb
Ulm
Mchn
Datex-P
■ ... Standorte DVST-P
u. Verbindungsleitungen
● ... Konzentratorstandorte

Planungswerte

Der Netzzugang ist vorgesehen über:

- Direktanschluß
- Fernsprechnetz
- Datex- und Telexnetz

Erstausbau (1980) geplant für:

2000 Datenendeinrichtungen (DEE)
   5 Vermittlungsstellen (DVST-P)
   1 Netzkontrollzentrum (NKZ)
$\sim$15 Konzentratoren (KZ)

Weitere Entwicklung gemäß Tabelle:

Jahr	DEE	DVST-P	KZ	NKZ
1980	2000	5	$\sim$15	1
1981	+2000	-	-	-
1982	+3000	4	4	-
1983	+3000	4	4	evtl. +1
1984	+3000	4	4	-
Σ	13.000	17	27	2

4 Verhältnis des Datex-P-Dienstes zu anderen DBP-Diensten

4.1 Allgemeines

- Der paketvermittelte Datexdienst zielt vornehmlich auf Rechnerverbundnetze sowie auf Dialoganwendungen insgesondere auch solche
  mit Kompatibilitätsdienstleistungen.

- Soweit jedoch Konkurrenzsituationen zu bestehenden Dienstleistungen entstehen, soll dem Teilnehmer die freie Wahlmöglichkeit erhalten bleiben.

4.2 Zu möglichen Konkurrenzverhältnissen von HfD, Datex-L, Datex-P

- Konkurrenzverhältnisse gibt es nur, wenn die unterschiedlichen
  technischen Leistungsmerkmale nicht dominieren.

- Die eventuelle Konkurrenz leitungsvermitteltes Datex-Netz zum
  HfD-Netz entscheidet sich nach wirtschaftlichen Kriterien.

- Wenn man leitungsvermitteltes Datex-Netz, HfD-Netz und ein
  paketvermitteltes Datex-Netz betrachtet, kann es im Bereich
  niedriger Betriebsstundenzahlen (bzw. niedriger übertragener
  Datenmengen) nur eine Konkurrenz Leitungs/Paketvermittlung und
  bei höheren Betriebsstundenzahlen nur eine Konkurrenz Paketver-
  mittlungs/HfD geben.

- Das leitungsvermittelte Datexnetz bleibt bei niedrigen monat-
  lichen Betriebsstundenzahlen besonders bei stapelartigen Anwendungen attraktiv.

4.3 Verhältnis Datex-P zu Bildschirmtext (BT)

4.3.1 Allgemeines zu den Diensten

- Bildschirmtext
  . BT ermöglicht Zugriff breiter Kreise auf BT-Zentralen
    zum Abruf gespeicherter Information und Austausch
    individueller Mitteilungen
  . BT-Teilnehmer können über BT-Zentrale nicht von DBP betriebene
    EDV-Anlagen erreichen
  . Streng formatgebundener Informationsaustausch
- Datex-P
  . Datex-P-Dienst ermöglicht Austausch von Daten zwischen
    allen Hauptanschlüssen des Netzes
  . Datex-P-Dienst ermöglicht Übergang in und aus anderen
    öffentlichen Wählnetzen

4.3.2 Realisierung der Dienste

- Bildschirmtext
  . Zugang Terminal-Teilnehmer zur Bildschirmtextzentrale:
    Fernsprechnetz mit Bildschirmtextmodem
  . Verbindung Bildschirmtextzentralen und externe Rechner:
    Datex-P-Dienst
- Datex-P
  . Datex-P-Netz besteht aus Hauptanschlüssen, Netzknoten und
    Verbindungsleitungen
  . Übergang Datex-P-Netz auch zu Fernsprechnetz, Datex-L-Netz,
    Telexnetz

4.3.3 Gebührenrelationen

- Bei Bildschirmtext werden für Datenübertragung zwischen
  Bildschirmtextzentrale und externen Rechnern die Gebühren des
  Datex-P-Dienstes angewandt
- Beim Übergang Fernsprech-/Datex-P-Netz soll ein entsprechender
  Modemtyp wie bei Bildschirmtext zu vergleichbaren Gebühren
  angeboten werden.

4.3.4 Nutzungsgesichtpunkte

- "Terminal"-Teilnehmer benutzen
  . Bildschirmtext, wenn sie die BT-typischen Dienstleistungen
    wünschen
  . Datex-P, wenn sie kostengünstige Datenübertragung für
    kommerzielle Anwendungen wünschen (bei wenig Verkehr
    Fe-Netz + Datex-P, bei viel Verkehr HAs an Datex-P)
- "Rechner"-Teilnehmer benutzen Hauptanschluß Datex-P für
  . Bildschirmtext-Verbindungen
  . Andere Verbindungen über Datex-P

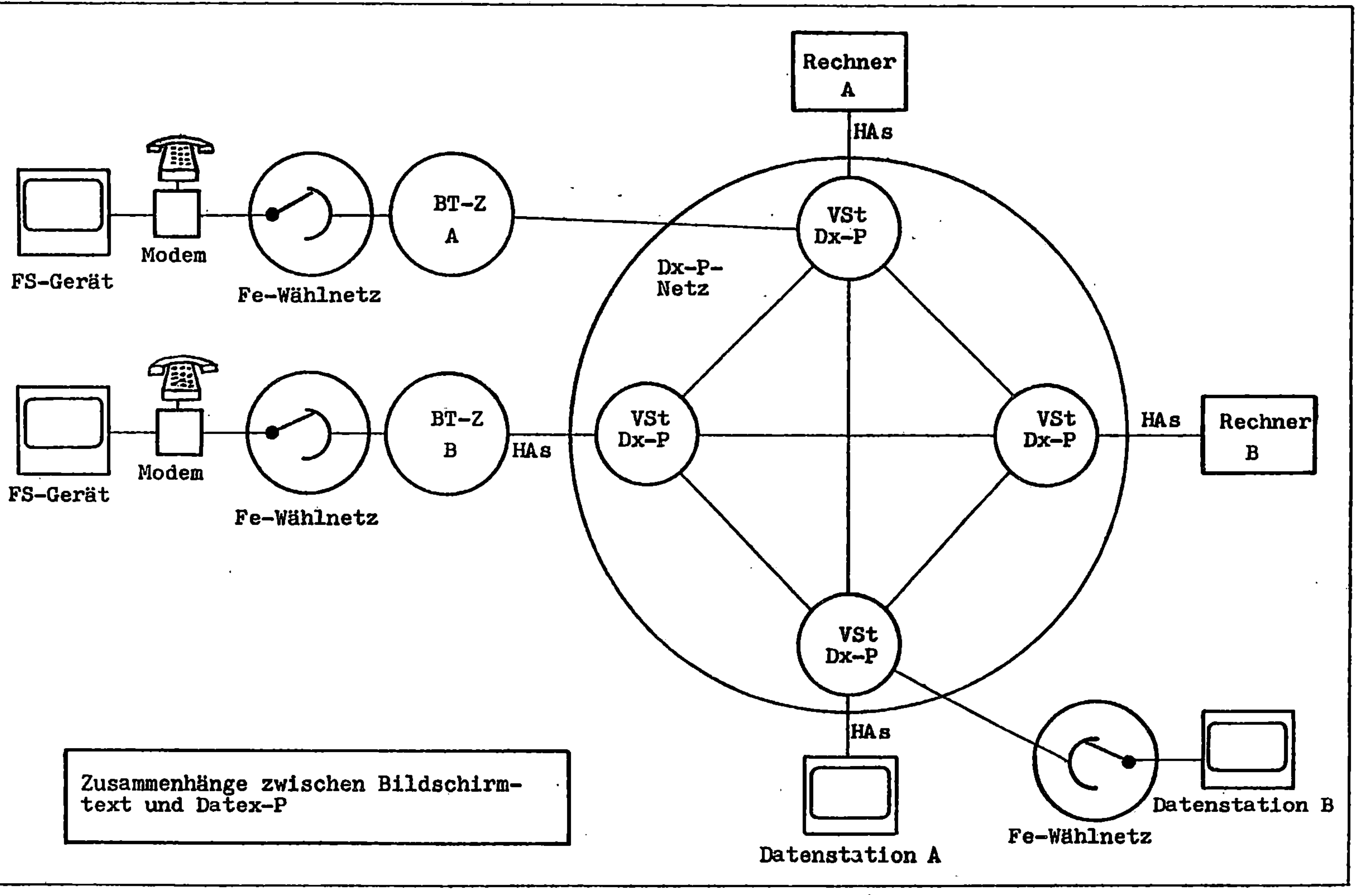

FS-Gerät
Modem
Fe-Wählnetz
BT-Z A
Dx-P-Netz
Rechner A
HAs
VSt Dx-P
FS-Gerät
Modem
Fe-Wählnetz
BT-Z B
HAs
VSt Dx-P
VSt Dx-P
HAs
Rechner B
VSt Dx-P
HAs
Datenstation A
Fe-Wählnetz
Datenstation B
Zusammenhänge zwischen Bildschirm-
text und Datex-P

5 Beispiele

5.1 Anwendungsbereiche der Netzzugänge

5.2 Dialoganwendungen

5.3 Stapelanwendungen

5.4 Verzögerungszeiten

5.1 Anwendungsbereiche der Netzzugänge

5.1.1 Überblick

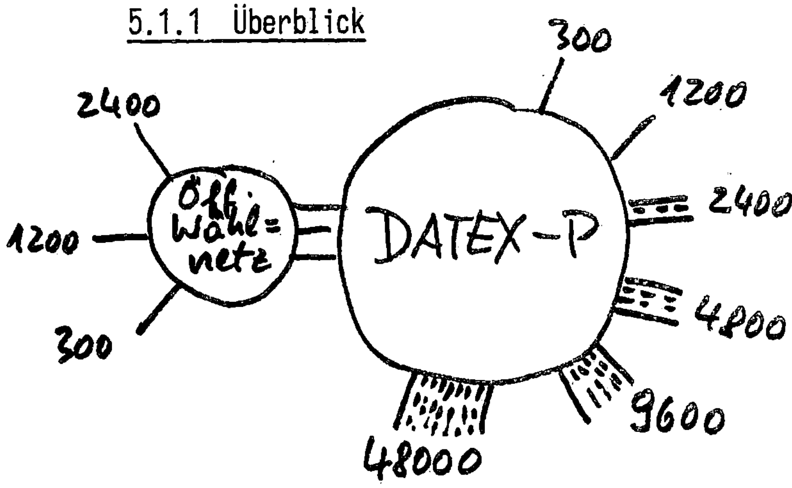

Alle Hauptanschlüsse mit Datenraten in bit/s

- Alle HAs und Zugänge sind in Netzzusammenhang
- Auswahl nach monatlichem Volumen und Übertragungszeit-
  anforderungen
- Mit wachsendem Verkehr/Datenvolumen
  . Übergang Einwählzugang zu HAs
  . HAs höherer Geschwindigkeit
- Mit wachsenden Anforderungen an Übertragungszeiten
  Wahl schnellerer Zugänge oder HAs
- Auswahl flexibel änderbar mit wachsendem Verkehr

5.1.2 Netzzugänge im Basisdienst (Verkehr von X.25-HAs)

- Einkanalanwendungen: Mit wachsendem Volumen oder wachsenden
  Anforderungen an Aufbauzeit Ausbau von 2 400 bit/s (200 DM)
  auf 48 000 bit/s (600 DM)
- Mehrkanalanwendungen
  . 1...4096 logische Kanäle: 5 DM/je zusätzlicher Kanal
  . Mit höherem Volumen und/oder kürzeren Übertragungszeiten
    Ausbau nach höheren Geschwindigkeiten
  . Praktischer Bereich:
    2400 bit/s mit 2 logischen Kanälen: 205 DM/Monat
    48000 bit/s mit 100 logischen Kanälen: 1 095 DM/Monat
    48000 bit/s mit 300 logischen Kanälen: 2 095 DM/Monat

- Kostenstruktur
  . In weitem Bereich variabel
  . Folgt flexibel Verkehrsbedarf
  . Niedrige Einstiegskostenschwelle

Beispiel: 1 200 bit/s - Zugang für Terminal

Fall A: Fe - HAs + BT - Modem + Fe-Nahgebühr + Zugangsgebühr
Fall B: Datex - P - HAs

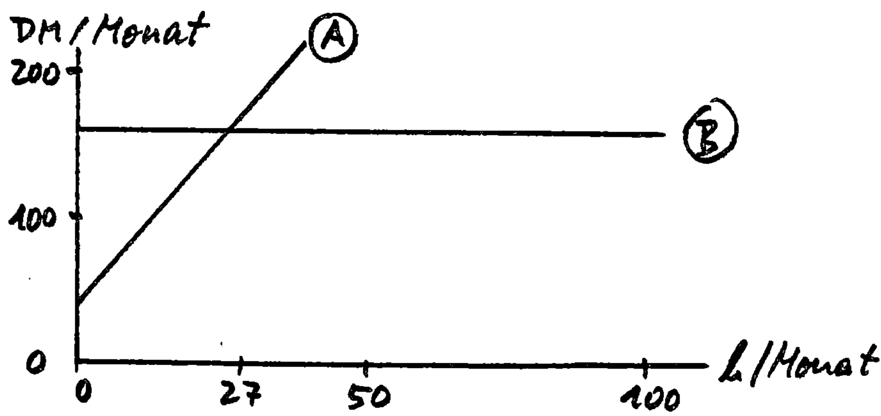

- Fall A: Niedrigkostenzugang für kleine Anwender mit wenig
  Verkehrsbedarf
- Fall B: Zugang für kommerzielle Nutzer mit relativ viel
  Verkehr
- Kurzfristiger Wechsel durch Anwender möglich
- Kostenstruktur
  - In weitem Bereich variabel
  - Folgt flexibel Verkehrsbedarf
  - Niedrige Eintrittskostenschwelle

Beispiel zu PAD-Benutzung an HAs

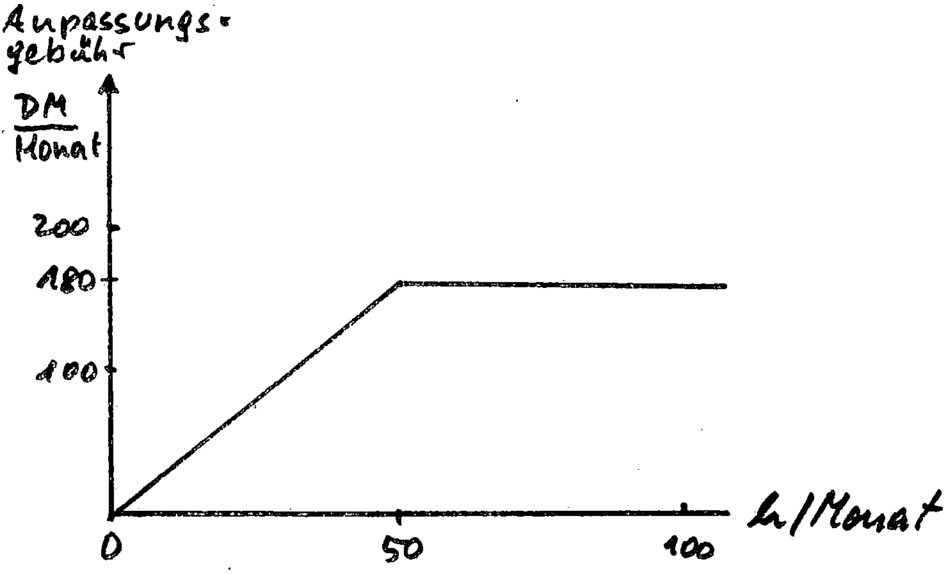

- Kleiner und großer Anwender kann zu jeweils akzeptablen
  Gebühren Anpassungs-Dienstleistung in Anspruch nehmen
- Gebührenerhebung für die Anpassung führt zu Marktdruck,
  X.25-Terminale anzubieten

5.2 Beispiele für Dialoganwendungen

Konfiguration

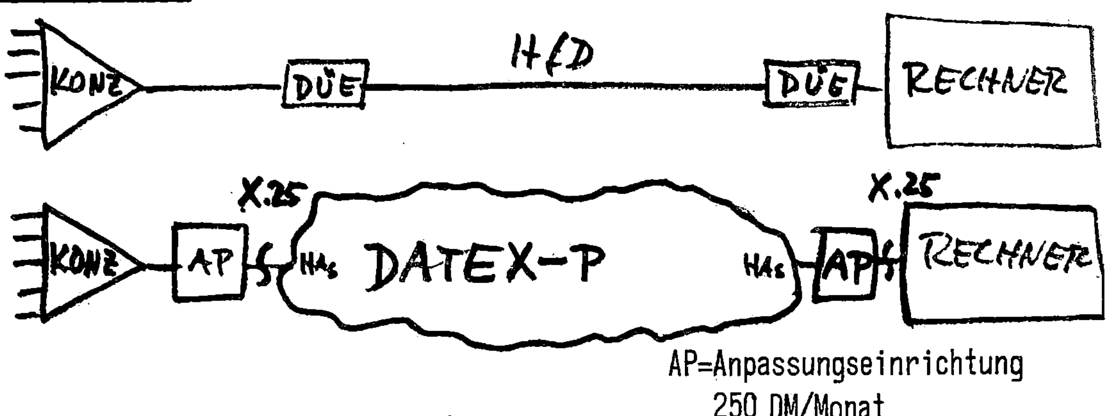

AP=Anpassungseinrichtung
250 DM/Monat

Verkehr je Terminal

Dialog	Zeichen/Transaktion	100 ... 1000
	Segmente/Transaktion	5 ... 15
	Transaktionen je Stunde	60 ... 30
	Segmente/Stunde	300 ... 450

Annahme: 400 Seg/h, 100 h/Monat

Ergebnis

Fall	Terminale am Konzentrator	HAs./HfD bit/sec	Grenzentfernung oberhalb derer Datex-P billiger ist bei 100 Betriebsstunden/Monat
A	1	1200	30 km
B	4	2400	40 km
C	16	4800	50 km

Grenzentfernung sinkt mit

- geringer Betriebsstundenzahl
- Mehrfachnützung AP und HAs am Rechner bei Datex-P
- geringere Kosten für AP

5.3 Beispiele für Stapelanwendungen

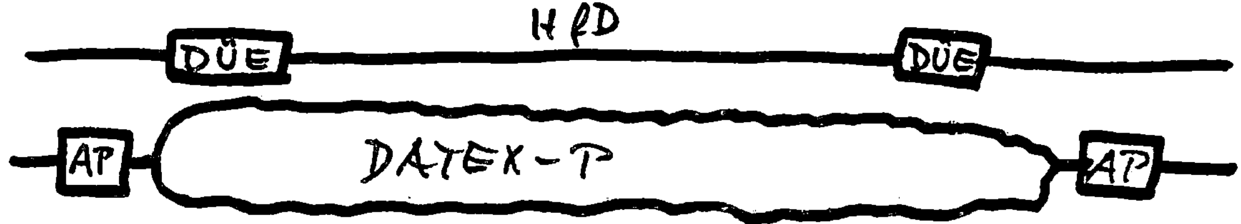

AP = Anpassungseinrichtung (250 DM/Monat)

Annahmen:

- Halb–Duplex–Übertragung
- Taggebühren
- Ausnutzung der Datenrate 0,7

Ergebnis: Grenzentfernung, oberhalb derer Datex–P billiger als
HfD ist als Funktion der Betriebsstundenzahl

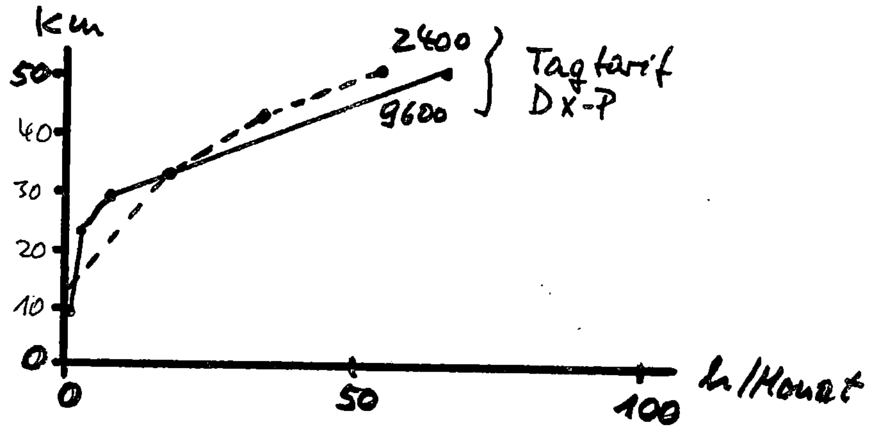

Grenzentfernung sinkt mit

- Teilweiser Übertragung in Nacht I oder II
- Geringere Kosten für AP

5.4 Beispiele zu Verzögerungszeiten

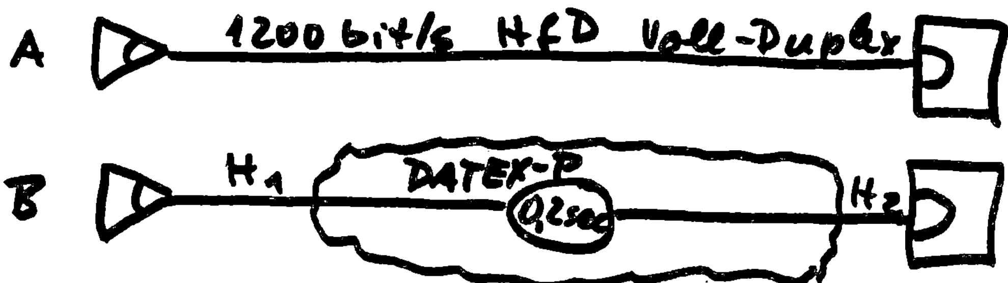

Annahmen

- Dialog
  Gepufferter Terminal
- Verzögerung von 1 Block von 128 bytes = 1000 bit
- 100 Betriebsstunden/Monat

Vergleich 1 (Bei B zwei HAs a 1200 bit/s)

- Übertragungszeiten: · A   0,8 sec
  - · B   (0,8 + 0,2 + 0,8) sec = 1,8 sec
- Wirtschaftlichkeit
  A teurer bei Entfernungen > 30 km (vgl. 5.2)

Vergleich 2 : Bei B zwei HAs a 4800 bit/s

Übertragungszeiten: · A   0,8 sec
- · B   (0,2 + 0,2 + 0,2) sec = 0,6 sec
- Wirtschaftlichkeit:
  - · Mehrkosten für schnellere HAs bei B : 280 DM/Monat
  - · A teurer bei Entfernungen > 40 km

Ergebnis

- Übertragungszeitberechnung ist kompliziert
- Datex-P hat wegen Speichervermittlung "technischen Startnachteil"
  und "ökonomischen Startvorteil"
- Bei Datex-P können mit einfachen und sehr ökonomischen Mitteln kurze
  Übertragungszeiten erreicht werden (schnellere HAs bis 48000bit/s)

6 Schlußbemerkungen

- Teure Betriebsmittel (Hauptanschlüsse, Vermittlungsrechner,
  Verbindungsleitungen) werden bei paketvermittelten Netzen
  weniger individuell Anwendungen/Anwendern reserviert, sondern
  gemeinsam genutzt und daher besser ausgenutzt.

- Datex-P ist ein sehr flexibles, zuverlässiges und kostengünstiges
  Datentransportsystem

- Anwender brauchen keine eigenen Netze (Vermittlungsrechner und
  HfD) mehr zu betreiben; sie schließen Terminale und DVA an
  DBP-Netz an.

- Kommunikation zwischen allen Anschlüssen mit genormten Schnittstellen

- Flächendeckendes und entfernungsunabhängiges tarifiertes Dienstleistungsangebot gibt Anwendern Planungsfreiheit für DVA- und
  Terminalstandorte

- Benutzungsabhängige Tarifierung führt zu einer geringen Einstiegskostenschwelle im Vergleich zu Netzen mit HfD und privaten
  Netzknoten.

The Addressing Requirements of a Transport Service

P.F.Linington
Data Communication Protocols Unit

and

V.Hathway
Division of Numerical Analysis and Computer Science

National Physical Laboratory, Queens Rd.,
Teddington, Middlesex TW11 OLW, England.

1.   Introduction

This paper discusses the addressing facilities and mechanisms required to support the operation of a general Transport Service. The concepts described result from discussion and development during the last five years amongst users of the British Post Office's Experimental Packet Switched Service (EPSS) and intending users of their Packet Switched Service (PSS). The activities centred on the committee which has become Study Group 3 of the PSS User Forum.

Much of the material is contained in the PSS Study Group 3 proposals for a Transport Service (1), but many of the ideas date back to its predecessor, the EPSS Bridging Protocol (2). The responsibility for the discussion and elaboration falls, however, on the authors of the present paper.

We concentrate here on the issues of identification; the paper describes the facilities required to name and allow access to user applications. The subject is central to the specification of a transport service because a communications channel cannot be specified without the ability to identify its desired object or endpoint. Indeed, the full advantage of inter-network gateways will not be realised unless messages establishing a connection across one network can carry addressing information for extending the connection across subsequent networks.

The mechanisms described here are simple yet powerful; while some of the examples are complex in order to demonstrate this power, the common uses are not. For example, in a simple case, where the desired connection is to one of a limited number of application processes accessed via a single X.25 network, the mechanisms would reduce to the unaugmented X.25 addressing.

2. The Transport Service

The aim of the Transport Service is to provide a clear boundary between the user of communications and the supplier of communications, either public or private; it allows all user applications to be constructed on the same standardized base, and allows any communication medium to be employed without modification of the application. Different communication schemes can be used both as alternatives and in combination.

The service provided is connection oriented; an association is established between two parties, who can continue to exchange information for as long as the association exists. The Transport Service is defined in terms of a number of service primitives, representing the set of actions that can be performed by the user and the set of stimuli that he may receive. The primitives are:

```
CONNECT      request a connection,
ACCEPT       confirm the connection,
DISCONNECT   terminate the connection,
FINISHED     terminate the connection on receipt,
DATA         transfer data,
INTERRUPT    signal some special event,
ADDRESS      transfer an address for later use,
PUSH         request transmission of buffered data,
RESET        resynchronize activity across the connection.
```

The direct use of addresses is confined to connection establishment; once the connection has been established, messages can pass along it without further guidance; the only addressing issue is then how addresses themselves are to be passed for future use. Thus in the remainder of this paper, we will only be concerned with the three primitives CONNECT, ACCEPT and ADDRESS. (There are, in fact, also some uses of addresses to localize errors, but these contribute nothing new to the discussion of addressing problems.)

3.   Names

In order to form a transport service connection to any endpoint, one must quote the name of the endpoint. The form of the name will vary among systems, from the purely numeric string to a descriptive natural language phrase. There is no need to be concerned here with the variations; a name is some string of characters conforming with the accepted usage of the local system.

If connection to a particular object is desired, then the name used must identify that object uniquely. Each network must be administered so that names issued within the network have the required uniqueness; to ensure this all names are issued or approved by a <u>naming authority</u>. The region within which a naming authority has control is its <u>naming domain</u>; the control may be over an area of any size, varying from operation within a single system to the coordinated control of many interlinked networks.

The international connection of PTT networks is an example of interlinked systems with a common naming plan. Worthy of note here are two draft recommmendations that have been produced by CCITT for the international connection of PTT networks. Firstly the recommendation X.75 (3) will permit international network level interconnection between PTT packet switched networks. The second recommendation is of much greater interest here. X.121 (4) is a draft for an "International Numbering Plan for Public Data Networks". The purpose of the X.121 International Numbering Plan is to facilitate the introduction of public data networks and provide for their interworking on a worldwide basis. This is a welcome development which enables us, from a Transport Service view point, to consider the resultant PTT conglomerate as a single network with a single naming domain. This is a significant advance but still leaves the requirement for a more general mechanism for naming endpoints in domains not encompassed by X.121.

At the other extreme, it is often desirable to allow the endpoints of a connection to be in the same machine. The Transport Service may be used for inter-process connection and communication under the control of a single operating system. In this case a single naming domain is involved: that of the operating system's process name space.

An object can have several different names with different degrees of permanence. The published name of a widely accessible service cannot be changed lightly, but the location of the machine providing the service may vary to allow growth or to circumvent failure. The properties required of names vary considerably, but for present purposes we can distinguish two kinds of name: a <u>title</u>, which indicates what an object is, and which is permanent and may be widely distributed, and an <u>address</u>, which specifies the current location of the object. (Some authors have used slightly different terminology when making this distinction. See, for example, Shoch 1978, (5).) To permit system reconfiguration, a title is (in principle) translated into an address each time it is used, so as to allow a connection to be established to the current location of the object. If the names in a system are fixed with no possibility of reconfiguration, or if changes of published name are acceptable, the distinction between title and address need not be made. The system can then be made simpler but less flexible.

The distinction between titles and addresses is, however, a relative one. As the situation is examined in progressively greater detail, further mechanisms are revealed, and with them corresponding choices that must be made in forming a connection. These choices now relate the name previously viewed as an address, but now in the role of a title, to a more specific address.

For example, in a database system some data item title is bound first to a file name, then to a location, and finally to a specific route to that location, as progressively finer detail is considered.

Title	Choice	Address
Data Item Name	which component file	Filename + pointer
Filename	physical location of file	System address + file
System address	route within network	Path name

In many cases, connection is required not to a definite object, but to an indefinite member of a class of similar objects. For example, on initial connection to a time sharing service, any free port to the service is suitable. In such cases, a name for the class, called a <u>generic name</u> is used.

4.   Multiple Domains

The objects named in a particular domain need not all be connection
endpoints. Indeed they cannot be, or connection to objects outside the
current domain would not be possible. Some of the names allocated in the
domain represent access points to other domains, where names in those
domains can be interpreted.

Thus, 01-246 8000 is a name, issued by the PTT, of a telephone giving
access to a domain in which Tom, Dick and Harry are valid names. The
prescription for making a connection is "phone 01-246 8000 and ask for
Harry". Note that this is an addressing operation and that, in the
caller's domain, the desired logical object might have been titled "the on-
call engineer".

At any stage in the interpretation of a name there is a part which is
interpretable within the current domain (the active part), and there may be
a further part which is not (the dormant part). This implies that the
active part can always be extracted from a longer string which may require
the definition of local termination conventions. At any location there is
available, as a result of interpreting the name, a local routing operation
and a name suitable for use after performing that operation.

The sequence of operations as a connection is created can be
illustrated as follows:

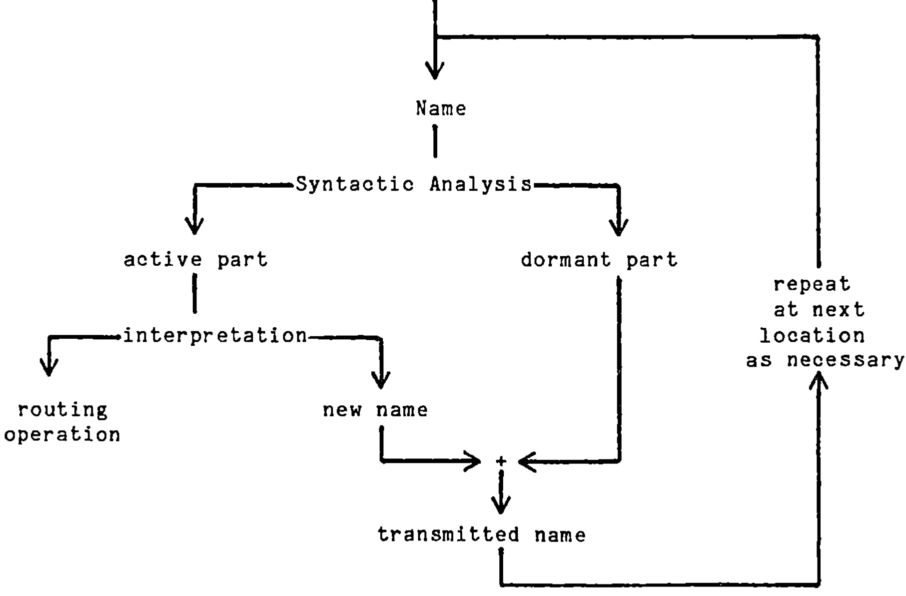

The various familiar routing strategies can fit within this framework; they differ in the nature of the transformation applied to the active part. If the identity transformation is used, the result is hop-by-hop routing; if the active part is deleted entirely, the result is source routing. There are many more complex possibilities for the transformation.

Some illustration may clarify the possibilities. The first example of distributed routing is the analysis of a postal address:

> 5, Dull Street,
> Grey Town,
> Badland.

The address is analysed repeatedly by different sorting offices, yielding in turn the routing operations "send to Badland", "send to Grey Town", etc. At each stage the complete address is passed on because it is written on the letter, but it is often more convenient to transform the address by discarding used fields as the analysis proceeds. For example, a human enquirer searching for a certain lady might:

1) Ask for "the Driver's Brother's Wife's Mother"
2) Find "the Driver" and ask for his "Brother's Wife's Mother"
3) Find "the Brother" and ask for his "Wife's Mother"
4) Find "the Wife" and ask for her "Mother"
5) Find "the Mother"

The appearance of multiple components in a name may not necessarily mean that it must be analysed repeatedly, as the driver might have known that the named object was in the back of the car at step (2). However, the analysis as a single operation would only be possible if the complete name was valid in the Driver's domain; if he did not recognise the lady, the analysis would have to proceed a step at a time, even if this generated a looped route.

In general, choice of alternate routes can only take place when there is knowledge of the correspondence of the identifiers of the possible alternative paths. Such facts cannot be deduced from analysis of the names; it derives from previous knowledge of the world. This distinction between the expected result of using a name (its intention) and the actual result of using it (its extension) is a familiar one in linguistic philosophy and is the foundation of the Electra paradox.

Of the above, the postal approach to addressing may be acceptable where there is a centrally organised hierarchical system of domains, while the second example might be more suited to a series of independent interlinked organisations, such as linked computer networks. There must, therefore, be conventions for the ordering of fields, such as left to right ordering, to allow the relevant active parts to be accessed in the order the domains are traversed.

The domains we are concerned with may not all be involved in the establishment of a transport service connection. It is quite possible for there to remain, after the creation of a connection, some piece of addressing information which is handed to the called party. Such information may select initial options, or determine aspects of the nature of the object addressed; this can be viewed as selecting an object from a set of possible virtual objects. Indeed, the division between the part of the address used by the transport service and that handed to the called party may vary if it is decided later to provide different options as separate services. There is, of course, nothing to stop such selections being performed by explicit negotiation, rather than addressing, and this may be more appropriate in cases where the options can later be re-negotiated.

5.   The Distributed Binding of Titles

The conversion of titles into addresses need not take place as a single operation. Generally it will only be performed when the active point of interpretation is within the region where reconfiguration is possible. If the title is bound to an address too early, the versatility of the title is lost, because the correspondence of title and address has been distributed too widely. The larger the region in which the correspondence is known, the more costly it is to update; the later the binding, the easier it is to reconfigure. For example:

	Title		Address
1)	The Network Group Common Room		--
2)	The Common Room	in	The Red Brick Building
3)	--		the third room on the left

At (1) there is no commitment to location. At (2), the group is located to a particular building, but there is no commitment as to a fixed location for the room. Control of the translation allows the site management to re-allocate buildings without invalidating the published name of the group's home. The elaboration at (3), taking place once the correct building has been reached, allows the building management to reallocate rooms without externally visible effect.

6.   The Size of Domains

There are undoubted advantages in making title domains as large as possible, by co-operation between naming authorities, so as to make the titles reasonably site independent. However, the mechanisms for the transport of a dormant part of the name are essential for the orderly management of separate installations.

The ideal from the point of view of uniform addressing is the agreement of a global naming scheme, in which the address of an object is valid in the same form everywhere. There are, however, problems with this approach (see Girard, (6)). The addresses are necessarily large, and the administration difficult. This may lead to implementors making simplifying assumptions about the set of addresses to be used, and then using this set, without some common prefix, as if it were the global set. Once such short cuts have been taken, and are hallowed by established usage, the return to the original global scheme will be difficult. Worse, it is impossible to incorporate separate communities not previously included in the supposedly global scheme without requiring incompatible change.

7.   Names and Connections

The above sections have described the naming of a process to which connection is desired. There are, in addition, aspects of naming associated with the establishment of a connection. The series of routing operations performed in setting up or tracing out a connection form a pathname. (This name will generally be an address, since it gives the current location of the endpoint.) Each endpoint of a connection will have a pathname giving access to the other endpoint; in one case the name will be formed from the routing operations actually used to create the path, while in the other the operations making up the name will be the inverses of those actually performed.

The pathname specifies a single object, the one to which connection has been made, even if a generic name was originally specified. It can therefore be used in principle to remake the connection, although some of the routing operations may not in fact be permitted if the connection has ceased to exist. For example, the provider of a service referenced by a generic name may not allow connection to a specific occurrence except as a result of their intervention.

As each link of a path is traversed by a CONNECT or ACCEPT message, the name of the reverse routing operation is added to an accumulating pathname. In this way the CONNECT message delivers the address of the calling process while the ACCEPT message returns the address of the process actually called; this is called the recall address, since it is suitable for connection re-establishment by the originator. The calling pathname can be used by the called party to return the call, but some of the routing operations on the path back to the calling party may not be valid because the corresponding links can only be created in the forward direction.

The generation of these path related addresses may involve transformations more complex than simple concatenation. Within a naming domain, a series of routing steps may be contracted into a single address; there may also be some replacement of addresses by the equivalent titles, allowing recall by alternative paths.

In addition to their use for reconnection, the pathnames provide some level of mutual identification for the endpoints connected. The identification provided is only as reliable as the network furnishing it, but for many purposes it may give a useful level of security. This aspect of the provision of recall addresses is particularly important in networks providing call redirection.

A quite distinct set of identifiers is generated as a result of the management of multiple connections. These are the identifiers issued to connections to distinguish between them where they use a common resource, such as a shared link. Connection identifiers are ephemeral and cease to have their allotted meaning once the connection is terminated. They form a totally different naming system from that of the object names, and do not interact with them.

8.   Examples of Address Manipulations

In the examples which follow, where endpoint names and pathnames are specified, the permanence of a name is not distinguished explicitly because it does not affect the illustration; conversion of titles to addresses is a local matter. The term 'address' is therefore used in the examples, as it represents the simplest case.

8.1   Example 1

The simplest example of addressing is in the use of a single network connecting one user to a system capable of providing only one function. In this case, the addressing requirements reduce to the network addressing, and there is no dormant address information transferred across the network. This assumes that the network provides calling address information.

Figure 1 shows the values of each address parameter at each endpoint and in the message in transit. The left hand side of the figure traces the address transformations accompanying the passage of the CONNECT message; the right hand side shows the recall address construction as the ACCEPT message is returned.

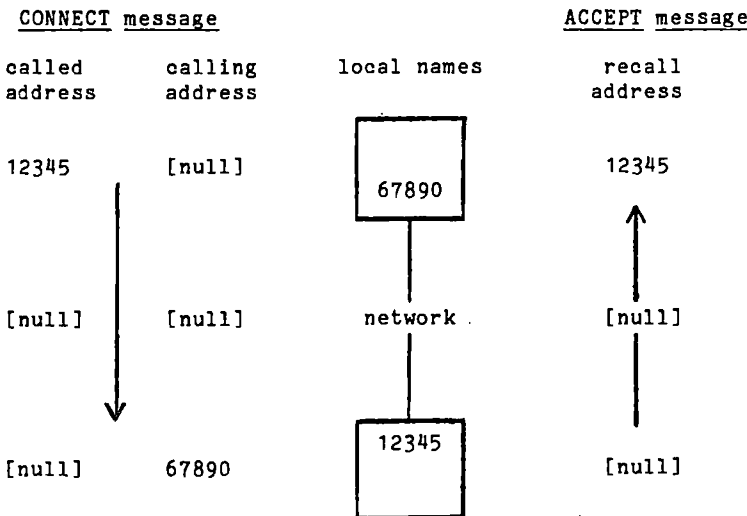

Figure 1 A simple case of addressing

8.2 Example 2

The situation is more complex if the network address gives access to several services, capable of supporting many users simultaneously, or if a concentrator connects multiple terminals to the network from the same address. The name of the service must now be carried across the network to specify the type of process to be created to service this call, and the identity of the created process must be returned to the caller if the process is subsequently to be referred to. Similarly, the identity of the terminal is passed, and could be used for authentication purposes.

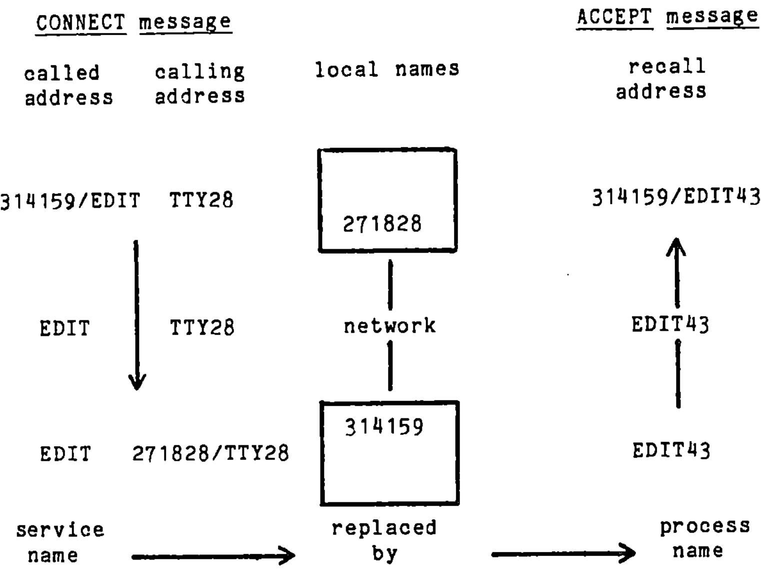

Figure 2   Use of address components and generic names

8.3 Example 3

A complicated example of the address manipulations is given in figure 3. In this example a connection is established over three networks, here supposed to be two private networks joined by a public data network. The first and last networks use the character '/' as an address terminator, while the interface to the public network uses '+'. These are, of course, arbitrary local choices.

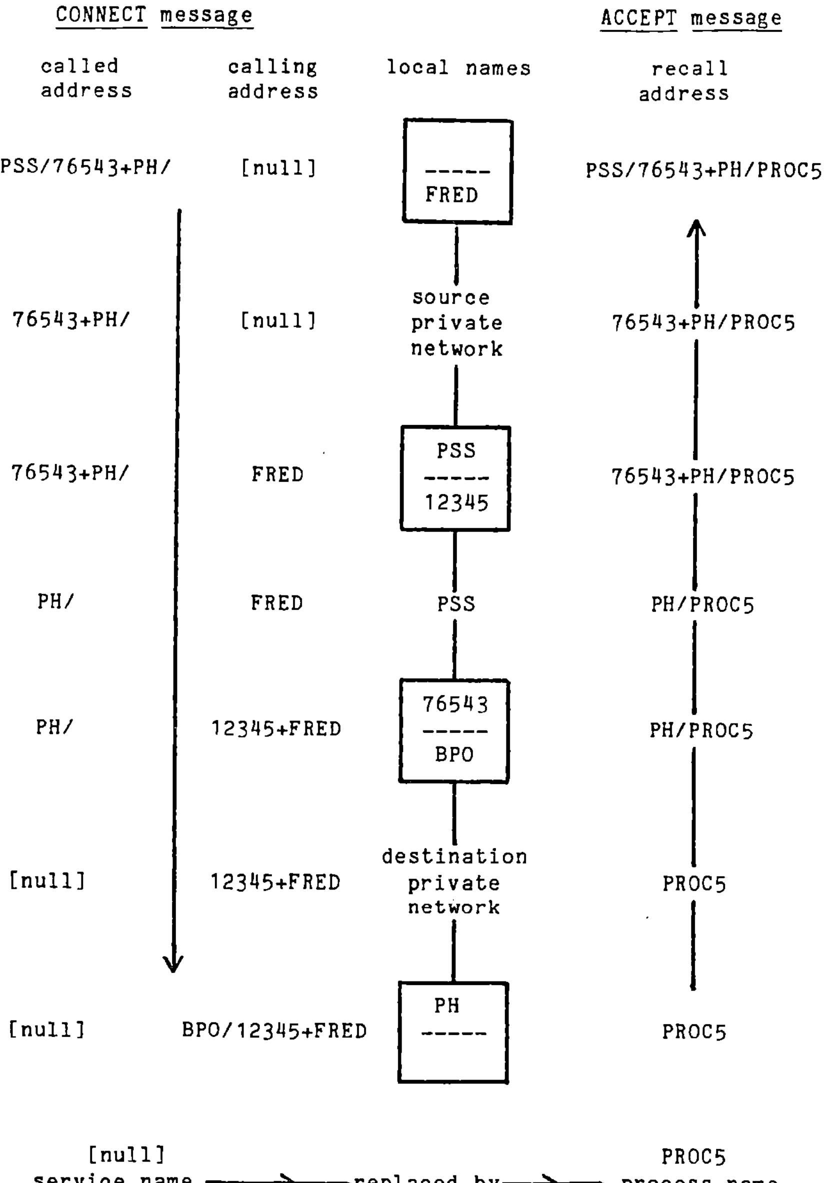

Figure 3 Address transformations in a sequence of networks and nodes. The boxes represent nodes. The strings within a box denote the addresses of that node in the corresponding networks.

9. Use of Addresses by Applications

More complex applications, such as Remote Job Entry, may be implemented using several associated calls. Thus applications will require to extend addresses to obtain the addresses for associated calls. To be consistent with the field structure described above, this must always be done by adding or deleting characters at the end of the address.

Since addresses are context dependent, they must be known to the transport service, and applications must not transmit addresses without the knowledge of the transport service. It is, of course, permissible to transmit strings which are to be appended to addresses as in the previous paragraph.

The transport service provides mechanisms for the explicit transport of addresses, which it then undertakes to maintain in a valid state. The transformation applied will be that normally applied either to a called or to a calling address, depending on whether the movement is towards or away from the object referenced (see figure 4).

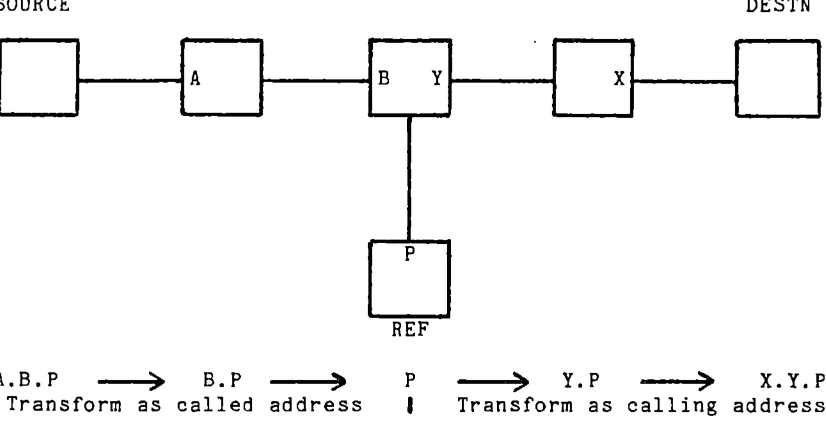

Figure 4   Movement of the address of REF from SOURCE to DESTN, with the transformations necessary to keep it valid at each point.

10. Knowledge of the Domain Structure

Examination of a name can reveal the structure of domains which its use will involve. Various sub-strings within the name may be related to different domains. However, the user of the name need not be aware of the internal structure; to him it is just a string which references a particular object. To take an example from personnal naming, "Ivan Ivanovich" is the name of an individual, within which can be discovered the name of the individual's father. Awareness of the derivation of the patronymic is not needed in order to talk to the man.

The allocation of a name to a newly created object is done entirely within a single domain. The more complicated names are produced as a result of movement of the viewpoint (see section 9); the new child was named by his parents simply "Ivan". He becomes "Ivan Ivanovich" and later "Ivan Ivanovich from Omsk" as a result of passage of his name between other individuals. To the individuals using the names, however, there need be no understanding of their structure.

11. The Treatment of Addressing in the ISO Reference Model

Sub-committee 16 of the International Standards Organization Technical Committee 97 has been working on a Reference Model for Open Systems Interconection (7); this description contains (in section 3.3) a discussion of identifiers. The model describes a layered subdivision of communications matters, and the discussion of naming is presented in this context.

The ISO model makes a distinction between titles and addresses. Further, it identifies two types of title, global titles and local titles; it is assumed that local titles are transformed to global titles before use. The field of application is thus restricted to situations in which global addressing can be employed, which can, as explained above, be a severe restriction in situations where continued evolution is expected to occur.

Addresses are defined to be service access point addresses, and specify points of attachment for particular entities. The description thus places emphasis on the connection, by associating the address with the access point rather than the entity served. Implicit in this distinction is a rigid approach to the management of entities and their connection to

services; the initiative is seen to be on the part of the service, whi··
provides labels for a possibly varying set of entities, rather than a
collection of labelled entities with varying associations to the services.

The division into layers is assumed to be mirrored by the addressing.
At each layer, there can be an addressing structure, but the addressing
structures are distinct at the different levels. This implies that if an
entity has more than one address from the lower layer, there is no
awareness of the correspondence, and alternative routings cannot therefore
be chosen from within a lower layer.

Finally, the model defines an identification of connections. This is
done in a way that overlays the connection names onto the set of names for
objects to which connections can be made, and assumes that the service
access point has the same address both when seen from above and when seen
from below.

In general, the treatment of identifiers presented is more limiting
than that presented here. It assumes that all systems involved can accept
the expense and upheaval of using global titles, and that there is an exact
parallel between the structuring of addresses and the layering of services.
These must be recognised as restrictions.

12.   Conclusions

This paper has attempted to illuminate the major issues involved in the
construction of an addressing scheme. It has outlined the need for
flexibility of use and management, and the needs when communicating between
systems with different naming authorities.

Mechanisms have been described that will allow these requirements to be
satisfied, without constraining local choice of addressing conventions and
name allocation. The mechanisms are simple in concept yet very powerful;
without such mechanisms, interconnection of separately developed and
managed components will be very difficult.

References

(1) A Transport Service, P.F. Linington (Editor), PSS Study Group 3, BIG CP(79)7.

(2) Bridging Protocol Specification, M.J.T. Guy (Editor), EPSS Study Group 3 BIG CP(75)7.

(3) X.75, M. Amano (Editor), CCITT COM VII-No. 207-E, May 1978

(4) X.121, H. Bieler (Rapporteur), CCITT COM VII No. 209-E, May 1978

(5) Shoch, J.F., Inter-Network Naming, Addressing, and Routing: IEEE-CS Compcon 78 Fall.

(6) Girard, P.M., Transport Level Addressing, DCPU Transport Service Workshop, December 1978.

(7) ISO Reference Model of Open Systems Interconnection, ISO/TC97/SC16 N227 June 1979.

DESIGN AND FORMAL SPECIFICATION OF AN X.25 BASED

OPEN TRANSPORT LAYER AND ITS PROTOCOLS

S. Schindler, D. Altenkrüger, U. Flasche,

J. Schulze, M. Steinacker

Technische Universität Berlin

Fachbereich Informatik

Abstract

The paper presented should be a kind of tutorial for those who have a basic understanding of the open systems interconnections philosophy as well as of software
technological problems in developing reliable systems. It mainly consists of four
parts, namely

- it explains the requirements for the Transport Layer as given in the Reference
  Model (of Open Systems Interconnections) document;

- it gives a general design for the RM Transport Layer meeting these requirements;
  this design is based on simple building blocks that may be easily described
  and specified;

- it characterizes a subset of the building blocks of the general design suitable
  for an X.25 based RM Transport Layer (having almost identical services used
  and provided as those presently discussed in the PIX group);

- it discusses the simplifications obtained from this decomposition of the whole
  Transport Layer into uniform building blocks and the technique we apply for
  formally specifying the modules (the building blocks contain) as well as the
  building blocks, themselves.

The intention of this paper is to provide a sound basis for a common understanding
of

- what intentions the Reference Model document associates with its Transport
  Layer, as well as

- how a layer may be designed such that advanced technologies for producing reliable software may be applied.

Table of Contents

1.   <u>Introduction</u>

Presently the discussion about the ISO Reference Model (RM, [1],[2]) is hardly understandable for insiders – there is no chance for outsiders to find out from the documents, what is going on. The two main reasons for this situation seem to be that we are concerned with an area in which the semantical notions (it is based on) are not yet really understood and which must span the huge distance between communications oriented towards telephone lines and communications oriented towards human beings.

One way out of this unsatisfactory situation might be to try to immediately improve the notions and notations used in the RM in order to make it comprehensive, for insiders as well as for outsiders. We do not take this approach – simply because the chance of success of merely theoretical and/or conceptual efforts might be questionable. Instead, one may try to contribute to improving the RM by elaborating on the structure proposed by the RM and designing/specifying/implementing systems neatly realizing it. For outsiders, systems of this kind would make it easier to get familiar with the functional decomposition of the communications area, as recommended by the RM; for insiders they are necessary, as well, for improving our today's understanding of the peculiarities of the various parts of this area. Notions and notations then may be adjusted appropriately.

In this paper we go a couple of steps on the latter way: Starting from the assumption that there is a commonly accepted understanding of what functions are to be realized on the layers 1,2, and 3 of the RM, [0.5], [0.7], we design (and specify in [0.9]) a set of services, protocols, and functions for the layer 4 of the RM. All these designs

- avoid incorporating any functions or services belonging to higher layers of the RM, nevertheless

- provide to the Session Layer   all the services as prescribed by the RM, and

- are implementable in a reasonable way over any RM network service.

In addition, the paper depicts a particularly actual case, in which

- it assumes X.25 based network services (on top of which to build the transport entities), and

- it provides for only those services offered in the PIX proposal, [3].

In other words: The Transport Layer designed and discussed in this paper is based, eventually, on the DATEX-P network services provided by the Deutsche Bundespost, as described in [4], and provides those transport services, that the PIX group is going to implement in their pilot project, HMINET II, [3].

The specification technique we apply, [0.2], [0.6], is strongly based on ideas from [5,6]; and has been developed having in mind the particular requirements of distributed systems. It is a formal specification technique allowing for automatically deriving executable code as well as the invariants required for proving the correctness of this code; in that our technique differs from the technique applied in [3,7,8] for describing a Transport Layer.

The paper presented contains - in addition to this introduction - three more chapters. Chapter 2 describes the requirements the RM imposes on the Transport Layer. In chapter 3 we design a Transport Layer meeting these requirements and discuss our design philosophy; we terminate this chapter by explaining the simplifications introduced into the design by restricting it to X.25 network services used and to the services to be provided, as described in [3]. While the chapters 2 and 3 are
concerned with conceptual discussions of the RM philosophy, the chapter 4 describes briefly the formal specification technique applied, i.e., it is concerned with new software technological tools developed for designing/specifying/implementing distributed systems. Thus the chapters 2 and 3 try to provide a sound basis for a common understanding of what intention the RM document relates to its Transport Layer. While the chapter 4 explains, why our design for the Transport Layer is particularly suitable for keeping its formal specification as simple as possible. In total, the paper should be a kind of tutorial for those who have a basic understanding of the RM philosophy as well as of the technological problems of producing reliable software.

2.   The RM Requirements for the Transport Layer

The text of this section consists, basically, of excerpts from the RM document, [1], and some comments and explanations we added for improving their understandability. In order to clearly separate the original RM text from our interpretations we enclose all quotations into "..." . Finally, we frequently shall make use of the term "RM X Layer" in order to abbreviate the phrase "RM requirements for the X Layer", or, more explicitly, "requirements for the X Layer, as prescribed by the RM document".

2.1   General Characterization of the RM Transport Layer

"The Transport Layer exists to provide the transport service in association with the underlying services provided by supporting layers". I.e.: The Transport Layer provides for the 'transport services'; the transport services are realized by means of the services provided by the underlying RM Network Layer.
"The transport service provides transparent transport of data between session entities. Transport Layer relieves the transport users from any concern with the detailed way in which reliable and cost effective transfer of data is achieved."

Some more comments about these quotations, based on the RM philosophy and terminology:

- "Transparent transport of data between session entities" means that the Transport Layer provides transport connections between session entities for transferring data between them without respect of the meaning of these data to the connected session entities.

- "Reliable transfer of data" means that the transport service user may select the quality of service from a limited number of available classes of services, guaranteeing more or less reliability or convenience.

- "Cost effective transfer of data" means that "The Transport Layer is required to optimize the use of the available communications resources to provide the performance required by each communicating transport user at a minimum cost. This optimization will be achieved within the constraints imposed by considering the global demands of all concurrent transport users and the overall limit of resources available to the Transport Layer. In particular, multiplexing at a higher layer is not expected to reduce the cost of providing the transport service between those higher layer entities although it may be quite valid in pursuit of some other (higher layer) objective."

The transportation means presently under considerations are telecommunications means, solely. I.e.: In particular, buffering must be restricted such that managing of large storage capacities is not required. The design of the Transport Layer should

"facilitate the use of more than one communication resource in tandem (e.g., the
network service may be built by the use of a packet switched network, used in tandem
with a circuit switched network)." And finally: "All protocols defined in the Transport Layer will have end-to-end significance, where the ends are defined as the cor-
respondent transport entitities."

Let us conclude this section with a comment concerning the "functions internal to
the Transport Layer". In order to meet the requirements, as prescribed by the RM document, the Transport Layer must provide appropriate services to the Session Layer
and must not use other services than those provided to it by the Network Layer. This
implementing of "services provided to the Session Layer" on top of the "services used
from the Network Layer" is done by means of functions internal to the Transport Layer.
I.e.: The Transport Layer contains various "functions that are necessary to bridge
the gap between the services provided by the Network Layer and the services needed
by the Session Layer". While these both sets of services are prescribed by the RM
document we should be completely free to design all internal functions at will. Conceptually, at least, we should be free. Unfortunately, some other concept is per-
sued in the present version of the RM document: Its description of the internal
functions has a drastic feedback on the services to be provided. We explain this
weak point in the present RM document in more detail in [0.9], and ignore it here.

Thus, we can give an example for the freedom mentioned above. The design for the
Transport Layer from [3] and the one in this paper have identical services (identical services provided as well as identical services used) but have vastly different
internal functions. The reason for developing our solution is our aim that our X.25
based Transport Layer be a special case of our RM Transport Layer efficiently implementable over any RM network service.

The rest of this chapter discusses the RM requirements for the services to be provided by and the services available to the Transport Layer. In the next chapter we
shall describe our design of a Transport Layer meeting these requirements.

2.2   The Services to be Provided by the RM Transport Layer

The services to be provided to the Session Layer are prescribed in two sections of
the RM document, namely in the characterization of the Session Layer, i.e., in
5.3.3 ("services required from the Transport Layer") and in the characterization of
the Transport Layer, i.e., in 5.4.2 ("services provided to the Session Layer").

As usual, the services can be considered in three groups, each of them associated with the corresponding phase of the connection concerned, i.e., here, of the transport connection. A transport connection always is in exactly one of the three phases: establishment, data transfer, and termination phase.

The establishment services must allow for "dynamical transport connection establishment" (between two session entities) and "class of service selection", where the selection is to be made from a limited number of available classes of services, each class characterized by various parameter combinations. Parameters may be throughput, transit delay, connection set-up delay, and reliability of the transport connection (with respect to its properties, such as alteration, loss, duplication, disordering, or misdelivery of data transmitted).

The data transfer services must distinguish between two kinds of data flow, normal and expedited. The normal data flow must meet the service requirements as selected during transport connection establishment. The transport data unit is unbounded in size for the normal data flow and may be bounded in size for the expedited data flow. "An expedited data unit will be delivered before the next submitted normal data unit will be delivered." Quality and flow control mechanisms may be different in both kinds of data flow, in particular, they must have separate flow controls.

The termination services must provide for the means to terminate a transport connection; this means (or an equivalent means) must be accessible to a transport entity, as well, if an unrecoverable error occurred.

2.3   The Network Services Available to the RM Transport Layer

The requirements for the Network Layer are described in two sections of the RM document, namely in "services required from the Network Layer" in section 5.4.3, and "services provided to the Transport Layer" in section 5.5.2.

The services provided by the Network Layer to the Transport Layer are characterized in the RM document as follows:

"The supporting Network Layer is required"

    1. "to provide a service for the transfer of network-service-data-units
       between entities in the Transport Layer." (This transfer may be unreliable.)

2. "to provide uninterpreted transfer of all data submitted."
3. "to provide all available knowledge with respect to the quality of service
   · offered."
4. "to provide the Transport Layer with a network connection endpoint identifier."
5. "to provide all its services at a known cost to the Transport Layer."

We still mention, here, some more RM requirements and nonrequirements for the network services. The network connection between two transport entities may be either
permanent (e.g., permanent virtual channel or in the case of datagram flow) or
established for a limited amount of time and then released. The network service data
units may be limited in size. Depending on the provided type of service, transferred
network service data units are not necessarily in sequence. The occurrence of errors
during network transmission is not excluded and may, dependent on the service class,
be notified to the Transport Layer.

2.4   The Importance of the Transport Layer for Network Interconnections

We did not yet mention an important aspect of the services a Transport Layer provides
to its users: It hides from its users all peculiarities of the underlying networks,
even if several of them are involved in an end-to-end transport connection. Thus,
for a transport service user's point of view - i.e., from above layer 4 - different
interconnected networks behave just like one single uniform network. I.e.: If a
transport connection is established by traversing serially a packet switched network
with datagram service, another one with virtual circuit service and a line switched
network, the users of this transport connections·on both sides need not care for
that. Except minor changes in the transport connection establishment phase, they
should be able to behave as if they were connected by only one single network.

There are two - qualitatively different -.advantages of this uniformity, namely

a) simplification of accesses to resources (processes) of anyone of several
   interconnected open systems from any point (process) in anyone of these
   systems;

b) simplification of plugging local networks - in many cases the only economical
   kind of computer system - into open network systems.

Obviously a) should increase drastically the value of anyone of the interconnected
open systems. But b) probably has even more importance: This allows for a structural
change in the whole development of computer equipments, in that a degree of power is
given to cheap local networks, one previously could not expect from them. The only requirements a cheap local network must meet in order to be interconnectable to some

particular open system are

- it must be able to support a gateway which would provide for an interface
  (to this open system) fulfilling the RM requirements on the layers 1,2, and 3

- the network services available in its host computers allow for a reasonable
  implementation of the Transport Layer of the open system to which it is interconnected. (More precisely: Those parts of the Transport Layer that actually
  must be implemented in these hosts, namely all its global protocols and the
  services it provides for.)

3.   <u>The Design of an RM Transport Layer</u>

When designing an RM Transport Layer, one has to overcome two problems, namely

- in addition to a minimal service provided by the Transport Layer, it should provide more convenient services to a transport user. This increased convenience results from the properties of the transport connection established, such as high reliability, high throughput, low cost, etc. A transport user should be able to select the service most convenient to him by appropriately setting the parameters involved in the transport connection establishment phase.

- the design must be implementable efficiently over any RM network, where the network services these networks provide to the Transport Layer may be pretty different from each other. For example the network services may or may not have the following properties:

    - normal and/or expedited network service data units are very limited in size,
    - network service data units are delivered in the same sequence in which they were transmitted to the network,
    - the throughput parameters of the network connections fit to the throughput parameters of the transport connections.

Thus, various transport services to be provided must be designed/implemented on top of different network services available.

We have two possibilities to organize a design for the Transport Layer, indicated in the two subsequently given graphics, where TS.1, TS.2,..., TS.T are the various transport services, and NS.1, NS.2, ..., NS.N are the network services provided by the network.1, network.2, ..., network.N, respectively.

This problem of "portability of a design" is known since many years, already, [9], and it is clear that the approach shown in Figure 2 must be taken: Here, the only part to be highly portable over the various networks is the BTS. Note that this understanding of portability has nothing to do with what FORTRAN/COBOL program users would associate with this term: Namely porting some application programs written in FORTRAN/COBOL from one FORTRAN/COBOL compiler to another one. In the software engineering area a system is called portable, if it is designed/implemented/documented in a way such that

    - it clearly shows what efforts are required to port it from one underlying system to another one, and

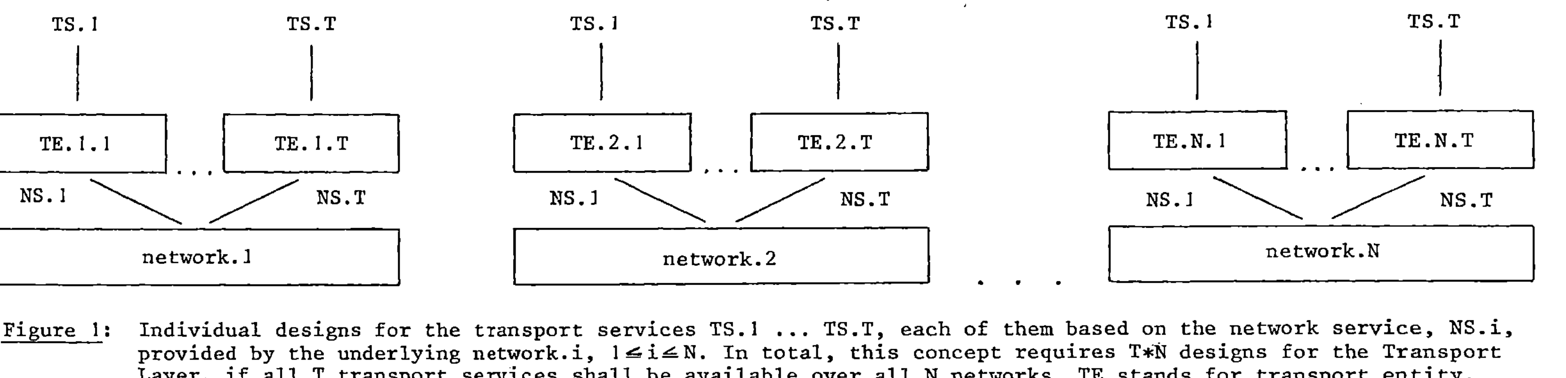

Figure 1: Individual designs for the transport services TS.1 ... TS.T, each of them based on the network service, NS.i, provided by the underlying network.i, $1 \leq i \leq N$. In total, this concept requires T*N designs for the Transport Layer, if all T transport services shall be available over all N networks. TE stands for transport entity.

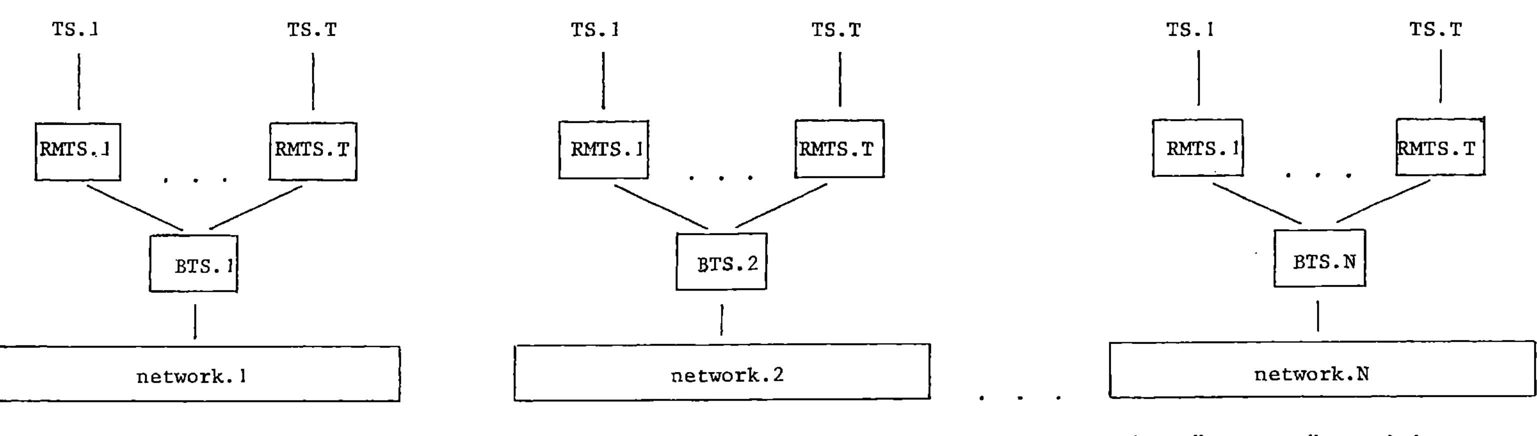

Figure 2: One single design for each of the T transport services, based on BTS. This BTS is a "sublayer" providing for a network independent base of the transport services. One single design of BTS over each of the N networks; each of them provides for the same services to the RMTS. In total, this concept requires T+N designs, if all T transport services shall be available over all N networks. One transport entity over network.i now consists of the BTS.i and RMTS.k, if it provides transport service TS.k.

- these efforts are reasonably low, i.e.; are negligible as compared to re-implementing the system on this other underlying system.

Fortunately, all these underlying systems (i.e., underlying networks) over which BTS must be portable, are pretty similar in that the services they provide would fulfill the RM requirements. Therefore it is possible to construct the BTS from a few building blocks, each of them providing for a particular facility to the RMTS such as sequencing/resequencing, assembling/disassembling, multiplexing/demulti-plexing, blocking/deblocking. Depending on the services providable by a particular network, only a subset of these building blocks may be necessary in the BTS over this network. A particular building block may be missing in this BTS if the facility it would have provided for

- either is superfluous over the network considered (because the facility provided by this building block is included, already, in the services used from this network. For example: If the underlying network maintains the sequences in both flows then the building blocks providing for sequencing/rese-quencing may be missing in the BTS),

- or there is no need for it (because only a restricted transport service is required by the transport user, and therefore the RMTS would not use the fa-cility provided by this building block. For example: No expedited transport service is required).

This chapter mainly is concerned with explaining the structure of our BTS and RMTS i.e., with explaining the building blocks of both of them and how they are integra-ted. Section 3.1.1 describes the BTS, and section 3.1.2 describes the RMTS. In the final part of this chapter, in section 3.2, we shall consider the simplifications obtained, if the underlying network services are X.25 based. The services provided as well as the services used are the same as in [3] (more precisely: they are the same, except the unbounded ETSDU's, our transport service allows for, while [3] allows for ETSDU's of one octett, only; in addition, our service provided will be more cost effective in many cases, if the tariff structure of the Deutsche Bundes-post is assumed).

3.1   The General Structure of our Design for the RM Transport Layer

3.1.1   The Building Blocks of the Basic Transport Services, BTS

In this section we shall describe the building blocks of the BTS, i.e., T_NPDU_ASS/DIS, T_EPDU_ASS/DIS, T_NNSDU_SEQ/RES, T_UP_MUX/DEM, T_DOWN_MUX/DEM, T_NNSDU_BLO/DEB. After having introduced them in sections 3.1.1.1 - 3.1.1.4 we discuss their interrelations to each other in section 3.1.1.5; reading this final section sometimes may be helpful when reading the sections 3.1.1.1 - 3.1.1.4, in particular its Figure 3. The abbreviations used here are almost selfexplaining: T stands for Transport Layer, NPDU, EPDU, NNSDU stand for "normal protocol data unit", "expedited protocol data unit", and "normal network service data unit", respectively, and the rest of the name indicates the function performed.

3.1.1.1 Assembling/Disassembling of TPDU's into NSDU's

In our design of the Transport Layer the transport service data units (TSDU's) will have the same size as and are identical to the transport protocol data units (TPDU's), except for the headers of the TPDU's, not yet available in the TSDU's. Transferring the TPDU's is done by means of the network service data units (NSDU's). The NSDU's may have arbitrary size or a very limited size, only, and they may be different for normal and expedited data flow. Thus, we introduce two building blocks for these assembly/disassembly purposes potentically required, called T_NPDU_ASS/DIS and T_EPDU_ASS/DIS, where the former/latter one is responsible for the Transport Layer normal/expedited protocol data units assembly/disassembly facility, respectively.

Either one or both of them may be absent in a BTS over a particular network, if the service data units of this network are of arbitrary size, respectively.
For the case of underlying X.25 based RM network services, the NNSDU's provided would be of arbitrary size, in general, while its ENSDU's would be 1-octett in size. Thus, over an X.25 network a BTS may not contain the building block T_NPDU_ASS/DIS, but must contain T_EPDU_ASS/DIS. We shall see in 3.1.1.3 that it may be reasonable to include the T_NPDU_ASS/DIS over a network service providing NNSDU's of arbitrary size, as well. This is the case if very large NTPDU's shall be

- "downward multiplexed" onto several network connections in order to speed up their transfer to the peer transport entity, or
- "upward multiplexed" without monopolizing by this large NTPDU's the network connection used.

Note: We obviously assumed that any RM network service provides two data flows, a
normal data flow (which might get blocked because of traffic overload) and an expedited data flow (which never gets blocked and which transfers its expedited data
units not slower than the normal data flow transfers its normal data units). This
assumption is necessary because any RM Transport Layer must provide two data flows,
a normal and an expedited one, and this requirement cannot be fulfilled in a reasonable way unless the underlying network provides an expedited data unit transfer, in
addition to its normal data unit transfer. Unfortunately, the RM document says:
"the provision of expedited NSDU transfer is for further study". We hope that this
inconsistency will be eliminated from the RM by these further studies.

3.1.1.2   Sequencing of NSDU's

The RM requires from any design of the Transport Layer to deliver all TSDU's to the
destination session entity in the same sequence as they were transmitted to it by the
source session entity. This implies: If the underlying network service may deliver
NSDU's to their destination (i.e., destination transport entity) in another sequence
than the one in which they were transmitted to the network (by the source transport
entity), then BTS must contain the building block T_NSDU_SEQ/RES, sequencing and
resequencing the departing/arriving network service data units correctly. I.e., we
here assume that – if the underlying network service does not preserve data flow sequencing – any NSDU of an RM network may carry a sequencing number.

In the case of ENSDU's this assumption may be unrealistic, because sequencing numbers may be too expensive if the ENSDU's are very short. This case occurs with the
X.25 interrupt packets, e.g.

We therefore would not include a T_ENSDU_SEQ/RES in the BTS over an X.25 network.
Instead, in this case, we prescribe that the T_EPDU_ASS/DIS would not transmit
another ENSDU (one for each direction) to the network connection before receiving an
end-to-end delivery confirmation; this guarantees, obviously, that ETPDU's are assem-
bled from ENSDU's in the same sequence in which they were disassembled. Thus, finally, overtaking of NSDU's – if it is possible at all, in the underlying network –
shall not be visible above the BTS, in any case, normal and expedited data flow.

3.1.1.3   Multiplexing of Transport Connections to Network Connections

By multiplexing of transport connections to network connections two different results are achieved, namely,

    a) extending and/or improving the quality of the transport service over the service provided by the Network Layer, and

    b) cost optimization of the service provided by the Transport Layer.

a) may be achieved by upward as well as by downward multiplexing. By upward multiplexing we may increase the number of transport connections above the number of network connections available; by downward multiplexing we may increase the throughput of a single transport connection above the maximal throughput of anyone of the network connections available. Note that one could design different multiplexing facilities for the two transport data flows, normal and expedited; in our design both flows of a particular transport connection are multiplexed to the same network connection(s). The building blocks for multiplexing are called T_UP_MUX/DEM and T_DOWN_MUX/DEM; in our design a transport connection may go through only one of them, i.e., we exclude – in favour of simplicity – the possibility of simultaneously upward and downward multiplexing for a single transport connection.

b) is achieved by using the facilities introduced for a). Upward multiplexing may reduce the total transport cost of several transport connections by multiplexing and paying one single fast network connection (see [4] for details) instead of paying one slow network connection for each transport connection. Downward multiplexing may reduce the transport cost for those transport users which need a network service at a time at which network services paid already are not used by those who paid them (e.g., permanent virtual circuits).

At a first glance the simplification mentioned above (not to multiplex a transport connection simultaneously upward/downward) looks like a restriction for optimizing cost effectiveness of transport connections. At a second glance one sees that not imposing this simplification would allow for serious "fragmentation problems", as they are known from the memory management area. It is well kown that avoiding this problem by dynamic compactification is expensive. Therefore it is an open question whether the above simplification really constitutes a restriction with respect to transport cost optimization.

3.1.1.4   Blocking/Deblocking of NNSDU's

Depending on the tariff structure of the underlying network it may be economical to block several short NNSDU's, i.e., short NTPDU's (plus some sequencing and multiplexing headers, if the building blocks for sequencing and multiplexing are present)

into one single NNSDU, [10]. As blocking is performed on short NNSDU's, only, header
informations should be compressed as far as possible because in this case the header
informations may make a nonignorable part of all the data to be transferred. If this
compression is performed when blocking takes place, then deblocking must re-establish
the complete header informations. The building block for these tasks is called
T_NNSDU_BLO/DEB. Blocking of ENSDU's is not intended in our X.25 based design.

3.1.1.5   A Summary of the BTS

Each of the building blocks BLO/DEB, MUX/DEM, SEQ/RES, and ASS/DIS might appear
twice, conceptually, one for the normal and one for the expedited data flow. Struc-
turally, each of these blocks consists of several modules. In this section we describe informally which modules each of the building blocks comprises and how these
modules are interrelated. More precisely, we only describe the modules required for
interconnecting the building blocks of the BTS and the modules enforcing the end-to-
end protocols of these building blocks. This description of a building block's internal structure still is incomplete and will be given in more detail in chapter 4.

Figure 3 gives an overall view of our design for the BTS. This design is a consider-
able generalization of the one proposed in [11]; the latter one is suitable for a
low service Transport Layer over an X.25 network, only, while the one presented in
this paper should be suitable for all kinds of underlying RM network services (and
offers a substantially more convenient and economical service).

The building blocks of the BTS within one transport entity cooperate with each other
through queues they use in common; a queue name consists of the initial letters of
the names of the building blocks it connects. Note that N_BD/MD_Q would connect
N_BLO/DEB and N_MUX/DEM, while E_BLO/DEB and E_MUX/DEM are connected by E_BD/MD_Q,
etc.

Each of these building blocks of a transport entity requires an end-to-end significant protocol of its own in order to be able to communicate with its corresponding
building block in the peer transport entity; in many cases this protocol will be
trivial, obviously.

Remember, finally, that BLO/DEB and/or SEQ/RES and/or ASS/DIS (and the related
queues) may be missing and MUX/DEM may be used   to mapping one-to-one a transport
connection onto a network connection (i.e., neither providing upward nor downward
multiplexing). These simplifications depend on the services used from the underlying

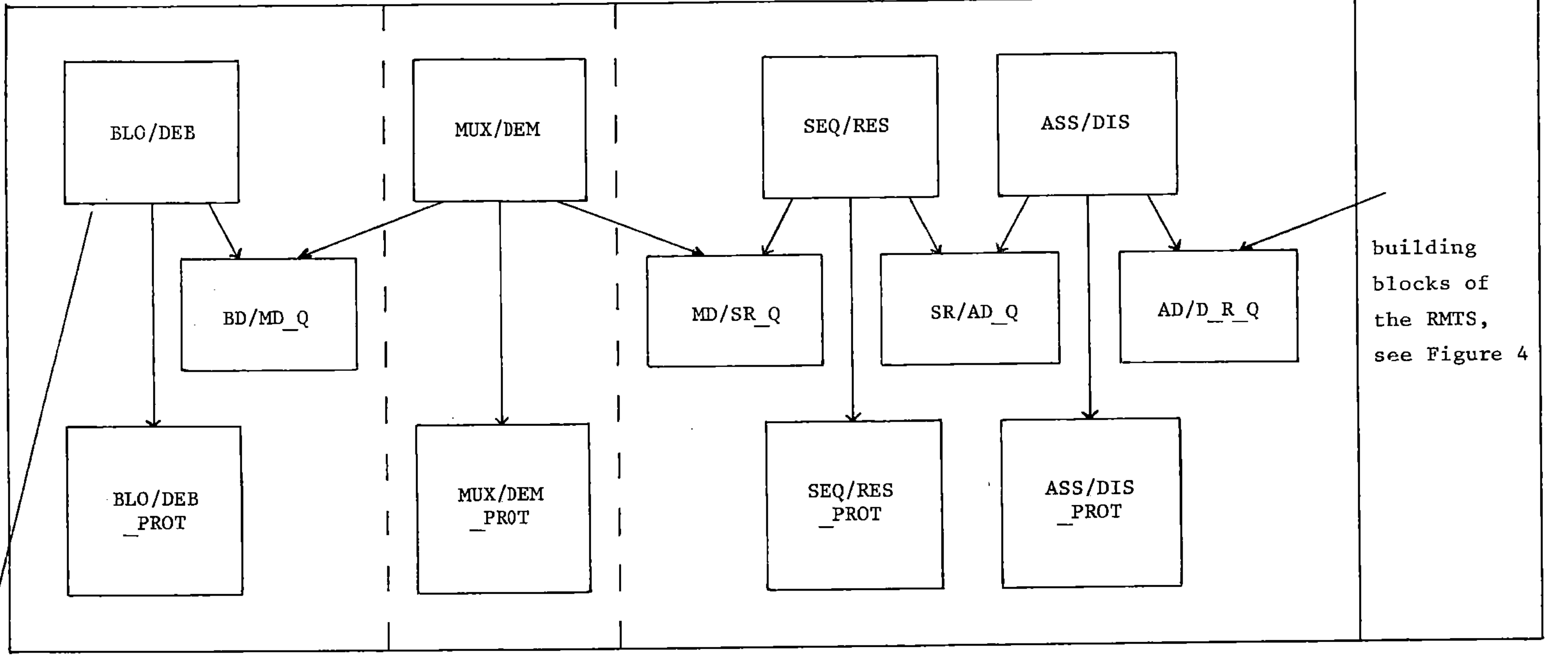

Figure 3: The building blocks of a (maximal) transport entity, here the BTS. For one transport connection all modules of the BTS may be pairwise, conceptually. Note that

- the storage requirement for one Q module would be the same as for these many Q modules.
- there is only one BLO/DEB building block for one network connection and all transport entities using this network connection.
- there is only one UP_MUX/DEM and one DOWN_MUX/DEM building block for all transport entities, i.e. for the whole Transport Layer.
- SEQ/RES, ASS/DIS and RMTS are private for each transport entity.

Network Layer and the services to be provided by the Transport Layer (to be designed on top of this BTS).

Let us conclude this section with a conceptual remark concerning the BTS. One could think of calling this set of building blocks "virtual network service" instead of "basic transport services". Although this term is very appealing it does not characterize what actually is provided by this set of building blocks, namely various functions needed for transport cost optimization and transport convenience, implemented by means of protocols having end-to-end significance; according to the RM document these functions and protocols clearly belong to the Transport Layer.

3.1.2   The Building Blocks of the RM Transport Services, RMTS

In this section we describe the RM transport services of our design as provided by the RMTS to the Session Layer. In section 3.1.1 we described the BTS which provides its services not to the Session Layer but to RMTS. The only purpose of the BTS is to make the design of RMTS independent of the network services available over a particular network; this enables us to design RMTS in such a way that its building blocks immediately correspond to the facilities/services, the RMTS provides to the Session Layer.

The building blocks of the RMTS are DU_REL, FLO_REL, FLO_CONT, TSDU_PACK, and TRANSACT. Depending on the service selected at transport connection establishment, all building blocks but FLO_CONT may be absent from the transport entity; moreover, a transport entity cannot contain TSDU_PACK and TRANSACT simultaneously.

In the BTS we only had the choice between incorporating a building block and leaving it away; in the RMTS, in addition to this choice, we may make the building blocks incorporated more or less powerfull (except TSDU_PACK, which is not variable). For this purpose, they are made variable by composing them of several building parts. I.e.: Each of the variable building blocks is a kind of product of several building parts; which building parts are chosen, actually, for a particular building block, depends on the semantical power required for it because of the service selected. While the building blocks are involved sequentially, one after the other, in transferring data units between the Session Layer and the Network Layer, the building parts actually constituting a building block would be used simultaneously in each transport data unit transfer. There is a simple reason why we designed the building blocks of the RMTS to be variable, whereas those ones of the BTS are unchangeable: We are not convinced that it would pay off to introduce this complexity into the BTS, while it is indispensable in the RMTS if the class of services provided by the Transport Layer shall be as large as required by the RM document.

Before describing the building blocks of our design of the RMTS (and their building parts), we first explain what services, at all, our design for an RM Transport Layer shall provide for.

3.1.2.1   The Class of the Services Provided by our Transport Layer

The BTS contains facilities, already, on which the services (to be provided by an RM Transport Layer) may be based. For example, these facilities may be used for

- transport cost optimization,
- extending the throughput classes and the number of network connections available over some particular network,
- handling arbitrary size NTSDU's and ETSDU's,
- etc.

Those facilities of the RM transport services not supported by the BTS or supported incompletely, only, must be provided for by the RMTS. In addition to transport connection establishment/termination services, the RMTS may provide improvements of

a) reliability of the transport connections,
b) convenience of using the transport services, and, in addition,
c) transport cost optimization.

Selection of a particular class of service is performed by the transport user through the local protocol (either at transport connection establishment time for the whole duration of a connection, or dynamically, i.e., during a session; prior to that, this may be done, too, possibly at user subscription time - an aspect not considered here). The particular class selected is indicated by appropriate actual parameter values transmitted according to the local protocol between a session entity and the Transport Layer.

Without going into details we next characterize a) - c) briefly, starting with the simpler topics b) and c).

For the sake of convenience (i.e., b)), as far as not yet covered by a) and c), RMTS provides for a transaction service, saving a transport user the effort to go through the three phases of a transport connection if he has to transmit one single (normal

or expedited) TSDU, only. The reliability classes available here are the same as for
normal transport connections; an additional parameter could indicate whether a local
or an end-to-end delivery confirmation (to the transport user) is selected, if a delivery confirmation is requested, at all.

For the sake of optimizing transport cost, once more (i.e., c)), RMTS offers a packing
facility and a flushing facility. If the packing switch is on (packing may be switched on and off during the transfer phase) small NTSDU's would·be packed into·larger
NTPDU's before transmitting them; this packing is performed according to the values
the relevant parameters had, when the packing facility was selected at transport connection establishment; in our design ETSDU's may not be packed in this way. Flushing
would always involve resetting of the transport connection into the initial state
and has a uni- or bidirectional effect, depending on the value of the relevant parameter when the flushing facility was selected at transport connection establishment
time. Packing/unpacking achieves cost reduction via a similar way as blocking/un-
blocking does. The differences between these two facilities are that

- in the former case TSDU's are packed, while in the latter case NSDU's
  are packed; these NSDU's may be very small (iff they are pure transport
  protocol control informations) or larger than TSDU (which they may
  enclose),
- in the former case packing is performed on a transport connection private
  base, while in the latter case blocking is done on a network connection
  private base.

The reliability class of the transport connection selected by the transport user
(i.e., a)) may concern the flow of NTSDU's or/and their contents; in our design
transmission of ETSDU's is highly reliable, a priori, and may not be reduced by the
user. Note that appropriate protocols must be selected for RMTS in order to enable
it to guarantee the selected reliability of the transport connection. These protocols differ from each other in their flow control mechanisms as well as in the
NTPDU-oriented redundancy insertion/evaluation mechanisms. Based on the reliability
properties of the underlying network service these protocols may be determined automatically (dynamically at transport connection establishment time, or statically and
a priori). Note, finally, that convenience is improved here once more: Obviously a
transport connection becomes more convenient as it becomes more reliable, in particular, if automatic retransmission is guaranteed (after an error was detected at one
side), relieving the transport user partly from maintaining things like checkpoint
informations, recovery blocks, etc.

3.1.2.2   The Building Blocks concerned with Reliability, DU_REL and FLO_REL

The building blocks DU_REL/FLO_REL are the lowest building blocks of the RMTS (see
Figure 4); they are responsible for maintaining the data unit/flow reliability,
respectively, of the transport connection, as selected at its establishment.

The data unit/flow oriented reliability, respectively, as provided by the BTS is
approximately the same as the one of the underlying network service; the BTS here
does not provide an improvement. For the normal data flow the reliability (i.e., bit
error rate, loss of NTSDU's, etc.) may be chosen arbitrarily at transport connection
establishment time. By this choice a protocol is determined responsible for insert-
ing/evaluating the required amount of redundancy into/in the (packed or non packed)
NTSDU's. Transport connection errors which cannot be corrected automatically in a
building block would be indicated to the next higher building block.

DU_REL is the lowest building block and is responsible for the integrity of any single data units received from the BTS. For this purpose the peer DU_REL must insert
into any data unit to be transmitted appropriate redundancy such that - when receiving a data unit - the probability of detecting a transmission error by DU_REL is
sufficiently high. We do not go here into the question what kind of redundancy would
be cost effective, in this case; but obviously the data unit oriented reliability of
a network connection (inclusively BTS) can be made arbitrarily high, i.e., it can be
adjusted to what has been selected by the transport user.

FLO_REL is the next higher building block and is responsible for the integrity of the
data flow received from the BTS. For this purpose the peer FLO_REL must insert into
the single data units to be transmitted identifiers indicating their sending sequence (so-called sent sequence numbers) and store   the data units sent until they
are no longer needed for retransmission. Note that the reliability of the protocol
control informations of this protocol - as well as of any higher one - is supported
by DU_REL. Thus it is possible to make the flow arbitrary reliable, i.e., it can be
adjusted to what has been selected by the transport user.

It is easily seen how both building blocks may be put together from different
building parts. DU_REL may contain various completely independent building parts
concerning different redundancy insertion/evaluation mechanisms. FLO_REL may contain
a retransmission building part or not; in the latter case it would only detect flow
errors (without being able to correct them automatically).

The technique discussed in this section (for improving the reliability of a transport connection) is completely independent of the kind of flow considered, i.e., it

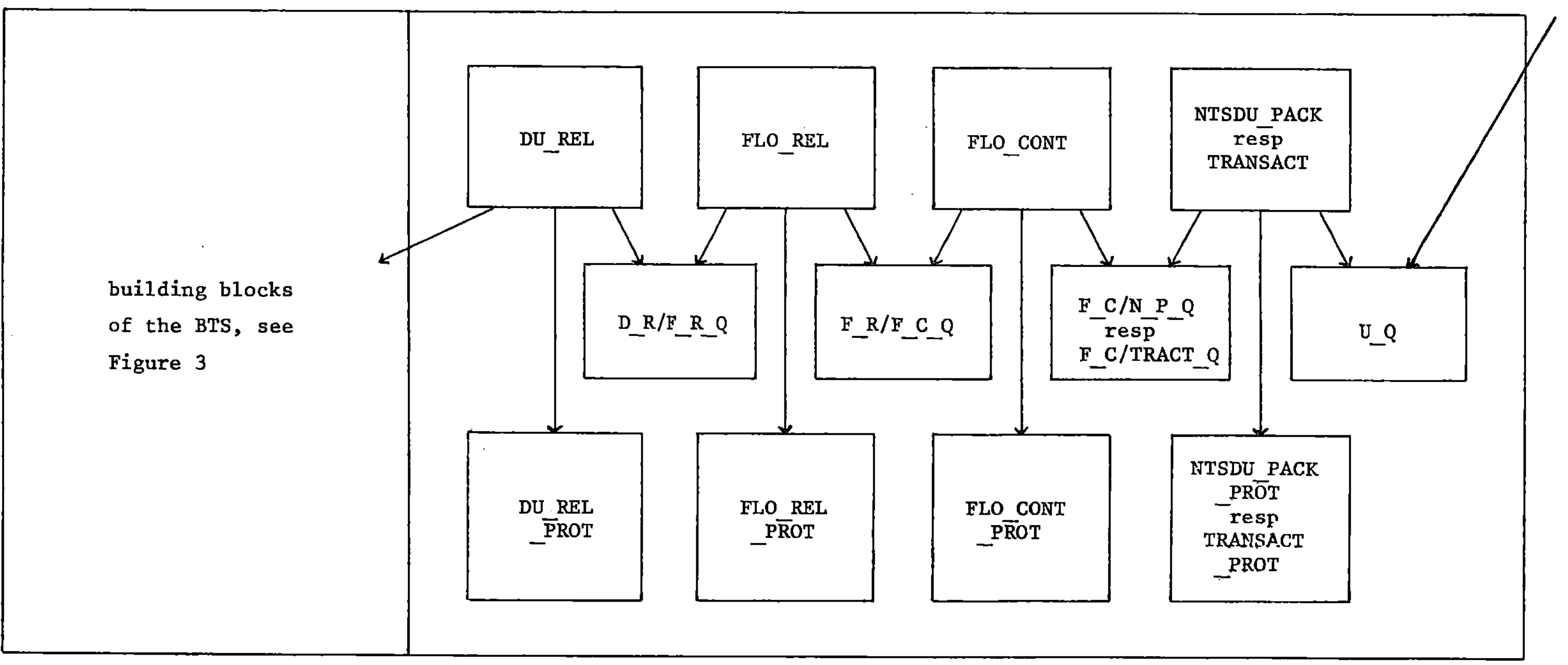

Figure 4: The building blocks of a (maximal) transport entity, here the RMTS. If the TRANSACT service is requested, NTSDU_PACK is absent.

is applicable to the normal as well as to the expedited data flow. Thus, in our design we have four building blocks, EDU_REL/NDU_REL, and EFLO_REL/NFLO_REL. We shall continue the discussion of the expedited data flow in section 3.1.2.4.

3.1.2.3   The Building Block concerned with Flow Control, FLO_CONT

FLO_CONT provides two different kinds of services, namely
   a) transport connection establishment and termination services, and
   b) flow control services for the transfer phase of a transport connection established.

Because of a) the building block FLO_CONT never may be left away completely; presently, only one establishment and one termination service are designed.

For flow control during the transfer phase FLO_CONT may provide various facilities for resetting (with or without flushing) the transport connection and controlling the amount of incoming data per time unit. All these flow control facilities may be left away completely; i.e.: if anyone of them is needed for a transport connection, it must be requested when establishing this connection. Resetting may be explicitly initiated by the transport user any time, while the "backpressure control functions" may not be called explicitly.

Flushing resetting differs from non flushing resetting in that in the latter case no data units are discarded, while in the former case each building block's queues are cleared as soon as it gets a flushing reset request; a reset request for a transport connection reinitializes all building blocks that are private to this transport connection. It is not quite obvious, what backpressure control mechanisms are the most convenient ones, the most cost effective ones, etc. But this is a minor problem because this facility is provided by a very simple and small building part of FLO_CONT; probably convenience and cost effectiveness of all reasonable mechanisms are about the same.

Note, finally, that FLO_CONT is the highest building block of RMTS if NTSDU_PACK and TRANSACT are absent.

3.1.2.4   The Expedited Data Flow

If not needed by a transport user the expedited data flow may be left away from the
transport connection he establishes. In this case certain flow control mechanisms
would not be possible, and this transport connection would not meet the RM requirements unless the flushing reset facility is available.

If an expedited data flow is requested the corresponding building part of FLO_CONT
and the building blocks EFLO_REL and EDU_REL are included into the transport entity.
EFLO_REL is very simple: its only purpose is to store the last ETSDU sent until it
is no longer required for retransmission. EDU_REL is independent of the reliability
requested by the transport user, i.e. it always provides for a high reliability.
Thus these two flows are subject to different sets of transport service characteristics and have separate flow controls.

Conceptually, we could have designed a separate building block EFLO_CONT, and thus
separated completely the N data flow from the E data flow; but in this case certain
synchronizations between the two flows are required, making this design more complicated than our design.

3.1.2.5   Packing/Unpacking NTSDU's by NTSDU_PACK

If the TSDU's (to be exchanged between the communicating session entities) are small
transport cost optimization requires to pack several of them into a TPDU, if the
delay caused by this packing is affordable. This is true, in particular, if NFLO_REL
assures high reliability of the normal data flow. Packing/unpacking is performed by
the optional building block NTSDU_PACK, located on top of FLO_CONT. If NTSDU_PACK
has been included into a transport entity at transport connection establishment,
packing may dynamically switched on/off by the transport user; in addition, he may
request at any time to transmit the NTSDU's packed at this time. The size of the
buffer for this packing of NTSDU's and the frequency for transmitting it automatically would be determined by the transport user at transport connection establishment, as normal.

3.1.2.6 Handling of single TSDU's by TRANSACT

TRANSACT is the only building block primarily concerned with convenience; besides
it may save some cost by reducing the amount of time a network connection is required for transmitting a single TSDU. There are separate building blocks for normal
and expedited transactions, ETRANSACT and NTRANSACT; the reliability properties of
the transaction services are the same as those ones of the normal/expedited data
flows, resp. Obviously NTSDU_PACK may not be used by the transaction services.

3.2   Our Design for an X.25 based RM Transport Layer

Starting from the general design as given in section 3.1 we now simplify it (by
leaving away several building blocks) such that we obtain a design for a Transport
Layer implementable over an X.25 network and providing the services as described in
[3]. Figure 5 shows this simplified design.

Because of the underlying X.25 network services the BTS may be reduced by the following building blocks:

- N_ASS/DIS is not necessary, because the NNSDU's may have arbitrary size.
  I.e.: The facility that would be provided by N_ASS/DIS is provided by the network service, already. Leaving away N_ASS/DIS might result in monopolizing a
  network connection by very large NNSDU's, if upward multiplexing of several
  transport connections onto one network connection is performed. In general this
  will be a minor problem and therefore may be ignored, here.

- DOWN MUX/DEM is left away because of simplicity. This makes it impossible to
  provide to a transport user a transport connection with a higher throughput
  capacity than the fastest network connection has. I.e.: Without DOWN_MUX/DEM
  we cannot put together a high throughput capacity (requested for a transport
  connection being established) from various slow network connections. Note that
  this does not only touch the aspect of convenience, but there is some cost aspect, too. If, namely, several slow permanent virtual channels are available,
  now a fast transport connection cannot be downward multiplexed onto them but
  another switched virtual circuit must be requested and payed.

- N_SEQ/RES may be left away, because an X.25 network connection maintains the
  sequence of the NNSDU's sent, and downward multiplexing of a transport connection is no longer possible in this design. (Note: The X.25 recommendation does
  not state explicitly, that virtual channels would preserve the ordering of
  packets to be transferred, [0.16]. Nevertheless, the common interpretation of
  the X.25 recommendation is, that a virtual channel would preserve this ordering).

- E_SEQ/RES is left away, because the E_ASS/DIS we have in our design operates
  with windowsize=1; i.e.: the global protocol between our E_ASS/DIS building
  blocks (in the peer transport entities of a transport connection) enforces the
  correct sequence in the transfer of ENSDU's between the communicating DTE's by
  not sending another ENSDU before the previously sent ENSDU has been received
  by the remote DTE. This restriction to windowsize=1 for the expedited data flow
  of an X.25 virtual channel is pretty inefficient and could have been left away,
  if the X.25 recommendation would have determined, that interrupt packets are

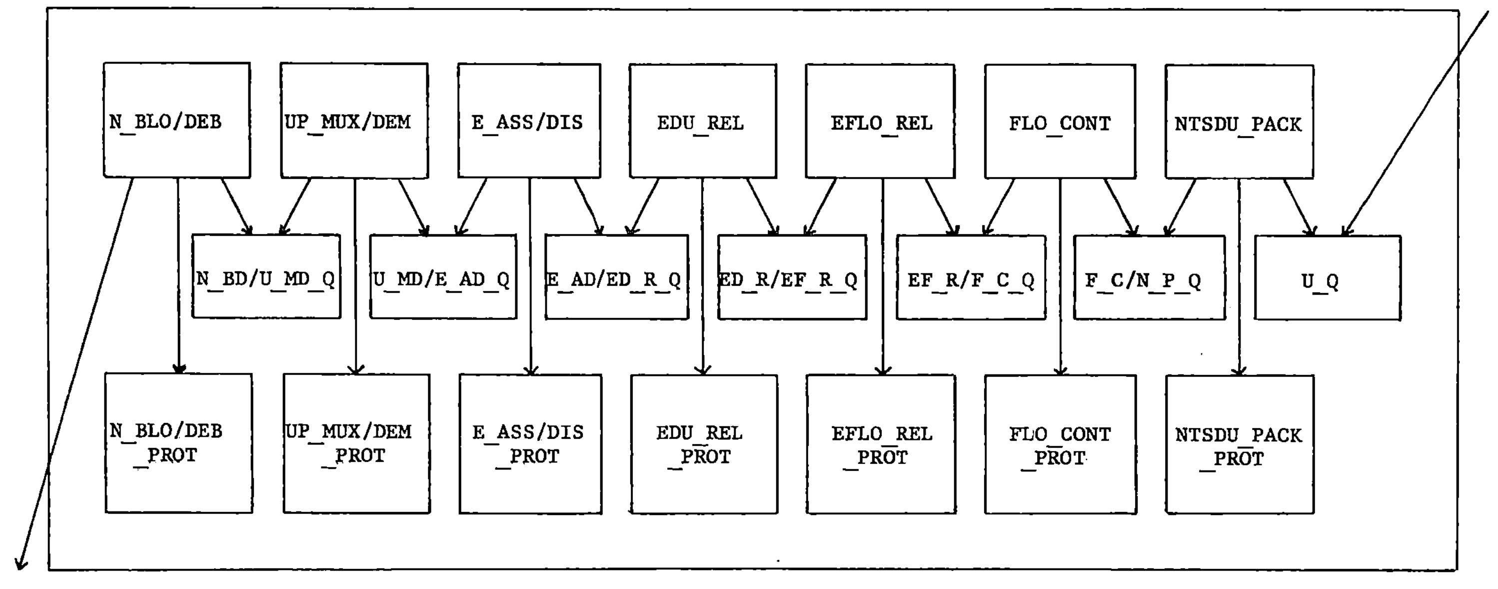

Figure 5: The X.25 based design

transmitted between the DTE's preserving the sending sequence (see [0.16]).

- E_BLO/DEB for the X.25 expedited data flow makes no sense.

- N_BLO/DEB could be left away, here because the design of [3] does not have it.
  Nevertheless we keep it in our design, because in the DATEX_P net of the Deutsche Bundespost leaving it away may result in a drastic increase of transport
  cost in certain cases (up to a factor of 10 and more). Note that N_BLO/DEB is
  optional in a transport entity and makes no sense in a transport connection,
  that has a network connection of its own; efficient handling of short NTSDU's
  of a single transport connection is achieved by NTSDU_PACK (The remaining short
  data units to be transmitted, the control information NTPDU's, probably cannot
  justify maintaining N_BLO/DEB in this case).

- UP_MUX/DEM in our design might be reduced to a mapping one-to-one transport
  connections onto network connections, just as done in [3]. For transport cost
  optimization purposes, again, we maintain the possibility of building several
  slow transport connections on top of a single fast network connection. In many
  cases this upward multiplexing would reduce the transport cost by a factor of
  2, (if a 48000 bit/sec line may be fully occupied, this factor may go up until 5).

Thus the only mandatory building blocks in our X.25 based BTS are E_ASS/DIS and
UP_MUX/DEM; optionally N_BLO/DEB may be requested and then would be included in the
two transport entities for this connection being established.

The only mandatory building blocks in the RMTS are EDU_REL, EFLO_REL and FLQ_CONT.
If only these building blocks are requested for the RMTS (at transport connection
establishment) then we obtain a RM transport connection with a highly reliable expedited data flow and a normal data flow having the reliability of the underlying
network. Our X.25 based simplified design would contain only these three building
blocks, and NTSDU_PACK, in addition.

Note that - if no expedited data flow is required on the transport connection -
the only building blocks needed for a transport entity would be FLO_CONT (without
its building part concerned with the expedited data flow) from the RMTS and
UP_MUX/DEM from the BTS.

Let us conclude this section by two remarks concerning protocols and service data
units in our designs.

Protocol definitions are completely left away, here. Because of the grain of decomposition of the design into building blocks all the protocols, the local as well
as the global ones, are very simple. ([0.9] contains all details). In order to
avoide having different interfaces in different designs we simply took the service
data units and the parameters from [3], where their meaning is described, too.

4. The Formal Specification of a Design

In this chapter we do not go down to the level of technical detail on which any formal specification of a software product actually would be located; these technical details may be found in [0.9]. Instead, in section 4.1, we start with summarizing various pretty recent insights from the area of producing reliable software and from the area of distributed systems. Our design and specification philosophies are strongly based on these insights.

An example for a design derived following this philosophy was given in chapter 3; in section 4.2 we shall make this design more complete and explain its feasibility for formally specifying it. The main part of this chapter, section 4.3, will be concerned with discussing the technique we developed for formally specifying communications control software products.

In order to avoid misunderstandings we would like to emphasize that we are not going to discuss how to formally specify a layer of the RM document. This would be a very interesting task, but presently there are too many open questions concerning important areas of the scope of the RM document; some of them are pointed out in [0.13, 0.14]! But, we are going to present a technique for formally specifying the design of a software product meeting the requirements of an RM Layer, in this case the Transport Layer. Thus, the usual terminology (and even the title of this paper) are somewhat misleading but should be harmless after this remark.

4.1 Some General Remarks about Formal Specifications

First of all there is the question what is ment by "formally specifying a design". Obviously there must be, a priori, a design which is to be formally specified and which is described in some informal way. Still pretty obviously, specifying a design means describing this design in a precise way (at least, in a more precise way than it was described before). Thus, the remaining question is, what properties a specification of a design must have in order to be formal. We consider a specification to be formal if there is a set of formal rules which are applicable to the specification and - iff applied - derive from it a set of boolean expressions stating uniquely for any point in time and for any function what the effect of executing this function is (and whether it is executable, at all). A formal specification may be given in a graphical notation, a language notation, or whatsoever; the only thing that matters is the set of formal rules to derive from the specification the set of predicates it stands for, determining uniquely the precise meaning of the specification given. Any correct implementation of the design would consist of programs leaving these predicates true at run time at those points in time, for which they are to hold.

The next question probably would be, what advantages formally specifying (a design) has as compared to informally specifying it. Obviously there is the important advantage just mentioned, that formal specifications provide for the invariants required for proving the correctness of an implementation. But another aspect seems to be at least as important as   proofs of correctness: It is a common experience that writing formal specifications for a design brings up a great deal of the bugs and holes of the design and where it differs from what it intuitively was expected to be. There are commonly accepted figures indicating what percentage of all errors occuring during the design and implementation of a product not formally specified one may detect by writing a formal specification for the design: [12] talks about more than 50%, [13] about approximately 75%. It is well known that these errors of a design are difficult to identify and to eliminate – if not detected early enough. These figures match to our experiences and it was primarily this effect resulting from writing formal specifications that makes us strongly advocate them and made us develop a formal specification technique, particularly suitable for communications control software products.

4.2   Designs for Communications Control Software Products

There are various particularities of software for communications control purposes that clearly must be understood in order to avoid designs for which it is hard to write a formal specification. In this section we shall explain two of them, indicated be the terms 'protocols' and 'exception handling'.

Concerning protocols: Experience shows, that complex protocols are extremely error prone. For example the X.25 Layer 2 and 3 protocols are pretty hard to understand [0.15, 0.16, 0.17] and are the sources of many errors. As we go to higher layers in a communications system the services of these layers become more flexible, requiring even more complex protocols (global as well as local ones) than the X.25 protocols. The only way out of this problem is not to design a single monolythic protocol for a layer, but to support the various facilities provided by a layer by separate single protocols. This results in having several global protocols for a single layer, as opposed to the layers 2 and 3, where one single protocol has to support all the facilities of these layers (see [0.5] and [0.7] for more about that). A further measure of separation of concerns is taken by encapsulating a protocol into a module of its own. Having the data flow in different modules then the protocol separates the activities controlled by this protocol from its implementation. This considerably simplifies the overall structure of the design by reducing the complexity of the single modules (being the specification units) and allowing for clear interfaces between them.

Concerning exception handling: in a distributed system exception handling must be done, sometimes, in a different way than in a centralized system. In a centralized system the attempt to execute a function in an exceptional situation in most cases would result in simply rejecting this attempt. In a distributed system the rejection mechanism often is useless, because here it is too expensive (technically) and deadlock prone (logically), [0.2]. Instead, the occurance of exceptional events often must lead to performing some reinitialization operations (e.g. reset operations, or clear operations). Considering this "exit mechanism" within one module, we could overcome all problems (related to specifying it) by means of an appropriately chosen semantic of our specification construct for protocol sequences, [0.2, 0.5]. But difficulties arise when trying to specify the impact, taking an exit in one protocol has for another protocol. This problem may be reduced by enforcing (by the design) that it is tackled in a uniform way throughout the design, i.e. without respect of the actual protocol taking an exit. In our design we enforce this uniformity by a uniform building block structure, i.e. by putting the design together from quite uniform building blocks, each of them allowing only one global protocol.

4.3   The OSA Approach

In our OSA project (OSA = Open Systems Architecture) we try to integrate
- the standardization efforts of the CCITT,
- the conceptual and standardization efforts of the ISO and the DIN
- the new software technologies for producing reliable software.

With respect to the last point we consider it to be utmost important to have a design technique supporting formally specifying a design. The design philosophy and specification technique we developed in the OSA project are based on this insight. In this section we shall show that our designs actually are suitable for being formally specified and how we proceed when doing so.

4.3.1   The Structure of our Formal Specifications

At a first glance the structure of our formal specifications is the same as the
structure of the design to be specified, because we give the formal specifications
for all the elements of our design (i.e. for all its building blocks and the modules
the building blocks consist of) element by element. Looking closer at it, we shall
see that formally specifying a module is strongly different from formally specifying
a building block; this is shown next.

Let us start with modules. A module is the specification unit for a set of functions
constituting a very basic part of the whole design and appearing at various places
of it. Typical examples are queue modules, stack modules, protocol modules, memory
modules. From a programming language point of view these modules are nothing else
but data type definitions (like class declarations in SIMULA), or speaking more
general, they provide for abstract data types. From the design point of view the
functions these modules specify are not yet available outsides of the layer being
designed. They are "layer internal" functions because their only purpose is to serve
as a basis for implementing the facilities/services to be provided by the layer.
I.e. they are semantically still pretty weak and completely independent of the functions specified in other modules. Specifying a module's functions under these circumstances is possible by means of several wellknown techniques, e.g. SPECIAL. If
we are concerned with a module specifying functions, the use of which is restricted
by a strong protocol - and this frequently is the case in the communications area -
the specification technique we developed is much simpler, [0.2, 0.5, 0.8], than what
was available previously. Thus writing down the formal specification for modules in
our design is a straight forward activity.

Now let us consider building blocks. Each building block is designed to provide some
particular service/facility. A building block consists of a set of modules (in our
design, between 7 and 11 modules, depending on the grain of the module structure).
In general, all the functions specified in the modules a building block contains are
visible to this building block. But there are modules, too, where it knows only
about some of their functions; an example for those modules are the Q-modules connecting two building blocks. A building block exports all the functions imported to
it from its modules; it does not know or specify any additional function. Nevertheless a building block is another specification unit for the functions it exports
(another one than the modules importing these function to it) in that it changes
their semantic by restricting their executability rules such that executing them,
actually, results in performing the service/facility the building block provides.
Thus, all a building block is responsible for, that is to control the cooperations
between its modules, i.e. to enforce some synchronization rules. Specifying these

synchronization rules is semantically something quite different than specifying a module's functions.

Note that, in our specification structure, we first specify in a module a set of elementary functions required for some administrative task, like buffering, protocol enforcement, etc; then we couple several of these modules together in a building block and specify in this building block the admissible sequences for executing these functions. On the specification level we therefore completely separate the concern of "what to do" from the concern of "when to do it".

The specification philosophy we persue for specifying modules is drastically different from the one we persue for specifying building blocks. In the former case our philosophy says, that a function being called for execution is executable, actually, only if this function's execution at this point in time is explicitly admitted by the module's specification. In the latter case our philosophy says, that a function being called for execution (and being executable according to its module's specification at this point in time) should remain executable, actually, unless the building block's specification explicitly disables this function's execution at this point in time.

The advantage of proceeding the way we did - namely, completely specifying in the modules the elementary functions needed and, separately, specifying in the building blocks the minimal restrictions for their execution sequences - should be obvious: We thus avoid to determine unvoluntarily the dynamical behaviour of the product we are specifying. An implementation following the same philosophy would allow for greatest flexibility when changes of the dynamical behaviour of the product are required. Such changes frequently are required if a system of this kind shall work efficiently, either because the traffic has changed, or because the equipment has changed, or, last not least, because the tariff has changed.

4.3.2   <u>The Basic Building Block</u>

Our design philosophy is based on two requirements, namely, the building blocks of a design
- should be that simple that writing formal specifications for them is simple
- should be that similar to each other, that they have a relatively large part in common.

In this last section we sketch this common part of all building blocks, the so called basic building block.

First of all, our maximal design for the Transport Layer contains 14 building blocks;
each building block contains up to 11 modules (in our present design, the most of
them not mentioned in this paper). Many of these modules are Q-modules or trivial.
The basic building block keeps away from the actual and substantial specification
activity any care for these routine specifications. Any one of the specifications
for the 14 building blocks starts with a "standard prelude", standing for the complete specification of the basic building block. This would not yet be particularly
helpful, if the amount of routine specifications were small as compared to the individual specifications required for a building block. Fortunately the contrary is
true: Because of the simplicity of the facility/service a building block is responsible for, the individual specifications consist of a few lines, only, per building
block specification.

Note, that these few lines of individual specifications per building block are only
a part of the differences between two.different building blocks: Most of the corresponding modules in different building blocks differ from each other, e.g. the global protocol modules, the various local protocol modules, the various memory modules. But all these module specifications are simple and small. What easily compli-
cates writing the formal specifications for a design, that are the building block
specifications. We avoided this problem by determining a uniform internal structure
for the building blocks which is flexible enough to allow to specify all building
blocks we need and which is simple enough to remain manageable reliably. It is due
to this uniform internal structure of the building blocks that the basic building
block (i.e. the part they have incommon) is that large.

General References

[1] Reference Model of Open Systems Interconnection, ISO/TC97/SC16, N227, Aug. 79

[2] The Reference Model-Open Systems Architecture, ISO/TC97/SC16, N117, Open Systems Interconnection, Paris, 78

[3] F. Vogt, E. Dregger, H. Eckert, B. Lausch: Specification of a Transport and Session Layer Protocol Based on the Message Link Protocol, Version 1.0, September 79

[4] Datex-P Benutzerhandbuch (unvollständige und nicht endgültig abgestimmte Fassung - vor Auftragsvergabe). Fernmeldetechnisches Zentralamt, 6100 Darmstadt ... 79

[5] E.W. Dijkstra: A Discipline of Programming, Prentice-Hall, Englewood Cliffs, N.J., 76

[6] D.L. Parnas: The Use of Precise Specifications in the Development of Software, Proceedings of the IFIP Congress 1977, North Holland Publishing Company, 1977

[7] G.V. Bochmann: Formalized Specification of the MLP. Department d'informatique et de recherche operationelle, Universite de Montreal, June 1979

[8] G.V. Bochmann: An Analysis of the MLP. Departement d'informatique et de recherche operationelle, Université de Montreal, June 79

[9] The UNCOL Project, Summerschool on Software Engineering, München, 73

[10] E. Raubold: Proposal for Message-Blocking Facility in MTC (agreed by ML-implementation-group, Berlin, March 79)

[11] S. Schindler, M. Steinacker: A Uniform Protocol Machine Organization for the Transport Layers of the ISO/TC97/SC16 Reference Model. Trends & Applications 1979: Advances in System Technology, May 17, 79, Gaithersburg

[12] C.R. Vick: Software Engineering Tools, Past, Presence and Future, Proc. of the 4th International Conference on Software Engineering, Munich, September 17-19, 1979

[13] Ramamoorthy et al.: A Systematic Approach to the Development and Validation of Critical Software for Nuclear Power Plants, Proc. of the 4th International Conference on Software Engineering, Munich, September 17-19, 1979

The OSA Project

[0.1]   S. Schindler: The OSA Project, Memo I, May 24, 1979 (project members are
presently the students D. Altenkrüger, .   U. Flasche, K. Gelhard,
H.G. Haase, T. Luckenbach, H. Marxen, B. Messer, B. Müller-Zimmermann,
M. Neumann, W. Schröder, J. Schulze, Z. Tosun, all of them working towards
their master's degree (i.e., for their Dipl.-Inform.), and the Assistent
Dipl.-Math. M. Steinacker, working towards his Ph.D. degree (i.e., Dr.-Ing.).

[0.2]   S. Schindler: The OSA Project: Specification of Data Types for Distributed
Systems, TU Berlin, FB 20, TR 79-13

[0.3]   T. Luckenbach, W. Schröder: The OSA Project: Specification of a Level 2
(LAP) Protocol Maschine, Studienarbeit TU Berlin, August 1979

[0.4]   D. Altenkrüger, U. Flasche, J. Schulze: The OSA Project: Study of the Design and Formal Specification of Transport Layer Protocols as Proposed by
the Reference Model, Studienarbeit TU Berlin, August 1979

[0.5]   S. Schindler, T. Luckenbach, W. Schröder: The OSA Project: Formal Specifications of the X.25 Layer 2 Protocols, Comments on Their Suitability for an
Open Link Layer, TU Berlin, FB 20, TR 79-11

[0.6]   S. Schindler, H. Marxen: The OSA Project: Translating RSPL Specifications,
TU Berlin, FB 20, TR 79-19

[0.7]   S. Schindler,   K. Gelhard, H.G. Haase, B. Messer, Z. Tosun:
The OSA Project: Formal Specification of the X.25 Layer 3 Protocol, Design
and Formal Specification of an Open Network Layer, TU Berlin, FB 20,
TR 79-10·

[0.8]   S. Schindler: The OSA Project: RSPL - A Reliable Software Production Language,draft available

[0.9]   S. Schindler, D. Altenkrüger, U. Flasche, J. Schulze, M. Steinacker: The OSA
Project: Design and Formal Specification of an Open Transport Layer and its
Protocols, TU Berlin, FB 20, TR 79-12

[0.10]   S. Schindler, H. Marxen, B. Müller-Zimmermann: The OSA Project: Automatic
Generation of Efficient Code for RSPL Specifications, TU Berlin, FB 20,
TR 79-16

[0.11]   S. Schindler, D. Altenkrüger, U. Flasche, J. Schulze, M. Steinacker: The
OSA Project: Design and Formal Specification of an X.25 Based Open Transport
Layer and its Protocols, Proceedings of the Conference on Communication in
Distributed Systems, December 3-4, 1979, Berlin

[0.12]   S. Schindler: Algebraic and Model Specification Techniques, Proceedings of
the 13th Hawaii International Conference on System Sciences, Honolulu,
January 3-4, 1980

[0.13]   S. Schindler, D. Altenkrüger, U. Flasche, J. Schulze, M. Steinacker: The OSA
Project: The Reference Model Transport Layer, Proceedings of the Pacific
Telecommunications Conference 1980, January 7-9, 1980, Honolulu

[0.14]   S. Schindler: Open Systems' Requirements - A Survey, Proceedings of the Conference on Computer Architecture and Operating Systems, March 19-21, 1980,
Kiel

[0.15] S. Schindler, T. Luckenbach, W. Schröder: The OSA Project: Open Questions
          About the X.25 Layer 2 Protocols (LAP A/B), in preparation

[0.16]   S. Schindler,   K. Gelhard, H.G. Haase, B. Messer, Z. Tosun:
          The OSA Project: Open Questions About the X.25 Layer 3 Protocol, in prepa-
          ration

[0.17]   S. Schindler: X.25 Considered Harmful? TU Berlin, FB 20, August 1979, sub-
          mitted for publication

[0.18]   S. Schindler: The ISO Reference Model and the CCITT X.25 - Chances and
          Problems for International Standards for Open Systems, Proceedings of the
          6th International Congress Data Processing in Europe, March 17-21, 1980,
          Wien

[0.19]   S. Schindler, D. Altenkrüger, U. Flasche, J. Schulze, M. Steinacker: Er-
          läuterungen und Beispiele zum Gebührenmodell für die Datex_P Dienste der
          Deutschen Bundespost, Entwurf vom Dezember 1979

Benutzerschnittstelle des
P I X
End-zu-End Protokolls

H. Eckert
Gesellschaft für Mathematik und Datenverarbeitung
- Institut für Datenfernverarbeitung -
6100 Darmstadt, West-Germany

Zusammenfassung:

Innerhalb von PIX[*] wurde in den letzten Jahren
eine Reihe von Protokollen für die unterschiedlichen Ebenen der Kommunikation erarbeitet.

Das vorliegende Papier beschäftigt sich mit dem
Protokoll, das allgemein der Ebene 4 und Ebene 5
(ISO-Architekturmodell) zugeordnet wird.
Insbesondere wird die Dienstleistung (Service)
beschrieben, die von dieser Ebene den darüber
liegenden Schichten angeboten wird.

[*] PIX: Pilotkomplex technisch-wissenschaftlicher
Rechnerverbundvorhaben

1. Einleitung

In den letzten Jahren wurden innerhalb von PIX eine Reihe von
Kommunikations-Protokollen erarbeitet, die auf verschiedenen Ebenen
der Kommunikation Mittel sind, das Kompatibilitäts-Problem zu überwin-
den und einen freizügigen Datenaustausch zwischen DV-Systemen unterschiedlicher Herkunft zu ermöglichen.

Der konkrete Aufsetzpunkt für die Entwicklung der höheren Kommunikationsprotokolle war die Empfehlung X.25 de CCITT, welche eine Schnittstelle zwischen einem Endbenutzer und einem öffentlichen Paketvermittlungsnetz beschreibt.

Folgende Architektur ergab sich für die höheren Protokolle (s. Bild 1):

Basierend auf den drei Ebenen von X.25 wurde das Message-Link-Protocol
(MLP) konzipiert, welches die zwei wesentlichen Aufgaben der End-zu-
End Prozeß-Verbindung und der allgemeinen Synchronisation erfüllte.

Darauf setzen die applikations-orientierten Protokolle auf (virtuelles
Terminal, Remote Job Entry, File Transfer, Remote Data Access), deren
Strukturierungs- und Synchronisationsmittel dem Modell der Kommuni-
kationsvariablen folgen.

Die Modellvorstellungen und damit auch die Modellierungssprache war
funktionsorientiert, d. h. die Protokolle wurden durch Funktionen
beschrieben, welche gesteuert durch äußere Ereignisse von den
Kommunikationspartnern ausgeführt wurden.

Alle grundlegenden Arbeiten an den Protokollen waren bereits abgeschlossen, bevor erste Ergebnisse, des im März 1977 gegründeten
ISO/TC 97/SC 16, vorlagen. Der jetzt erreichte Stand der Normungsarbeit (dokumentiert in ISO/TC 97/SC 16 N 227) hat im wesentlichen
die Modellvorstellungen in PIX bestätigt.

Selbstverständlich haben die laufenden Arbeiten von ISO und DIN die
detaillierte Analyse der PIX-Protokolle, insbesondere das Message-
Link-Protocol, beeinflußt. Dabei fand, ohne substantielle Änderung
eine Umorientierung in zwei Punkten statt:
- Die Schichtenbildung wurde verfeinert,
- der funktionellen Beschreibung wurde die Servicebeschreibung
  vorangestellt, d. h. das was die einzelnen Ebenen leisten

wurde explizit ausgedrückt und die Funktionen und ihre
Zerlegung innerhalb einer Schicht nach dem von ihnen zu
erbringenden Service ausgerichtet.

Dies brachte zwei wesentliche Vorteile mit sich:

1. Eine klare Gliederung der Verfeinerungsschritte beim Entwurf
   der speziellen Komponenten eines Protokolls:

   - Der Zerlegung eines Protokolls in überschaubare, insbesondere
     für eine Verifikation handhabbare Bausteine. (Connect-Proto-
     col, Disconnect-Protocol, Synchronization-Protocol, ...)

   - Eine präzise Unterscheidung der notwendigen Ereignisse und
     Informationen, die an den lokalen Service-access-point auf-
     treten, von denen, die End-zu-End Bedeutung haben (protocol-
     data-unit, interface-data-unit). Dadurch wird es möglich,
     klare Regeln für die Inanspruchnahme eines Service an einer
     Benutzungsschnittstelle zu geben und sie vom eigentlichen
     Protokollablauf zu unterscheiden.

2. Es wird eine Überprüfung der Funktionen in bezug auf den von
   ihnen zu erbringenden Service möglich.

Nachdem nun die wesentlichen Arbeiten am Message-Link-Protocol in bezug
auf eine
   - Service-Beschreibung
   - Funktionelle Beschreibung
   - Protokoll- und Schnittstellen-Beschreibung
abgeschlossen sind, kann man folgendes feststellen:

   - Das Message-Link-Protokoll (MLP) paßt in den konzeptionellen
     und funktionellen Rahmen, der durch das 'Reference Model of
     Open Systems Interconnection' vorgegeben ist.

   - Es hat bezüglich der Spezifikation seiner Dienstleistungen
     und Protokolle einen genügend großen Detaillierungsgrad
     erreicht, um implementiert zu werden.

2. Struktur des MLP

Ausgehend vom ISO-Architekturmodell, müssen einige Festlegungen getroffen werden, um zu einem implementierbaren Protokollentwurf zu gelangen.

Für Protokolle der Ebene 4/5 sind Annahmen notwendig bezüglich

1. der Relation zwischen den Instanzen benachbarter Ebenen,
2. des Service der von der Ebene 3 vorausgesetzt wird,
3. des in gewissem Sinne minimalen Umfangs an Dienstleistung, den die Ebenen 4/5 den darüber liegenden Schichten bereitstellen müssen, damit Instanzen dieser Ebene eine gesicherte Kommunikation durchführen können.

Die Annahmen zu 1. haben in der Hauptsache Auswirkungen auf die Zuordnung von Instanzen der verschiedenen Ebenen und damit auf Namens- und Adressierungskonventionen.

Es wird für das MLP angenommen, daß es zu einem Zeitpunkt einer Prozeß-Prozeß-Verbindung folgende eins-zu-eins Relation zwischen Instanzen der Ebenen 3, 4/5, höhere Ebenen gibt:

Application/Presentation-Connection end-point

Session/Transport-Connection end-point

Network-Connection end-point

Dies bedeutet keine Einschränkung in folgenden zwei Punkten:

- Ein Prozeß kann zu anderen Prozessen zu einem Zeitpunkt mehrere Session-Connections parallel unterhalten.

- Während der Lebensdauer einer Session-Connection können mehrere Network-Connections (allerdings zeitlich nacheinander) benutzt werden.

Zu Punkt 2: Der Service, der von der Ebene 3 vorausgesetzt wird, ist derjenige, welcher für die Durchführung der Ebene 4/5-Funktionen erforderlich ist (es wird angenommen, daß ein VC eines Paket-Vermittlungsnetzes (X.25) die geforderten Dienstleistungen erbringt). Möglicherweise sind die Anforderungen nicht minimal (besonders bezüglich expedited data flow).

Zu Punkt 3: Aus der Sicht eines Applikations-Prozesses sollten von der
Ebene 4/5 global folgende Dienstleistungen erbracht werden:

(1) Etablieren einer Prozeß-Prozeß-Verbindung,

(2) Stabilisieren der Verbindung als Funktion der Zeit,

(3) Zuordnung/Freigabe der Übertragungsressource,

(4) Unterstützung/Durchführung von Prozeß/Prozeß-Synchronisation,

(5) Abbau einer Prozeß-Prozeß-Verbindung,

(6) Übertragung von Benutzer(-Prozeß)-Daten (Messages).

Abhängig vom Service der unterlagerten Ebene 3 und der Qualitätsanfor-
derung der Applikationsebene an eine Transportverbindung kann es notwendig sein, eine scharfe Trennung der Ebenen 4 und 5 vorzunehmen.

Damit ist die Ebene 4 diejenige Stelle innerhalb eines Schichtenmodells,
die

"die Benutzer des Transport-Service von allen Problemen eines
zuverlässigen und kosten-effektiven Datentransports befreit."
(s. 7)

Nach der derzeitigen Tarifstruktur bei öffentlichen Paket-Vermittlungs-
netzen wäre eine mögliche Ebene-4-Dienstleistung, die der Kostenmini-
mierung dient, eine Blockungs-Funktion [10], die es erlaubt, mehrere
Nachrichten der Applikationsebene in eine vollständige Paketfolge
abzubilden.

Selbstverständlich ist die Ebene 4 auch die geeignete Schicht, in der,
unter Berücksichtigung der Qualitätsanforderungen und der Verfügbarkeit,
eine Auswahl aus verschiedenen Datennetzen getroffen würde.

Für die Ebene 5 blieben dann, abgesehen von der Herstellung einer
Verbindung zwischen Instanzen der höheren Schicht, Services der allgemeinen Prozeß-Prozeß Synchronisation, welche sind:

- Kontrolle des Datenaustausches
- Erzeugen von abgesicherten Rücksetzpunkten
- Zurücksetzen auf solche Punkte der Kommunikation
- Eröffnen und Abschließen von Kommunikations-Phasen.

Das MLP bietet dem Benutzer eine kombinierte Schnittstelle der Ebene 4/5 an. Dabei
werden aus der Ebene 4 die Dienstleistungen CONNECT (RESUME) und DISCONNECT (RELEASE)
dem Benutzer explizit sichtbar. Dies ist durchaus mit dem ISO-Architekturmodell
verträglich, zumal die Ausführung dieser speziellen Services zeitlich getrennt von
allen Dienstleistungen der Ebene 5 ablaufen.

3. Die Benutzer-Schnittstelle des MLP

Der Benutzer des MLP, welches die globalen Service-Leistungen (1)-(6)
erbringt, hat Zugang zu den Dienstleistungen dieser Ebene (4/5) über
einen lokal zu realisierenden Service-access-point. Der Service, den
der Benutzer in Anspruch nimmt, wird ihm von der unterlagerten Schicht
als ganze erbracht, welche somit als ein verteiltes System, bestehend
aus den Instanzen der Ebene 4/5 und der Ebene 3, gedacht werden kann
(s. Bild 2).

3.1 Beschreibungsmethode

Bei der Beschreibung einer Benutzer-Schnittstelle, d. h. eines
Service-access-point, ist zweierlei zu beachten:
    Einerseits ist die Beschreibung des Service, der von einer
    Ebene erbracht wird, essentieller Bestandteil der Architek-
    tur eines Open-Systems und jede Beschreibung, die dies
    außer Acht läßt, bleibt vage.
    Andererseits muß die Beschreibung so weit wie möglich
    unabhängig von speziellen Implementationsvorstellungen
    sein, um einen Service-access-point abhängig von den
    lokalen Gegebenheiten (Operating System, Implementation-
    Language) an unterschiedlichen Stellen eines verteilten
    Systems realisieren zu können.

Die Methode, die für das MLP zur Beschreibung des an der oberen Schnittstelle erbrachten Service, gewählt wurde, beruht auf dem Konzept der
Service-Primitive.

Ein Service-Primitiv ist ein modularer Baustein eines Service, welcher
im Grunde durch Abstraktion der Interprozeß-Kommunikation entstanden
ist, wie sie in realen Systemen vorgefunden wird.
Beispiele dafür sind: Subroutine-Calls, Makro-Aufrufe, Exit-Routinen.
Ein Service-Primitiv kann von beiden Seiten einer Schnittstelle auf-
gerufen (d. h. die Ausführung des Service angestoßen) werden. Die
Leistung eines Primitive (sein Service) wird durch die Angabe von
"Ein-/Ausgabeparameter" beschrieben.
Dazu ein Beispiel:
    Es soll das Etablieren eines X.25 Switched-Virtual-Channel
    (SVC) beschrieben werden.

Betrachten wir zunächst den Fall, daß ein Benutzer der
Ebene-3-Schnittstelle einen SVC einrichten möchte. Er
muß dazu alle Informationen, die für den Aufbau eines
Call-Request-Packet erforderlich sind, bereitstellen.
(Distant network address, facilities, user data, etc..)
Als Antwort erwartet er, ob der Call angenommen wurde
oder nicht.
Dies wird im folgenden etwas formalisiert:
Die gesamte Dienstleistung, vom Auftrag einen SVC zu
etablieren, bis zur positiven oder negativen Bestätigung
über das Gelingen, soll (in Großbuchstaben) mit INIT
(initialisiere SVC) bezeichnet werden. Die Parameter,
die beim Aufruf mitgegeben werden, sind durch →
gekennzeichnet; diejenigen welche nach der Durchführung
zur Verfügung gestellt werden, durch ← kenntlich gemacht.

Damit wird der Service wie folgt beschrieben:

```
    INIT (→ distant network-address,
          → facilities,
          → user data,
            .
            .
            .
          ← accepted : boolean
          ← reason (if rejected))
```

Die gleichen Überlegungen können nun für den Fall angestellt
werden, daß in der Ebene-3 ein Incoming Call empfangen wurde
und die Ebene-3 den Benutzer darüber informiert, eine Antwort
erwartet, um daraufhin ein Call-accepted- oder ein disconnect-
packet der Partner-Instanz zu schicken.

Man stellt bei genauer Beobachtung fest, daß über die Schnittstelle hinweg die gleichen Informationen ausgetauscht werden;
nur in umgekehrter Richtung.

Um dies einheitlich in kompakter Schreibweise auszudrücken,
werden zwei weitere Symbole eingeführt:
Wird das Service-Primitiv INIT vom Benutzer der Ebene-3
angestoßen, schreiben wir ↓INIT, wird es von der Ebene-3
selbst angestoßen, schreiben wir ↑INIT. Somit läßt sich
der gesamte Service der Initialisierung eines VC in der

Form schreiben:

        ↓ or ↑ INIT

                    (→ distant network-address,
                      → facilities,
                      → user data,
                          .
                          .
                          .
                      ← accepted : boolean
                      ← reason (of rejected))

Diese Beschreibungsmethode hat folgende Vorteile:
  - Sie modularisiert die gesamten Interaktionen, die an eine
    Benutzerschnittstelle bei der Benutzung des Service einer
    Ebene notwendig sind.
  - Sie gibt ein formalisiertes Mittel, um präzise den Service,
    der an einer Schnittstelle geboten wird, zu beschreiben.
    -- Der Service einer Schnittstelle wird repräsentiert durch
    die Menge der Service-Primitive. --
  - Sie erlaubt es - in Bezug auf eine Verifikation - lokale
    Regeln für die korrekte Abfolge der Ausführung von Service-
    Primitiven zu formulieren. (Bemerkung: Zur Formulierung
    des Protokolls und dessen globaler Eigenschaften müssen
    neben den lokalen Regeln noch die globalen Zusammenhänge
    mit End-zu-End Bedeutung der Service-Primitive angegeben
    werden.
  - Für eine Implementation können aus der Beschreibung die
    zu realisierenden Schnittstellen-Ereignisse und die damit
    verbundenen Übergabedaten leicht konstruiert werden.

3.2 Die Service-Primitive der ML-Benutzerschnittstelle

Wie in den vorangehenden Abschnitten angedeutet, werden an den Benutzer-
Schnittstelle des ML-Protokolls sowohl Services der Transport-Ebene
(Etablieren einer Transport-Connection), als auch Services der Session-
Ebene (Synchronisationsdienste) angeboten.

Diese Services werden mit der Methode der Service-Primitive beschrieben.

Mit jedem angebotenen Service (konkret Service-Primitiv) ist ein weitgehend selbständiges von anderen Primitiven unabhängiges Protokoll
verbunden. Der Zusammenhang der Services wird durch die lokalen Anwen-
dungsregeln (hier nicht näher ausgeführt, s. [4, 5, 6]) bestimmt.

Beispiel:
      Es gibt die Service-Primitive CONNECT und
      DISCONNECT. Zu beiden gehört ein Protokoll.
      Sie sind über folgenden Zustandsautomaten
      miteinander gekoppelt.

      DISCONNECT   CONNECT

      Zustand: $\emptyset \;\hat{=}\;$ non existent; $1 \;\hat{=}\;$ existent

Diese Unabhängigkeit der Service-Primitive und damit der Protokolle
erlaubt es dem Benutzer, die Services des ML-Protokolls angepaßt an
die Bedürfnisse seiner Anwendung zu benutzen. So kann er z. B. nach
Einrichtung einer Transportverbindung sofort mit dem Austausch von
Daten mit seinem Partner beginnen, oder die beiden Kommunikationspartner können zunächst einen gesicherten Wiederaufsetzpunkt in ihrem
Dialog einrichten.

      Diese Unabhängigkeit der Services erlaubt:

- aufwärtskompatible Protokollerweiterungen
- Kommunikation mit Hilfe unterschiedlich stark
   ausgebauter Protokollversionen (natürlich auf
   der Basis einer Absprache über die gemeinsam
   in Anspruch zu nehmenden Services).

Zur Lokalisierung der ML-Benutzerschnittstelle in existierenden Fern-
verarbeitungssystemen sei bemerkt, daß sie in den vergleichbaren
Dienstleistungen auf der Ebene von ACF/VTAM oder DCAM angesiedelt sein
könnte [11, 12, 13, 14, 15].

Nicht unmittelbar vergleichbar sind dagegen die zugehörigen Protokolle,
da im Bereich Open-Systems-Interconnection ein höherer Grad an
Verteilung und Gleichberechtigung von Funktionen einer Ebene berücksichtigt werden muß.

3.2.1 Service Primitive mit rein lokaler Wirkung

Es gibt in Bezug auf einen Dialog zwischen zwei Prozessen im wesentlichen zwei Service-Primitive mir rein lokaler Wirkung:

- ✦ ALLOCATE und
- ✦ DEALLOCATE

Die Leistung dieser Primitive besteht darin, eine Applikation mit den lokal notwendigen Hilfsmitteln für eine Kommunikation auszustatten, bzw. nach deren Beendigung die benutzten Ressourcen wieder frei zu geben.

Die Allocation (bzw. Deallocation) muß von den Kommunikationspartnern für jede Session-Connection an der sie beteiligt sind, getrennt vorgenommen werden. Ihnen werden dabei logisch System-Prozesse zugewiesen, die in der Lage sind, eine Session-Connection zu unterhalten.

Sie erbringen die Dienstleistung, wie sie in den nachfolgenden Primitiven formuliert sind. Diese Systemprozesse sind daher im wesentlichen zweiseitig, event-getrieben; einerseits durch den Applikations-Prozeß am oberen Interface, andererseits durch ihren Partnerprozeß, der wiederum durch Events am Interface zur unterlagerten Schicht (Ebene 4 oder 3) sichtbar wird.

Wie stark der Vorgang der Allocation (Deallocation) dynamisiert werden kann, hängt von der Implementation und dem Leistungsumfang der Betriebssysteme ab.

Ebenso hängt die Realisierung der Interface-Events von den lokalen Gegebenheiten ab.

Festzuhalten bleibt, daß diese System-Prozesse, welche in der Lage sind, eine Session-Connection zu unterhalten

- als zuteilbare Ressource angesehen werden,
- vor der Aufnahme einer Kommunikation zugeteilt sein müssen,
- exklusiv einer Session-Connection zugeordnet werden.

Die in existierenden Systemen vergleichbaren Funktionen sind YOPEN / YCLOSE-Makros in DCAM und die OPEN/CLOSE Makros in ACF/VTAM.

Service-Primitive, die an der Applicationsschnittstelle sichtbar werden
und ihrem Service nach zur Transportebene gehören, sind

            ↑ or ↓ CONNECT (→ network-connection parameter,
                            → (distant) transport-address,
                            → service class,
                            → break recovery : boolean,
                            → protocol identifier
                            ← accepted : boolean
                            ← reason (if rejected)

und   ↑ or ↓ DISCONNECT (→ reason)

Nachdem eine Applikation erfolgreich den ALLOCATE-Service in Anspruch
genommen hat, kann sowohl sie zu anderen Applikationen, als auch
Kommunikationspartner zu ihr eine Transport-Connection aufbauen.

Der Aufbau einer solchen Verbindung hat zwei Aspekte und erfolgt daher
auch in zwei Schritten (nicht sichtbar an der Benutzerschnittstelle)

            1.) Herstellen eines Connections-Gedächtnisses
            2.) Requirieren eines Übertragungskanals
                (z. B. X.25 VC)

Zu 1.) Das Connection-Gedächtnis besteht aus einem Paar von Transport-
Adressen, oder äquivalent dazu Namen, unter denen die beiden Kommunikationspartner diese Transport-Connection betreiben wollen.

Dieser Name (resp. Adresse) muß vor der Einrichtung der Verbindung dem
Partner bekannt und im Zielsystem eindeutig sein. Eine Connection
existiert so lange, wie das Connection-Gedächtnis auf beiden Seiten der
Kommunikation vorhanden ist.

Das zugehörige Connection-Protokoll sorgt für die Herstellung und
Synchronisation des Gedächtnisses zwischen beiden Partnern.

Zu 2.) Da ein Übertragungskanal, als eine zuordbare   Resource ange-
sehen wird, muß eine Allocation vor der Übertragung von Daten erfolgen.
Dabei ist es möglich, daß in zeitlicher Abfolge zu einer Transport-
Connection mehrere Kanäle (Network-Connections) zugeordnet werden.
(Dies kann mit den beiden Service-Primitiven RELEASE / RESUME während

einer Transport-Connection veranlaßt werden.
(Diese Primitive sind hier nicht weiter beschrieben.)
Aus dieser dynamischen Zuweisung einer Network-Connection resultieren
zwei Probleme, die vom CONNECT / DISCONNECT-Protokoll - genauer dem
Transmission-Resource-Allocation (TRA-) Protokoll - gelöst werden.

Erstens ist es bei gleichberechtigten Partnern möglich, daß einer
Transport-Connection zwei Network-Connections zugeordnet werden; dies
ist der Contention-Fall.

Zweitens kann von Applikationen, die nicht miteinander in Kommunikation treten wollen, versucht werden, die gleiche Network-Connection
zu requirieren; dies ist der Collision-Fall.

Ein Vergleich zwischen mir bekannten existierenden Systemen und dem
CONNECT / DISCONNECT-Service ist nur schwer möglich, da er, insbesondere aber das zugehörige Protokoll, sehr stark die Gleichberechtigung
der Kommunikationspartner und den dynamischen Aspekt des Connection-
Gedächtnisses betont und unterstützt.

3.2.3 Service-Primitive der Session-Ebene

Die Services der Session-Ebene erfüllen drei Aufgaben:

1.) Einrichten und Auflösen einer Session-Connection
2.) Kontrolle des Datenaustausches und Synchronisation zwischen den
    kommunizierenden Applikationsprozessen
3.) Datenaustausch

Zunächst sei folgendes bemerkt:

Da diese Service-data-units (Df. siehe [7]) der Session-Ebene, im
Falle fehlender Optimierungsprotokolle in der Transport-Ebene eins-zu-
eins auf Service-data-units der Transport-Ebene abgebildet werden, ist
es möglich, daß Applikationsprozesse ohne Benutzung der Session-Ebene
kommunizieren können.
An der Schnittstelle würden dann nur die Service-Primitive CONNECT;
DISCONNECT; SEND; RECEIVE benutzt.

Allerdings wäre dies eine ungesicherte Kommunikation, bei der die
Applikationen alle Probleme, die aus der Network-Ebene entstehen
könnten, selbst behandeln müßten.

Die gesamten Sicherungs- und Synchronisationsdienste (incl. Einrichten
und auflösen einer Session-Connection) beruhen auf zwei Zählern,
einem Send-Zähler (NS) und einem Receive-Zähler (NR), die von der
Session-Ebene jeweils an der Benutzerschnittstelle (den Service-
Access-points) geführt werden und dem two-way-handshake-Mechanismus
(s. Bild 3 und Bild 4).

Von den beiden Zählern NS, NR werden die Messages (session-service-
data-units) gezählt, die durch die Service-Primitive SEND und RECEIVE
an der Schnittstelle zur Applikation übergeben werden.

Damit die Zählerpaare der Kommunikationspartner sinnvoll verwendet
werden können, müssen sie selbstverständlich auf beiden Seiten das
gleiche "Stück Information" zählen. (S. dazu Definition von service-
data-unit in [7]).

Weiterhin müssen die Applikations-Prozesse in Bezug auf das Abgeben
und Aufnehmen der Session Service Data-Units sequentiell sein, da
sonst über die Schnittstelle 4/5 zu höheren Ebenen keine Identifikation der Messages möglich ist.

Bei jedem Synchronisationsvorgang werden die Zähler (NS, NR) der
Kommunikationspartner ausgetauscht und von den Instanzen der Ebene 4/5
verglichen. Die Differenzen stehen den Applikationen als Ergebnis des
Synchronisationsservice zur Verfügung.

Der two-way-handshake-Mechanismus, als eigentliches Mittel der
Kommunikation der Session-Instanzen, betont in starkem Maße die
Gleichberechtigung der beiden Partner.

Er kann angesehen werden als eine verschränkte Überlagerung von zwei
Master-Slave Beziehungen ausgedrückt mit "Command-Response".

Ein Partner gibt ein "Command", erwartet ein "Command" der Gegenseite
und falls beide ein "Command" gegeben und empfangen haben, werden die
"Responses" ausgetauscht.

(Bemerkung: Die Zähler NS, NR werden in den "Responses" mitgeteilt).

3.2.3.1 Service-Primitive für den Datenaustausch

Die Service-Primitive für den Datenaustausch sind

       ↓ SEND (→ session-service-data-unit
             ← accepted : boolean)

und

       ↑ RECEIVE (→ session-service-data-unit
             ← accepted : boolean)

Den Service-Primitiven können jeweils zwei Schnittstellen-Events zugeordnet werden.

    1. Übergabe der Session-Service-data-unit,
       falls dies möglich ist,
    2. Bestätigung der Annahme.

Der zweite Event hat nur lokale Bedeutung, d. h. er wird erzeugt, falls
entweder die Applikation, oder die Session-Ebene die Information auf-
genommen hat. Er bedeutet im Falle von SEND nicht, daß der Partner die
Information bereits erhalten hat.

Selbstverständlich wirkt sich auf die Ausführung der Service-Primitive
die Flußkontrolle des benutzten Kanals als Rückstau aus.

Die Übergabe der entsprechenden Zähler NS NR (s. einleitender Abschnitt)
an die Applikation kann für Recovery-Fälle sehr sinnvoll sein und
sollte bei lokalen Implementationen berücksichtigt werden.

3.2.3.2 Service-Primitive für Bind-Unbind

Die folgenden Service-Primitive werden zur Errichtung (resp. Auflösung)
einer Session-Connection angeboten:

    ↓ or ↑ OPEN   (→ open-data 1,
                 ← open-data 2,
                 → mode,
                 → checkpoint-hierarchy-range: integer,
                 ← open (accepted, rejected (reason)))

```
↓ or ↑   CLOSE   (→   close-data 1,
                  ←   close-data 2,
                  ←   n1, n2 lost n.s.s.d.u.)
```

Die Parameter haben folgende Bedeutung:

- open-data 1, open-data 2, close-data 1, close-data 2 sind Daten, die
  die beiden Applikationen während der OPEN- (bzw. CLOSE-) Operation
  austauschen können. Sie sind für die Ebene 5 transparent.

- mode legt das Kommunikationsverhalten der beiden Partner fest, welches
  sie durch die OPEN-Operation etablieren wollen. Die Bedeutung des
  mode-Parameters ist für die Ebene 5 transparent. Die von den beiden
  Partnern angebotenen modes werden jedoch auf Gleichheit geprüft und
  und eine Nicht-Übereinstimmung führt zu einem Mißlingen der OPEN-
  Operation.

- Checkpoint-Hierarchy-range: integer
  Mit diesem Parameter wird der Wertebereich 0 bis 255 der expedited
  data (z. B. X.25 Interrupt) in zwei Teile geteilt. Der Bereich 0
  bis checkpoint-hierarchy-range wird für den TELEGRAM-Dienst (hier
  nicht näher ausgeführt) benutzt, der Bereich von checkpoint-
  hierarchy-range bis 255 dient den CHECKPOINT-Services.

- open (accepted, rejected (reason))
  Hier wird der Ausgang der OPEN-Operation mitgeteilt.

  Zu einem Mißlingen kann es kommen durch

      - Nicht-Übereinstimmung der modes
      - Nicht-Übereinstimmung der checkpoint-hierarchy-range
      - Ablehnung durch den Partner
      - irreparable Fehler des Transportsystems (z. B. RESET, CLEAR)

- n1, n2 lost n.s.s.d. u (im CLOSE)

  n1, n2 sind die Zähler-Differenzen von NS (bzw. NR), die während der
  Kommunikation seit der letzten Synchronisation aufgetreten sind.

  Allgemein ist zum Service der OPEN und CLOSE Primitive zu sagen, daß
  sie die geeigneten Elemente sind; um eine Kommunikation sicher zu
  beginnen und zu beenden, da sie für den Austausch der definiert
  ersten (bzw. letzten) Protokollelemente einer Kommunikationsphase
  sorgen. Konkret werden durch sie die SEND/RECEIVE Zähler in einen
  Anfangszustand gesetzt und miteinander abgestimmt.

Das OPEN-Primitiv sorgt weiterhin für den <u>ersten</u> gesicherten
Rücksetzpunkt in der Kommunikation. Dieser ist dann unbedingt erforderlich, wenn im weiteren Verlauf der Kommunikation solche Punkte
definiert und im Fehlerfall auf sie zurückgegangen wird.

3.2.3.3 Service-Primitive für Synchronisation

Neben den speziellen Synchronisier-Services OPEN und CLOSE, die Anfang
und Ende einer Session markieren, gibt es eine Reihe von Service-
Primitiven, die von den Applikationen an beliebigen Stellen innerhalb
einer Session (natürlich in Abstimmung mit dem Partner) benutzt werden
können.

Diese sind:
-      Das allgemeine SYNC-Service-Primitiv

       ↓ or ↑ SYNC   (→ sync-data 1,
                       ← sync-data 2,
                       → mode,
                       ← sync (accepted, reject (reason)),
                       ← n1, n2 lost n.s.s.d.u)

Die Bedeutung der Parameter ist logisch äquivalent zu denen in den
OPEN und CLOSE-Primitiven.

Dabei kann der mode-Parameter, abhängig von den Applikationen, beliebige Bedeutung haben.

Eine mögliche Anwendung des SYNC-Service-Primitivs wäre die Kontrolle
der Zähler, NS, NR in bestimmten Abständen während des Datenaustausches.
Damit wird eine Übertragung der Zähler für jede session-service-data-
unit überflüssig. (Sie ist für erste Implementationen auch nicht vorgesehen.)

Allerdings kann dann aus der Tatsache n1 $\neq$ $\emptyset$ oder n2 $\neq$ $\emptyset$ nicht ge-
schlossen werden, daß es sich bei den verlorenen data-units um die
zuletzt gesendeten handelt.

- Die beiden Check POINT-Services-primitive:

↓ or ↑ SET CHECKPOINT (→ checkpoint-data 1,
                        ← checkpoint-data 2,
                        → checkpoint-priority,
                        ← checkpoint (accepted, rejected (reason)),
                        ← n1, n2 lost n.s.s.d.u.)

↓ or ↑ CHECKPOINT RESTART (→ checkpoint priority,
                           ↑ abandoned)

Mit dem Primitive SET CHECKPOINT sind logisch zwei Absprachen bei
den Benutzern verbunden.

1. Die Übereinkunft einen Checkpoint der gleichen Priorität gemeinsam
   zu schreiben.

2. Den vorangehenden Checkpoint der gleichen Priorität aufzugeben.

Diese Strategie beinhaltet, daß zu jedem Zeitpunkt, zu jeder
Priorität, nur ein gültiger Checkpoint existiert.

Für das Gelingen einer SET CHECKPOINT Operation gilt analog das zu
OPEN gesagte.

Insbesondere gelingt sie nicht, wenn n1 oder n2 nicht gleich $\emptyset$ sind,
oder wenn die von den Partnern angebotene Checkpoint-priority nicht
übereinstimmt.

Zum Wiederaufsetzen auf einen geschriebenen Checkpoint wird das
Service-Primitive CHECKPOINT RESTART benutzt. Zur Übertragung der
Checkpoint-Priorität werden die Expedited-data-units der Transport-
Ebene (oder Network-Ebene) benutzt (z. B. X.25 Interrupt).

<u>Bemerkung</u>:
Da mit dem Primitive CHECKPOINT RESTART in der Kommunikation auf
einen Übertragungszustand zurückgesetzt wird, bei dem alle gesendeten
service-data-units auch empfangen wurden, könnte die Checkpoint-
Priority auch auf einen qualifizierten RESET der Network-Ebene abgebildet werden.

Die Ebene 5 überprüft die von den beiden Applikationen gegebene
Checkpoint-Priority auf Gleichheit. Wird keine Übereinstimmung
festgestellt, so wird der CHECKPOINT RESTART Service mit höherer
Priorität ausgeführt. Dies wird im Parameter abandoned mitgeteilt.

Die Bedeutung des PURGE Service-Primitives liegt weniger in einer Prozeß-Prozeß Synchronisation als vielmehr in der Indikation des Datenverlustes, der im Übertragungskanal stattgefunden haben kann.

↓ or ↑   PURGE (← n1, n2 lost n.s.s.d.u)

Selbstverständlich kann ein solcher Verlust auch auf Initiative eines Applikationsprozesses erfolgt sein.

Der PURGE-Service löst (wird ausgelöst durch) ein RESET der unterlagerten Ebene aus. Falls ein Datenverlust eingetreten ist, wird dies durch die Zählerdifferenzen n1 und n2 mitgeteilt. Die weitere Reaktion auf diese Indikation bleibt den Applikationen überlassen. Für den Fall, daß die Kommunikation durch Checkpoints gesichert ist, würden die Benutzer mit CHECKPOINT RESTART fortfahren.

Literatur:

[1]   F. Hertweck, E. Raubold, F. Vogt
        X.25 based process-to-process communication
        "Computer Networks", Oct. 1978

[2]   F. Hertweck, E. Raubold, F. Vogt
        The ML Protocol description
        PIX/HLP/TEK/78/01

[3]   G. v. Bochmann, F. Vogt
        Message Link Protocol
        Functional Specification
        ACM-SIGCOMM
        "Computer Communication Review
        (Volume 9, Number 2)
        and
        HMI-B 284 Dec. 1978
        NI-16.1/6.2 (71-78 and NI- 16.2 (110-78)

[4]   G. v. Bochmann
        Specification of the Services provided by the MLP
        Département d'informatique et de recherche opérationelle,
        Université de Montréal
        April 1979

[5]   G. v. Bochmann
        Formalized Specification of the MLP
        Département d'informatique et de recherche opérationelle,
        Université de Montréal
        June 1979

[6]   G. v. Bochmann
        Analysis of the MLP
        Département d'informatique et de recherche opérationelle
        Université de Montréal
        June 1979

[7]   ISO/TC 97/SC 16/ N 227
        Reference Model of Open Systems Interconnection
        Version 4, August 1979

[8]   G. v. Bochmann
        A General Transition Model for Protocols and Communication
        Services
        Département d'informatique et de recherche opérationelle,
        Université de Montréal
        Mai 1979

[9]   C.C.I.T.T.
        Provisional Recommendation X.3, X.25, X.28, X.29 on packet
        switched data transmission services
        Genèva 1978 ISBN 92-61-00591-8

[10]   E. Raubold
        Proposal for message-blocking facility in ML
        GMD-Darmstadt (23.3.79)

[11]   SIEMENS Transdata
        Datenfernverarbeitung mit BS 2000
        DCAM-Programmschnittstellen (Einführung)
        (Februar 1979, Version 5.0)

[12]   SIEMENS Transdata
        Datenfernverarbeitung mit BS 2000
        DCAM-Makroaufrufe (Programmierhandbuch)
        (Juli 1978, Version 4.0)

[13]   IBM
        Advanced Communications Function for VTAM
        (ACF/NTAM) General Information
        GC38-0254-3
        Fourth Edition (January 1978)

[14]   IBM
        Advanced Communications Function for VTAM
        (ACF/VTAM) Concepts and Planning
        GC38-0282-1
        Second Edition (August 1977)

[15]   IBM
        VTAM Macro Language Guide
        VTAM Level 2
        GC27-6994-2
        Third Edition (June 1976)

[16]   F. Vogt, E. Dregger, H. Eckert, B. Lausch
        Specification of a Transport and Session
        Layer Protocol based on the Message Link Protocol
        (Version 1.0)
        September 1979

Bild 1: Location of ML-Protocol in a layered protocol
hierarchy

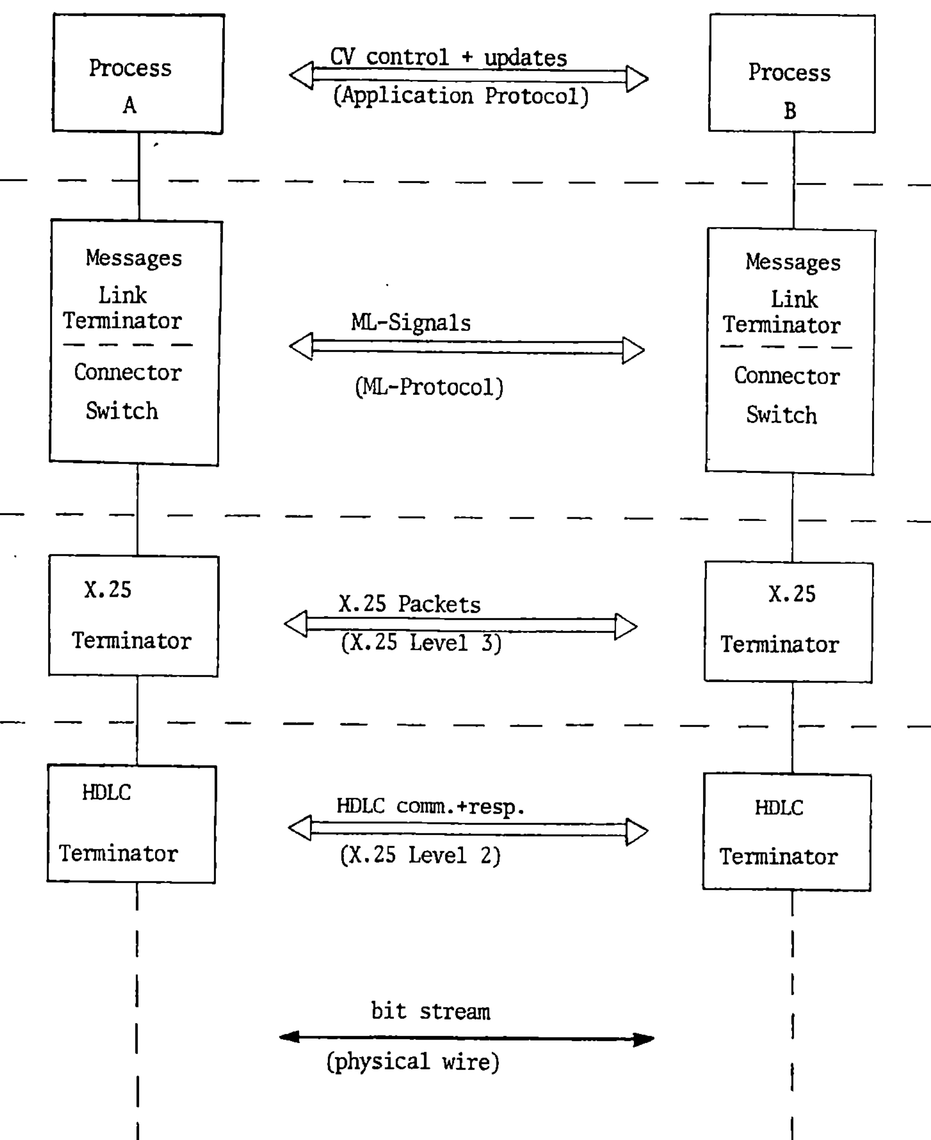

Bild 2: Modell einer Ebene mit Betonung des Service-Aspekts

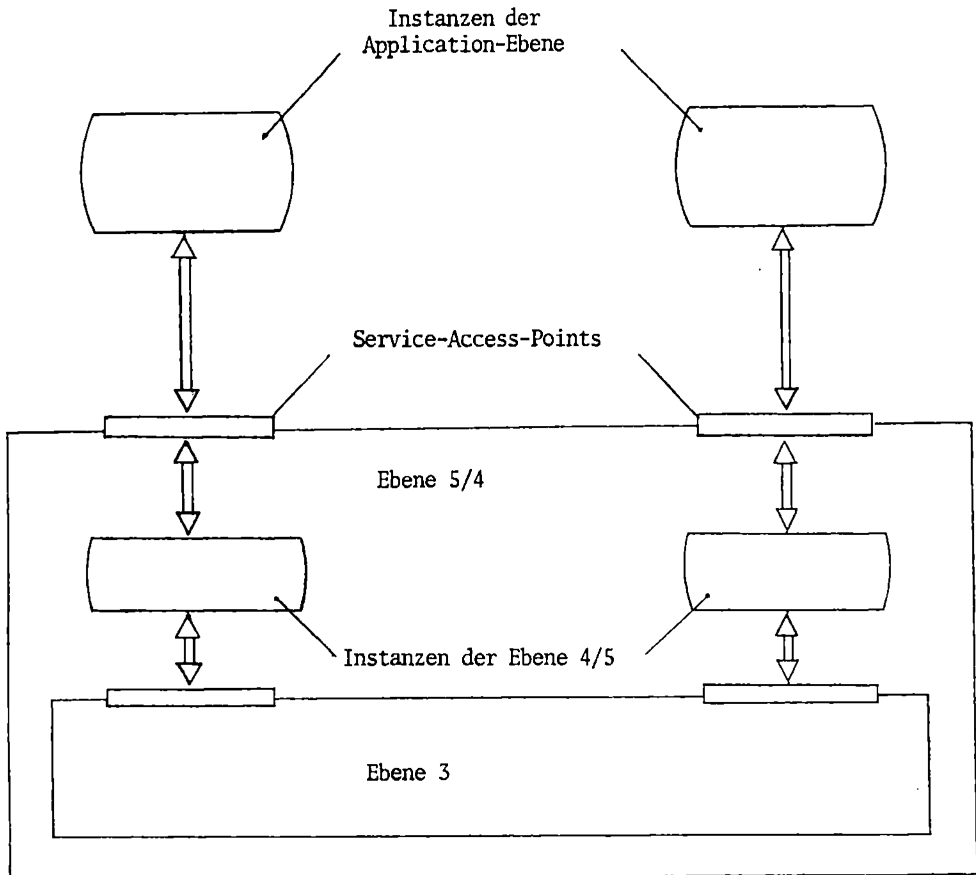

Bild 3: Zähler der Session-Ebene an den
Service-Access-Points zur Applications-Ebene

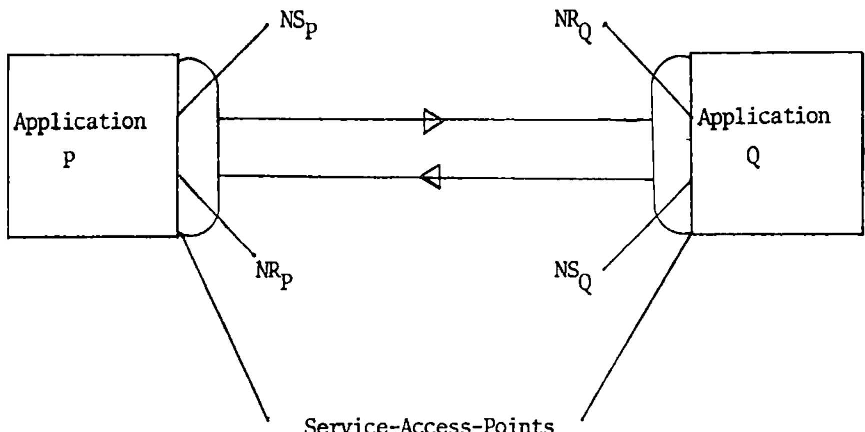
NS_P
NR_Q
Application
P
Application
Q
NR_P
NS_Q
Service-Access-Points

<u>Bild 4</u>: Synchronisation-convention

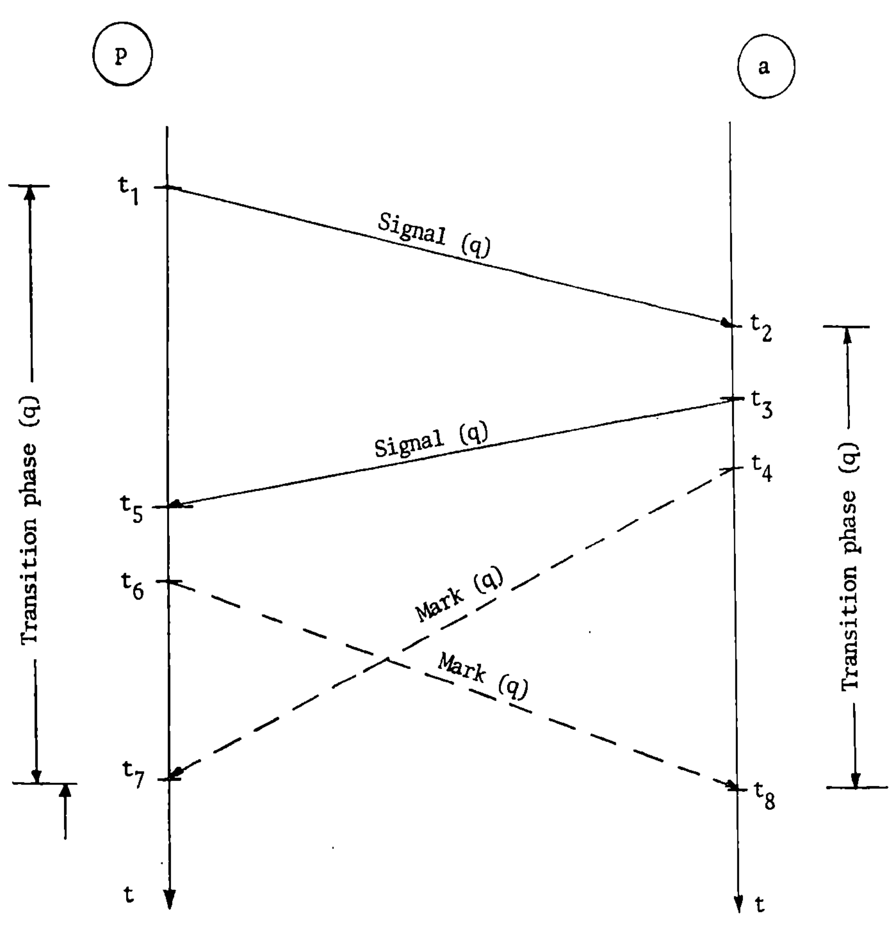

timing rules:

$$t_4 = \text{Max} \ (t_2, \ t_3)$$

$$t_6 = \text{Max} \ (t_1, \ t_5)$$

Transition phase p: Min $(t_1, \ t_5)$ ... Max $(t_6, \ t_7)$

Transition phase a: Min $(t_2, \ t_3)$ ... Max $(t_4, \ t_8)$

<u>UK NETWORK INDEPENDENT FILE TRANSFER PROTOCOL</u>

by Dr. D. Rayner
Division of Numerical Analysis and Computer Science
National Physical Laboratory
Teddington, Middx. U.K.

and A.W. Jones
Computer Aided Design Centre
Madingley Road, Cambridge, U.K.

<u>ABSTRACT</u>

The UK Network Independent FTP was specified in December 1977 and has
since remained unchanged. Its structure will be outlined and its
relation to both the underlying Transport Service and application
interfaces will be discussed. File management and data presentation
problems will be identified. These and other deficiencies have their
solution in a longer-term standard File Handling Protocol.   In the
meantime, this FTP will be enhanced and will become a UK interim
standard. Five independent implementations have been tested over
EPSS.   The lessons from this testing will be discussed and the need
for a Certification Centre to support the interim standard will be
identified.

1. INTRODUCTION

The definition of a Network Independent File Transfer Protocol (FTP) was finalised by the UK High Level Protocols Group in a document [1] published in December 1977. This group was associated with the UK Post Office Experimental Packet Switched Service (EPSS) as EPSS Study Group 2. It has now ceased to meet and the Department of Industry Data Communication Protocols Unit (DCPU) has taken over the distribution of the specification document. Interest in the protocol has been received from many groups worldwide and well over 1000 copies of the document have been distributed.

At least nine independent implementations have been produced, on a variety of different machines. Five of them have been tested together in various combinations over EPSS. Since two of these are actually in systems on other networks connected to EPSS, namely ARPANET and the NPL local network, the protocol is already being tested in a multi-network environment. Many more implementations are planned, some for use on EPSS, some on its successor, the X.25 based PSS, and some on private networks. The DCPU supports a group, called the FTP Implementors' Group, to co-ordinate these implementations, to let implementors benefit from each other's experience, and to resolve any ambiguities and uncertainties in the protocol definition.

1.1 Progress towards a standard

This protocol was the starting point for the work of a British Standards Institute (BSI) working group of the committee on "Open Systems Interconnection" (DPS 20 WG 6). Although this FTP only provides for the transfer of complete sequential files, this BSI group has produced a specification of a Filestore Image [2] to be used as the basis for a more comprehensive long-term standard "File Handling Protocol" (FHP). It is envisaged that this would include file access and management functions, as well as file transfer, operations on sets of files and part-files, as well as complete files, and the handling of indexed sequential and random access files, as well as sequential ones. BSI is, however, unlikely to approve such a standard until it has been approved by the International Standards Organisation (ISO). The output of the group is, therefore, produced as input to the ISO committee on "Open Systems Interconnection" (TC 97 SC 16).

At the current rate of progress, it will probably be five years before a standard FHP emerges from ISO. CCITT (Comite Consultatif International Telegraphique et Telephonique) is likely to produce a Teletex protocol standard in the meantime and, since this will perform a restricted kind of file transfer, it could become a base for a future FHP. A more comprehensive filestore image would have to be defined to underlie such an FHP. CCITT is, however, not well suited to this task, so it may have to be left to ISO.

1.2 A UK interim standard

Unfortunately, five years is too long to wait for a standard in this area, since users of the emerging public data networks will want to move files between various systems in the interim. In the UK PSS is currently scheduled to start in March 1980, so there is already mounting pressure for an agreement on an interim standard It is becoming widely accepted that this UK interim standard will be the current FTP, possibly with minor modifications and extensions to overcome some of its known deficiencies. This protocol will, therefore, be used extensively in the UK for at least the next five years.

The remainder of the paper is devoted to considering in detail certain aspects of this FTP and the lessons that have been learned from it so far.

2. STRUCTURE OF THE PROTOCOL

The protocol concerns the exchange of messages in three phases. The first, the negotiation phase, and the last, the termination phase, use an integrated set of commands, considered to be at one level (Level 0). The second phase is the data transfer phase, during which both commands and data are exchanged. These commands are considered to be at a second level (Level 1) and the data at a third (Level 2).

At Level 0 the initiator of the exchange, known as P, has control, but the negotiation concerns 25 attributes stored at the other end, known as Q, in a system-independent image of its filestore. P starts by sending a Start File Transfer (SFT) command with all the necessary parameters to specify its requirements for file access and transfer attributes, including the direction of transfer. Q responds with either a positive (RPOS) or negative (RNEG) reply command with appropriate parameters. If P receives an RNEG or an RPOS with unacceptable parameters, it then immediately enters the termination phase by sending a STOP command If, however, P receives an acceptable RPOS, it enters the data transfer phase by sending a GO command. When the data transfer phase is ended and the end is acknowledged by the receiver of the data, then P enters the termination phase and sends a STOP command. In the case of more drastic abort action within the data transfer phase, the underlying Transport Service connection is closed without a STOP being sent.

Once Level 1 is entered (by the sending or receiving of a GO command) the sender of the file assumes control. The sender can be either P or Q, since the direction of transfer is one of the transfer attributes agreed by the negotiation. The commands at Level 1 are all fixed format and introduced by a special zero header byte to distinguish them from the data, which is transmitted in records, each split into a number of sub-records introduced by a non-zero header byte. The sender uses commands to:

(a) indicate the start or restart point (SS);
(b) put restart marks in the data stream (MS);
(c) indicate a change of character code in the data (CS);
(d) indicate the end of the data or the temporary end of the data flow (ES).

The receiver uses commands to:

(a) request a restart from a given mark point (RR);
(b) acknowledge mark points (MR);
(c) request termination of, or a temporary pause in, the data flow (QR);

(d) acknowledge receipt of the end of the data (ER).

The use of each of the more advanced facilities, such as restarts and temporary pauses in the transmission, is subject to negotiation.

3. RELATION TO THE TRANSPORT SERVICE

From the outset, the protocol was intended to be network independent. The Transport Service (TS) was already being seen as the layer that would separate applications-oriented protocols from the communications sub-network, by providing a set of network-independent primitive operations at its upper interface. It was, therefore, assumed that the protocol would be implemented directly above a suitable TS.

3.1 What was assumed

Since there was not even any thought of an interim standard TS at that time, the assumptions made about the underlying TS had to be minimal and as general as possible. Three assumptions were specified as being essential. These were:

(a) The TS should provide two independent synchronised streams of bytes, one from P to Q, the other from Q to P, each with a well-defined starting point. The TS must regulate the flow of data in each stream so as to limit the demands on the receiver of data.

(b) The TS is responsible for error detection and network-independent error recovery. Undetected errors should be sufficiently rare (according to some user-chosen "quality of service") and all detected but uncorrected errors should be reported to both ends in a manner that permits recovery of synchronisation. Such an event is called a TS Reset. If such a Reset cannot be given, then both processes must be warned that the communication has broken down irrecoverably.

(c) There must be a function to force delivery of any currently buffered data.

It was also seen as desirable, but not essential, that the TS should allow either process to issue a Reset command with the same resynchronising effect as an internally generated one. A further implied but unstated assumption was that the TS should provide an adequate multi-network addressing capability.

3.2 What was not assumed

The assumptions stated above are so minimal that they should be met by any reasonable TS. It is what could not be assumed that has shaped the FTP.

Firstly, it was not assumed that, if blocks of data were presented to the TS at one end, the boundaries of the blocks would be preserved when the data was delivered at the other end. This meant that message boundaries had to be explicitly encoded in the FTP.

Secondly, it was not assumed that communication would be free from data loss. This meant that restart marks, mark acknowledgement and restart requests had to be included in the FTP. However, further consideration has lead to the conclusion that these facilities should always be provided in an FTP, because the use of them requires a knowledge of both the application and the filestore that no lower level can possess.

Thirdly, it was not assumed that the TS would perform any data compression or code conversion; so facilities for these had to be included in the FTP and made subject to negotiation.

Finally, it was not assumed that a process could change any timeout values used in the TS implementation. It was likely that some TS implementations would use a shorter timeout when queued data was not being read by the intended recipient, than when there was inactivity but no queued data at all. Therefore, a facility was included for agreeing on a temporary pause in the data flow at the receiver's request. This allows the queues to be emptied prior to a period of inactivity.

3.3 UK interim standard TS

Currently, within the UK, an interim standard TS is being finalised, following the publication of a draft for comment [3]. The draft has a byte stream interface and a set of seven primitive operations: Connect, Accept, Disconnect, Reset, Data, Push, and Disconnect Request. Current discussions suggest that Disconnect Request might be discarded and that two new primitives might be added: Address and Interrupt. These changes need not concern the FTP implementor because none of the three primitives under question is needed by FTP. The other six primitives are all needed, although Reset is more necessary as a response than as a command.

4. RELATION TO THE APPLICATION PROCESS AND THE USER

Whilst assumptions are made about the relation of FTP to the level below it, no assumptions are made about what is above it. Most implementations will provide an interface to application processes. This will allow the process to specify some or all of the parameters for the SFT command and receive any incoming messages, a notification of the final "state of transfer" and, possibly, progress messages. This interface might be a candidate for standardization, but there is currently no proposal for an interim standard for the application interface to correspond with that for the protocol.

An interface to a human user is something that can be provided by one possible form of application process. Its standardization is, therefore, considered to be an entirely separate matter, which is not necessary for many uses of FTP.

5. RELATION TO FILE MANAGEMENT

Although the protocol is primarily concerned with the activity of file transfer, it has not cleanly divorced this from file management activities. The "mode of access" attribute, whose main function is to specify the direction of transfer, can also be used to specify file deletion. Several parameters, such as "kinship", which is used to supplement the "filename", can be used in the SFT to enquire about certain attributes of a file without needing to transfer it. The "file size" and "mode of access" attributes can be used together to specify the reservation of a certain amount of new file space.

This causes problems for both implementors and users. For example, it is not clear what the effect of requesting deletion should be. How quickly should the deletion take place? Should it take place even if the file transfer ends in failure? If deletion was requested in a separate command-response exchange, the second question would not arise and the first question could be answered in a parameter of the response. A similar approach could be taken for other file management activities. It is, therefore, hoped that a future FHP will make this kind of clean separation of activities

6. DATA PRESENTATION ISSUES

One of the major problem areas that has not yet been adequately researched is that of data presentation. Problems have been uncovered by both implementors and users. There are two different possible user requirements: one is for the file to be transferred completely unchanged; the other is for the file to be converted to a form that gives it the same meaning on the destination system as it had at the source. The former is handled by binary file transfer and the latter by text file transfer.

6.1 Binary files

Since binary files cannot be assumed to contain characters, they are considered to be divided into "words", of a machine-dependent length, rather than "bytes". This poses no problem for "words" with lengths that are a multiple of 8 bits, but for those that are not there is the problem of mapping them onto the TS byte stream. This can be done either by packing the "words" together or by padding out each "word" to align the next on a byte boundary. Accordingly, there is a "binary mapping" attribute that specifies the word length and whether "packed" or "aligned" mode is to be used. Unfortunately, packed mode, as specified, does not work for "word" lengths less than 8 bits, because it is not always possible to tell how much padding is used at the end of each sub-record.

6.2 Data Codes

Text files give rise to rather more problems. Firstly, it is necessary to specify the code in which the file is to be transferred, so that code conversion can be performed if necessary and so that characters that have formatting significance (called "format effectors") can be identified. There is, therefore, a "codes" attribute. However, it has been discovered that it is not sufficient just to identify the code used in the transfer; it is also necessary in some circumstances to specify the code to be used for storage, so that a file deposited in a remote filestore can be usefully recovered later. The addition of a "code for storage" attribute is, therefore, one of the likely minor extensions that will be made before the interim standard is finalised.

Secondly, the "codes" attribute specifies four possible parity bit options, but it does not cater for "parity bit set to 1", which is the option that some implementors would prefer to use. There may, therefore, need to be another extension to cover this.

Thirdly, the "codes" attribute is used together with the "code select" command in the data transfer phase to cater for mixed code files. It is not, however, known to what extent users require mixed code file transfer. It is also unclear how "codes for storage" can be unambiguously specified in such cases. One suggestion is to restrict mixed code files to using one text code and binary, but this would preclude the use of IA5 with a private code. Implementors have also identified the need to distinguish clearly the case of a mixed code file from the one where a file can be transmitted in either one of two codes. A solution to this problem would be to use a bit in the "codes" or "facilities" attribute to specify whether or not it was a mixed code file.

Some implementors and users have also found a problem with private codes, because the protocol assumes that the specification of "private code" in the "codes" attribute is unambiguous. This is not always the case, so an attribute is needed to name the private code concerned.

6.3 Format effectors

It is necessary to specify how formatting is indicated or implied in a text file. Three techniques are catered for in a "format effectors" attribute. The first is the use of the end of a record to imply the start of a new line. The second is the use of the first character in each record as an ANSI (Fortran) carriage control character. The third is the use of explicit formatting characters, such as "carriage return" and "form feed", within the data, optionally with the additional implication that "carriage return" implies "line feed" or vice versa.

One problem is that the default is specified as being the first of these techniques, although this requires most sending implementations to scan the data for "end of line". Some implementors have found that explicit formatting characters are much easier to handle because then, in many cases, the data does not need to be modified.

Another problem occurs when a particular formatting character has not been agreed upon. If at all possible, the sender should replace any occurrence of the character in the source file by other characters to give the same formatting effect. This can then lead to an expansion of the file that was not anticipated when the "maximum transfer size" or "file size" attributes were agreed. One solution would be to preprocess every file that might need expanding before agreeing on values for these other attributes. This would clearly cause a delay and, in any case, would only be applicable to Q. P would not necessarily discover that expansion might be needed until the response was received from Q; in which case, P might have to terminate the transfer attempt and start again.

An associated problem is that some formatting characters, such as "form feed", can only be interpreted if the intended page size is known. Another possible extension is, therefore, to add attributes to specify the virtual page size, both length and width.

7. TESTING IMPLEMENTATIONS

7.1 4-stage testing schedule

Experience of testing FTP implementations on EPSS has shown that it is desirable to start by adopting a four stage testing schedule. This uses back-to-back testing initially, while the silly bugs are removed, to give the implementor confidence that his implementation is self-consistent. This gives controlled conditions in which any errors that occur must be local in origin. Site-to-site testing is used to complement this, because it enables misunderstandings of the protocol definition to be discovered. It also reveals the behavior of the implementation to circumstances unforeseen by the implementor, often as a result of the two implementations being under different operating systems. The result will be two mutually compatible implementations, but testing with a third independent site will be necessary to give confidence that both are not defective in some way.

The first stage is back-to-back testing of Level 0 commands. Experience shows that this is best done by starting with a fairly full implementation of P and a minimal Q, used simply as a debugging aid for P. Once the implementor has confidence in P, then Q can be more fully developed and the roles reversed. Only two sequences can be tested at this stage, SFT-RNEG-STOP and SFT-RPOS-STOP.

The second stage is back-to-back testing of Levels 1 and 2. This requires the implementation of a Sender and Receiver, normally in separate processes. The first test to be passed is the transfer of a null file, that is where the "end of data" command immediately follows the "start of data" command. The main purpose of this test is to check that the inter-process communication works. After that the goal is to transfer a file in each direction without data corruption. Once this has been achieved for a small file, it should be repeated for larger files.

The third stage is basic site-to-site testing, repeating the exchanges tested during the first two stages. Ideally, only one of the implementations will be under development, in order to simplify the action of locating and correcting any bugs exposed. Experience has shown that, until the two sites become well-acquainted, there is a time-consuming overhead in setting up a site-to-site test, so it is important that as many bugs as possible are removed in the first two stages. Time can also be wasted unless both sites are fully informed about what is happening at all times. This means that both sites should monitor all bytes sent and received and that there should be a reliable independent means of communication between the people at each site, whether by telephone or by a separate terminal-to-terminal connection.

The fourth stage is more thorough site-to-site testing, exploring variations of SFT parameters and Level 1 commands sequences. This is the stage that testing on EPSS has reached, but it has not progressed beyond making a few ad hoc changes to parameters and file types. What is required is a set of standard tests to be performed at this stage.

7.2 A Certification Centre

While this testing schedule is satisfactory for an implementation that is to be used in a closed environment to perform certain known types of file transfer, it fails to establish that the implementation truly conforms to the protocol definition. Once FTP becomes a UK interim standard and is marketed as a generally available product by software vendors, this is far from good enough. What is then required is the establishment of a Certification Centre, which will test implementations for conformity, acceptability and performance and issue appropriate certificates. Indeed, potential vendors of FTP packages have indicated that, before they commit resources to developing such software, they need to see the interim standard being supported by a declaration from the UK government that it will establish just such a centre.

Discussions that could lead to the setting up of a Certification Centre in the UK are currently in progress. This Centre would be required to test and issue certificates for implementations of both TS and FTP interim standards. Testing for conformity with the standards would include testing an implementation's reactions to error situations as well as to correct protocol. Nevertheless, the Centre should not restrict itself to testing for conformity, because it is possible to conform to such high-level protocol standards without being of any use. For example, an FTP implementation could conform whilst courteously rejecting every attempt at a transfer. It is, therefore, also necessary to test for acceptability. As yet, the concept of acceptability is imprecise, but it must include acceptable performance, because it is little use an implementation conforming if it takes hours to respond.

7.3 Acceptability tests

It is likely that a set of acceptability tests will be devised and published, so that implementors will know what is expected of them. Implementations intended for general use will be expected to pass most, if not all, such tests. However, it will not be a matter of passing or failing the whole set, but rather the certificate will have to list the achievements of the implementation for each of the tests. Implementations designed to meet specific needs might, therefore, be expected to pass only a subset of the tests. For instance, an implementation might be a Sender but not a Receiver, or might only handle binary files. It will be up to the user to decide what tests must be passed to meet his specific needs.

The danger of this flexibility is that it will sanction incompatible implementations, so lessening the possibility of being able to move files between any two systems on an open network. To avoid this, one subset of the acceptability tests must define the minimum achievement necessary to ensure real compatibility.

7.4 Research and development needed

The technical problems involved in establishing a Certification Centre should not be underestimated. Nobody yet actually knows how to devise appropriate tests for a protocol as complex as FTP. There will, therefore, necessarily have to be a major research and development project to solve the technical problems. The setting up of this project is still under discussion, but it is hoped that the formal declaration of intent to establish a Certification Centre will be made when it starts, to give encouragement to potential vendors of TS and FTP packages.

Establishing a Certification Centre for interim standards will allow techniques for testing high-level protocols to be developed and tried out in practice, in preparation for the certification of a future internationally accepted FHP standard. Nevertheless, testing is an inherently incomplete way of checking conformity, so it will also be necessary to develop formal specification and verification techniques for application to such longer-term standards.

8. CONCLUSIONS

The UK network independent File Transfer Protocol (FTP) has remained stable for nearly two years and has been shown to work satisfactorily in most cases for complete sequential file transfer. There are, however, several data presentation problems, most of which can be resolved by enhancing the protocol prior to it becoming a UK interim standard.

The general demands made of the supporting Transport Service are quite minimal. The ability to select options within the FTP, however, allows implementations to make use of more advanced facilities that a Transport Service might offer, without unnecessary redundancy in the FTP.

Although it is not clear that a standard application interface is necessary, the lack of an agreed specification for such an interface is seen by some as a deficiency.

Other deficiencies exist in the scope of the protocol. In particular, file management activities are inadequate and the handling of part-files, indexed sequential and random access files, and sets of files is non-existent. The solution to these problems cannot be expected to appear in the UK interim standard, but should be included in any future longer-term international File Handling Protocol standard.

Finally, the current ad hoc methods of testing FTP implementations on EPSS will not be sufficient once the protocol becomes a UK interim standard. A Certification Centre will then be needed, to test implementations for conformity, acceptability and performance and to issue appropriate certificates. Discussions are, therefore, under way to set up a research and development project to solve the technical problems involved in this concept.

REFERENCES

1. Linington, P.F. (ed.), A network independent file transfer
   protocol, prepared by the UK High Level Protocols Group,
   HLP/CP(78)1, December 1977, available from Dr. P.F. Linington, Data
   Communication Protocols Unit, Computer Laboratory, Corn Exchange
   Street, Cambridge, CB2 3QG, U.K.

2. Open systems interconnection - the filestore image - definition,
   prepared by BSI DPS 20 WG6, BSI/DPS20/WG6/38 (also BSI/DPS20/363
   and ISO/TC97/SC16 WG2 London 79 - 17), 1979, available from Dr.
   P.F. Linington, address as in [1].

3. Linington, P.F. (ed.), A transport service, draft for comment,
   prepared by the Post Office Packet Switching Study Group 3,
   BIG/CP(79)7, April 1979, available from Dr. P.F. Linington, address
   as in [1].

$$\text{Das "Virtual device protocol" (VDP)}$$

Oswald Fundneider
Siemens   AG
München

1.   Entstehung:

Das Virtual device protocol entstand durch gemeinsame Bemühungen der Firmen CII-HB, ICL und Siemens.
Ziel war der Entwurf eines längere Zeit tragfähigen Terminalprotokolles, das einschlägige Erfahrungen der genannten Hersteller integriert. Der Vorschlag wurde bei den zuständigen nationalen Standardisierungsgremien (AFNOR, BSI, FNI) und bei ECMA eingereicht.
Die folgenden Ausführungen beziehen sich auf VDP Version 5.

2.   Übersicht:

Das VDP unterstützt die Kommunikation eines Steuerprogrammes in einem Terminal, an dem geeignete Geräte angeschlossen sind, mit einem Programm in einem Verarbeitungsrechner oder mit einem Steuerprogramm in einem anderen Terminal. Um nicht jedes Terminal mit allen Funktionen des VDP belasten zu müssen, werden mehrere Terminalklassen mit unterschiedlichen Funktionsmengen vorgesehen; innerhalb einer Klasse sind außerdem einige Funktionen wahlfrei. Das VDP macht die Kommunikation der Terminals von hersteller- und anwendungsspezifischen Eigenschaften unabhängig und ermöglicht dadurch freie Kopplung in offenen Systemen. Unterschiedliche Terminalklassen sind nicht kompatibel.

Die Kopplungspartner vereinbaren beim Verbindungsaufbau die Terminalklasse und die wahlfreien Parameter; dadurch wird sozusagen ein gedachtes (virtuelles) Terminal erzeugt, das der jeweilige Kopplungspartner anschließend sieht und anspricht. Das VDP be-

schreibt nicht die Abbildung der Eigenschaften dieser gedachten
Terminals auf die Bedienerschnittstelle und Geräte durch das Steuerprogramm im Terminal; dies bleibt dem jeweiligen Realisierer
des Terminals überlassen, der für die vorgesehene Anwendung optimieren kann. In Version 5 enthält das VDP noch nicht die bitmäs-
sige Codierung der Protokollelemente; sie kann aber leicht ergänzt werden.

Das VDP ist ein "presentation protocol" im Sinne des ISO-Refe-
renzmodelles. Es werden einige Anforderungen an die Session-
Schicht gestellt, die hier nur kurz behandelt werden.

Genauer eingegangen wird auf die Erzeugung des virtuellen Terminals und dabei wiederum auf das Datenspeichermodell des VDP
als der wichtigsten Terminaleigenschaft. Abschließend werden
noch kurz die Funktionen gestreift, die beim "erzeugten" Terminal genutzt werden können.

3.   <u>Anforderungen an die Session-Schicht</u>

Von der Session-Schicht wird die Unterstützung der folgenden
Funktionen erwartet:

- Aufbau und Abbau der Session
- Funktionen der Datenübertragung

    o fehlerfreier Datentransport in beiden Richtungen ohne Reihen-
      folgeveränderung

    o Unterstützung der wechselseitigen Übertragung (turn; demand
      turn)

    o Nachrichtenstrukturierungs-Unterstützung (Session-service-
      data-unit, quarantine-unit, session-interaction-unit).

    o Kanal für Kurzinformation in beiden Richtungen, der nicht
      der Nachrichtenflußsteuerung unterliegt.

- Mechanismus zur Auswahl und Parametierung der höheren Protokolle (Select..., Acknowledge...)

4. Das Erzeugen des virtuellen Terminals

4.1 Allgemein

Beim Verbindungsaufbau müssen sich die Kopplungspartner auf die
Verwendung des VDP, die Terminalklasse und die Parameter innerhalb der Terminalklasse einigen; dadurch wird ein virtuelles Terminal mit genau definierten Eigenschaften erzeugt. Die Eigenschaften dieses Terminals können später noch geändert oder auf den An-
fangswert zurückgesetzt werden.
Für das Erzeugen des virtuellen Terminals stehen beim VDP folgende Eigenschaften zur Auswahl:

a) Terminalklassen:
   - Basisklasse
   - Basis- und Formatklasse
   - (später Grafikklasse usw.)

b) Kopplungsfälle:
   - Terminal-Terminal
   - Terminal-Verarbeitungsrechner

c) Eigenschaften der Geräte
   - Datenspeicherstruktur
   - Adressierungsmöglichkeiten im Datenspeicher
   - Eingabe/Ausgabe/Ein-Ausgabe
   - Zeichenvorräte (z. B. unterschiedliche nationale Varianten
     des ISO-7 Bit-Codes)

d) Verschiedene wahlfreie Funktionen in der Formatklasse

4.2 Terminalklassen

Das VDP unterstützt derzeit zwei Terminalklassen, jede deckt eine
wichtige Terminalkategorie ab:
Die Basisklasse die nicht formatiert arbeitenden alphanumerischen
Terminals, die Formatklasse die formatierten alphanumerischen Terminals.

Als zukünftige Erweiterung wird an eine Grafikklasse gedacht.
Beispiele für die Terminalklassen:
Basisklasse:

Schreibstationen, Zeilendrucker, Seitendrucker, Kartenleser
und -stanzer, Datensichtstationen, Lochstreifengeräte.

Formatklasse:

Formatfähige Terminals (z.B.Datensichtgeräte mit oder ohne
Diskette als Formatspeicher)

Graphikklasse:

Graphische Sichtgeräte und Plotter

4.3   Kopplungsfälle:

Beim VDP wurde größter Wert auf Symetrie gelegt, um die Kopplungsfälle Terminal-Terminal und Terminal-Verarbeitungsrechner
möglichst gleich erscheinen zu lassen. Nur an wenigen Stellen
mußte die Symmetrie verlassen werden, um nicht beim Terminal
auf wichtige Funktionen verzichten zu müssen, die für das Programm im Verarbeitungsrechner unsinnig wären.

4.4   Struktur und Adressierung des Datenspeichers bei der
Basisklasse:

4.4.1 Dimensionen des Datenspeichers

Gerade in diesem Punkt unterscheiden sich Terminals heute stark:
wir finden einzeilige Bildschirme, unterschiedlichste Papier-
formate usw. Das VDP integriert in seinem Datenspeicher-Modell
diese Unterschiede zu einer flexiblen, homogenen Lösung. Beim
Erzeugen des gedachten Datenspeichers gleichen die Kopplungspartner ihre Wünsche und Möglichkeiten ab.
Der Datenspeicher kann mit ein, zwei oder drei Dimensionen definiert werden, jede Dimension mit einer festen (begrenzten) oder
undefinierten (unbegrenzten) Länge.

<u>Dimension x:</u> (Zeilenterminal)

Diese Dimension muß als einzige immer vorhanden sein und enthält
einen eindimensionalen Bereich für alphanumerische Zeichen, den
man sich zum Verständnis als horizontale Zeile begrenzter (fester)
oder unbegrenzter (undefinierter) Länge vorstellen kann, wie sie
praktisch z. B. beim einzeiligen Bildschirm oder beim Lochstrei-
fen vorkommt.

<u>Dimension y:</u> (Seitenterminal)

Diese Dimension kann fehlen. Ist sie definiert, dann ergänzt sie
die x-Dimension zu einem zweidimensionalen Bereich für alphanumerische Zeichen, den man sich als Seite vorstellen kann, die aus
Zeilen mit alphanumerischen Zeichen besteht. Auch die y-Dimension
kann feste oder undefinierte Länge haben.
Ein praktisches Beispiel eines Datenspeichers mit x- und y-Dimension fester Länge ist z. B. der Bildschirmspeicher eines Daten-
sichtgerätes; ein Beispiel für feste x-Länge und undefinierte y-
Länge ist der Fernschreiber mit seinem Endlospapier.

<u>Dimension z:</u> (Buchterminal)

Auch diese Dimension kann fehlen; wenn vorhanden, ergänzt sie die
xy-Dimensionen zu einem dreidimensionalen Bereich, den man sich
am besten als eine Folge von Seiten vorstellt, die jeweils aus
Zeilen für alphanumerische Zeichen bestehen. Auch diese Dimension
kann mit begrenzter oder unbegrenzter Länge definiert werden. Ein
praktisches Beispiel ist z.B. ein Datensichtgerät mit einem Ar-
beitsspeicher, der gleichzeitig mehrere Bildschirminhalte faßt.
Einen Datenspeicher mit xy fester Länge und mit z undefinierter
Länge hat z.B. der Seitendrucker mit Endlospapier.

<u>Dimension w:</u> (Archivdimension)

Diese wahlfreie Dimension ist ganz anderer Art als die x-, y- und
z-Dimension. Sie ist eine nicht adressierbare "Archivdimension".
Sie darf nur definiert sein, wenn x, y und z, soweit überhaupt definiert, feste Länge haben und damit einen fest umgrenzten Bereich
beschreiben. Die w-Dimension sagt dann aus, wieviele durch x, y, z
(soweit definiert) definierte Bereiche im Terminal-Archiv zwischengespeichert und damit dem Terminalbediener noch zugänglich sind.
Dem Kopplungspartner ist der Archivinhalt nicht mehr zugänglich.

Auch die Dimension w kann wie die anderen Dimensionen feste oder
unbegrenzte Länge haben. Feste Länge finden wir z. B. bei Bild-
schirmgeräten mit begrenztem Archivspeicher, unbegrenzte Länge bei
Papiergeräten mit Endlospapier. Diese Dimension fehlt bei Bild-
schirmgeräten ohne Archivspeicher.

4.4.2 Datenspeicherstruktur bei der Basisklasse

Durch die jeweils begrenzt (feste Länge) oder unbegrenzt (undefinierte Länge) definierten Dimensionen x, y, z wird ein ein-, zwei-
oder dreidimensional gedachter Datenspeicher aufgespannt, der in
einzelnen adressierbaren Zeichenpositionen organisiert ist. Wahl-
weise kann jede vorhandene Dimension x, y oder z zusätzlich mit
Tabulatormarken strukturiert werden. Die Archivdimension w braucht
hier nicht weiter behandelt werden, da sie vom Kopplungspartner
nicht adressiert werden kann.

4.4.3 Adressierung des Datenspeichers bei der Basisklasse

a) Implizite Adressierung.
   Die gedachte Schreibmarke zeigt zu Beginn auf den Anfang des
   in einen oder mehreren Dimensionen definierten Datenspeichers,
   d. h. auf den Ursprung des Koordinatensystems (o, o, o). Jedes
   Zeichen, das in den Datenspeicher geschrieben wird, verursacht
   ein implizites Vorrücken der Schreibmarke um eine Stelle in
   Richtung der x-Dimension. Ist die x-Dimension mit begrenzter
   Länge definiert, dann stößt die Schreibmarke früher oder später an dieser Grenze an. Sie bleibt dort solange in einer gedachten Warteposition haften, bis das nächste Zeichen geschrieben werden soll. Noch vor dem Schreiben wird dann die y-Adresse
   implizit um 1 erhöht und die x-Adresse auf 0 gesetzt:
   Es wird also am Anfang der nächsten Zeile weitergeschrieben.
   Diese implizite Inkrementierung der y-Adresse erfolgt aber nur
   dann, wenn y überhaupt definiert ist und wenn die y-Adresse
   nicht am Anschlag ist; sonst bleibt die Schreibmarke in der
   Warteposition stehen. Entsprechend sind die Überlaufregeln
   von der y- zur z-Dimension definiert; auch hier erfolgt die
   implizite Erhöhung der z-Adresse nur dann, wenn z definiert
   und noch nicht am Anschlag ist. Die z-Dimension ist die höch-
   ste beim VDP definierte Dimension; wird sie begrenzt definiert,

so kann die Schreibmarke nie über diesen Wert hinausgehen.

b) Explizite Adressierung
   Beim Verbindungsaufbau werden für jede Dimension die zuge-
   lassenen Methoden der expliziten Adressierung vereinbart.
   Folgende Adressierungsmethoden stehen für jede Dimension zur
   Auswahl:

   a) Sequentielle (relative) Vorwärtspositionierung auf die
      nächsten Zeichenpositionen

   b) Sequentielle (relative) Vorwärtspositionierung auf die
      nächste Tabulatormarke

   c) Direkte (absolute) Adressierung einer Zeichenposition;
      die Adresse gibt dabei den Abstand zur zugehörigen Koor-
      dinatenachse an. Die direkte Positionierung ist nur für
      Dimensionen mit begrenzter Länge vorgesehen. Außerhalb
      des definierten Teiles liegende Adressen sind ungültig.
      Auf eine explizite Adressierung folgender Text wird nach
      den gleichen Überlaufregeln behandelt, wie sie für die
      implizite Adressierung beschrieben wurden.

   Bild 1 und Bild 2 erläutern die expliziten Adressierungsmöglichkeiten für die x- und y-Dimension in einem
   eindimensionalen bzw. zweidimensionalen Datenspeicher.

4.4.4 <u>Textattribute</u>

Für jede Zeichenposition im Datenspeicher der Basisklasse und
Formatklasse kann die Art der Darstellung und die Schriftgröße
festgelegt werden, die dem Bediener sichtbar werden soll. Da-
für steht dem Kommunikationspartner ein besonderer Befehl zur
Verfügung.
Bei der Art der Darstellung kann gewählt werden zwischen

-   betont / normal / zurückgenommen / unsichtbar
-   auffallend / nicht auffallend.

Wie diese Attribute tatsächlich dem Bediener dargestellt werden,
ist im VDP offen gelassen; so könnte z. B. "betont" bei einem

Gerät als rot, bei einem anderen als überhell abgebildet werden,
oder "auffallend" als blinkend interpretiert werden.

4.5 Struktur und Adressierung des Datenspeichers bei der Format- klasse

4.5.1 Formatierung

Einem Datenspeicher mit Basisklassen-Struktur werden ein oder
mehrere Formate zugeordnet, er wird "formatiert". Die Formate
werden vorher definiert und lokal oder beim Kopplungspartner
gespeichert. Fern gespeicherte Formate müssen natürlich für die
Formatierung zum Terminal übertragen werden. Solange der Datenspeicher formatiert bleibt, sieht der Kopplungspartner nicht
mehr die Basisstruktur, sondern nur die darüberliegende Formatstruktur.
Ein Format enthält meist viele Felddefinitionen:
Für jedes Feld ist neben dessen Namen die relative Lage des
Feldes zum Formatanfang und die Feldlänge angegeben, außerdem noch Feldattribute, darunter die für die Datenspeicherstruktur wichtige Aussage, ob es sich um ein Feld mit festem
oder variablem Inhalt handelt: Nur Felder variablen Inhalts
sind nämlich für den Kommunikationspartner sichtbar; die Felder festen Inhalts dienen nur der lokalen Unterstützung des
Terminalbedieners.

4.5.2 Struktur des formatierten Datenspeichers

Nach der Formatierung ist die ursprüngliche Datenspeicherstruktur mit ihren x, y oder z-Dimensionen verschwunden.
An ihre Stelle tritt eine neue zwei- oder dreidimensionale
Formatstruktur, die nur mehr Formate mit Feldern variablen
Inhalts enthält, da nur diese für die Kommunikation benutzt
werden können. Die Dimension r entspricht den einzelnen Positionen innerhalb eines Feldes, s den Feldern eines Formates und die wahlfreie Dimension t den Formaten selbst; t existiert nur, wenn mehrere Formate gleichzeitig dem Datenspeicher zugeordnet werden. Die Länge der einzelnen Felder und
die Anzahl der Felder wird bei der Formatdefinition vorgegeben.

Werden alle zugeordneten Formate entfernt, dann nimmt der Datenspeicher wieder die ursprüngliche Struktur der Basisklasse an.

Bild 3 zeigt als Beispiel eine zweidimensionale Datenspeicherstruktur.

4.5.3 Adressierung

Im Unterschied zur Basisklasse ist hier für jede Dimension nur eine einzige explizite Adressierungsmethode zugelassen, und zwar werden Positionen innerhalb eines Feldes (r-Dimension) direkt (absolut) adressiert, während die einzelnen (variablen) Felder eines Formates (s-Dimension) über Namen adressiert werden. Die Auswahl eines Formates aus mehreren gleichzeitig zugeordneten Formaten wird ebenfalls über Namen getroffen (t-Dimension).
Das Überschreiten einer Feldgrenze ist nur durch explizite Adressierung möglich.

4.5.4 Feldattribute

Bei der Formatdefinition werden jedem Feld Attribute zugewiesen, die bis auf wenige Ausnahmen bei formatiertem Datenspeicher nicht geändert werden können. Die Attribute lassen sich in mehrere Gruppen einteilen:

a) Das Attribut zur Unterscheidung fester und variabler Felder wurde schon behandelt; nur die variablen Felder sind im formatierten Datenspeicher für den Kommunikationspartner sichtbar.

b) Mehrere Attribute regeln die Datenerfassung durch den Bediener. Es sind dies:

   - geschützt / ungeschützt / Eingabe zwingend
   - markierbar / nicht markierbar
   - Ausrichten des Inhaltes: nach rechts / nach links / nein
   - Ein Satz verfeinerter Plausibilitätsprüfungen
     (z. B. numerisch usw.) ist als wahlfreie Funktion

vorgesehen, aber noch nicht im Detail beschrieben.

c) Zwei Attribute steuern die zugelassenen Wege für Feldinhalte:
Normalerweise werden alle variablen Felder zum Kommunikations-
partner gesendet; zur Optimierung der Übertragung können eini-
ge davon ausgeklammert werden (transmittable/non transmittable)
Das andere Attribut (printable/non printable) regelt, welche
Felder lokal abdruckbar sind.

d) Ein Standardwert für Textattribute kann jedem Feld ausserdem
zugeschrieben werden; er gilt immer dann, wenn nicht innerhalb
des Feldes explizit andere Textattribute verlangt werden. Die
Textattribute regeln wie bei der Basisklasse Darstellung und
Schriftgröße.

5.   Funktionen des erzeugten virtuellen Terminals

Die Funktionen des virtuellen Terminals schlagen sich im VDP als
Befehle und Meldungen nieder.
Die wichtigsten Funktionen sind im folgenden grob aufgelistet.

5.1   Gemeinsame Funktionen beider Terminalklassen

- Textattribut wählen
- Status abfragen
- Geräte aktivieren

5.2   Funktionen der Basisklasse (zusätzlich zu 5.1)

- Text übertragen
- Adressieren; entsprechend den vereinbarten Datenspei-
  cherstrukturen und Adressierungsmethoden.

5.3 Funktionen der Formatklasse (zusätzlich zu 5.1)

- Format definieren
- Format übertragen
- Format abrufen

- Format zuordnen
- Format entfernen

- Format benutzen
    - o Adressieren
    - o Text übertragen
    - o Feldattribut ändern
    - o Markieren.

6. Verfügbarkeit

Das VDP wurde von den drei Herstellern gemeinsam erarbeitet und abgestimmt, um die Normung auf diesem wichtigen Gebiet voranzubringen. Vor kurzem haben die nationalen und internationalen Gremien begonnen, dieses Feld konkret zu bearbeiten. Wir hoffen auf gute Fortschritte und werden rechtzeitig Geräte mit dem schließlich genormten, virtuellen Terminalprotokoll auf den Markt bringen.

7. Quellen und Literatur

7.1 Quellen

a) Virtual device protocol; Version 5
   (CII-HB/ICL/Siemens)
   (DIN/NI 16.2-2679)
b) Reference model of open systems interconnection.
   (ISO/TC97/SC16/N227) (Juni 1979)

7.2 Literatur

a) Standard ECMA-48:
   Additonal controls for character imaging
   i/o-devices (Sept. 76)

b) Bauwens, E., Magnee, F.;
   "Definition of the Virtual Terminal Protocol
   for the Belgia University Network"
   (Computer Network Protocols Symposium
   Proceedings, Liege, 13-15 Februar 1978

c) Dünki, A., Schicker, P.;
   "Virtual terminal definition"
   (Computer-networks, Sept. 77)

d) Data entry virtual terminal protocol
   for Euronet (DEVT);
   (EEC/DG-XII/EURONET/VTP-D/3, Sept. 77)

e) Proposal for a standard Virtual
   Terminal Protocol
   (IFIP, Working group 6.1, Februar 1978)

f) Schicker, P., Zimmermann, H.;
   "Proposal for a Scroll mode Virtual
   Terminal in European Informatics Network"
   (EIN/CCG/77/02, Januar 77)

g) Schulze, G., Börger, W.;
   "A Virtual Terminal Protocol Based on
   the communication Variable",
   (Computer Network Protocols Symposium
   Proceedings, Liege 13-15, Februar 78)

h) The PIX virtual terminal protocol
   (PIX/VTP/TEK/78/01)

i) Magnee, F., Endrizzi, A.;
   "Virtual Terminal Protocols - A Survey"
   (EIN/CCG/EUR/78002)

j) Terminal access protocols
   (ISO/TC97/SC16 N58)

k) CCITT-Empfehlung X3, X28, X29.

l) CCITT/COM VIII, Rapp. Gr. on Teletex
   Terminals
   (Mai 1979, Genf, Dok. 135)

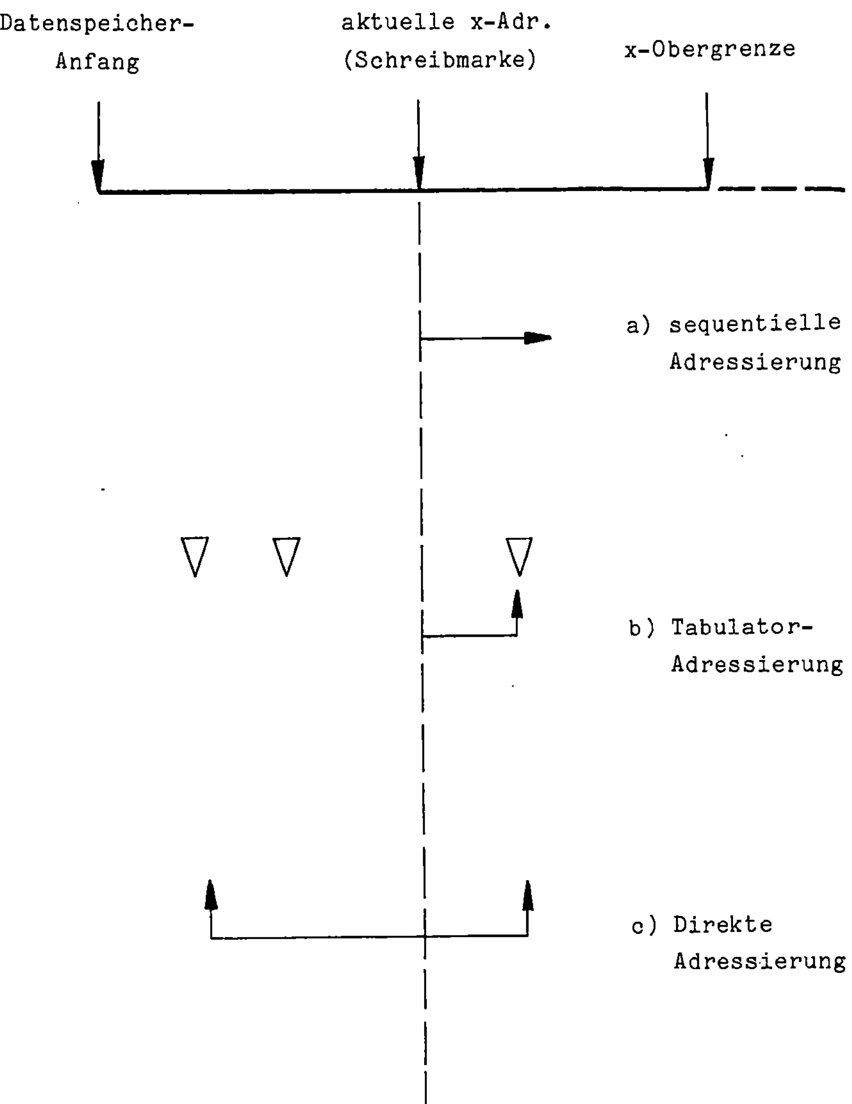

Bild 1:

<u>Adressierung in der x-Dimension.</u>
Eindimensionaler Datenspeicher begrenzter Länge (y- und z-
Dimension fehlen).

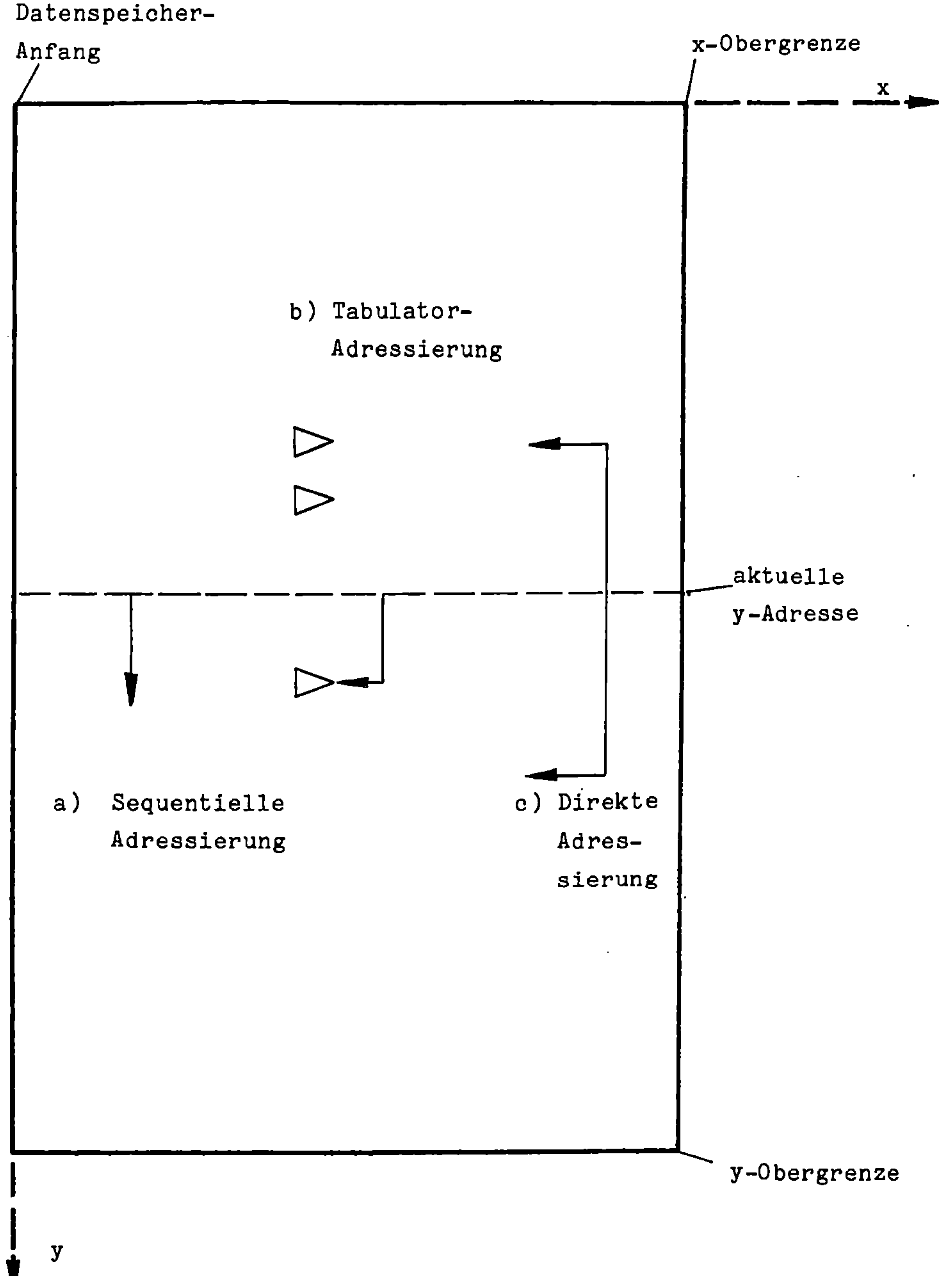

Bild 2:

Adressierung in der y-Dimension.
Zweidimensionaler Datenspeicher begrenzter Länge (z-Dimension
fehlt).

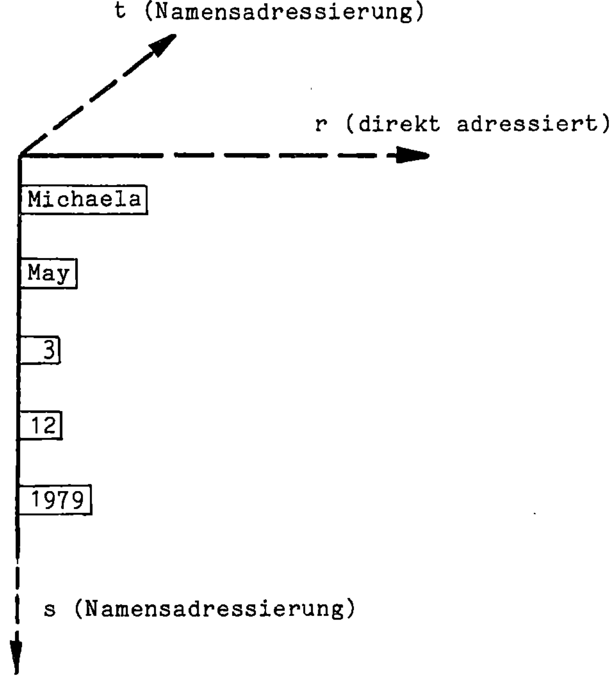

a) Datenspeicher aus Sicht des Bedieners

b) Gedachte Datenspeicherstruktur, wie sie der Kommunikation
    mit dem fernen Partner zugrundeliegt.

Bild 3:   <u>Zweidimensionale Datenspeicherstruktur</u>
           nach dem Formatieren (Dimension t fehlt)

JOB TRANSFER IN OPEN SYSTEMS

=============================

H. Kerutt , R. Speth
Universität Düsseldorf
Rechenzentrum

Abstract

The general understanding of Job Transfer/Remote Job
Entry in an Open System Architecture is outlined and
functions necessary to perform a Job Transfer service
according to that understanding are discussed. Guide
line for the discussion is the idea of job networking.
In a slightly different way most of existing JT/RJE
protocols apply this netjob idea. The description of
a netjob and its execution according to the communication protocol are explained. On that basis and with
regard to the ISO layered model the question of how
to proceed with standardisation is discussed.

Contents

1. Scope

In present days networks of heterogenous computers
mostly the following network services are provided:

- a "Virtual Terminal" service to support networkwide access from heterogenous terminals to dialogue
  applications on arbitrary hosts
- a "File Transfer" service to support the usage
  of files beeing stored on or retrieved from
  remote hosts
- a "Job Transfer" service to support local submission
  and remote execution of batch jobs. Sometimes this
  kind of service in an Open System is called "Remote
  Job Entry" but throughout this paper the first
  entitling is chosen(for clarification see chapter 3)

Other services are for instance for Remote Data Access,
Prorgam-Program Communication,etc. According to the general
demand for that kind of services there are plans (proposals) from the relevant ISO/TC97/SC16 committee to start
standardisation projects on some of these services. Although because of the growing of the importance of dialogue
applications most effort is done in the field of the Virtual
Terminal there is still a certain demand for services connected with bulk data transfers as file and job transfers.
Job transfer for instance will be the first service to be
implemented in two presently planned computernetworks - the
network for the public administration and universities in
Nordrhein-Westfalen (DVS NW) and the PIX-network for universities and scientific institutions in West Berlin(BERNET)
and other institutions in the BRD.

This article generally deals with the Job Transfer(JT)
service and reviews problems related to it with the following aims:

- to separate the JT process from other Open System(OS)
  processes which reside in the upper layers, the Application and Presentation Layer, of the ISO reference model
- to define what functions a JT service in an Open
  System should comprise
- to compare existing JT/RJE protocol proposals in order
  to possibly extract common ideas
- to discuss the interface to lower layers and give
  an example

and finally

- to mention problems to be solved in applying the ISO
  model to the JT application.

2. Job Transfer and Network Standards

Network standards are well known for other OS services as
for instance the "Virtual Terminal(VT)" or the "Virtual
File Store(VFS)". Before looking to Job Transfer under
the viewpoint of network standards the situation for VT
and VFS is briefly displayed.
The functional behavior of an abstract networkunique VT
is fixed in the VT description and the communication
about that functions is done according to the VT communication protocol. The "understanding" between the VT and
the real terminal is done by mapping the VT capabilities
to the existing terminal (and host) properties. The dialogue application - that is the communication above VT
level between the user at the terminal and a program/
dialogue system - is performed according to the conventions of the specific application.
That means there is a direct connection between the user
and the attached application system, say the editor. This
may be visualized by figure 1.

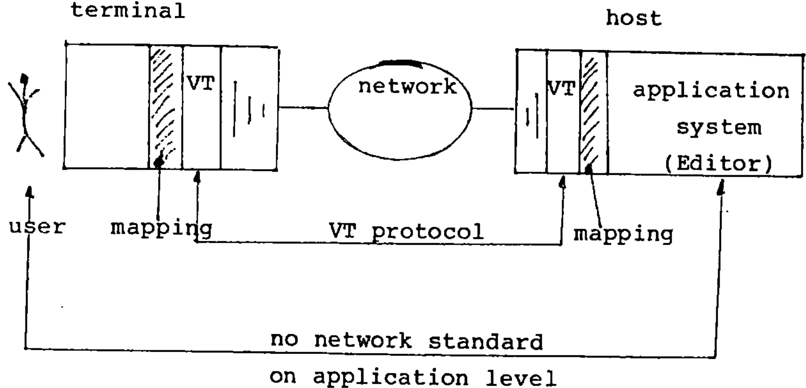

Figure 1

For a File Transfer service (and in extension more generally
for a Remote Data Access service) a networkunique description of a Virtual File Store is used. Beside aunique record
and file structure description a VFS includes also a certain
set of common file store manipulation and administration
commands. The user or a program may directly contact the
VFS and so beeing freed from knowing the different local
file stores of the hosts in the network. This gives a
slightly different picture as in the VT case (see figure 2).
In using the VFS no direct connection between the local
requestor(user, program,...) and the remote server (local
data management system of the remote host) exists: the user
only talks to "his" Virtual File Store in a "language" this
store understands.
Naturally again mapping functions have to be used to finally
get data stored or retrieved at the local file system of the
remote host. The applicability of the VFS model is therefore
limited with respect to the complexity of file data and
file manipulation structures where no mapping relation can
be set up.

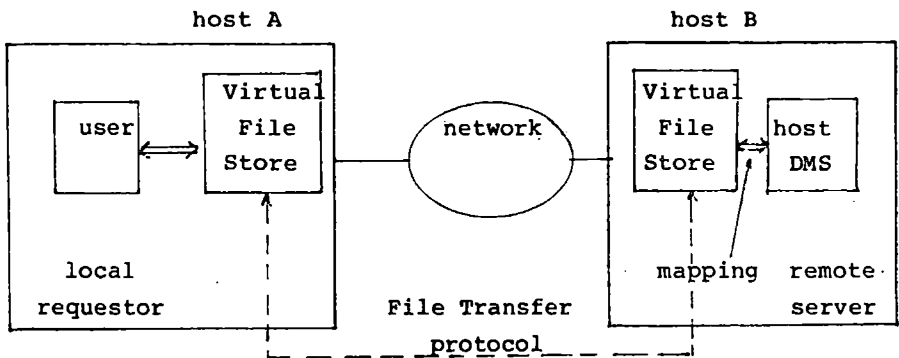

Figure 2

Coming to the Job Transfer service a quite natural extension
of the preceding ideas would be to have no direct (logical)
connection between the user and the remote host - that is
the distinct usage of the job control language(JCL) of the
execution host - and to define a network internal Virtual
Job Description and Manipulation. Quite in analogy to figure
2 this would look as shown in figure 3.

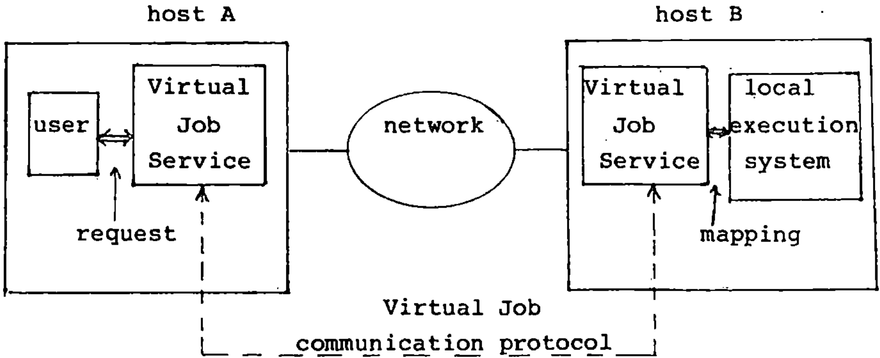

Figure 3

To provide this kind of Virtual Job service one would have
to worry with the old problem of a common job control
language and this is certainly no reasonable starting point
to set up a standardized batch service in an Open System.
Therefore a first working assumption (which can also be
found in nearly all JT protocol proposals) is

to use the natural JCL on each host.

The user has to specify his job according to the JCL of the
host on which he wants to execute the job. That restricts
our problem "merely" to the transfer problem and additional
services which will be discussed in the next chapter.
Concluding from this point of view - and this may be essential for the user of the network services - one can say that

- a dialogue application uses standardized level 6 presentation conventions ("the Virtual Terminal") but let
  the dialogue itself up to the user/progamm conventions
- demanding for remote file data one can apply a standardized Virtual File Store interface where most of the VFS
  description may be seen on the level 6 of the ISO model
- for job execution one has to know the JCL and execution
  conventions of the desired execution host. Descriptions
  necessary for this kind of service in an Open System
  may be distributed on level 6 and 7 of the ISO model.

An ISO/SC16 ad hoc group had tried to classify functions
belonging to level 6 and level 7 for these three items /1/.
The following figure 4 was drawn with the explanations added
but there was no real agreement about the exact boundary.

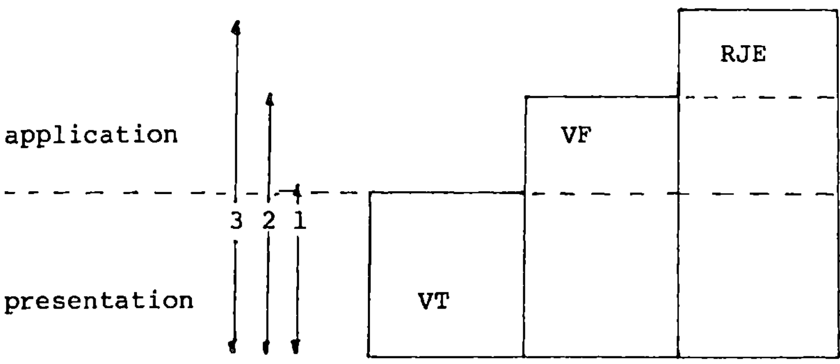

Figure 4

Explanation to figure 4:

(1) data and command structuring according to transformation rules

(2) file manipulation, management + (1) during file control and transfer

(3) station management and command language + (2) + (1)

3. Job Transfer and Supporting Services.

With the discussed restrictions with respect to the JCL Job Transfer in an Open System is reduced to a network internal transfer problem. Such a transfer service in a system of heterogenous computers in principle should provide a similar set of functions which are presently well known at homogenous central systems having a starshaped network of stations connected by "station protocols". Therefore JT in an Open System can be regarded "to be the network equivalent of todays remote job entry stations where the interaction is only between two systems" /2/. By this restriction job processing in an OS is separated from controlling networkwide task execution.
Beside the evident problem of transferring submitted jobs or produced printoutput to specific sites in the network additional services should be provided which a user knows from his local system as job or system status inquiries, routing facilities, broadcast/mailbox facilities, job manipulation facilities,etc. The user may request for these services via an appropriate JT user interface(see figure 5)

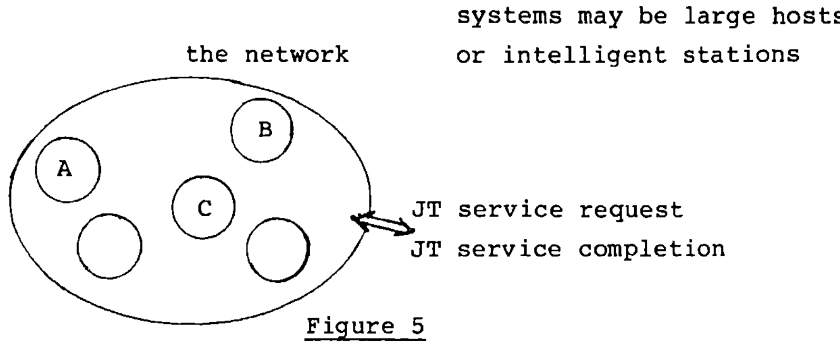

Figure 5

The following list of services may be provided by a JT
protocol. The list may be extended(/3/,/4/,/5/,/6/,/13/).
* job transmission facilities; to transfer a job to a
  specified host; the job to be transferred   can   be
  imaged as a jobfile or a cardimage; the job transmission has to take place in a device independent manner

* output transmission facilities; to route the produced
  output to any specified host; after execution of the
  job at the execution host various kinds of outputs are
  produced which can be one of the following categories:
  - compiler or run protocol
  - dayfile
  - system messages
  According to the user's specification the outputs associated with the received and executed job
  - shall be sent back to the originating host
  - shall be printed at the execution host
  - or shall be routed to a third host or station
    having for instance special hardware devices
    not available at the local host.
  The output transmission has to take place in a device
  independent manner.

* status inquiry facilities;
  status inquiries may concern the whole network situation, special netjob situation, special host or special
  job situation,etc.

* job manipulation facility, for example:
  - for cancelling a job
  - for holding a job (in the input queue)
  - for releasing a job from hold
  - for rerouting a job

* operator-operator communication facilities;
  they may be included in the job manipulation facilities.

* broadcast/mailbox facilities; these facilities may
  be seen to support communication between the network
  administration and the user

In order to support these service functions at any site
of the involved hosts there should exist the appropriate
subprocesses. The following figure 6 gives an example:

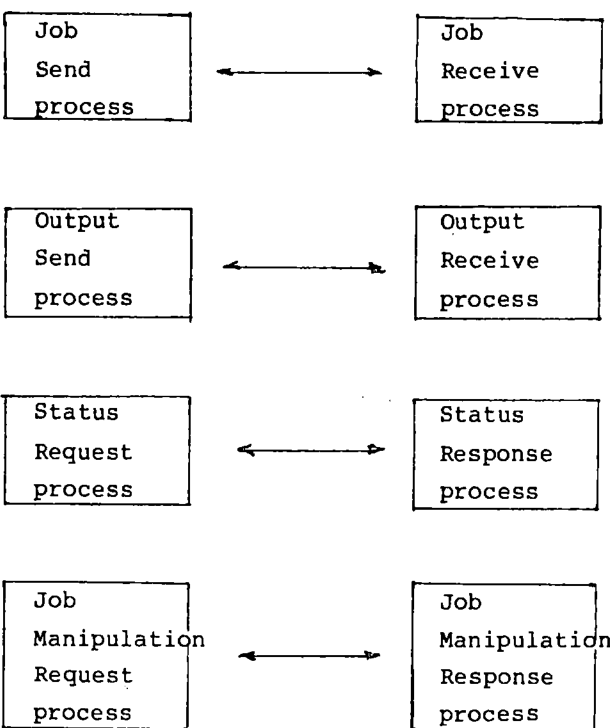

Figure 6

4. A Model of Job Transfer on the Basis of
Existing Protocols

Although we explicitely have excluded to deal with a
Virtual Job service on the basis of a common job control
language the introduction of an abstract network specific
model according to which the Job Transfer can be designed
seems to be recommendable. We will call it the "netjob"
model or the idea of "job networking" and it should be
stated here that the relevant ideas can be found in many
of the existing JT protocols.
In this chapter we shall try to display the idea of job
networking from two points of view:
- trying to understand job networking in a certain
  analogy with local job processing and
- examining existing JT protocols in order to evaluate
  comparable features

4.1 Job Networking - the Idea
Considering local batch processing well known features are:
- the processing unit called "job"
  which is a data stream consisting of a set of job
  control statements and data like a program or input
  data. The data stream is enclosed in a begin and an
  end of job card. The job is further attributed with
  some accounting and resource inquiring information.

- the job execution

- administration facilities for handling job input,
  job execution and output queues, which are
  supported by the local operating system.

In an extension the idea of "job networking" is to see
the network as a whole as a "job processing system"
providing similiar features as displayed for the local
job processing:

- the processing unit now called the "netjob"
  describable as a data stream which is now the user's
  job or output considered above beeing transparent
  to the job networking with respect to its syntax and
  semantics. In analogy to the job the data stream
  is enclosed in a begin and an end of netjob "card"
  represented as a starting and an ending message (see
  chapter 5); furthermore the netjob is completely
  described by attributes containing for example routing information and netjob characteristics.

- netjob execution
  which in job networking can be seen as the controlled
  submission of the netjob described by a communication
  protocol as for example outlined in chapter 5.

- netjob administration
  which should support for example correct netjob
  routing and status and control inquiries. Similiar
  to local operating system functions the netjob administration facility has to handle netjob queues
  containing the appropriate information (input, execution,output). These queues are referring to the de-
  stined host in the network.

In the following chapters the netjob as the processing
unit described by its attributes and the netjob related
administration facilities are outlined both on the
basis of existing protocols.

4.2 Netjob Attributes
The netjob is completely described first by its structure
consisting of the begin and the end of the netjob and the
user's job file as the bulk data, and secondly by some attributes which are assigned to the netjob during the whole
netjob execution. The structure of the netjob is reflected
in the communication phases of the jobtransfer protocol
(see chapter 5).

In the following we shall consider a fundamental set of
attributes found to be necessary after considering some
existing protocols /3/, /4/, /5/, /12/, as there are:
- remote host identification
     -- for the destined execution host
        (called execution node name in JES2 /3/)
     -- for the output print host
        (called punch node or print node name in JES2)
  it must be uniquely declared by each computing centre
  included in the network suitable to a network wide
  standard format.

- user identification
     -- for the destined execution host
     -- for the output print host
  because the user must have the allowance to use
  resources of the remote host and for accounting.

- password
  for each target host

- mode of output (/12/)
  which should be a specification for the special hardware device at the output print host. For example it
  should be a special printer using multiple character
  sets, a card puncher, a disk or a plotter.

- netjob identification
  usually at any system the job during execution get some
  task sequence number by which it is uniquely identified
  in the local operating system. With the help of that
  identification a user can inform about his job's situation and furthermore the operator can cancel or manipu-
  late the job. In a network the netjob situation is
  comparable to that in a local system. For informing
  about or manipulating the netjob must be uniquely identified. For this some kind of netjob identification is
  necessary which is assigned to each netjob by the JT
  process before the netjob executed (/4/,/12/).

- coding of data

  in some protocols a standard coding of data for
  example IA5 is declared according to which the
  netjob is transferred. If no coding conventions
  are fixed each host must provide mapping functions
  from any source code existing at the included
  remote hosts

- record length

  a specification is needed if no standard length
  is declared as for instance max. 80 characters
  per line, e.g. card format (see /3/, /4/).

- output format

  it is necessary to declare the line and page format
  for the output print host if there is no standard
  format be given like in /4/ with the "Communication
  Variable" concept

Beside this fundamental set of attributes by which for
our opinion the netjob is completely described we found
additional attributes in the existing protocols but
they are very special for the considered network like
for example "priority for execution" or "priority for
output" /5/. It is not necessary for general understanding to consider them in this context.

4.3 Netjob Administration
In any existing operating system there exists some kind
of job administration facility like the handling of a job
input, job execution and output queue. For job networking
certain extensions in the operating systems or additional
facilities for handling the netjob in a similiar way must
be provided. It may be some kind of book keeping about
the received netjobs and their attributes . By this the
correct routing of the produced output, the status inquiries etc. can be performed.

For supporting a comfortable netjob administration the
following entries may be handled in such a book keeping
facility associated to one netjob:
    - the above described attributes
additionally
    - the receiving time and date
    - the execution time
    - the output spool time
    - the actual netjob situation in the execution
      system like
            -- waiting (for execution)
            -- in execution
            -- ready (in output queue)
            -- aborted

Into this administration facility relevant for netjobs the
implementor must map the existing job execution facilities
of the local operating system. Considering several existing
protocols we will view some different realizations of this
problem:
1) In the JES2 system /3/ the netjob is always associated
with a "jobheader" containing descriptive information about
the netjob mainly like the above described attributes. At
each node of the network, e.g. at each host of the network
that handles the netjob, some more information is added
to it like time and date .The jobheader is forwarded with
the netjob through the network. In this case the book
keeping facility is part of the netjob during the whole
netjob execution.

2) Considering the PIX RJE protocol /4/ there is made
a proposal for the introduction of a so called "RJE memory"
which should be installed at each network host. It is moti-
vated with the necessity for giving security and more
flexibility to the netjob handling but nothing is said
about the handling itself. The idea is that the processes
handling the netjobs like the job send/ receive and output
send/ receive process can update the entries in the RJE
memory. The status inquiring facilities should be realized

as requests to the RJE memory. Hereby the book keeping
entries besides the netjob attributes are not accompanying
the netjob from one host to the other. Each host has to
create new entries for each received network input.

3) In the JT-protocol /5/ we found an interesting realisation of a netjob administration facility, the "jobmill".
It can be regarded as an attempt to define some kind of
standardisation in administrating the netjobs. In the
jobmill there are three places where the netjobs are kept
while in the host:
- the input list
- the execution list
- the output list

The netjob may be in one list at any time. The netjob
beeing in the input list means it is received from the
network. Beeing in the execution list means the contents
of the netjob which is the user's job is in execution.
Nothing is said about netjob execution we defined above.
Beeing in the output list means that the output corresponding to a retrieved netjob is ready for transmission.
The netjob is represented by an entry containing the whole
characteristics of the netjob mainly described above and
some additional information which is dependent on that
special network configuration. We don't want to consider
them in details. For updating and handling the entries
only one process is responsible, the "jobmill interrogation
and control" process. For status requests and operator
messages a connection is established to that process.

From the viewpoint of the provided services the attempt
to generalize such netjob administration is a quite
supportable way to complete the model of job networking.

5. The Communication Protocol

Job networking ,e.g. the netjob execution, is performed by
cooperation of JT processes on the hosts/stations. This
cooperation on top of the communication hierarchy follows
certain rules: a peer to peer protocol (the "JT protocol")
will be run and protocol data units will carry appropriate
control information for that level. The communication is
done via the lower level service interface. An example for
such an interface and consequences for the design of the
JT protocol are given in chapter 5.2. The protocol will
have an internal structure adjusted to the idea of job
networking.

5.1 The Structure of the Protocol

The JT process consists of several subprocesses(see p.10).
On the basis of the netjob idea the job and output subprocesses may be structured into the following main activities
- submission of netjobs which is structured
     -- in an "opening phase" characterizing the begin
        of the netjob
     -- in the "bulk data transfer phase" which handles
        the transmission of the netjob datastream
     -- and in an "ending phase" characterizing
        the end of the netjob
  - control of the JT process communication
  - synchronisation of the communication steps between
    the peer partners
A list of additional activities as for example checkpoin-
ting, re-synchronisation ,etc. depend on the design of the
service interface (see chapter 5.2 for further discussion).

Naturally further definitions and conventions have to be
used discussed partially already in chapter 4.1 as for
instance record structure, device control related conventions, coding/decoding and compression/decompression

conventions. It should be mentioned here that definitions
of that kind can be assigned to the Presentation Layer
in the ISO model and may be discussed for example under
the viewpoint of a "Virtual Device" protocol. But presently
there is no general agreement on that problem (see p. 7)

As an example for the structure of the JT communication
two protocol proposals are reviewed here. In the first
example /4/ there is a halfduplex communication for the
netjob opening and ending phase and a simplex structure
in the bulk data transfer phase.

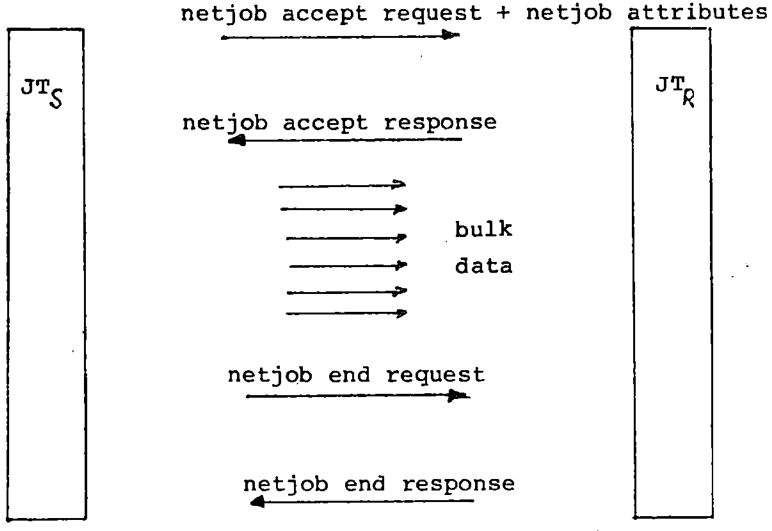

Figure 7

A similiar structure can be found in /5/ which beside
of slightly different attributes differs in the end
phase of the communication where no response step is
performed (figure 8)

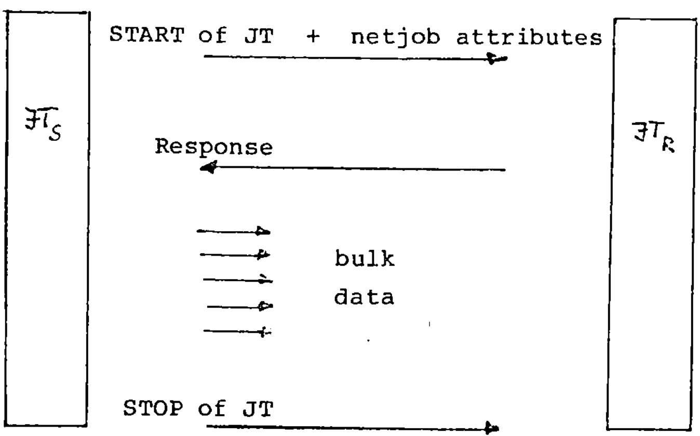

Figure 8

5.2 Lower Level Service Interface

Inspecting different JT protocols one can find that although
they provide comparable kind of network services (for instance according to the list of chapter 3) internally they
have different communications specific functions. Evidently
this depends on the kind of the lower level service interface the JT process can use. As an example checkpoint and
resynchronisation mechanisms are mentioned. If one adopt the
argument that these two special functions are needed by
most of the application processes one can perform them on
levels below the application process. An interface which is
designed according to these assumptions may provide the
following services (for further discussion and explanation
see /7/):

CONNECT	: establishment of transport connection bet- ween application processes
DISCONNECT	: termination of transport connections
DATA	: exchange of normal data units
TELEGRAM	: exchange of expedited data units
PURGE	: purge between co-operating processes, restart of data flow

```
OPEN            : binding co-operating modes of operations,
                  providing the synchronisation services
CLOSE           : unbind co-operating modes of operation
SYNCH           : synchronisation between co-operating
                  processes
SET CHKPT       : set checkpoints
CHKPT RESTART:  restart on previously set checkpoints
```

6. How to Proceed for Standardisation

There are two main points to be discussed first:
* What network services should be provided by the JT
  communication process? Examples are given in chapter 3.

* Could a design guide line be agreed on? Job networking
  seems to be a usable framework for this according to
  which many existing protocols are designed.

Beside these decisions some other issues have early to
be investigated:
* What kind of lower level service interface will be
  used ? This question is closely connected with the
  interpretation of the upper layers 6 and 7 of the ISO
  reference model. Three ways of interpretation may be
  outlined here:
    - try to keep the seven layers in the severe archi-
      tectural sense. This means however to fix an exact
      boundary between application and presentation layer
      and examine criteria for positioning the boundary.
      This problem was discussed within an ad hoc group /1/
      of ISO/SC16/WG2 and " no rigorous criterion could
      be identified which was entirely satisfactory"
    - try to keep layer 6 and 7 be separated from the lower
      levels as one building block what means that one dif-
      ferentiates a "communication service" (layers 1-5)
      from the "users of communication service". This kind
      of view is proposed by /8/ and is shown in figure 9.

156

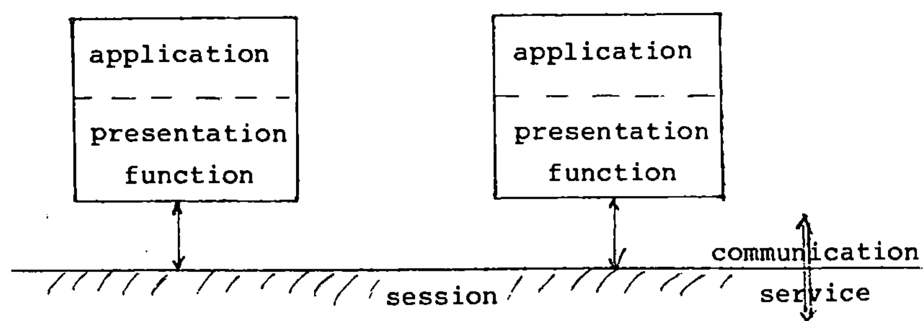

Figure 9

- in an even more simplified model /9/ one only has
  one individable entity called "application entity"
  above the transport service according to figure 10.

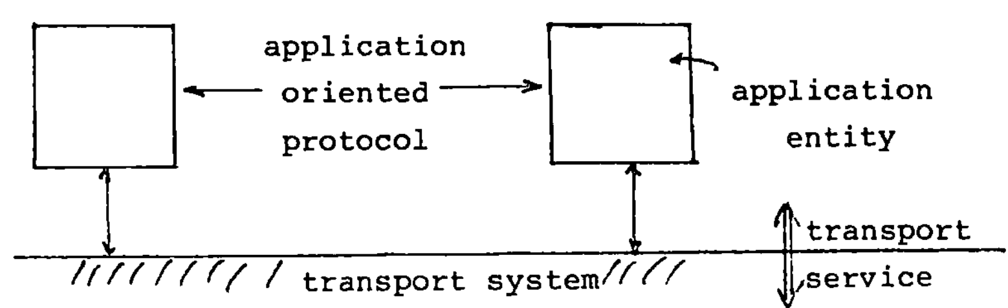

Figure 10

Then the ISO model can be assigned as follows: the
transport service contains layer 1-4 and the adres-
sing functions of layers 5 and 6 while the application entities contain all the other functions found
before in layers 5,6 and 7

* In addition to these different approaches to understand
  and interpret the upper layers of the ISO model there
  are proposals to describe the Presentation Layer in
  using an abstract model based on the idea of a shared
  store owned and communicated about by the remote

processes /10/. This idea was applied to describe JT
communication /4/ but can also be found in other pub-
lications for instance /8/ . The general applicability
of this model to support application level communication may be discussed.

* An essential task of Job and File Transfer protocols
is to handle the transfer of the bulk data. Somewhere
/11/ it is proposed to use a common bulk data transfer
service for several applications which is shown in
figure 11. Similiar ideas are reported in /14/ where
Job Transfer/RJE is performed in connection with File
Transfer based on a common "Data Transfer". These
points have to be discussed mainly under the viewpoint
of consistency with the ISO architecture.

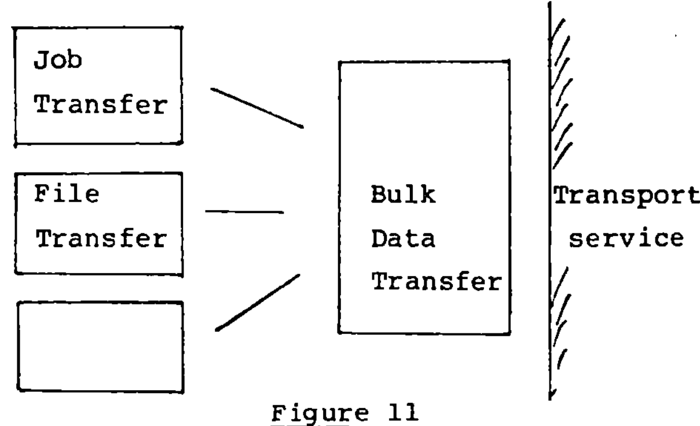

<u>Figure 11</u>

As one can see from the mentioned points some very basic
problems have to be solved first but apart from this
it should be possible - if one adopts for instance the
idea of job networking - to start specifying the netjob
description and structuring the protocol.

7. Conclusion

Job Transfer in an Open System can be modelled according to the execution of an abstract "netjob" in the network environment. This idea of job networking found in most of existing Job Transfer protocols can be applied in a machine independent manner.

With respect to the ISO layered model functions to be performed within the JT protocol may be found but the well known difficulties for applying a level 6 and level 7 separation are existing further. Job networking and related conventions however may be discussed apart from that difficulties.

8. Literature

/1/ Report on the Third Meeting of ISO/TC97/SC16/WG2,
    June 1979 London; SC16/N220,Annex C

/2/ Computer Networks and their Protocols
    D.W.Davies,D.L.A.Barber,W.L.Price,C.M.Solomonides
    J.Wiley & Sons, N.Y., 1979

/3/ Network Job Entry Facilities for JES2
    R.O.Simpson, IBM SYS J.,Vol 17, No 3, 1978

/4/ The PIX RJE Protocol
    W.Heinze,B.Struif,M.Wilhelm, GMD Darmstadt 1978

/5/ Job Transfer Protocol
    M.A.Mc Conachie, Univ. Nottingham, 1976

/6/ RJE Protokoll im Datenvermittlungssystem Nordrhein-
    Westfalen, DVS NW , Landesamt für Datenverarbeitung
    und Statistik NW, 1979

/7/ Specification of a Transport and Session Layer
    Protocol
    E.Dregger,H.Eckert,B.Lausch,F.Vogt
    PIX/HLP/TAG/79/05 GMD Darmstadt, 1979

/8/ KOOPA ADV Zwischenbericht der ad hoc Gruppe "Höhere
    Kommunikationsprotokolle"; Bundesminister des
    Innern, Bonn, 1979

/9/ German Position to Future Program of Work of
    ISO/TC97/SC16 ;   ISO/TC97/SC16/N208 , 1979

/10/ Application Protocol Design Based on a Unified
     Communication Model ; E.Raubold et al.,
     ICCC Kyoto 1978

/11/ A Proposal for a Bulk Transfer Protocol;
     A.Belloni,M.Bozzetti,G.Le Moli,
     INWG Gen. Note 196 , 1979

/12/ A Proposal for a Batch Service 1 & 2;
     A. Belloni, M. Bozzetti, G. Le Moli,
     C.R.E.I., Centro Rete Europea di Informatica
     Politecnico de Milano - Milano,
     EIN/CREI/76/ , 1976

/13/ Remote Job Entry Protocol
     R.Bressler,R.Guida,A.Mc Kenzie
     The ARPA Protocol Handbook
     RFC 407, 1972

/14/ An RJE Protocol for a Resource Sharing Network
     J.Day, G.R.Grossmann
     CAC University of Illionois
     ARPANET RFC No.725 , 1977

RECHNERVERBUND IM BILDSCHIRMTEXT

Dipl.-Phys.   Jürgen Döring

DATEL GMBH - danet
Bartningstraße 55

6100 Darmstadt

I N H A L T

1. Zusammenfassung

Das Bildschirmtext-System wird im Gegensatz zu ähnlichen
Systemen (Viewdata, Prestel, Datavision etc.) ein zusätzliches
Leistungsmerkmal aufweisen, den Rechnerverbund.

Hierdurch wird es dem Benutzer ermöglicht, mit seinem Bild-
schirmtext-Terminal (Fernsehgerät) mit den DV-Anlagen der
Informationslieferanten in einen Dialog zu treten, die am
Rechnerverbund angeschlossen sind. Die Voraussetzung für
eine solche Kommunikation ist die Existenz eines Kommunika-
tionsprotokolls. Bildschirmtext kann als eine Applikation
angesehen werden, die ein offenes System nutzt. Daher sollte
Bildschirmtext in die allgemeine Philosophie der 'open systems'
passen.

Im Feldversuch wird zunächst ein einfaches Protokoll verwendet, das den dort auftretenden Anforderungen und der Konfiguration im Bildschirmtext-Feldversuch gerecht wird.

2. Heutige und zukünftige Kommunikation im BT-Rechnerverbund

Das heutige Bildschirmtext-System im nicht-öffentlichen Versuch
beziehungsweise das Prestel-System in Großbritannien im Test-
Dienst erlaubt dem Benutzer lediglich die Kommunikation mit der
örtlichen Bildschirmtext-Zentrale. Der Benutzer stellt die Verbindung zur Bildschirmtextzentrale mit Hilfe eines LSI-Modems
mit automatischem Kennungs- und Wählimpulsgeber oder manuell
über einen normalen Modem (in Deutschland D 1200 S) her. Die
Übertragung von der BT-Zentrale zum Decoder des TV-Terminals,
der mit einem Speicher für einen Seiteninhalt versehen ist, erfolgt mit 1200 bit/sec asynchron. Die Benutzer-Eingabe wird auf
dem Hilfskanal mit 75 baud zur BT-Zentrale übertragen und dem
Benutzer im Echoplex-Verfahren auf dem Bildschirm dargestellt
(siehe Bild 1).

Der Benutzer hat in diesem Dialog zwei Dienste zur Verfügung:

- das Abrufen von Informationsseiten aus der BT-
  Datenbank durch Fortschreiten im Suchbaum der BT-
  Zentrale oder Direktwahl von Informationsseiten.

- Eingeben von Daten in die BT-Zentrale in beschränk-
  tem Umfang unter Verwendung sogenannter Dialog-Seiten.
  Hierbei wird die eingegebene Information im peripheren
  Speicher der BT-Zentrale solange gehalten, bis sie vom
  gleichen oder einem anderen Benutzer abgerufen wird.

Aus diesen beiden Dienst-Merkmalen wird ersichtlich, daß lediglich
Mensch-Maschine-Kommunikation möglich ist, wobei die Maschine immer
die lokale BT-Zentrale ist. Auch bei Existenz anderer BT-Zentralen
ist keine Kommunikation zwischen den BT-Zentralen bzw. zwischen dem
Benutzer und einer entfernten BT-Zentrale möglich (siehe Bild 2).

Für den öffentlichen Dienst in England wird ein Sternnetz vorgesehen. Es handelt sich aber um reine Maschine-Maschine-Kommunikation.

Der Zweck der hiermit verfolgt wird ist, in einem zentralen
Update-Zentrum die Datenbank zu führen und die sogenannten
Service-Zentren regelmäßig mit einheitlichem Inhalt zu versor-
gen. Das Update-Zentrum ist im Prinzip eine normale Prestel-
Zentrale, die allerdings nur von den Informations-Lieferanten
über das Wählnetz erreicht werden kann. Der Benutzer wählt
automatisch immer das Service-Zentrum in seinem Ortsnetz
(siehe Bild 3).

Die Kommunikation zwischen dem Update-Zentrum und den Service-
Zentren erfolgt entweder über überlassene Stromwege oder über
ein Paketvermittlungsnetz. In jedem Falle ist oberhalb der
Transportebene ein Protokoll der höheren Ebenen notwendig.

2.1 Zukünftige Konfiguration im Bildschirmtext

Wie wird nun die zukünftige Konfiguration für den Bildschirmtext-Rechnerverbund in Deutschland aussehen ?

Zunächst sollen die Anforderungen an das Gesamtsystem beschrieben werden. Das System wird folgende Leistungsmerkmale aufweisen:

- die lokalen Bildschirmtext-Zentralen werden einen
  allgemeinen Datenbank-Teil enthalten, der in allen
  BT-Zentralen gleich ist;

- die BT-Zentralen werden einen lokalen Datenbank-Teil
  enthalten, der spezifisch für diese BT-Zentrale ist;

- externe Datenkbanken werden so an das System angeschlossen werden, daß jeder Benutzer jede externe
  Datenbank, die von einem Informationsanbieter auf
  einem eigenen System betrieben wird, erreichen kann.

Es sind also entscheidende Leistungsmerkmale im Vergleich zu
den heutigen Leistungsmerkmalen des Systems hinzugekommen,
die das gesamte BT-System zu einem flächendeckenden, verteilten
Datenbanksystem machen.

Einen vergleichbaren Ansatz zur Integration von privaten Datenbanken in das öffentliche Viewdata-System gibt es nur im französischen Videotext-System. Das englische Prestel-System, auf dem
die Technik für den Bildschirmtext-Feldversuch basiert, sieht nur
ein öffentliches, verteiltes Datenbanksystem vor. Zudem werden
dort alle Datenbanken durch ein synchrones Updating versorgt und
besitzen alle den gleichen Inhalt (Bild 3).

Die Konfiguration für Bildschirmtext ist wesentlich komplexer.
Es wird zwei Bereiche der Datenkommunikation geben. Der erste Be-

reich umfaßt die Kommunikation zwischen den BT-Zentralen.
Die BT-Zentralen tauschen Information, die an den Benutzer
durch dessen lokale BT-Zentrale weitergeleitet wird, aus.
Der zweite Bereich der Datenkommunikation betrifft den Datenaustausch zwischen BT-Zentrale und externen Rechnern. Auch
hier steht die Kommunikation zwischen BT-Benutzer und der
Datenbank des externen Rechners im Vordergrund.

Beide Kommunikationsformen sind sehr ähnlich, jedoch funktionell zeigen sich einige Unterschiede, wie im Folgenden gezeigt
wird. Als Übertragungsnetz wird das Paketvermittlungsnetz der
DBP, Datex-P, verwendet. Damit ergibt sich die in Bild 4 darge-
stellte Konfiguration.

Die Verbindung zwischen den BT-Zentralen bzw. zwischen BT-
Zentrale und externem Rechner wird über permanente oder ge-
schaltete virtuelle Verbindungen (PVC oder VC) hergestellt.
PVC's wird man für den Fall häufig benutzter Verbindungen ver-
wenden, während VC's für selten benutzte oder häufig wechselnde
Verbindungen geschaltet werden.

Auf die über X.25-Ebene 3 liegenden Kommunikationsprotokolle
für Bildschirmtext wird in Kapitel 2.3 eingegangen.

2.2 Dienste und Anwendungs-Funktionen

Der Rechnerverbund im Bildschirmtext bietet funktionell in
zwei Bereichen Dienste und Funktionen an

- Information retrieval
- Datensammlung.

Beide Bereiche beziehen sich sowohl auf kommunizierende Bildschirmtextzentralen als auch auf die Datenübertragung zwischen
BT-Zentrale und externen Rechnern.Zusätzlich sind die Funktionen
der

- expliziten Weitervermittlung

und

- impliziten Weitervermittlung

vorgesehen, wobei die implizite, vom Benutzer nicht wahrgenommene
Weitervermittlung, nur zwischen BT-Zentralen stattfindet.

2.2.1 Kommunikation zwischen BT-Zentralen

Die BT-Zentralen enthalten in ihren baum-strukturierten
Datenbanken einen globalen Teil, der in allen BT-Zentralen identisch ist, und einen lokalen Teil, der für jede BT-Zentrale spezifisch ist. Zusätzlich kann im globalen Teil der Fall eintreten,
daß eine BT-Seite zwar global definiert ist, jedoch nur in einer,
bzw. nicht in allen, BT-Zentralen gespeichert ist. Dies ist der
Fall, in dem implizit, d.h. ohne explizite Anforderung durch den
Benutzer, eine Verbindung über PVC oder VC zu der BT-Zentrale
hergestellt-wird, die die gewünschte BT-Seite enthält. Selektiert
der Benutzer nun in dieser entfernten BT-Zentrale eine Seite, die
in einer dritten BT-Zentrale gespeichert ist, wird automatisch
die erste Verbindung abgebaut, und eine Verbindung zur dritten
BT-Zentrale hergestellt.

Weiterhin kann der BT-Benutzer explizit den lokalen Teil einer
beliebigen anderen BT-Zentrale selektieren und dort Information
abrufen. Dies erfolgt über eine Gateway-Funktion, d.h. Auswahl
einer speziellen Gateway-Seite in der lokalen BT-Zentrale.

Bei der Kommunikation zwischen BT-Zentralen steht hauptsächlich
der Informationsabruf (Information retrieval) im Vordergrund.
Die Funktion Datensammlung kommt mehr bei der Kommunikation mit
externen Rechnern zum Tragen, obwohl diese Funktion auch zwischen
BT-Zentralen möglich sein wird. Auf die Datensammlung wird genauer im folgenden Abschnitt eingegangen.

Ein weiteres Leistungsmerkmal des Rechnerverbundes zwischen Bildschirmtextzentralen ist das identische Updaten, d.h. Verteilen ge-
änderter Informationen für den globalen Teil der BT-Zentral-
Datenbanken. Dieser Vorgang findet dann statt, wenn ein Informations-
lieferant eine BT-Seite, die in mehreren oder allen BT-Zentralen
gespeichert werden soll, editiert. Die BT-Seite wird hierbei in den
Zentralen eingespeichert, die auf der sogenannten Verteilliste für
diese Seite stehen.

2.2.2 Kommunikation zwischen BT-Zentralen und externen Rechnern

Bei dieser Kommunikationsform im BT-Rechnerverbund existiert die
Funktion des impliziten Verbindungsaufbaues nicht. Der Hauptgrund
hierfür ist die Tatsache, daß die Struktur der externen Datenbanken
frei ist, d.h. nicht notwendigerweise baumstrukturiert und somit
nicht unbedingt in eine Gesamt-BT-Datenbankstruktur integrierbar
ist.

Der Informationsseitenabruf erfolgt identisch wie bei der Kommunikation zwischen BT-Zentralen über die Gateway-Funktion.

Ein wesentliches Leistungsmerkmal im BT-Rechnerverbund ist die
Funktion der Datensammlung. Dies ist insbesondere für Betreiber
externer Rechner von Interesse, da hierbei der BT-Benutzer in
einem Dialog mit einem privaten Datenverarbeitungssystem treten
kann. Der Benutzer verwendet sein BT-Terminal hierbei nicht nur

zum Abrufen von Information, sondern ist in der Lage Daten,
die an den externen Rechner weitergleitet werden, über eine
Tastatur an die BT-Zentrale einzugeben. Hierbei übernimmt die
BT-Zentrale die Funktion, die asynchron vom Benutzer eingegebenen
Daten zu sammeln, zwischenzuspeichern und an den externen Rechner
zu übertragen. Die Struktur der Felder, d.h. die Maske auf dem
Bildschirm des Benutzers, wird vom externen Rechner definiert und
übertragen. Der Vorgang der Datenerfassung kann in folgende
Schritte zerlegt werden:

- der Benutzer selektiert eine Datensammlungs-Seite
  im externen Rechner über die BT-Zentrale;

- der externe Rechner überträgt die Datensammlungsseite
  mit den entsprechenden Felddefinitionen an die dem Benutzer zugeordnete BT-Zentrale;

- die BT-Zentrale überträgt den darstellbaren Inhalt der
  Datensammlungsseite an den Decoder des Benutzer-Termi-
  nals und speichert die Felddefinition ab;

- der Benutzer gibt über seine Tastatur die Daten ein, die
  von der BT-Zentrale im Echo-Verfahren an das Benutzer-
  Terminal zurückübertragen und in der BT-Zentrale ge-
  sammelt und zwischengespeichert werden;

- der Benutzer signalisiert das Ende der Dateneingabe zur
  BT-Zentrale;

- die BT-Zentrale überträgt den Block der gesammelten Daten
  an den externen Rechner.

Hierbei übernimmt die BT-Zentrale in gewisser Weise PAD-Funktionen
für das asynchrone BT-Terminal.

Ansonsten entsprechen die beschriebenen Funktionen denen eines
einfachen Asynchron-Sichtgeräts.

Wesentlich ist, daß der externe Rechner mit jedem Teilnehmer
in einen freien Dialog treten kann, d.h. jede beliebige Information im Rahmen des erlaubten Codes vom Benutzer
erhalten kann. Dies gilt natürlich nur unter der Voraussetzung,
daß der Benutzer über eine entsprechende Tastatur verfügt.

2.3 Kommunikationsprotokolle

Wie in anderen Vorhaben wird auch in Bildschirmtext an der
Definition von Kommunikationsprotokollen gearbeitet. Das Modell
der "open systems architecture" von ISO mit seiner Schichten-
struktur findet auch hier weitgehend Eingang.

In jedem Falle wird die Tendenz dahingehen, bis in die Präsentationsschicht ein allgemeines Kommunikationsprotokoll, das
einem Standard entspricht, zu nehmen und nur die anwendungsspezifischen Funktionen für Bildschirmtext spezifisch zu definieren.

Hier soll lediglich eine Liste der möglichen Eigenschaften für
ein Kommunikationsprotokoll angegeben werden, vor allem auch des-
wegen, um in Kapitel 3.3 dagegen prüfen zu können, welche die
Eigenschaften im Feldversuch schon realisiert sind. Im wesentlichen gibt es zwei Bereiche zwischen Paketvermittlungsebene
(Datex-P) und der BT-spezifischen Anwendung, die hier relevant sind:

- Transportschicht

und

- Präsentationsschicht (siehe auch Bild 5).

Funktionen, die im ISO-Modell in der Session-Schicht untergebracht
sind, können u.U. zur Aufwandsersparnis in die Transport- oder Präsentationsschicht verlegt werden.

Folgende "Primitive" sind in der Transport-Schicht (über die Service-
Schnittstelle erreichbar) denkbar:

		Funktion
1.	CONNECT (aktiv)	aktiver Verbindungsaufbau
2.	CONNECT (passiv)	Erklärung der Bereitschaft zum Verbindungsaufbau mit Empfänger-angabe
3.	ACCEPT	positive Bestätigung einer Ver-bindung

Funktion

4.	REJECT	Ablehnung einer Verbindung
5.	COLLISION	Feststellung der Kollisions-Situation beim Verbindungsaufbau
6.	RECONNECT	Wiederaufbau einer zusammengebrochenen Verbindung
7.	RESYNCH	Resynchronisieren und Check-point setzen
8.	RESET	Wiederaufsetzen beim letzten Check-point
9.	DATA	Datenübertragung
10.	PUSH	Leeren des Übertragungskanals
11.	EXPEDITED	Übertragen vorrangiger Daten
12.	INTERRUPT	Übertragen von Steuerinformation mit höherer Priorität
13.	DATAGRAM	Übertragen einer Nachricht ohne Sequenzkontrolle und expliziter Empfangsbestätigung
14.	DISCONNECT	Auflösung einer Verbindung
15.	ADRESSING	Adressierung von Sender und Empfänger
16.	MULTIPLEXING	Multiplexen mehrerer Sitzungen oberhalb eines PVC oder VC
17.	FLOWCONTROL	Flußkontrolle für einen Sub-PVC oder -VC.

In der Präsentationsschicht lassen sich "Primitive" wie in der Transportschicht nicht so einfach definieren. Folgende Dienste sind aber nach ISO-Modell als Unterstützung der Anwendungen zu sehen:

- Verwaltung der Eintragung von Daten
- Nachrichtenaustausch
- Darstellung der Daten
- Verwaltung der Datenstrukturen.

3. Bildschirmtext-Feldversuch

Im BT-Feldversuch sind im Vergleich zum späteren Dienst folgende
Einschränkungen gegeben:

- zunächst wird das Datex-P-Netz nicht
  verwendet,

- es findet keine Kommunikation zwischen den BT-
  Zentralen statt.

3.1 Konfiguration im Feldversuch

Im Feldversuch wird zwar kein Paketvermittlungsnetz verwendet,
jedoch wird die Schnittstelle X.25 nach Datapac mit symmetrischer
LAP-B auf Ebene 2 implementiert. Dies erlaubt jederzeit den Übergang auf ein DPV-Netz. Lediglich die BT-Zentrale muß dann vom DCE-
Verhalten auf DTE umgestellt werden. Für den externen Rechner ergibt sich keine Änderung (siehe Bild 6 und 7).

Wie aus den Abbildungen ersichtlich ist, ist der Anschluß von externen Rechnern auf zwei Arten möglich:

- direkt an die Bildschirmtext-Zentralen über X.25
  nach Datapac mit symmetrischer LAP-B,

- über den Vorrechner, der zunächst eine Basic-Mode-
  Schnittstelle (BSC) zur Verfügung stellt (für Rechner, die nicht über X.25 verfügen). Im Laufe der
  Entwicklung wird sich herausstellen, ob es notwendig
  ist, weitere Prozedur-Varianten auf dem Vorrechner
  zu emulieren.

Insgesamt können 16 externe Rechner über den Vorrechner angeschlossen werden. Für direkt an die BT-Zentralen über X.25 angeschlossene
Rechner stehen pro BT-Zentrale 5 physikalische X.25-Ports zur Verfügung. Das bedeutet, daß ein Rechner, der an beide BT-Zentralen

angeschlossen wird, je BT-Zentrale einen physikalischen Port
belegt. Anders ist dies bei Verwendung von Datex-P. Dann besteht diese Einschränkung nicht mehr.

Die BSC-Anschlüsse werden im Multipoint-Verfahren betrieben.
Damit stehen jedem externen Rechner mit BSC-Anschluß 32 logische Adressen zur Verfügung und damit können theoretisch
32 Benutzer gleichzeitig mit dem Rechner kommunizieren. Diese
32 logischen Adressen werden auf je 16 PVC's jeder BT-Zentrale
im Vorrechner abgebildet. Den direkt über X.25 angeschlossenen
Rechnern stehen je 32 PVC's zur Verfügung. Damit enden in jeder
BT-Zentrale 256 PVC's von Rechnern über den Vorrechner und
160 PVC's von direkt angeschlossenen Rechnern. Die rund 200
Wählports werden im Betrieb dynamisch, je nach Anforderung, auf
die 416 PVC's abgebildet.

3.2 Dienste und Anwendungsfunktionen im Feldversuch

Die Dienste und Anwendungsfunktionen, die das BT-Rechnerver-
bundsystem im Feldversuch zur Verfügung stellt, entsprechen
im Wesentlichen den unter 1.2 beschriebenen. Allerdings gibt
es im Feldversuch keine Kommunikation zwischen den BT-Zentralen
für Benutzeranwendungen.

Folgende Dienste werden zur Verfügung gestellt:

- Information-Retrieval von externen Rechnern

  Der Benutzer kann über Gateway-Seiten eine Verbindung
  zum externen Rechner aufbauen und über diese Verbindung Information- bzw. Auswahl-Seiten aus der Datenbank des externen Rechners abrufen.

- Abrufen von Datensammlungs-Seiten (Masken) vom externen Rechner und Übertragung gesammelter Daten zum
  externen Rechner

  Auch hier erfolgt der Verbindungsaufbau über die Gateway-
  Seite.

Beide Anwendungen können gemischt verwendet werden, d.h. der Benutzer kann in einer Sitzung sowohl Information-Retrieval als
auch Datensammlung durchführen.

Der externe Rechner hat zudem die Möglichkeit, die Gateway-Seiten
in "closed user groups" zu legen.

3.2.1 Details zum Informations-Retrieval

Der Informationsabruf aus dem externen Rechner erfolgt aus der
Sicht des Benutzers (nachdem die Verbindung aufgebaut ist) in
der gleichen Weise, wie aus der BT-Zentrale. Der Unterschied

besteht in der internen Behandlung. Es gibt zwei Möglichkeiten:

- direkter Aufruf einer Seite durch Eingabe von
  * Nummer #

- Abruf durch Eingabe einer Auswahl-Ziffer.

In beiden Fällen wird ein "Page-Request" generiert.

3.2.2 Details zur Datensammlung

Der Betreiber des externen Rechners kann Datensammlungseiten
mit maximal 62 Eingabefeldern definieren. Jeder Datensammlungsseite folgen - unsichtbar für den Benutzer - bis zu 4 weitere
Datenseiten, die die Felddefinitionen und Hinweiszeilen zur
Bedienerführung (in Zeile 23 des Benutzerbildschirms dargestellt) enthalten (siehe Bild 8). Während der Datensammlung
stehen dem Benutzer folgende Funktionen zur Verfügung:

- Beenden Eingabe für ein Feld und Sprung des Cursors
  zum nächsten Feld (Eingabe von #)

- Backspace um eine Stelle und Löschen (Eingabe von **)

- Wiederholen der Seite mit Rücksetzen aller Daten-
  felder auf Blank (Eingabe von * 00)

- Absenden nach Beendigung der Eingabe ins letzte Feld
  einer Datensammlungsseite (Eingabe von #).

Zusätzlich zu normalen, vom Benutzer auszufüllenden Datenfeldern
kann der Betreiber des externen Rechnerns Name- und Adressfelder
definieren. Hierdurch wird erreicht, daß aus der BT-Benutzer-
Datei der BT-Zentrale Benutzerdaten in Datensammlungs-Blöcke für
externe Rechner eingetragen werden. Der Benutzer muß hierzu natürlich seine Einwilligung geben.

3.3 Realisierte Protokoll-Funktionen im Feldversuch

Die folgende Tabelle soll zeigen, welche der heute im Gespräch
befindlichen "Primitive" bzw. Dienste im Protokoll des Feld-
versuchs realisiert sind.

Primitive bzw. Dienst	im Feldversuch
CONNECT (aktiv)	ist durch CONNECTION REQUEST realisiert. BT-Zentrale ist immer Master und nur die BT-Zentrale kann CONNECTION REQUEST abgeben.
CONNECT (passiv)	nicht realisiert
ACCEPT	ist durch CONNECTION ACKNOWLEDGEMENT realisiert
REJECT	CONNECTION REFUSAL
COLLISION	kann nicht auftreten und ist somit nicht realisiert
RECONNECT	nicht realisiert
RESYNCH	nicht realisiert, da zunächst auf Transportebene nur eine Fenstergröße von 1 realisiert ist
RESET	nicht realisiert (Grund siehe RESYNCH)
DATA	durch FRAME DATA BLOCK realisiert Bestätigung in Sonderfällen durch ACKNOWLEDGEMENT explizit

Primitive bzw. Dienst	im Feldversuch
PUSH	nicht realisiert
EXPEDITED	nicht realisiert
INTERRUPT	nicht realisiert
DATAGRAM	nicht realisiert
DISCONNECT	DISCONNECTION REQUEST mit DISCONNECTION ACKNOWLEDGEMENT
ADRESSING	durch Session-Identifizierung (USER PAST) realisiert
MULTIPLEXING	nicht realisiert
FLOWCONTROL	wegen fehlendem MULTIPLEXING nicht notwendig
Verwaltung der Eintragung von Daten	Standard-Funktion der BTZ-Software
Nachrichtenaustausch	BT-anwendungsspezifisch (BTZ-Software)
Darstellung der Daten	BT-anwendungsspezifisch (BTZ-Software)
Verwaltung der Datenstrukturen	BT-anwendungsspezifisch (BTZ-Software)

Hieraus ist ersichtlich, daß im Feldversuch zwar die Transportebene
zu einem Großteil abgedeckt ist, die Präsentationsschicht jedoch
direkt in die Anwendung (BTZ-Software) integriert ist.

Decoder und
Bildspeicher
12oo b/s
Ortsnetz
LSI-Modem
75 b/s
BT-Zentrale

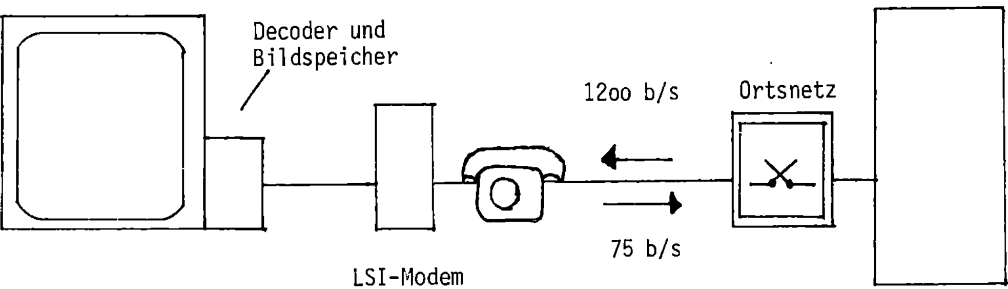

Bild 1

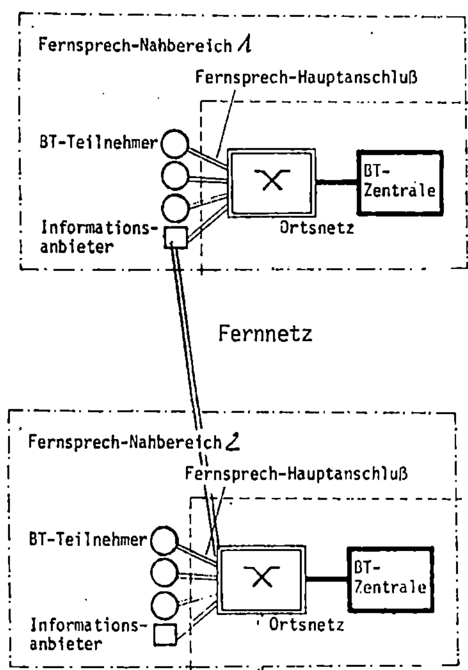

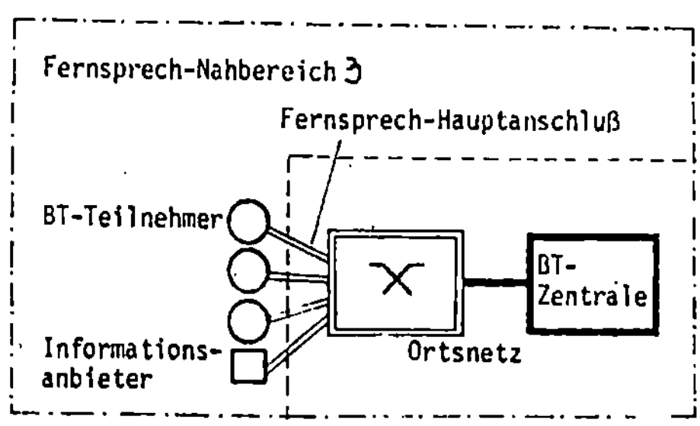

<u>Bild 2:</u> Bildschirmtext ohne Rechnerverbund

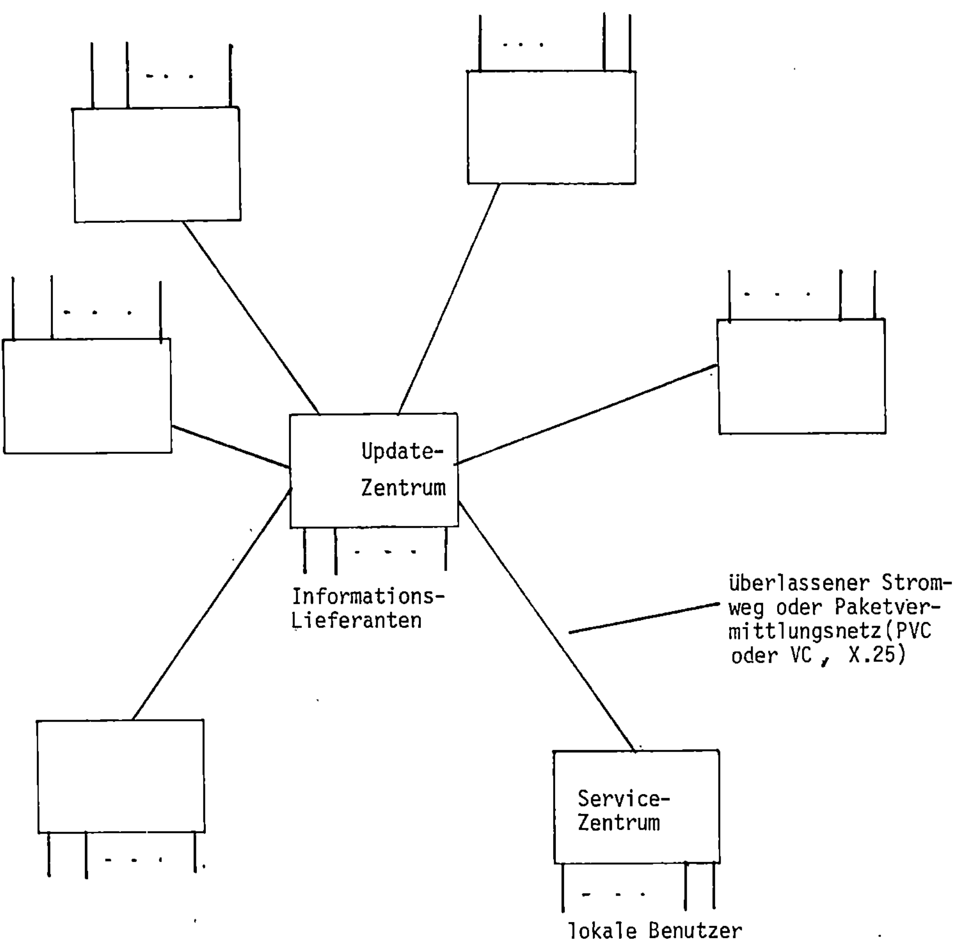

Bild 3: Englisches Prestel-System

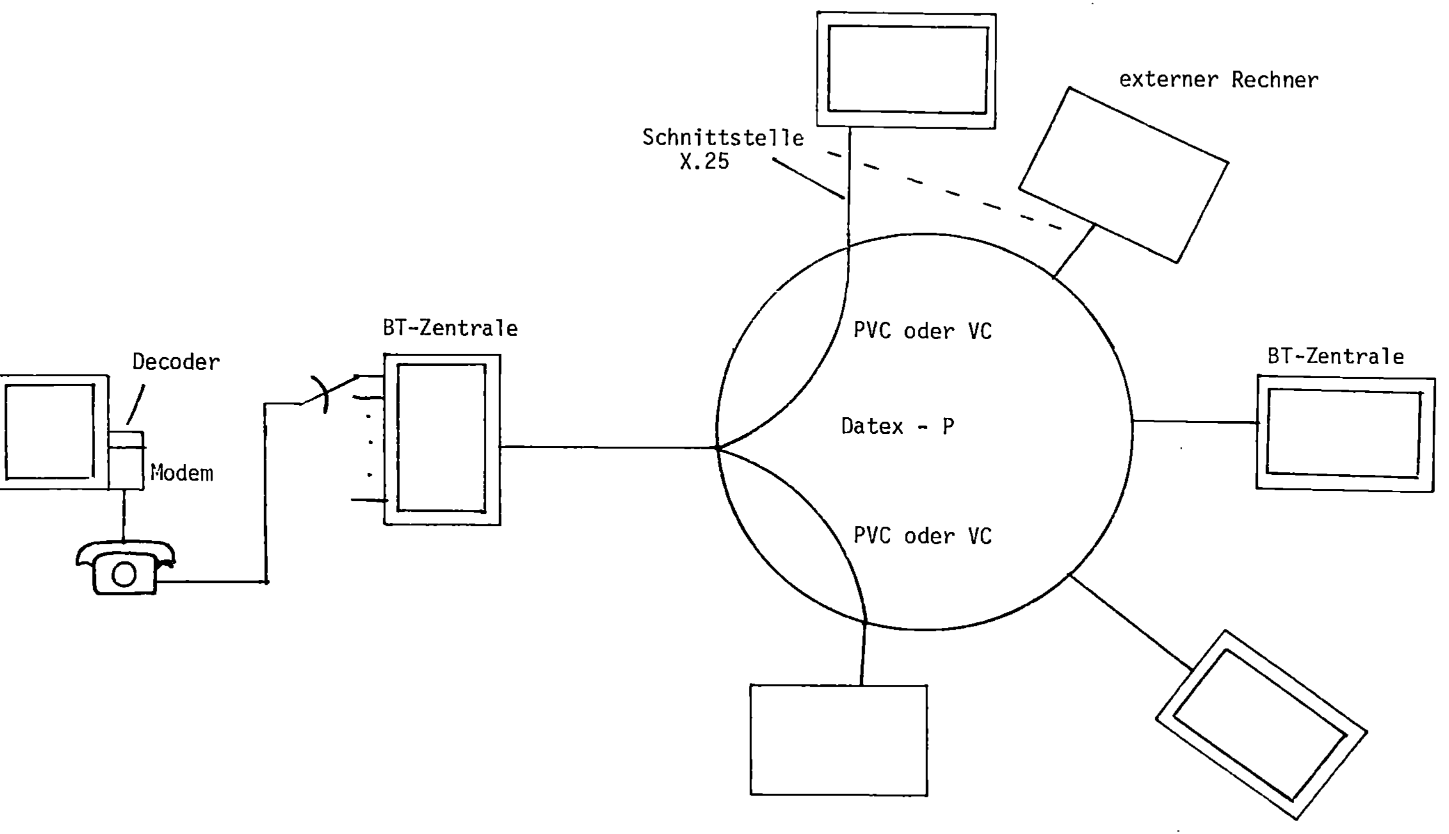

Bild 4:   Gesamtkonfiguration für den Rechnerverbund in Bildschirm-Text

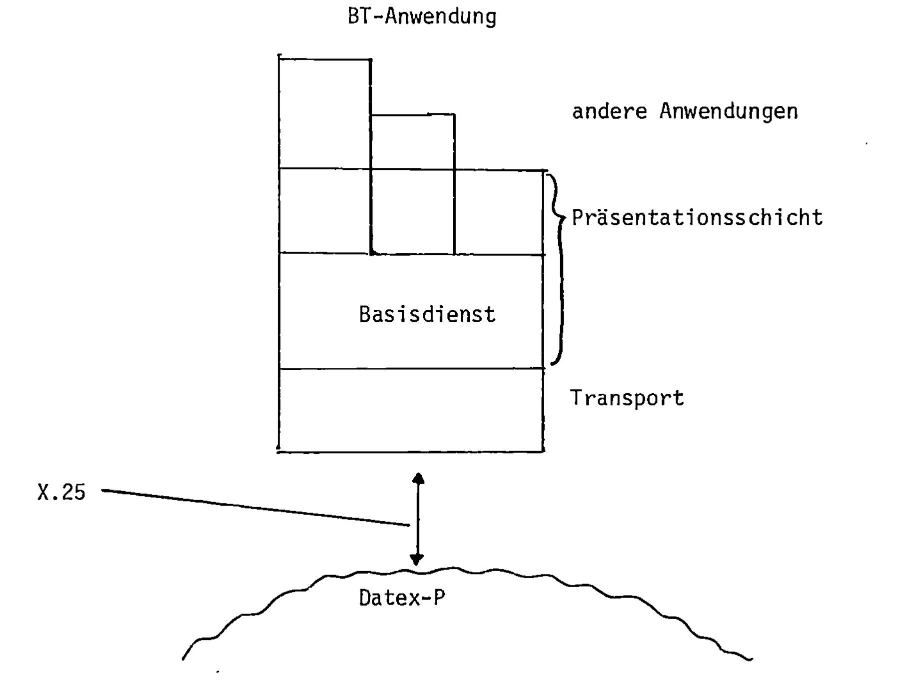

<u>Bild 5:</u>   Schichtenstruktur der Kommunikations-Protokolle für Bildschirm-RV

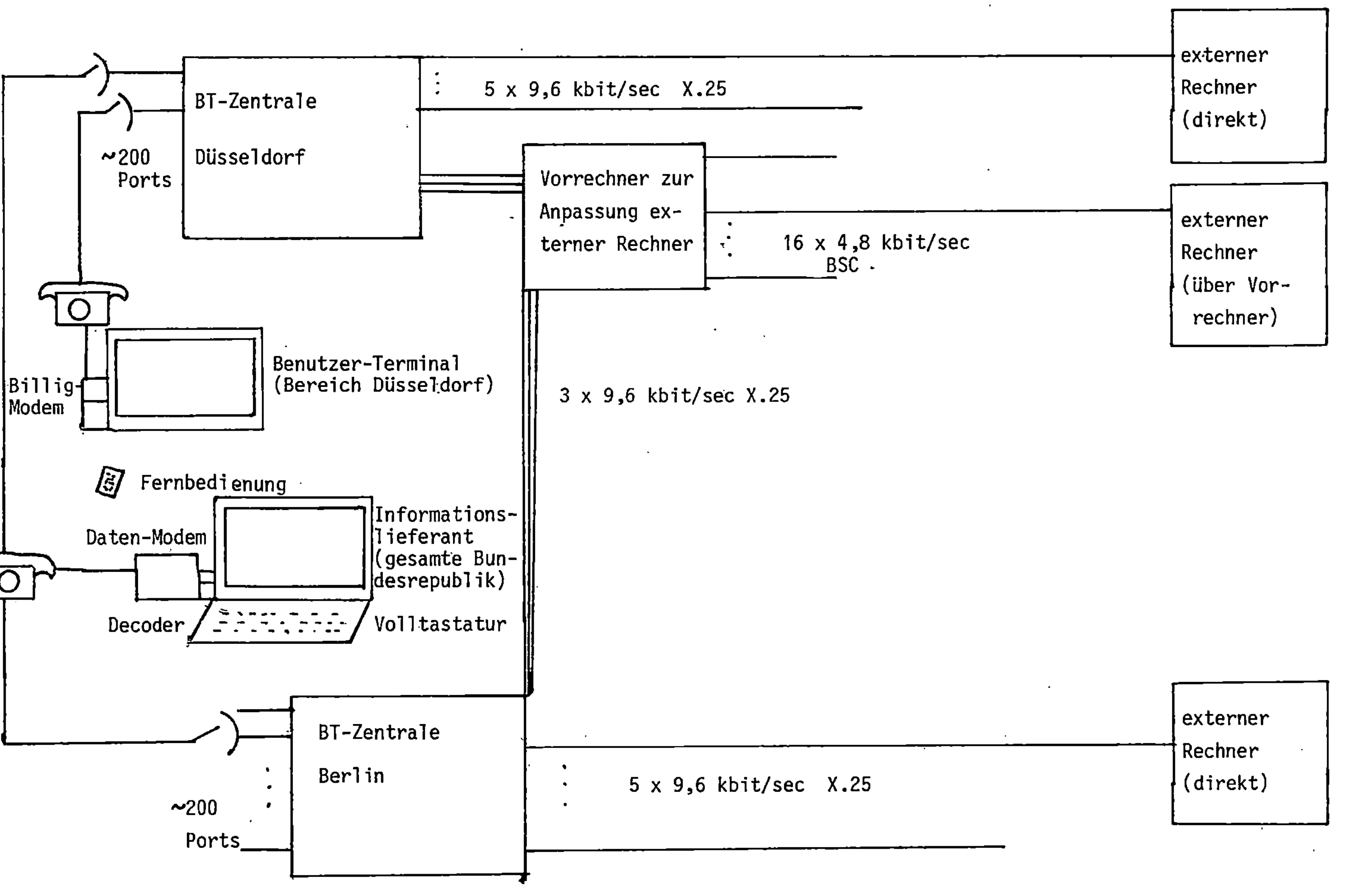

Bild 6: Konfiguration des Rechnerverbundes im BT-Rechnerberbund

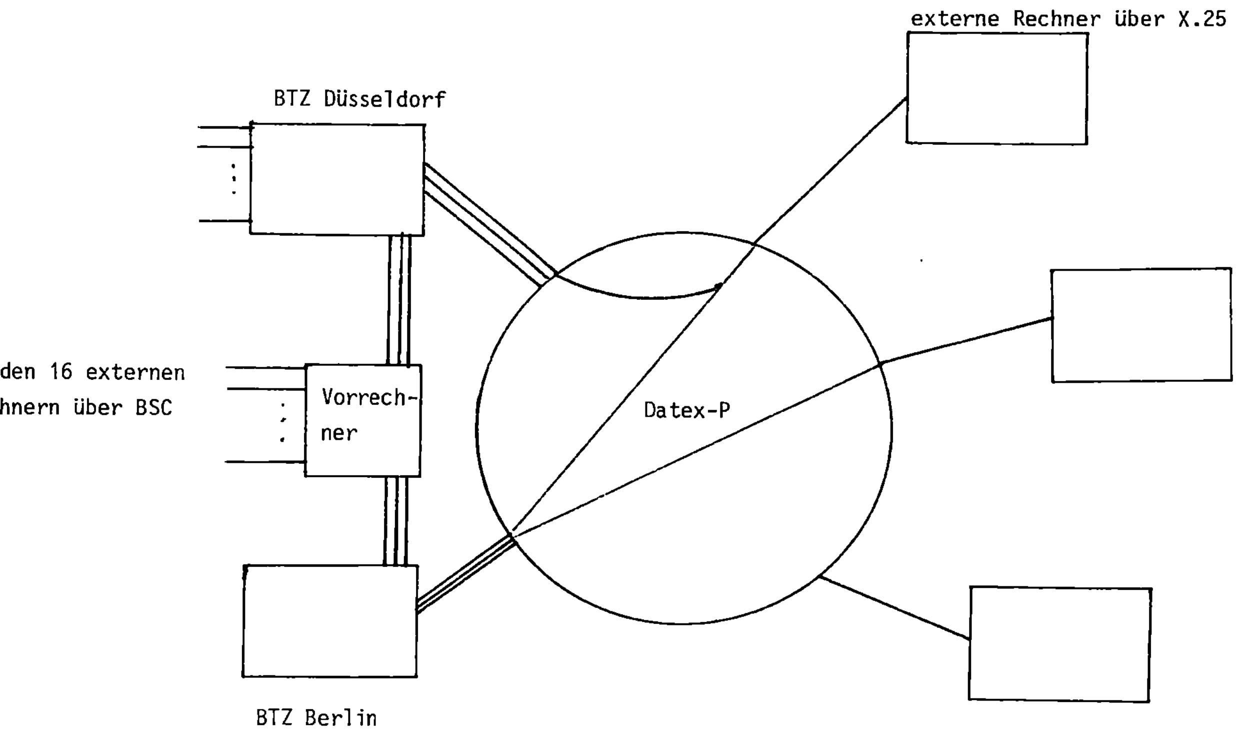

Bild 7: Zwischenschaltung von Datex-P im Feldversuch

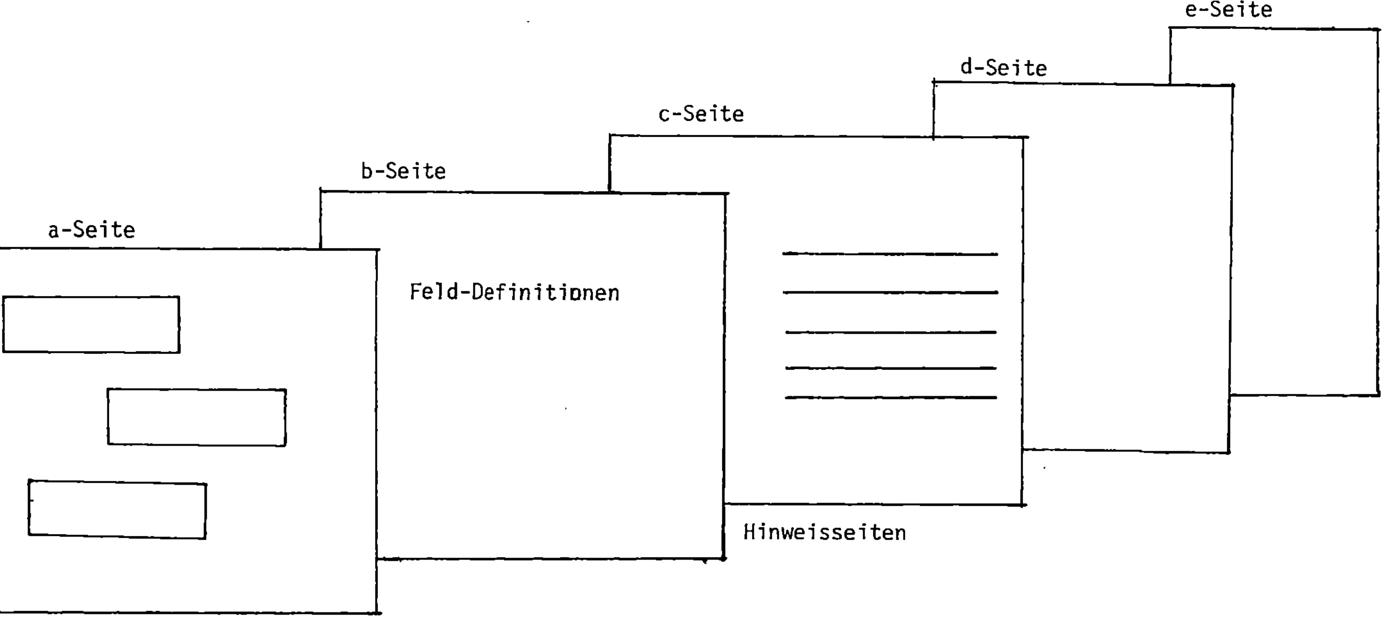

Bild 8: Aufbau einer Datensammlungsseite

STANDARDISIERUNGSFRAGEN UND REALISIERUNGSERFAHRUNGEN BEI
KOMMUNIKATIONSPROTOKOLLEN IN EINEM INHOMOGENEN RECHNERVERBUNDNETZ

W. Hartnick und Dr. B. Vogel
Landesamt für Datenverarbeitung und Statistik Nordrhein-Westfalen
4000 Düsseldorf

0. Einleitung

Die Standardisierung der Datenkommunikation in verteilten Systemen ist bereits unter
technisch-wissenschaftlichen Aspekten ein komplexes und ausreichend schwieriges Problem. Die Beziehung zur Anwendung impliziert weitere Randbedingungen.

Nach einem kurzen Überblick über generelle Standardisierungsprobleme wird im folgenden zunächst versucht, die besonderen Wünsche und Probleme von Anwendern zu artiku-
lieren. Als ein Diskussionsbeitrag wird dann die aktuelle Lösung eines Großanwenders
skizziert. Am Beispiel von Projekten im Bereich eines im Aufbau befindlichen Netzes
werden Probleme aufgezeigt, die bei der Realisierung eines inhomogenen Rechnerver-
bundnetzes mit herstellerunabhängigen Standards zu lösen sind.

1. Probleme bei der Standardisierung

Bei der Analyse der Situation im Bereich der Standardisierung von Schnittstellen für
die Datenkommunikation in verteilten Systemen ist eine Vielzahl von Schwierigkeiten
erkennbar. Die technischen Probleme sind auf Grund der schnellen technischen Entwicklung und der Vielfalt der vorhandenen bzw. denkbaren Systemkonzepte bereits
schwierig zu lösen. Weil die optimale Realisierung einer Schnittstelle eng an die
Systemfunktionen gekoppelt ist, darf das Kommunikationskonzept nicht losgelöst von
den Systemkonzepten der DV-Einrichtungen betrachtet werden. Kommunikationskonzept,
Systemarchitektur und Anwendung sind eng ineinander verflochten und können nur be-
dingt als unabhängige Probleme gesehen werden.

Weitere Schwierigkeiten entstehen, weil am Standardisierungsprozeß unterschiedliche
Interessengruppen mit unterschiedlichen kurz- bzw. langfristigen Zielsetzungen beteiligt sind. Große Hersteller, kleine Hersteller, Wissenschaft und Forschung sowie ver-
schiedenartige Anwendergruppen haben hier sicherlich völlig unterschiedliche Schwerpunkte und Wünsche. Diese Ausgangssituation der unterschiedlichen beteiligten Interessengruppen läßt leider auch eine gewisse Skepsis gegenüber einem baldigen Standar-
disierungsfortschritt gerechtfertigt erscheinen.

Die Grundforderung, wirtschaftliche und flexible Netze auf der Basis herstellerunab-
hängiger Standards einzuführen, führt somit zu einer Vielzahl von Einzelaspekten,
die nur sehr schwer optimal in ein Gesamtkonzept integriert werden können. Spezielle
Einzelaspekte sind:

- wirtschaftliche Realisierbarkeit auf den vorhandenen Systemen und kurzfristige
  Verfügbarkeit der Standards,

- langfristig wirtschaftliche und auf zukünftige Systeme ausgerichtete Konzeption,

- weitreichende Definitionen zur Sicherung der Kompatibilität unterschiedlicher
  Realisierungen und Möglichkeiten für unterschiedlich umfangreiche, aber miteinander kompatible Protokoll-Subsets,

- gründliche und theoretisch-wissenschaftlich fundierte Erarbeitung eines Standards,

- übersichtliche und durchschaubare Konzepte, sowie Sicherstellung transparenter
  Realisierungs- und Betriebsmöglichkeiten (Fehleranalyse, Datenschutz, Betriebs-
  sicherheit, Steuerung usw.),

- Dienstleistungen für eine Vielzahl von Systemfunktionen und Anwendungen.

Diese unvollständige Aufzählung verdeutlicht bereits, daß Prioritäten und Schwerpunkte gesetzt und Kompromisse eingegangen werden müssen, um zu praktikablen Ergeb-
nissen zu gelangen. Insbesondere sollten von vornherein Zwischenschritte bzw. Fortschreibungsmöglichkeiten einkalkuliert werden und für einzelne Teilbereiche unterschiedliche Strategien und Schwerpunkte gewählt werden. So verursachen z. B. spätere
Änderungen der Protokollarchitektur oder der funktionalen Struktur wesentlich mehr
Schwierigkeiten als einzelne Detailänderungen. Die Festlegung der Gesamtarchitektur
muß also frühzeitig und mit besonderer Sorgfalt erfolgen.

An dieser Stelle wird deutlich, daß die ausführliche Diskussion einer Vielzahl von
Strategien zu weit führen würde. Im folgenden Abschnitt wird daher lediglich versucht, einige aus der Sicht der Anwender besonders wichtige Aspekte zu erläutern und
zu bewerten.

2. Situation und Forderungen der Anwender

Bei der Datenkommunikation hat der Anwender mehrere Gesichtspunkte zu einem Planungs-
konzept zusammenzuführen. Einerseits fordert die rasch wechselnde und schwer vorher-
sehbare Marktsituation im Datenverarbeitungsbereich und besonders im Bereich Daten-

kommunikation eine schnelle Anpassung der DV-Konzeption des Anwenders. Andererseits
zwingt die beschränkte Anpassungsfähigkeit der Organisation auf Grund ihrer internen
Verflechtung mit der DV-Konzeption zu langfristiger und stabiler Planung.

Eine Komponente, die hier einbezogen werden muß, und die für viele Anwender eine gewisse Schlüsselposition inne hat, ist die Frage, ob herstellerabhängige oder herstellerunabhängige Netzkonzepte und Schnittstellen verwendet werden. Neben den Konzepten einzelner Hersteller stehen hier bestehende oder zukünftige Normen, Normvorschläge und eigene Protokolldefinitionen zur Wahl. Von der Grundidee her stellt die
Entscheidung für ein herstellerunabhängiges Konzept sicherlich die überzeugendere
langfristige Lösung dar. Das Fehlen ausreichender Standards bringt jedoch für die
Anwender hier erhebliche Probleme.

Bei der Standardisierung stellen also die Anwender als Gesamtheit eine besonders
wichtige Interessengruppe dar. Diese Gruppe nimmt jedoch aufgrund ihrer internen
Struktur und der geringeren technischen Sachkenntnis noch nicht den gebührenden Rang
im Spiel der Interessen wahr.

Als Anwenderforderung sind kurzfristig verwendbare Ergebnisse bzw. Zwischenschritte
zu nennen. Zunächst einmal resultiert der Wunsch nach kurzfristig verfügbaren Standards aus den aktuellen Planungsproblemen, insbesondere der großen Anwender. Bei der
Entscheidung zwischen herstellerabhängigen und herstellerunabhängigen Netzkonzeptio-
nen spielt der Umfang der bereits definierten Standards eine entscheidende Rolle.
Die baldige Verfügbarkeit würde außerdem die Einführungs- bzw. Verbreitungschancen
der Standards vergrößern, da andernfalls Herstellerdefinitionen und -konzepte wesentliche Zeitvorteile erhielten. Baldige Verfügbarkeit von realisierungsreifen Standards
ist somit aus Anwendersicht ein besonders gewichtiges Argument.

Diese Standards sollen zunächst an heutigen Systemen orientiert sein. Es ist besser,
eventuelle Überarbeitungen vorzusehen als die Durchsetzbarkeit durch schwierige
Realisierbarkeit zu gefährden.

Eine weitere Forderung ist die Transparenz der Normungssituation. Aufgrund der vielen
beteiligten und unterschiedlichen Gremien ist es sicherlich nicht möglich, eine langfristig verläßliche Zeitplanung für den Standardisierungsprozeß zu machen. Eine gewisse Transparenz sollte jedoch mindestens angestrebt werden, damit der Anwender
möglichst verläßliche Plandaten über den zu erwartenden Standardisierungsprozeß für
seine eigene Planung zur Verfügung hat.

Von besonderer Wichtigkeit als mehr technische Einzelheit ist noch, daß Funktionen
der Ebenen und die Services zwischen den Ebenen möglichst detailliert frühzeitig

festgelegt werden. Dann können Vorablösungen bzw. vorläufige "eigene Standards" hiermit kompatibel gehalten werden. Der Austausch einer Prozedur oder der Austausch von Prozedurteilen ist relativ einfach, wenn die Funktionen und insbesondere die Beziehungen zu anderen Ebenen unverändert bleiben.

3. Das Konzept des DVS

Mit der Einflußnahme auf langfristige Entwicklungen sind jedoch die aktuellen Planungsprobleme vieler Anwender nicht beseitigt. Wichtige Entscheidungen mit schwer überschaubaren langfristigen Konsequenzen sind häufig bereits jetzt zu treffen.

Für den Großanwender Land Nordrhein-Westfalen haben die Normungssituation, der Stand und die Möglichkeiten der DV-Technik und langfristige Gesichtspunkte zu besonderen Aktivitäten geführt, die eine gesetzliche Grundlage besitzen. Das Gesetz über die Organisation der automatisierten Datenverarbeitung in Nordrhein-Westfalen (ADVG NW) vom 12.2.1974 fordert den Verbund der DV-Einrichtungen des Landes in der Landesdatenverarbeitungszentrale, den Gemeinsamen Gebietsrechenzentren, den Fachrechenzentren, den Kommunalen Datenverarbeitungszentralen und den Hochschulrechenzentren in einem Landesinformationssystem. Eine technische Basis für den Verbund ist das Datenvermittlungssystem NW (DVS).

Ein einfacher Weg, um diesen Auftrag zu verwirklichen, wäre sicherlich das Abstützen auf internationale Normen und allgemeingültige herstellerunabhängige Netzkonzepte. Da aber solche Standards und solche Konzepte z. Z. noch nicht existieren, mußte in Nordrhein-Westfalen ein anderer Weg gefunden werden. Aufgrund der großen Zahl von am Verbund zu beteiligenden unterschiedlichen DV-Einrichtungen ergab sich unmittelbar die Zweckmäßigkeit einer Standardisierung, d. h. der Schaffung einer einheitlichen Schnittstelle zum Anschluß an das Verbundsystem. Die durch "Sprachumsetzung" zwischen jeweils zwei unterschiedlichen DV-Systemen gegebene Alternative würde langfristig eine um ein vielfaches größere Anzahl von Umsetzungen erfordern. Die Möglichkeit, das Verbundsystem aus Soft- und Hardware nur eines DV-Herstellers aufzubauen, kann bei der geplanten Größe des DVS nicht als echte Alternative gesehen werden.

Man hat sich daher für eine "eigene Standardisierung" entschieden. Ein solcher eigener Standard muß sich sicherlich an anderen Randbedingungen orientieren als eine langfristig gültige allgemeine Norm. Die Gegebenheiten und die Situation im Bereich der Standardisierung führten dazu, daß man sich möglichst weitgehend auf vorhandene Normen bzw. Normungsbestrebungen abstützt. Weiterhin wurde versucht, sich auf eine einfache, praktikable und auf z. Z. vorhandenen Systemen unmittelbar realisierbare Schnittstelle zu beschränken. Die enge Berührung einer solchen Realisierung mit vor-

handenen Systemfunktionen läßt sicherlich aufgrund der gegebenen Mittel und der Termin-
situation nur einen solchen einfachen Weg zu. Grundkonzept ist daher die Anlehnung
an Vorhandenes, eine einfache modulare Struktur, eine stufenweise Errichtung und eine
Hierarchie von Protokollebenen.

Bei der Definition der Protokolle wurde besonderer Wert auf weitgehende Unabhängigkeit zwischen den Protokollebenen und damit auf langfristig günstige Anpassungsmög-
lichkeit an Standards gelegt. Es steht völlig außer Zweifel, daß eine allgemeine Norm
einer Speziallösung vorzuziehen ist. Die Fortschreibung des DVS-Konzepts soll sich
daher an der Normungsentwicklung orientieren.

Ein wichtiger Gesichtspunkt für ein Datennetzkonzept mit einer einheitlichen Schnittstelle ist sicherlich auch die größere Transparenz dieser Lösung. In diesem Zusammenhang kann auch der Datenschutz als Argument für das DVS-Konzept angeführt werden.

Man hat sich in Nordrhein-Westfalen bereits sehr frühzeitig für die Verwendung der
Datenpaketvermittlungstechnik entschieden. Eigene Kommunikationsrechner mit Daten-
paketvermittlungstechnik stehen bereits zur Verfügung. Inzwischen hat sich die
Deutsche Bundespost entschieden, ein öffentliches Datennetz mit Paketvermittlungstech-
nik einzuführen. Es ist vorgesehen, daß das DVS auch diesen Dienst in Anspruch nimmt.
Ein eigenes Paketvermittlungstransportnetz ist kein notwendiger Bestandteil des DVS-
Konzepts. Durch Datex-P wird das DVS nicht gefährdet, sondern gefördert. Die Bereitstellung eines privaten Paketvermittlungsnetzes war bis zur Entscheidung der DBP für
Datex-P erforderlich und hat wichtigen Projektfortschritt ermöglicht. Aus der Sicht
des DVS-Projekts sind die Datex-P-Aktivitäten in jedem Fall sehr zu begrüßen.

4. <u>Funktionsschichten im DVS</u>

Im DVS sind 5 einheitliche, d. h. für die Nutzer verbindliche Funktionsschichten
oder Protokollebenen vorgesehen. Die Ebenen bzw. Funktionsschichten 1 bis 3 entsprechen der CCITT-Empfehlung X.25, wobei z. Z. in Ebene 2 zusätzlich zu LAPB eine
weitere HDLC-Leitungsprozedur, das sogenannte Symmetrische System angeboten wird. In
Ebene 3 wird zusätzlich zu den in X.25, Level 3, gebotenen Möglichkeiten ein einfacher Datagrammdienst angeboten.

Es ist vorgesehen, die X.25-Schnittstelle des DVS sobald möglich der Datex-P-Defini-
tion anzupassen. Auf diese Weise sollen für Hersteller und Projektträger unnötige
Kosten, die durch Speziallösungen entstehen, vermieden werden. Außerdem kann dann
der Datex-P-Dienst zusätzlich zum eigenen Paketvermittlungsnetz genutzt werden.

Über diesem reinen Datentransportbereich liegt als Ebene 4 die sogenannte DV-Strom-
Ebene. Auf dieser Ebene tauschen DV-Strom-Kontrollmodule (DKM) sogenannte Records
aus. Über die zugehörige Verbindung des Paketvermittlungsnetzes können mehrere DV-
Ströme geschaltet werden (Multiplexen). Die DV-Strom-Prozedur dient zur Synchronisierung der miteinander kommunizierenden Datenverarbeitungseinrichtungen. Die DV-
Strom-Prozedur hat eine sogenannte End-to-End-Sicherungsfunktion und stellt außerdem
ein einheitliches Netzzugriffsverfahren zur angeschlossenen Datenverarbeitungsanlage
dar.

Als Funktionsschicht 5 folgt schließlich die Dienstleistungsprozedurebene. Hier sind
anwendungsabhängig verschiedene Protokolle vorgesehen (z. B. RJE, Datei-Transfer,
Dialogverkehr, Transaction). Auf dieser Ebene tauschen Dienstleistungsprozesse sogenannte Nachrichten über den Nachrichtenstrom aus.

Die DVS-Ebenen entsprechen der Layer-Philosophie des ISO-7-Ebenen-Modells. Definitionen wie Entities, Connection, Protocol-Data-Units und Service-Data-Units ent-
sprechen also weitgehend den zugehörigen DVS-Begriffen. Die Funktionsschicht 4
(DV-Strom-Ebene) im DVS umfaßt die Funktionen von Transport-Layer und Session-Layer.
Die Funktionsschicht 5 (Dienstleistungsprozedurebene) umfaßt Presentation-Layer und
Application-Layer. Die definierten Dienstleistungsprozeduren sind als System-Protocols
zu sehen. Enterprise Specific-Application-Protocols, die entsprechende Presentation-
Layer-Funktionen umfassen, sind grundsätzlich verwendbar.

Man kann also zusammenfassend sagen, daß für das DVS relativ einfache Protokolle definiert wurden, die weitgehend mit der Normungsentwicklung kompatibel sind. Langfristig wird hier sicherlich eine Anpassung erforderlich sein. Dieser Gesichtspunkt
wurde jedoch bei der Konzeption so weit möglich berücksichtigt.

Aufgrund der derzeitigen Situation im Bereich der Standardisierung, in dem z. Z. noch
keine einheitlichen langfristigen Normen sichtbar sind, und aufgrund der engen, anfangs zitierten Verflechtung von Organisation und Datenverarbeitung ist der in
Nordrhein-Westfalen eingeschlagene Weg zu rechtfertigen. Für einen Anwender dieser
Größe ist es besser, zunächst mit Vorabnormen zu arbeiten und der gesamten Organisation entsprechend Zeit zu geben, die Verbundkonzeption in die Planung zu integrieren,
d. h. sich der technischen Möglichkeiten des Verbundes zu bedienen, als zu lange zu
warten und damit kostenaufwendige organisatorische Probleme hervorzurufen.

Zur Zeit stehen drei Netzrechner mit Paketvermittlung und mehrere unterschiedliche
getestete DV-Systeme mit Anschluß an dieses Netz zur Verfügung. Die Realisierung der
Funktionsschicht 4 (DV-Strom) ist für verschiedene DV-Systeme recht weit fortgeschrit-
ten. Der Einsatz wird im Dezember 1979 beginnen. Die Realisierung von Dienstleistungs-

prozeduren ist für April 1980 vertraglich festgelegt. Erste Betriebstests werden im
Januar 1980 beginnen.

5. Generelle Realisierungsprobleme

Die aufgezeigte Ausgangslage im Lande Nordrhein-Westfalen ergibt die Problematik,
verschiedene Rechner von IBM, Siemens, CDC, Honeywell-Bull, Nixdorf, Dietz u. a. an
das DVS anzuschließen. Schon beim Entwickeln des DVS-Architekturmodells und der Protokolle war man von der Randbedingung der einfachen Realisierbarkeit ausgegangen. So
ist z. B. die Funktionsschicht 4 des DVS u. a. im Hinblick auf Verträglichkeit mit
den Zugriffsmethoden der Hersteller konzipiert. Ansonsten wurde bereits aufgezeigt,
daß das DVS auf derselben Philosophie bezüglich Layer, Entities und Connections
basiert wie das ISO-Modell. Daher können die bei der Realisierung von DVS-Protokollen
gewonnenen Erfahrungen durchaus auf andere Projekte übertragen werden, denen ebenfalls
ein ISO-ähnliches Konzept zugrunde liegt. Sie können außerdem Konsequenzen für die
Fortschreibung von Protokollen und Realisierungskonzepten haben, da ein so komplexes
Gebiet nicht rein theoretisch zu bewältigen ist.

Bei den laufenden Implementierungen muß sich nun zeigen, inwieweit die Realisierbarkeit wirklich gegeben ist und sich das Schichtenmodell in einer modularen Software
widerspiegelt.

Die bisherigen Arbeiten am DVS haben erwartungsgemäß ergeben, daß für die Realisierung der herstellerunabhängigen Protokolle die bereits sehr weitgehende DFÜ-Hard- und
Software bei einzelnen Herstellern teilweise mehr Probleme als Hilfestellung bietet.
So lassen z. B. die Netzarchitekturen von IBM und Siemens, nämlich SNA und TRANSDATA,
gar keine offenen Netze im Sinne der ISO-Definition zu, da alle potentiellen Netz-
teilnehmer zur Generierzeit bekannt sein müssen. Außerdem ist es z. B. bei IBM z. Z.
noch nicht möglich, daß Applikationen (d. h. keine Terminals) mit TSO kommunizieren.

Bei der Planung der Realisierung ging man von den beiden Fragen aus, für welche Art
Anwendungen genau die Verbundprotokolle zur Verfügung stehen sollten, d. h. wie im
einzelnen die Interessen der Nutzer liegen, und wie intensiv die EDV-Hersteller an
der Entwicklung der zu erstellenden Software beteiligt werden können. Denn die Nutzer-
anforderungen bestimmen im wesentlichen die zu erfüllenden Grenzwerte (z. B. Zahl der
gleichzeitig möglichen DV-Ströme), und ohne die Mitarbeit der Hersteller scheint insbesondere bei den unteren Funktionsschichten eine optimale Implementierung kaum möglich, da man es dort i. a. unmittelbar mit Betriebssystemfunktionen zu tun hat.

Als Randbedingungen waren bei allen Überlegungen Kosten, Termine sowie das zur Verfügung stehende Personal (Quantität und Qualität) zu berücksichtigen.

Es wurden dann drei Problemkreise näher untersucht, um zu einer optimalen Lösung zu kommen, nämlich

a) verfügbare Systemsoftware zur Zeit der Implementation, d. h. u. a.

- Welche Protokolle sind als Standards enthalten (HDLC, X.25, usw.)?
- Wie groß ist der Speicherplatz in Vor- und Hauptrechner?
- Wie ist die Sicherheit gegenüber und beim Systemausfall?
- Wie hoch ist der maximale Durchsatz?
- Wie sind die Adressierungsmöglichkeiten?
- Wie werden die Systembenutzer untereinander koordiniert
  (Schutz von Benutzerspeichern usw.)?
- Welche Programmiersprachen stehen zur Verfügung?
- Wie wird der Datenschutz realisiert?
- Gibt es Prüfung auf Zugangsberechtigung?
- Welche Diagnosemöglichkeiten im Fehlerfall liegen vor?

b) Weiterentwicklung der Systemsoftware, d. h. u. a.

- Welche Änderungen einer Systemsoftware sind kurzfristig möglich und wie werden
  diese gewartet?
- Wird das Betriebssystem aufwärts kompatibel weiterentwickelt?
- Welche neuen Systemfunktionen sind in absehbarer Zeit zu erwarten?

c) zu erstellende Software, d. h. u. a.

- Wird zusätzliche Software benötigt, um in den Hauptrechner zu gelangen?
- Wird zusätzlich Testsoftware benötigt?
- Wer erstellt die Software (welche Kenntnisse)?
- Welche Unterstützung liefert der Hersteller?
- Ist die Definition von Ausbaustufen möglich?
- Wie sind die Fortschreibungsmöglichkeiten?
- Kann die Wartung zufriedenstellend geregelt werden?
- Welche Qualitätsanforderungen bezüglich Handhabbarkeit, Diagnosemöglichkeit,
  modularem Aufbau usw. liegen vor?

Diese Aufzählung erhebt keinen Anspruch auf Vollständigkeit, soll aber einen gewissen Überblick über die zu berücksichtigenden Gesichtspunkte geben. Die Bewertung der einzelnen Punkte mag dabei von Projekt zu Projekt verschieden sein. Da die Einzelprobleme nicht unbedingt die gleichen Konsequenzen für die Realisierungen haben, sondern im Gegenteil teilweise gegensätzliche Forderungen nach sich ziehen bzw. den erwähnten Randbedingungen entgegenstehen, kann jede Realisierung nur einen Kompromiß gemäß der erwähnten Bewertung darstellen.

6. Allgemeine Realisierungskonzepte

In der Praxis sind im wesentlichen drei Realisierungskonzepte bei der Implementation von Kommunikationsprotokollen anzutreffen:

1. In einem vorgeschalteten Rechner werden alle netzeinheitlichen Protokolle abgehandelt und zum Verarbeitungsrechner hin einfache Geräte emuliert.

   Vorteile dieses Ansatzes liegen auf den ersten Blick im Bereich von Kosten und Termineinhaltung. Außerdem brauchen die Betriebssysteme der Verarbeitungsrechner nicht geändert zu werden, es gibt keine Speicherprobleme im Verarbeitungsrechner und man ist insgesamt von Änderungen im Verarbeitungsrechner nur dann betroffen, wenn die Schnittstellen der emulierten Geräte sich ändern.

   Bei diesem Konzept sind allerdings im allgemeinen große Nachteile zu befürchten, insbesondere im Vorrechner bezüglich möglicher Grenzwerte, Durchsatz, Adressierungsmöglichkeiten, Speicherplatz, leichter Programmierbarkeit und ähnlichem. Man ist auf die Möglichkeiten des vorgeschalteten Rechners angewiesen und kann - dies ist vielleicht der größte Nachteil - keine Standards und Systemfunktionen des anzuschließenden Rechners nutzen, auch dann nicht, wenn der z. B. X.25 in sein Betriebssystem integriert.

   Das andere Extrem bei den Konzepten zur Realisierung von Kommunikationsprotokollen ist:

2. In einem vorgeschalteten Rechner wird höchstens die Leistungsprozedur abgehandelt, alle anderen Protokolle sind im Verarbeitungsrechner implementiert.

   Der Vorteil eines solchen Konzepts liegt darin, daß der Hauptrechner im allgemeinen mehr Möglichkeiten zur Implementation bietet und die Software leichter änderbar ist, sowie genügend Speicherplatz zur Verfügung steht. Nachteile sind vor allem im Durchsatz sowie in der Beeinträchtigung anderer Benutzer zu sehen. Außerdem wird im allgemeinen größere Zusatzsoftware nötig sein, um überhaupt in den Hauptrechner zu gelangen.

Zwischen diesen beiden Extremkonzepten kann ein Mittelweg gesucht werden, der zu folgendem Ansatz führt:

3. In einem vorgeschalteten Rechner werden die Transportprotokolle abgehandelt, die übrigen im Verarbeitungsrechner.

Dabei ist natürlich die Frage, wo genau die Transportprotokolle enden und die höheren Protokolle anfangen. Die Vor- und Nachteile dieses Konzepts ergeben sich größtenteils aus den Vor- und Nachteilen bei den beiden anderen Lösungen. Im übrigen entspricht dieser Ansatz den üblichen Herstellerkonzepten.

Wie man sieht, kann keine der Lösungen generell für jedes System bevorzugt werden. Außer von den Möglichkeiten der Systeme hängt es wie gesagt auch von Kosten- und Zeitvorstellungen ab, welche Lösung man wählt.

Bei den obigen Darstellungen ging man stets von einer Konstellation Vorrechner - Hauptrechner aus, obwohl etwa kleinere Systeme nicht alle einen Vorrechner haben, aber die für den Vorrechner oben angesprochenen Dinge wären dann zu übertragen auf ein sicherlich existierendes DFÜ-Modul. Grundsätzlich kann man bei der Implementierung von Kommunikationsfunktionen unterscheiden, ob sie im Vorrechner/DFÜ-Modul, durch Umsetzung auf Betriebssystemfunktionen oder als Anwendungsprogramme realisiert sind.

7. Realisierungen im DVS

Einen gewissen Einblick in die Probleme der Praxis mögen die Erfahrungen bei der Erstellung der Realisierungskonzepte für zwei Großrechner sowie kleinere Systeme geben.

1 Realisierung auf Siemens 7000 unter BS 2000 mit Vorrechner TD 968 X

Bei dem Anschluß der BS 2000-Rechner an das DVS konnte man zunächst von einer vorhandenen X.25-Software im Vorrechner TD 968 X ausgehen (von der GMD/Firma SESA erstellt). Dadurch ergaben sich zunächst für die Realisierung der Funktionsschicht 4 drei Alternativen, die eingehend untersucht wurden, nämlich

a) Funktionsschicht 4 wird vollständig im Hauptrechner abgehandelt,
b) Funktionsschicht 4 wird vollständig im Vorrechner abgehandelt.
c) der Verwaltungsteil von Funktionsschicht 4 wird im Vorrechner, die Steuerung im Hauptrechner abgehandelt.

Aufgrund der vorgegebenen Termine sowie der verfügbaren Systemsoftware konnte nur
Alternative 1 gewählt werden. Dabei werden die virtuellen Verbindungen von X.25
auf Siemens NEA-Verbindungen abgebildet, das DKM wird als DCAM-Applikation realisiert. Der Anschluß der Dienstleistungsprozesse an das DKM vollzieht sich über eigene Makros, die wesentlich schneller arbeiten als die DCAM-Makros. Soweit wie
möglich werden die Funktionen von NEA und DCAM ausgenutzt (asynchrone Verarbeitung,
Verteilcode usw.).

2 Realisierung auf IBM-Anlagen unter MVS mit Vorrechner 3705-II

Zunächst wurden Alternativen mit anderen Herstellern untersucht, die die 3705 ersetzen bzw. in ihre eigene Software einbringen wollten. Weil dabei zu viele Fragen
offen blieben, insbesondere bezüglich Unterstützung der Experten aus den USA, wurden daraufhin mit der IBM ähnliche Alternativen diskutiert wie beim Siemens-An-
schluß. Das Ergebnis war dann auch trotz etwas unterschiedlicher Sprachmittel ähnlich, die IBM paßte die für den TRANSPAC-Anschluß entwickelte X.25-Software an die
Erfordernisse des DVS an, so daß eine vergleichbare Ausgangslage bestand. Die
Funktionsschicht 4 wird vollkommen im Hauptrechner abgehandelt, nämlich als VTAM-
Applikation. Unterschiede liegen in der Kommunikation zwischen Vor- und Hauptrechner sowie im Anschluß der Dienstleistungsprozesse, die mit dem DKM über die ACF/
VTAM-Schnittstelle verkehren. Die Nutzung dieser VTAM-Schnittstelle gibt - genau
wie bei Siemens die Nutzung der DCAM-Schnittstelle - eine weitgehende Sicherheit
gegenüber Systemänderungen.

3 Realisierung bei kleineren Systemen

Auch bei den kleineren Systemen gibt es unterschiedliche Ansätze, welcher Teil der
Protokolle in DFÜ-Hardware, Systemsoftware oder als Anwendersoftware realisiert
wird. Damit die Prozessorbelastung nicht zu groß wird, sind im allgemeinen die
Grenzwerte wesentlich geringer als bei den Großanlagen, während am Protokoll keine
Einschränkungen gemacht werden dürfen. Wegen des meist geringen Speicherplatzes
können nicht unbedingt die DFÜ-Aktivitäten gleichzeitig mit den übrigen Anwendungen
auf diesen Systemen laufen. Es wird daher z. T. eine Overlay-Technik eingesetzt, bei
der sogar Module ausgelagert werden können, die nicht ständig benötigte Protokollfunktionen behandeln.

Bewußt nicht erwähnt wurde der Anschluß von Primitivterminals an das DVS. In ersten
Überlegungen zur Errichtung des DVS waren zwar sog. TAP's (Terminalanschlußprozes-
soren) vorgesehen, jedoch sehen wir heute keine Notwendigkeit für die Errichtung
solcher TAP's für die z. Z. bekannten Anwendungen mehr. Die Terminalbenutzer sind
nämlich direkt an Großrechner angeschlossen (bei unmittelbarer geographischer Nähe)

und können dort die nötigen Dienstleistungen für den DVS-Verbund aufrufen, oder sie haben "vor Ort" ein intelligentes Terminalsystem, das dann die DVS-Prozeduren integriert hat, was selbst bei einem kleinen 64-K-System wie der Nixdorf 8820 möglich ist.

Aufgrund der verschiedenen Systeme ist man bis heute jeweils zu einem unterschiedlichen Realisierungskonzept gekommen, obwohl alle diese Konzepte unter Mitarbeit von Vertretern des LDS entstanden sind, die die früheren Ansätze kannten. Wie bereits vermutet, gingen die eingangs aufgelisteten Gesichtspunkte wesentlich stärker in die Implementierungen ein als die Protokollfunktionen selbst. Es hat sich dabei bestätigt, daß eine enge Zusammenarbeit mit den Herstellern sowie eine möglichst genaue Kenntnis der Nutzerwünsche von grundlegender Bedeutung sind. Es kommt ja letztlich darauf an, welche Dienste dem Benutzer zur Verfügung gestellt werden sollen, und zwar hinsichtlich Qualität und Quantität, d. h. etwa wie viele gleichzeitige Verbindungen will der Benutzer mit welchen Kommandos ansprechen können.

SPEZIELLE VT-IMPLEMENTATIONSPROBLEME

B. Struif
Gesellschaft für Mathematik und
Datenverarbeitung mbH, Bonn

Zusammenfassung:

Bei der Implementation eines "virtual terminal"-Protokolls treten Probleme auf,
die durch die nötigen Abbildungen, die unterschiedlichen Betriebssystemphilosophien
sowie durch bestimmte Eigenschaften bzw. Ausprägungen der beteiligten Hardware
hervorgerufen werden. Einige dieser Probleme, u.a. initial control, Faltung, Sy-
stemzeilenunterstützung, werden systematisch untersucht und mögliche Lösungs-
wege aufgezeigt.

1. Einführung

Um verteilte DV-Resourcen ökonomisch nutzbar zu machen, muß der Zugang zu den-
selben auf möglichst einfache Weise realisierbar sein. Insbesondere für Dialoganwendungen gilt, daß der Benutzer von einem Terminal aus eine Verbindung unter
Nutzung von P.T.T.-services (öffentliches X.25-Netz) zu dem Zielsystem aufbauen
möchte, mit dem er in Kommunikation treten will. Da ein Zielsystem die Vielfalt
vorhandener Terminals aufgrund der unterschiedlichen Terminalfunktionen, Betriebs-
modi, Zeichensätze, Bildschirmgrößen, Leitungsprozeduren usw. nicht unterstützen
kann, muß dort eine Abbildung auf ein standardisiertes "virtuelles" Terminal (VT)
und auf der Benutzerseite eine Abbildung des standardisierten virtuellen Terminals
auf das jeweilige reale Terminal (RT) vorgenommen werden.
Die Abbildung des virtuellen Terminals auf das reale Terminal kann auf der Benutzerseite

— von einem PAD,

— von einem Kleinrechner, der einen RT/VT-Umsetzer enthält und je nach Typ
   auch lokale Verarbeitungsdienste bietet, oder

— direkt in einem programmierbaren Terminal

durchgeführt werden.

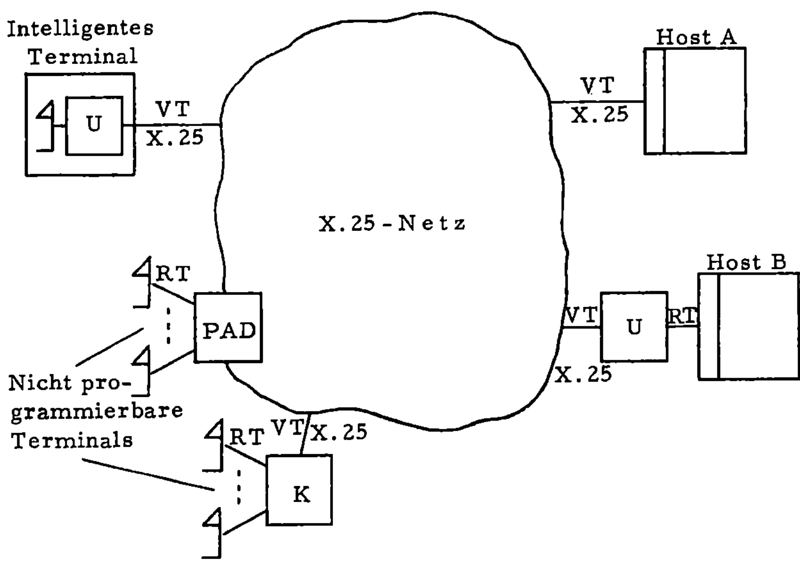

U = RT/VT-Umsetzer bzw. VT/RT-Umsetzer

PAD = Packet Assembler Disassembler (RT/VT-Umsetzer
am Netzrand)

K = Kleinrechner, der einen RT/VT-Umsetzer enthält und
ggf. weitere lokale Dienste bietet

Abb. 1 : Terminal/Host-Verbindung über ein X.25-Netz

Langfristig anzustrebendes Ziel wird jedoch sein, die realen Terminals direkt an
eine standardisierte VT- und Transport-Schnittstelle anzupassen, so daß keine Umsetzungen und Abbildungen mehr erforderlich sind. Dies bedeutet jedoch nicht, daß
alle Terminals den vollen VTP-Leistungsumfang unterstützen müssen, sondern daß
Terminal-Klassen durch Nutzung verschiedener VTP-subsets gebildet werden können.

Auf der Host-Seite sollte das virtuelle Terminal-Protokoll unmittelbar unterstützt
werden. Der Weg dahin ist jedoch noch sehr weit. Langfristig sollte hier versucht
werden, VT-Datenstrukturen direkt von den Programmiersprachen her zu unterstützen. Solange eine Unterstützung des VTP's direkt im Host nicht möglich ist, kann
vor dem Host eine Abbildung des virtuellen Terminals auf ein dem Host bekanntes
"reales" Terminal vorgenommen werden.

Die Abbildung sowohl auf der Host-Seite als auch auf der Terminalseite stellt nicht
nur hohe Anforderungen an die Flexibilität des virtuellen Terminal-Protokolls (VTP),
sondern birgt auch eine Reihe von Problemen in sich, die aus den unterschiedlichen

Systemphilosophien resultieren. Einige dieser Probleme sollen im folgenden näher analysiert werden.

2. VT-Implementationsprobleme

2.1 Verbindungsaufbau

Das VT-Protokoll beschreibt die Kommunikation zwischen zwei VT-Prozessen. Grundsätzlich sind beide Prozeßpartner gleichberechtigt, d.h. jeder hat das Recht, den Verbindungsaufbau anzustoßen. Prinzipiell ist jedoch zu klären, ob es aus der Sicht des jeweiligen Prozesses auch sinnvoll ist, von diesem Recht Gebrauch zu machen. Das Triggerereignis für den Anstoß des Verbindungsaufbaus beim terminalseitigen VT-Prozeß gibt der Benutzer selbst durch Angabe des gewünschten Zielsystems im lokalen Pre-Dialog. Das entsprechende hostseitige Triggerereignis müßte von einem Programm her kommen oder vom Betriebssystem, wenn dieses eine System- oder Benutzernachricht (z.B. Inhalt einer Benutzerdatei) auf dem betreffenden Terminal ausgeben will. Da nicht davon ausgegangen werden kann, daß das Zielterminal auch von dem gewünschten Benutzer besetzt ist, wäre bei dieser Vorgehensweise nur ein Monolog möglich. Implementierungstechnisch wäre hier zudem ein größerer Aufwand erforderlich, da das Zielterminal ggf. nicht sofort verfügbar ist (ausgeschaltet, belegt) und damit eine entsprechende Auftragsverwaltung mit Warteschlangen und Timer-Überwachungen notwendig wird. Weiterhin würde in dem Host eine Zielterminal-Adreßverwaltung benötigt. Aufwand und Nutzen stehen daher in keiner günstigen Relation, so daß ein Verbindungsaufbau vom Host her als wenig sinnvoll anzusehen ist.

2.2 Initial Control

Der Prozeß, der im Besitz der "initial control" ist, darf die Kommunikation eröffnen. Bei den meisten Anwendungen (z.B. File Transfer) ist a priori klar, welcher der Prozeßpartner die Kommunikation eröffnet und damit das Recht für das Senden der ersten Message besitzt. Bei der VT-Anwendung findet man jedoch auf der Hostseite unterschiedliche Startbedingungen vor:

- Host-Typ A geht nach der Herstellung der Verbindung in Wartestellung auf das "LOGON"

— Host-Typ B sendet nach der Herstellung der Verbindung eine LOGON-Eingabe-Aufforderung zum Terminal (z.B. PLEASE ENTER LOGON).

Hieraus entsteht eine "initial control"-Problematik, die auf folgende Arten gelöst werden kann:

1. Man veranlaßt den VT-Prozeß im Host-Typ A, daß er ebenfalls eine LOGON-Eingabe-Aufforderung sendet. In diesem Fall könnte die "initial control" eindeutig dem hostseitigen VT-Prozeß zugeordnet werden.

2. Der VT-Prozeß von Host-Typ B unterdrückt nach Verbindungsaufbau die LOGON-Eingabe-Aufforderung. In diesem Fall wäre die "initial control" eindeutig beim terminalseitigen VT-Prozeß.

3. Die "initial control" bleibt undefiniert. In diesem Fall muß man Lösungen für den Konflikt-Fall erarbeiten, daß beide Prozeß-Partner die Kommunikation eröffnen, um deadlock- oder undefinierte Protokollzustände zu vermeiden.

4. Beim Verbindungsaufbau wird mitgeteilt, welcher Prozeß-Partner die "initial control" besitzt, d.h. welcher Prozeß die Kommunikation eröffnen wird. Dies setzt voraus, daß sich dieses Problem beim Verbindungsaufbau konfliktfrei lösen läßt. Das ist aber nur dann der Fall, wenn mindestens ein Partner die Qualität hat, sowohl die Kommunikation selbst beginnen zu können als auch den Partner-prozeß die Kommunikation beginnen zu lassen. Eine solche Flexibilität ist auf der Terminalseite vorhanden, so daß der hostseitige Prozeß bei Verbindungsauf-bau mitteilen könnte, ob er die "initial control" beansprucht oder nicht.

Lösungen 1 und 2 erscheinen pragmatisch, liefern jedoch keinen prinzipiellen Bei-trag zur Eliminierung der "initial control"-Problematik, die auch bei anderen An-wendungen auftreten kann. Lösung 3 ist zwar machbar, jedoch schwer implemen-tierbar und birgt Probleme für die Realisierung des Prozesses als wohldefinierten Zustandsautomaten in sich. Variante 4 stellt wohl aus der Sicht eines Netzwerk-Architektur-Modells die "sauberste" Lösung dar. Es sollte daher ein "initial cont-rol"-Parameter zur Menge der Verbindungsaufbau-Parameter gehören.

2.3 Faltung

Eine dialogfähige Applikation arbeitet mit Ein- und Ausgabezeilen, deren Länge von der Anwendung her bestimmt ist. Die logische Zeilenlänge kann daher im konkreten

Fall länger als die physikalische Zeilenlänge des Terminals sein, von dem aus die Applikation gestartet wird. Die Lösung dieses Konflikts (Faltungsproblem) ist abhängig von der jeweiligen Betriebssystemphilosophie. Folgende Varianten sind hauptsächlich vertreten:

1. Darstellung des Überlaufs in der Folgezeile ohne Markierung des logischen Zeilenendes

2. Darstellung des Überlaufs in der Folgezeile mit Markierung des logischen Zeilenendes durch die Terminal-Hardware (sichtbare Darstellung der NL-Funktion z.B. durch hochgestellten Punkt oder durch nach links abknickenden Pfeil bzw. nach links abknickende Ecke)

3. Umgehung des Faltungsproblems durch die Applikation selbst, indem horizontale Sichtfenster-Verschiebungsfunktionen bereitgestellt werden (z.B. bei Editiersystemen)

4. Abschneiden der Überlänge.

Von dem VT-Protokoll ist die direkte dynamische Unterstützung der logischen Zeilenlänge zu fordern. Ist jedoch bei den VT-Datenstrukturen nur eine maximale Zeilenlänge von 80 Zeichen vorgesehen, entsteht ein Faltungsproblem, das nur durch eine zusätzliche, vom VT-Protokoll her nicht sichtbare Vereinbarung gelöst werden kann (z.B. durch Markierung der Überlaufzeile mit einem speziellen Endezeichen).

Bezüglich der Darstellung sowohl ein- wie ausgabeseitig von logischen Zeilen, die länger als die physikalische Zeile sind, müssen bei der RT/VT-Umsetzung Entscheidungen getroffen werden, die - hardwareabhängig - Variante 1 oder 2 unterstützen. Wenn die Hardware keine logischen Zeilen kennt und überlange Zeilen als 2 getrennte Zeilen behandelt, so ist zwischen Benutzer und terminalseitigem VT-Prozeß eine Zusatzvereinbarung nötig, d.h. der Benutzer muß die Überlaufzeile als solche explizit kennzeichnen in ähnlicher Weise, wie dies die beiden VT-Prozesse tun müssen für den Fall, daß die VT-Datenstruktur nur eine begrenzte Länge hat.

2.4 Grundrasterzeichen

Jedes VT-relevante Sichtgerät besitzt einen Bildwiederholungsspeicher, der im Grundzustand eine der folgenden Vorbesetzungen aufweist:

- NIL

- Blank

- Punkt

Sichtbare Grundrasterzeichen (NIL wird bei einigen Terminals als Punkt in halber Buchstabenhöhe dargestellt) dienen der lokalen Benutzerführung. Gleich, welche Voreinstellung für den Bildwiederholspeicher zutrifft, die VT-Datenstrukturen sind mit NIL vorbesetzt. Eine Benutzer-Eingabe vom Typ Buchstabe A, Cursor-Bewegung nach rechts, Buchstabe B (also keine Eingabe eines Zeichens auf Position 2) sollte also

- A, NIL, B   im Fall 1
- A, Blank, B   im Fall 2
- A, Punkt, B   im Fall 3

übertragen werden. Problematisch ist Fall 1, da die NIL-Behandlung in den verschiedenen Betriebssystemen sehr unterschiedlich ist. Eventuell muß der hostseitige VT-Prozeß das NIL eliminieren oder durch Blank ersetzen.

2.5 Systemzeile

Die Betriebssystemphilosophie bezüglich der Realisierung von Systemzeilen auf einem Bildschirm sind sehr verschieden. Folgende Varianten sind u. a. zu unterscheiden:

1. die unterste Bildschirmzeile ist für Systemmeldungen reserviert und steht einer Applikation nicht zur Verfügung

2. die unterste Bildschirmzeile ist für Systemmeldungen vorgesehen, steht aber normalerweise der Applikation zur Verfügung

3. die Systemmeldung wird irgendwo auf dem Bildschirm ausgegeben (abhängig von der aktuellen Situation).

Systemmeldungen (Operateur- bzw. Systemnachrichten) stellen asynchrone Ereignisse aus der Sicht des VT-Protokolls dar. Sie stammen zudem nicht von der normalerweise an den hostseitigen VT-Prozeß gekoppelten Applikation, sondern direkt oder indirekt vom Betriebssystem. Da normalerweise das VT-Terminal nur die beiden Zustände "Eingabezustand" und "Ausgabezustand" kennt, die im Wechsel durchlaufen werden, erfordert die Behandlung einer Systemmeldung im Terminal-Eingabe-

zustand zumindest für die Fälle 2 und 3 eine besondere Maßnahme: den Interrupt.
Mit seiner Hilfe kann der hostseitige VT-Prozeß seinen Wunsch, eine Systemmeldung absetzen zu wollen, verdeutlichen und das Update-Recht für die Systemzeile verlangen.

Im Fall 1 könnte der VT-Prozeß ständig das Update-Recht für die Systemzeile besitzen, d.h. das Absetzen eines vorherigen Interrupts wäre nicht unbedingt erforderlich. Um jedoch Unterschiede zu vermeiden, sollte Fall 1 wie die beiden anderen Fälle behandelt werden.

2.6 Steuerung der Ein- und Ausgabe

Zur Vermeidung von Benutzerfehlern haben einige Sichtgeräte die Fähigkeit, die Tastatur ganz bzw. für geschützte Felder z.B. beim formatisierten Arbeiten zu sperren. Diese Hardware-Eigenschaft ist jedoch nur nutzbar, wenn die VT-Datenstrukturen Signale enthalten, ob und bei welchen Cursor-Positionen eine Sperrung vorzunehmen ist, d.h. der terminalseitige VT-Prozeß muß wissen, ob der Benutzer ein Update-Recht für ein bestimmtes Feld hat oder nicht. Hieraus resultiert die Anforderung an das VT-Protokoll, die Update-Rechte für die definierten Datenstrukturen für jeden Prozeßpartner eindeutig und mit dem benötigten Differenzierungsgrad beschreiben zu können. Die Beschreibbarkeit der Update-Rechte im VT-Protokoll ist jedoch nur ein Teilproblem. Das andere Problem liegt im Erkennen einer Applikations-Eingabe-Forderung (Prompting Signal Problem). Das Aussenden einer Message von der Applikation auf ein Terminal bedeutet nicht unbedingt, daß die Applikation in den Eingabezustand übergegangen ist, da die Gesamtausgabe zwischen zwei Eingabezuständen aus mehreren Messages (Teilausgaben) bestehen kann.

2.7 Abbruch einer laufenden Applikation

Üblicherweise meldet sich eine Applikation am Sichtgerät, wenn eine Eingabe gefordert wird, bzw. der Kommando-Entschlüßler, wenn die eingegebenen Kommandos abgearbeitet sind oder ein Programmlauf beendet ist. Nun kommt es immer wieder vor, daß eine Applikation abgebrochen werden soll, weil sie sich z.B. in einer Schleife verfangen hat oder versehentlich mit falschen Parametern versorgt wurde. Da die Applikation sich von selbst wegen des fehlenden Triggerereignisses

"Eingabeforderung" nicht meldet, kann ein Abbruch nur über eine Betriebssystem-Funktion realisiert werden. Der Abbruch-Wunsch stellt ein asynchrones Ereignis dar, das Triggersignal hierfür muß der Benutzer liefern. Dies setzt voraus, daß ein "program function key" für diesen Zweck reserviert wurde bzw. der Abbruch-Wunsch durch Angabe eines bestimmten Interrupt-Codes in einer für solche Zwecke reservierten Terminal-Steuerzeile dem VT-Prozeß mitgeteilt werden kann.

2.8 Abbruch einer anstehenden Ausgabe

Immer wieder kommt es vor, daß ein Benutzer noch anstehende Ausgaben nicht sehen will, weil er sie schon kennt (z.B. längere Ausgaben von Programmen) oder weil er bei einem Kopier- oder Auflist-Vorgang die gesuchte Information schon gefunden hat. Er möchte also dem System mitteilen: skip vorwärts bis zur nächsten Eingabeforderung. Dieser Abbruchwunsch stellt ebenfalls ein asynchrones Ereignis dar, weil der normale Protokoll-Ablauf dadurch geändert wird und eine Neu-Synchronisation der beiden VT-Prozesse erforderlich ist. Für die Mitteilung dieses Skip-Wunsches müssen dem Benutzer analoge Mittel wie für den Abbruch einer laufenden Applikation zur Verfügung stehen. Das VT-Protokoll sollte daher so beschaffen sein, daß es diese Leistung erbringen kann, wobei das Wegwerfen der Information aus Gründen der Transportkapazitäts- und Kosten-Ersparnis auf der Host-Seite vorgenommen werden sollte.

2.9 Gesprächsabbruch

Ein Gesprächsabbruch unterscheidet sich von einer normalen Gesprächsbeendigung dadurch, daß die Dialogbeendigung mit einem Abbruch einer laufenden Applikation einhergeht. Insofern gibt es also eine Parallele zu dem Problemfall "Abbruch einer laufenden Applikation". Der Unterschied besteht jedoch darin, daß in jenem Fall die VT-Kommunikation fortgesetzt wird, in diesem Fall jedoch keine Fortsetzung erwünscht ist. Da der hostseitige VT-Prozeß sowieso die Fähigkeit haben muß, bei einem Netz-Zusammenbruch ein "LOGOFF" zu machen und sein Gedächtnis zu normieren, kann man einen Gesprächsabbruch über einen Verbindungsabbau realisieren. Den "disconnect"-Wunsch muß der Benutzer seinem lokalen VT-Prozeß wieder über einen "program function key" oder über die Terminal-Steuerzeile mitteilen können.

3. Qualität eines VT-Protokolls

Die Qualität eines VT-Protokolls hängt also nicht nur allein von seiner Mächtigkeit ab, verschiedene Terminal-Typen und Terminal-Funktionen unterstützen zu können, sondern auch von seiner praktischen Implementierbarkeit vor dem Hintergrund der hier aufgezeigten Problempalette.

Literatur

/1/   J. Börger, G. Schulze

The PIX Virtual Terminal Protocol
PIX/VTP/TEK/78/01
(zu beziehen durch: GMD-IFV, Rheinstr. 75, 6100 Darmstadt)

/2/   SESA Deutschland GmbH

Implementationsstudie des PIX-Virtuellen-Terminal-Protokolls
für das Hewlett-Packard Sichtgerät 2645 A
Frankfurt, 28.7.78

ARCHITEKTUR OFFENER KOMMUNIKATIONSSYSTEME

- STAND DER NORMUNGSARBEIT -

H. J. Burkhardt
Gesellschaft für Mathematik
und Datenverarbeitung GmbH
Institut für Datenfernverarbeitung
Rheinstr. 75
D-6100 Darmstadt

Abstract:

Die internationale Normungsarbeit an offenen Kommunikationssystemen
hat zum Ziel, Datenendeinrichtungen unterschiedlicher Hersteller in
die Lage zu versetzen, miteinander zu kommunizieren und zu
kooperieren.
Diese Fähigkeit erhalten die Datenendeinrichtungen dadurch, daß sie
ihr externes Verhalten bestimmende Protokollnorm einhalten, die einer
einheitlichen Kommunikationsarchitektur folgen.

Der vorliegende Beitrag beschreibt den aktuellen Stand der Normungsarbeit an dieser Kommunikationsarchitektur.

ARCHITEKTUR OFFENER KOMMUNIKATIONSSYSTEME

- STAND DER NORMUNGSARBEIT -

H.J. Burkhardt
Gesellschaft für Mathematik
und Datenverarbeitung GmbH
Institut für Datenfernverarbeitung
Rheinstraße 75
D-6100 Darmstadt

1. Einführung:

Das im März 1977 gegründete ISO/TC 97/SC 16 definiert als seine Aufgabe:

"Standardization in the area of open systems as it relates to systems interconnection. This will include the development of standards required for the reference model of Open Systems Interconnection and for exchange of information between open systems. This work will take into due account other standardization activities in this area."

Unter System wird jede autonome, räumlich abgegrenzte Einheit verstanden, die fähig ist, Information zu verarbeiten. Dieser Begriff schließt somit Rechner mit ihrer Peripherie und Software ebenso ein wie Benutzerstationen mit ihren menschlichen Bedienern.

Systeme werden zu offenen Systemen aufgrund der Fähigkeit miteinander zu kommunizieren und zu kooperieren [Kooperieren meint dabei die Zusammenarbeit zwischen (räumlich verteilten) Komponenten, um eine gemeinsame Aufgabe zu erledigen; die Vorstellungen hierzu sind gegenwärtig noch recht vage]. Diese Fähigkeit erhalten sie - unbeschadet ihrer internen Struktur und Herkunft - dadurch, daß sie ihr externes Verhalten bestimmende Normen einhalten. Diese Normen sind Protokollnormen; bekannte Beispiele für Protokollnormen sind 'Basic Mode Control-Procedures' und 'High Level Data Link Control-Procedures'.

Auskunft darüber, welche Protokollnormen nötig sind und in welcher Beziehung sie zueinander stehen, erwartet man von einem 'Reference Model of Open System Interconnection'. Es stellt die Basis für die Einordnung existierender Normen und die koordinierte parallele Entwicklung noch fehlender Normen dar.

Diesem Referenzmodell galt bisher die Hauptarbeit im SC 16. Der bisher erreichte Stand ist im Dokument ISO TC 97/SC 16 N 227 vom August 1979 dargelegt und wird im folgenden skizziert:

2. Strukturierungsprinzipien des Referenzmodells

Das grundlegende Strukturierungsprinzip des Referenzmodells ist nach wie vor das der Schichtung (layering), obwohl es als alleiniges und durchgängiges Prinzip zunehmend in Frage gestellt wird.

Bei der Schichtung wird jedes System als aus einem geordneten Satz von Untersystemen zusammengesetzt betrachtet (s. Bild 1). Ein Untersystem besteht aus einer oder mehreren Instanzen (entity).
Untersysteme der selben Ordnung bilden gemeinsam eine Schicht (layer).
Benachbarte Untersysteme kommunizieren miteinander über die ihnen gemeinsame Schnittstelle.
Jede Schicht - mit Ausnahme der höchsten - bietet der ihr überlagerten Schicht eine bestimmte Dienstleistung. Um diese Dienstleistung zu erbringen, werden Instanzen dieser Schicht in der Regel gezwungen sein, miteinander über Schichtenprotokolle (peer-to-peer-protocols) zu kooperieren. Um kooperieren zu können, werden die Instanzen jeder Schicht - mit Ausnahme der untersten - unter Inanspruchnahme der Dienstleistung der jeweils unterlagerten Schicht miteinander kommunizieren.

Es werden eine Reihe von Kriterien angeführt, die helfen sollen, zu entscheiden, wo in einem derartigen Schichtenmodell Schnittstellen angeordnet werden sollen und wieviel es insgesamt sein sollten. Zur Beantwortung der Frage nach der Anzahl der Schnittstellen werden im wesentlichen arbeitsökonomische Kriterien angegeben (z. B.: Kreiere genug Schichten, um überschaubare, unabhängig bearbeitbare Aufgaben zu erhalten, aber nicht mehr als ohne Schwierigkeiten zu einer Gesamtarchitektur zu integrieren sind). Die Kriterien zur Beantwortung der Frage nach dem Wo sind teils aus funktioneller Sicht gewählt, teils durch Abbildbarkeitsgesichtspunkte bestimmt (z. B. Kreiere immer dann eine Schicht, wenn es notwendig ist, verschiedene Ebenen der Abstraktion in der Behandlung von Daten zu unterscheiden, wie Morphologie, Syntax, Semantik; oder: Kreiere eine Schnittstelle dort, wo sie sich in Hard- oder Software entweder schon befindet oder aufgrund der absehbaren technologischen Entwicklung zweckmäßigerweise befinden sollte; oder: Kreiere eine Schnittstelle, wo es wünschenswert ist, irgendwann eine Schnittstellennormung vorzunehmen).

Die beschriebene Strukturierung in Schichten ist offensichtlich für Dienstleistungen sinnvoll, die in einer statischen, hierarchischen Beziehung zueinander stehen und sie hat dort Schwächen, wo sich hierarchische Beziehungen nicht herstellen lassen oder aber dynamisch ändern.

Für Dienstleistungen, auf die letzteres zutrifft, werden zwei andere Mechanismen diskutiert, nämlich "Sublayering" und "Protocol Switching".

"Sublayering" meint die Untergliederung einer Schicht in Unterschichten, die abhängig voneinander sind, weil sie den gleichen Instanzen und Verbindungen zugeordnet sind, und über deren Benutzung dynamisch entschieden werden kann.

"Protocol Switching" erreicht die Dynamik dadurch, daß zwischen verschiedenen Protokollen einer Schicht hin- und hergeschaltet werden kann.

3. Die Schnittstelle zwischen Transportbenutzern und Transportsystem

Der Begriff des Systems beschreibt die physische, räumliche Realität unter Abstraktion von ihrer spezifischen Ausprägung.

Die für das Referenzmodell gesuchte Kommunikationsarchitektur stellt eine logische, funktionelle Beschreibung des Kommunikationsvorganges unter Abstraktion von spezifischen Kommunikationsinhalten dar.
Eine erste grobe, aber wesentliche Abstraktion besteht darin, Kommunikation zu zerlegen in:
- Produktion von Information
- Transport von Information
- Konsumption von Information.

Produktion und Konsumption sind komplementäre Funktionen, die sich in informationsverarbeitenden Instanzen, Transportbenutzer genannt, abspielen, der Transport ist Dienstleistung eines unterlagerten Transportsystems (s. Bild 2).

Die Kommunikation zwischen Transportbenutzern ist inhaltlich durch die Aufgabe, der sie dient, das aber heißt durch die Anwendung, bestimmt.

Da die Bild 2 zugrundeliegende Abstraktion keine Voraussetzung über die Kommunikationsinhalte enthält, ist die Schnittstelle zwischen Transportbenutzern und Transportsystem anwendungsunabhängig. Da sie weiter keine Voraussetzung über die für den Transport benutzten Mittel macht, ist sie darüber hinaus auch transportmittelunabhängig.

Das Transportsystem baut so kostengünstig wie möglich Transportverbindungen gewünschter Güte zwischen Transportbenutzern auf. Die Transportbenutzer sind dem Transportsystem über die ihnen zugeordneten Transportadressen bekannt.
Über etablierte Transportverbindungen können in beiden Richtungen gleichzeitig Daten fließen. Die Reihenfolge der Daten bleibt beim Transport erhalten. Jeder Transportbenutzer hat die Möglichkeit der Flußkontrolle, d. h. er kann die Abnahme von Daten aus seiner Transportverbindung unterbrechen und damit einen Rückstau ins Transportsystem auslösen, der sich ggf. über die Transportverbindung bis zum einspeisenden Transportbenutzer fortpflanzt.

Eine Transportverbindung wird abgebaut entweder auf Anforderung eines Transportbenutzers oder als Folge eines nicht behebbaren Fehlers im Transportsystem. Daten, die der Abbauvorgang noch in der Transportverbindung antrifft, gehen verloren.
Übereinstimmung besteht darüber, daß die beschriebenen Basisdienstleistungen ergänzt werden müssen durch Mechanismen, die es erlauben, bestimmte Signalisierungsinformationen (z. B. Interruptsignale) zwischen den Transportbenutzern auszutauschen, auch dann, wenn Nutzdaten aufgrund eines Rückstaus nicht fließen können.

Zwei Mechanismen werden diskutiert. Der eine besteht darin, Signalisierungsinformation ohne Zerstörung der Nutzdaten auf einem zweiten unabhängigen Datenpfad (expedited data path) zu transportieren, der andere darin, die Signalisierungsinformation unter Zerstörung der Nutzdaten in der Transportverbindung zu transportieren (purge).

Den beiden Mechanismen liegen meiner Einsicht nach unterschiedliche
Vorstellungen über die Natur der über eine Transportverbindung kommu-
nizierenden Transportbenutzer zu Grunde. Die Befürworter des ersten
Mechanismus scheinen in einem Transportbenutzer mehrere parallele
asynchrone Prozesse zu sehen, während die Befürworter des zweiten Me-
chanismus in einem Transportbenutzer einen sequentiellen Prozeß sehen.
Da dies die weitere Modellbildung grundlegend beeinflußt, ist eine
Einigung hierüber dringend erforderlich.

4. Die anwendungsorientierten Protokolle

Das Transportsystem gewährleistet, daß der eine Transportbenutzer "hö-
ren" kann, was der andere "sagt" und umgekehrt. Ziel einer jeden
Kommunikation ist es jedoch, daß die Kommunikationspartner sich "verstehen".
Dies erfordert, daß die Information, die der eine Transportbenutzer
aktuell produziert, genau die Information ist, die der korrespondie-
rende Transportbenutzer aktuell fähig ist zu konsumieren. Oder anders
ausgedrückt, daß Produktion und Konsumption anwendungsorientierten
Protokollen zwischen den Transportbenutzern folgen.
Ganz allgemein gilt wohl, daß Verstehen vom Gesprächsthema abhängt
und eine auf gleichem Vorverständnis beruhende Übereinstimmung über
die Bedeutung des Gehörten erfordert. Dies könnte man seine inhaltli-
che oder semantische Komponente nennen.

Damit dies aber überhaupt zum Tragen kommen kann, ist Vorbedingung,
daß die gleiche Sprache gesprochen wird und daß bestimmte Konven-
tionen bezüglich der Gesprächseröffnung, Gesprächsführung und des Ge-
sprächsabschlusses eingehalten werden. Dies könnte man seine formale
oder syntaktische Komponente nennen.

Es ist unbestritten, daß die Protokolle zwischen Transportbenutzern
dieser Modellvorstellung entsprechende Elemente enthalten müssen.
Fraglich ist jedoch, ob diese Elemente, wie noch im gegenwärtigen Referenzmodell, weiterhin drei unabhängigen Schichten zugeordnet werden
können, nämlich der Anwendungsschicht (Application Layer), der Datendarstellungsschicht (Presentation Layer) und der Gesprächssteuerungsschicht (Session Layer) (s. Bild 3).
Als eine Alternative zu der Gliederung der Transportbenutzer in
Schichten wird ihre Gliederung in Unterschichten diskutiert.

In der Anwendungsschicht werden die eigentlichen anwendungsspezifischen Protokolle abgehandelt. Diese sind grob in die folgenden fünf
Kategorien eingeteilt:

Kategorie_1:

System management protocols (e. g. activation/deactivation management,
monitoring and error control).

Kategorie_2:

Application management protocols (e. g. authentication, access control,
accounting, deadlock recovery, and commitment protocols).

Kategorie_3:

System protocols (e. g. file access, remote job entry, and process
initiation).

Kategorie_4:

Industry-specific application-protocols (e. g. banking and airlines).

Kategorie_5:

Enterprise-specific application-protocols (e. g. company X's private
order entry system).

Protokolle der Kategorien 1 bis 4 werden als international normungs-
würdig angesehen; SC 16 sieht dabei für sich eine Zuständigkeit für
die Normung von Protokollen der Kategorien 1 bis 3.

Die Datendarstellungsschicht bietet der Anwendungsschicht vorgefertig-
te Datenmodelle (presentation images) zum Umgang mit strukturierten
Daten und befreit die Anwendung davon, sich mit spezifischen Eigenschaften physikalischer Medien zum Speichern, zur Ein-/Ausgabe und
Wiedergabe von Daten auseinanderzusetzen.

In der Gesprächssteuerungsschicht sind die Funktionen angesiedelt, die
zu Gesprächseröffnung und -abschluß und zur geordneten Gesprächsführung (Synchronisierung durch my turn/ your turn, Stützpunktschreiben,
Rücksetzen auf Stützpunkte ...) dienen.

Wegen der Unsicherheit, ob das Schichtenmodell zur Gliederung der anwendungsorientierten Protokolle tragfähig ist, wird in diesem Bereich

nicht weiter schichtenspezifisch gearbeitet, sondern versucht, die
drei gegenwärtig wichtigsten Anwendungsbereiche (einheitlicher Termi-
nalzugriff (Virtual Terminal), einheitlicher Speicherzugriff (Virtual
File Store), einheitlicher Rechnerzugriff (Job Transfer and Manipulation)) zunächst unabhängig funktionell zu gliedern. Erst danach soll
entschieden werden, wo Gemeinsamkeiten gemeinsame Protokolle nahele-
gen, bzw. Unterschiede unterschiedliche Protokolle fordern.

5. Die transportorientierten Protokolle

Das Transportsystem ist realisiert durch Transportinstanzen, die über
Transportprotokolle miteinander kooperieren und die dazu die Dienste
eines unterlagerten Netzes in Anspruch nehmen (s. Bild 4).

Das Netz stellt Netz-Verbindungen (network connections) zwischen
Transportinstanzen zur Verfügung.

Die Schnittstelle zwischen Transportinstanz und Netz ist unabhängig
von der spezifischen Ausprägung des Netzes, d. h. unabhängig davon,
ob eine Netzverbindung über ein Paketvermittlungsnetz oder ein Durch-
schaltevermittlungsnetz oder eine Kette dieser Netze führt (Network
independent interface).
Sie ist funktionell identisch mit der Schnittstelle zwischen Transportbenutzer und Transportinstanz. Im Gegensatz zu dieser ist sie in
bezug auf die Eigenschaften der Verbindung nicht bedarfsorientiert,
sondern angebotsorientiert.
Damit ist gemeint, daß die Eigenschaften von Netzverbindungen nicht
beliebig aus einem kontinuierlichen Spektrum wählbar sind, sondern
daß sie in diskreten Abstufungen angeboten werden; z. B. bietet ein
Durchschaltenetz Verbindungen mit Übertragungsgeschwindigkeiten von
600 b/s, 1200 b/s, 4800 b/s. Dieses Angebot ist bei öffentlichen Netzen mit bestimmten Gebühren verbunden.

Allgemeine Aufgabe der Transportschicht ist somit, die geforderte
Transportdienstleistung an die angebotene Netzdienstleistung qualita-
tiv anzupassen und Transportverbindungen kostenoptimal auf Netzverbindungen abzubilden. Die Transportinstanzen werden durch globale
netzweit eindeutige Netzadressen (general numbering plan) identifiziert.

Für den allgemeinen Fall, daß die Transportinstanz mehrere Transportbenutzer bedient (entspricht Funktion einer privaten Nebenstellenanla-
ge), sind mehrere Transportadressen mit einer Netzadresse assoziiert.

Ein Netz stellt Netzverbindungen zwischen Transportinstanzen zur Verfügung. Eine Netzverbindung führt jeweils über genau zwei Endknoten
und eine beliebige Anzahl von Zwischenknoten, wobei die Zwischenknoten
in der Regel Bestandteile öffentlicher Netze sind.

Ein Netz läßt sich funktionell in drei Schichten untergliedern (s.
Bild 5), die die Funktion
    - der Vermittlung (network layer)
    - der abschnittsweisen Sicherung (data link layer)
    - die Bitübertragung (physical layer)
ausführen.

Die Schicht 1 liefert als Basisbausteine Übertragungsteilstrecken, die
es erlauben, Bitströme zwischen Knoten zu übertragen. Störungen, die
auf diesen Teilstrecken auftreten, würden zur Verfälschung oder Verlust von Bits führen. Dagegen schützen Protokolle der Schicht 2, die
aus einer ungesicherten Teilstrecke einen gesicherten Übermittlungsabschnitt machen.

Die Schicht 3 schließlich hat die Aufgabe, die gesicherten Übermitt-
lungsabschnitte zu Netzverbindungen zu verknüpfen. In ihr sind somit
die Funktionen der Wegewahl und Vermittlung angeordnet.

Die Protokolle der Schichten 1 bis 3 kann man zusammenfassen unter dem
Begriff Zugangsprotokoll zu "öffentlichen" Datennetzen. Sie sind bei
den verschiedenen öffentlichen Datennetzen unterschiedlich, teilweise
schon begründet durch unterschiedliche Ausprägung der Schicht 1.

Durch die Art der Grenzziehung zwischen öffentlichem Datennetz und
privater Datenendeinrichtung sind die Technologien in der Datenendeinrichtung und die Vermittlungs- und Übertragungstechnologie stark miteinander verkoppelt (s. Bild 6). Wünschenswert wäre hier eine Entkopp-
lung und Vereinheitlichung durch mehr am Dienstbegriff als an der
Technologie orientierte Schnittstellen.

Die Bedeutung der Schnittstelle 3/4 liegt darin, daß sie in der Lage
ist, genau das zu ermöglichen, wenn man sie zur neuen Schnittstelle

zwischen Datenendeinrichtung und einer um die Funktionen der Schichten
1 bis 3 erweiterten Datenübertragungseinrichtung der Post macht.

Bild 7 zeigt noch einmal zusammengefaßt alle Schichten des Referenz-
modells.

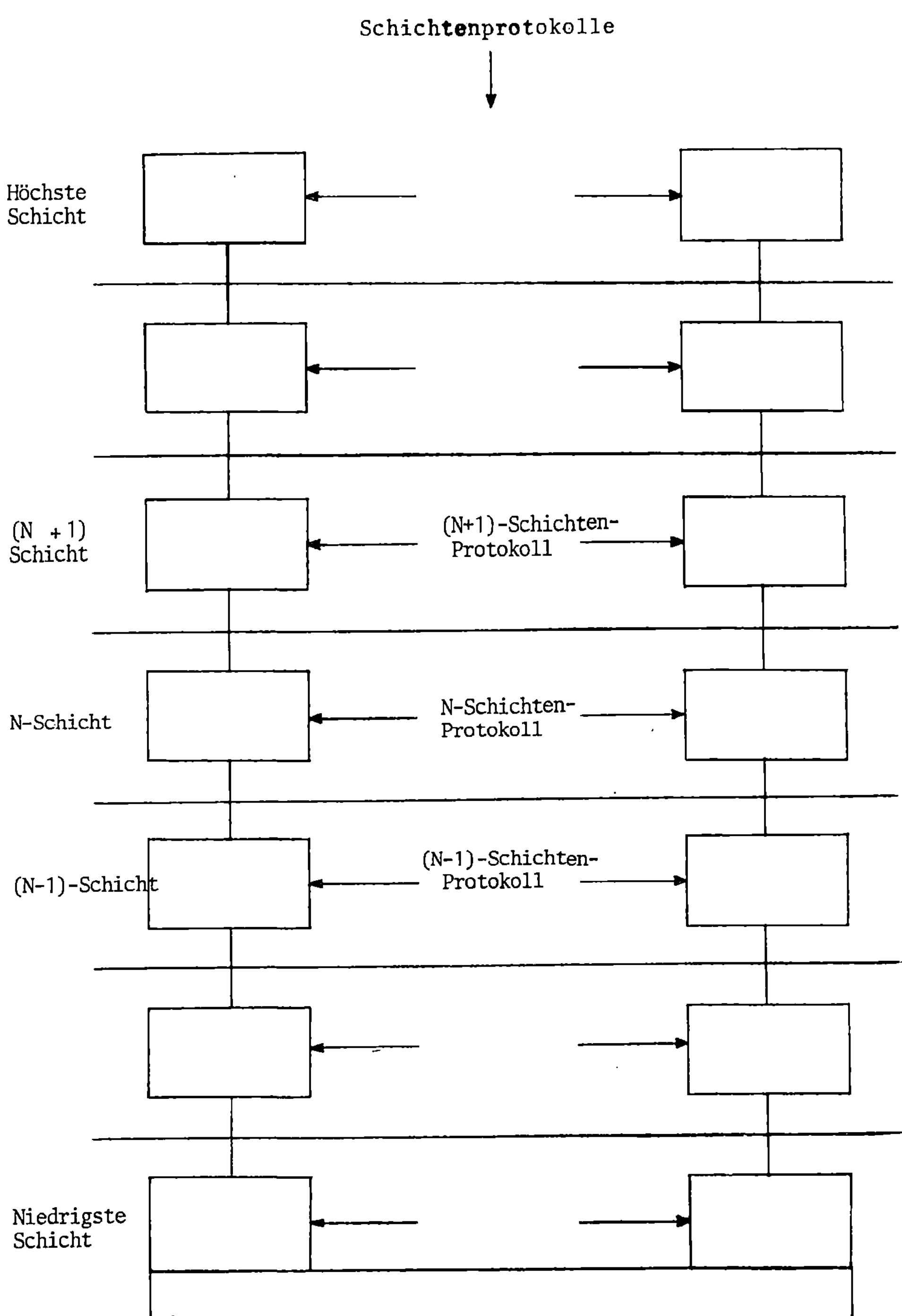

Bild 1: Das Strukturierungsprinzip der Schichtung

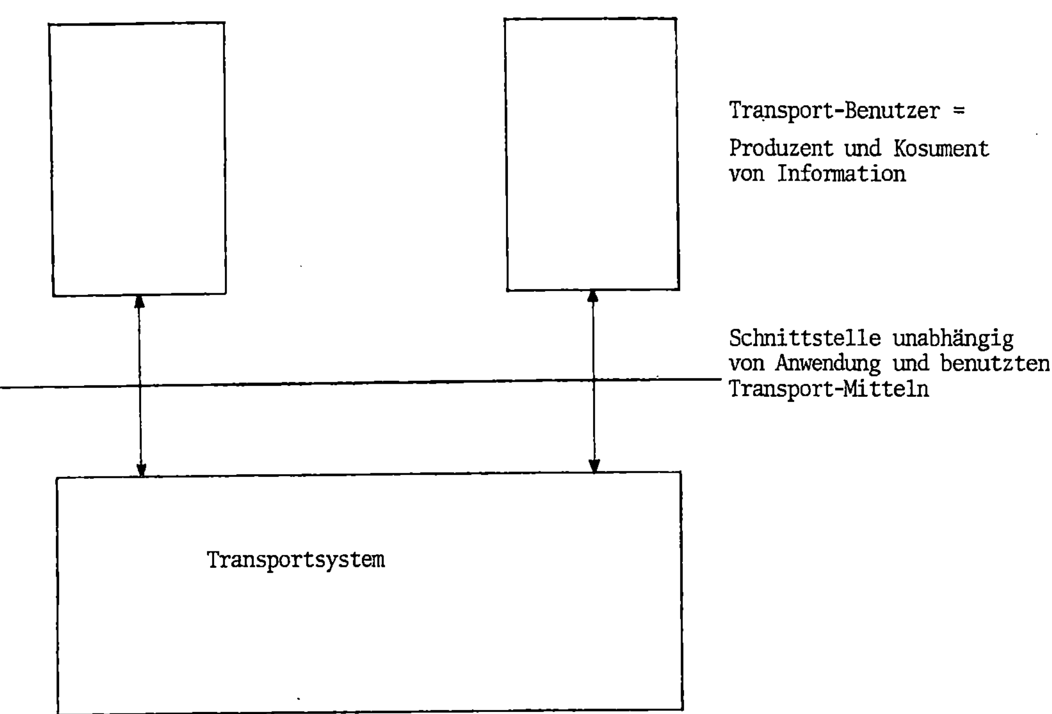

Bild 2: Die Schnittstelle zwischen Transportsystem und Transportbenutzer

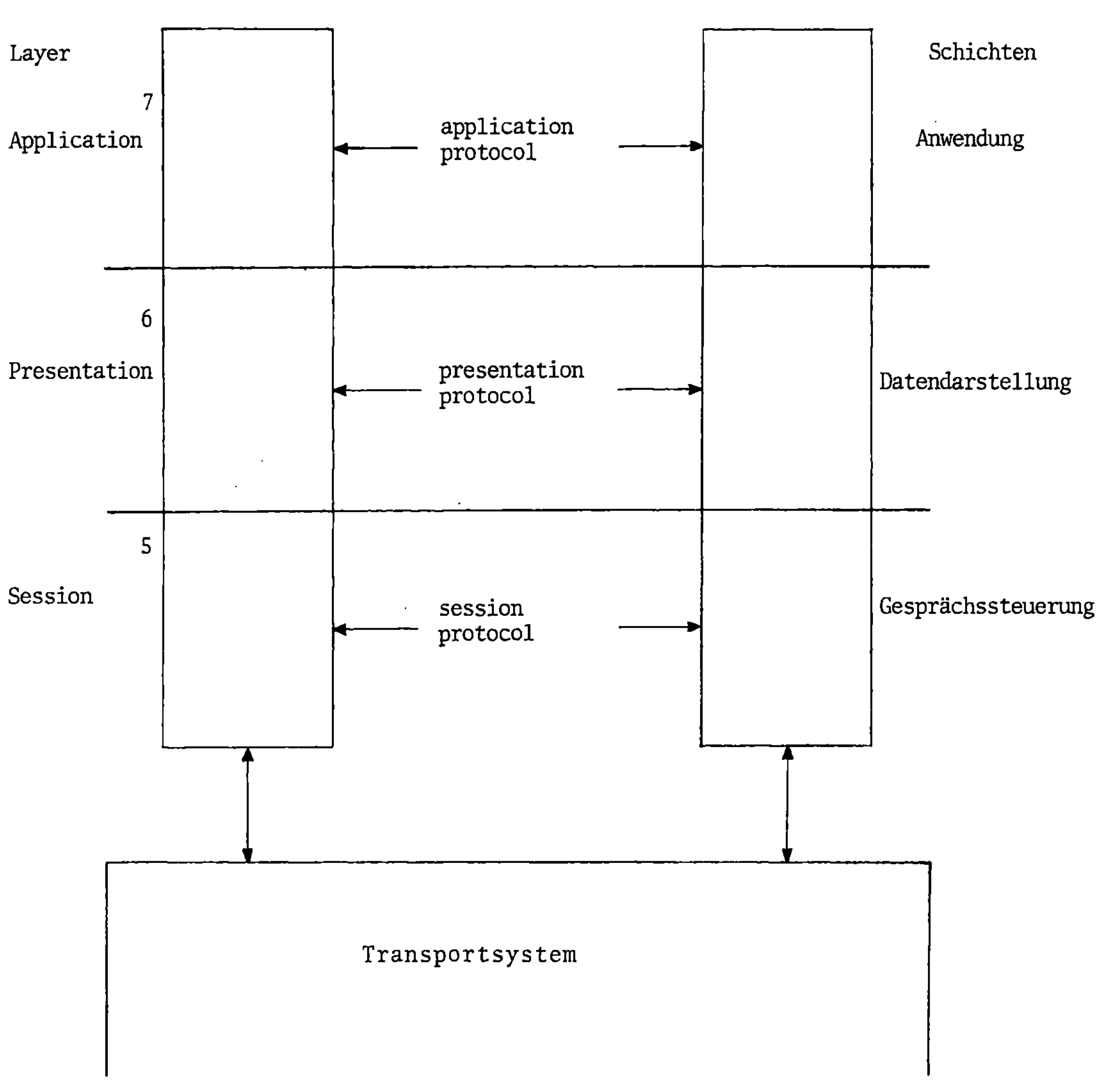

Bild 3: Die anwendungsorientierten Protokolle

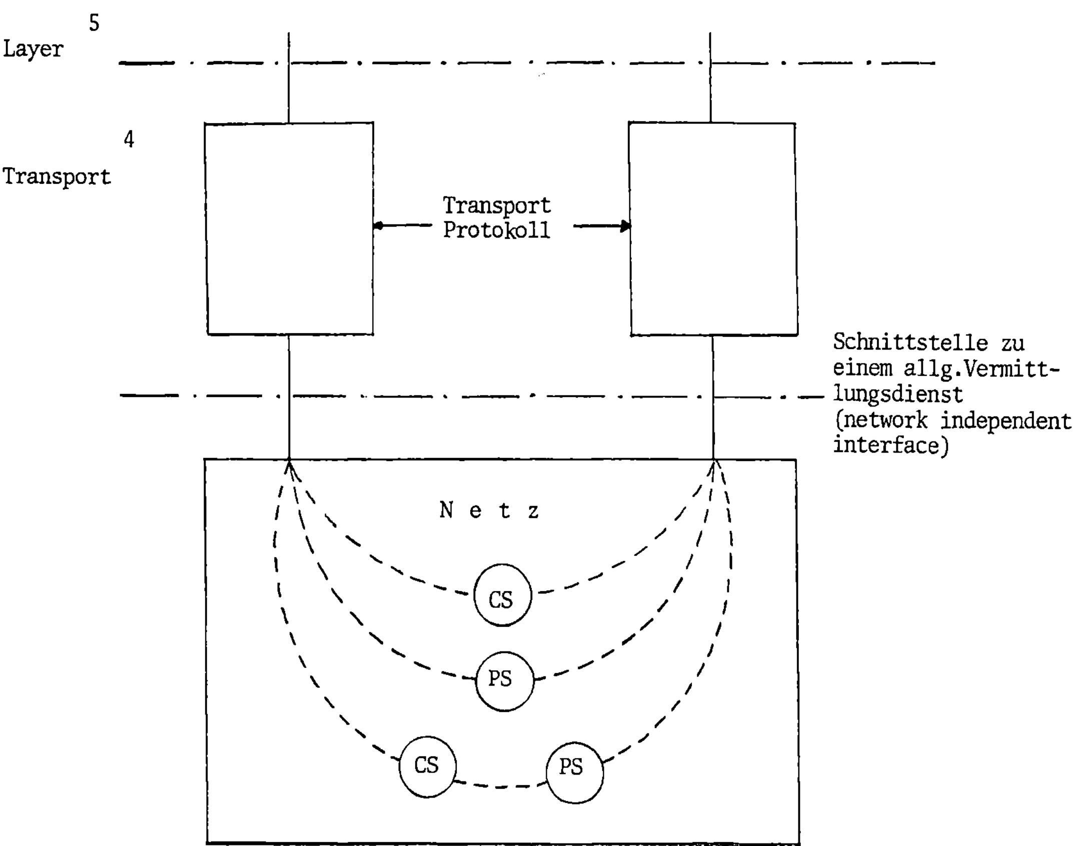

Bild 4: Die Schnittstelle zu einem allgemeinen Vermittlungsdienst

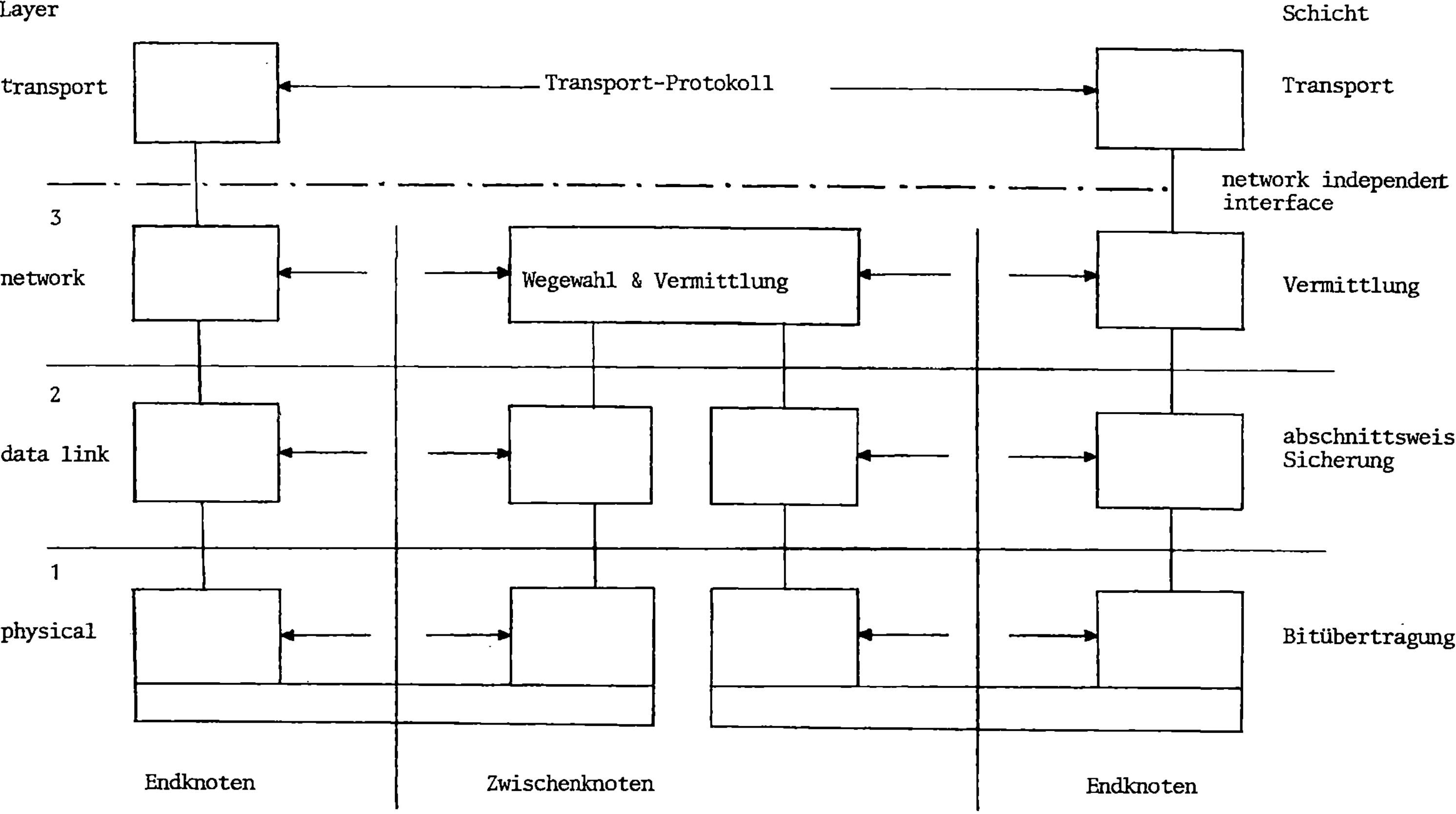

Bild 5: Funktionelle Untergliederung eines Netzes

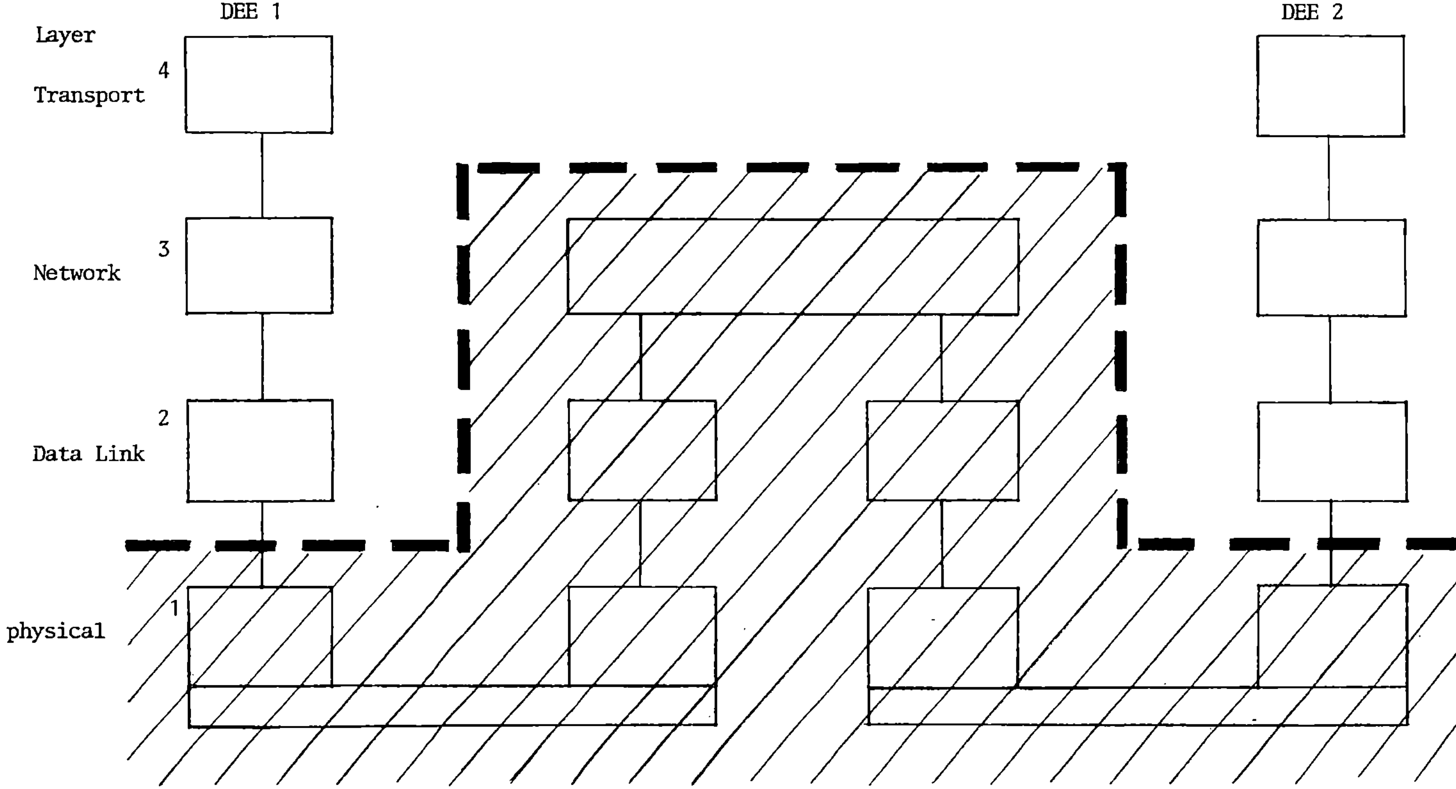

Bild 6: Gegenwärtige Abgrenzung zwischen privater Datenendeinrichtung und Posteinrichtungen

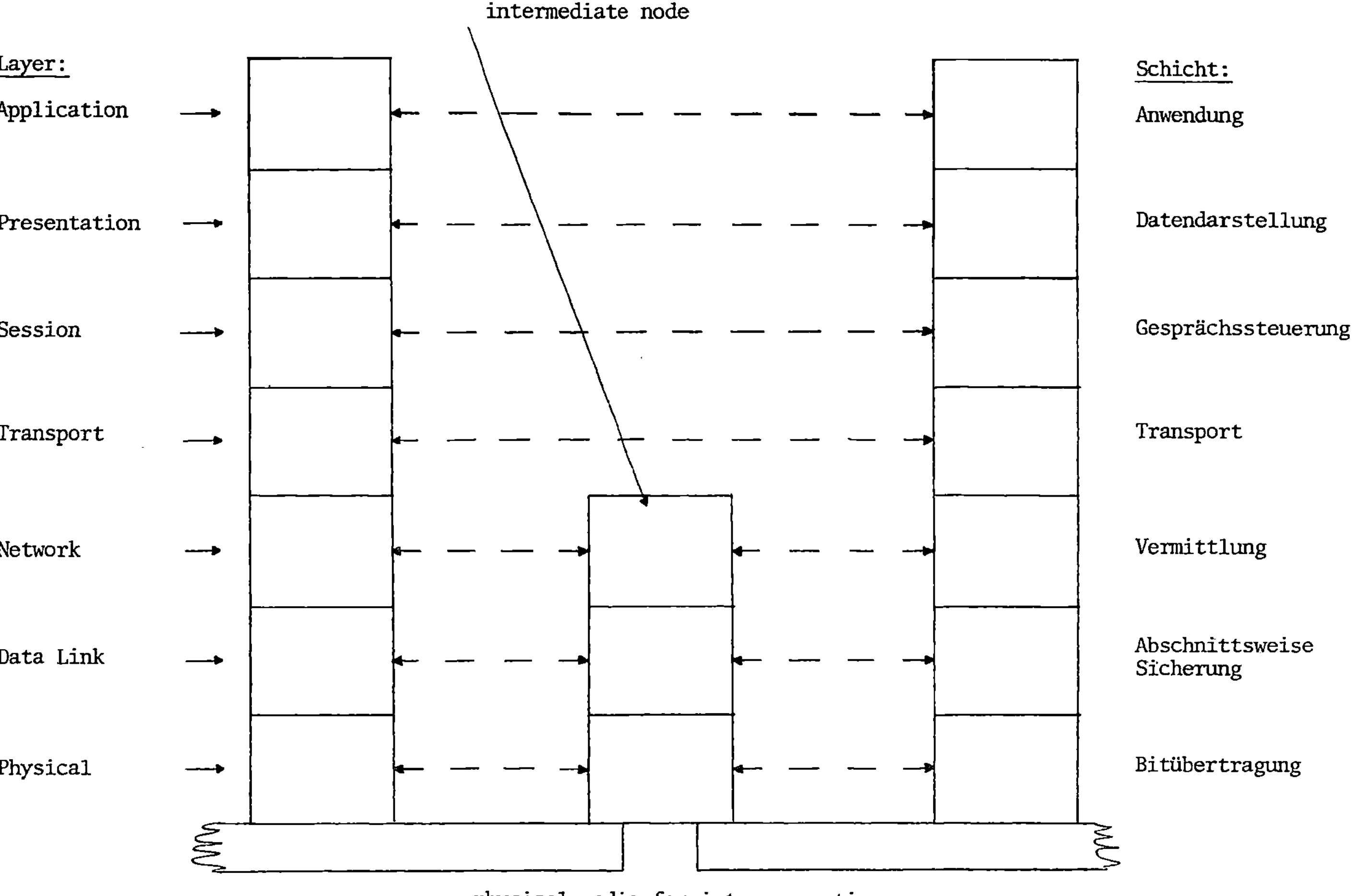

Bild 7: Die Schichten des Referenzmodells

<u>Literatur</u>:

[1] Reference Model of Open Systems Interconnection
(Version 4 as of June 1979) ISO/TC 97/SC 16 N 227

[2] E. Raubold
A model for application level networking protocols
PIX/HLP/GMD/78/01

[3] G. Schulze, J. Börger
A virtual terminal protocol based upon the
"communication variable" concept
Computer Network 2 (1978, pp 291-296

[4] J. Börger, G. Schulze
The PIX virtual terminal protocol
PIX/VTP/TEK 78/01

[5] W. Heinze, B. Struif, M. Wilhelm
The PIX RJE-Protocol
PIX/RJE/TEK 78/01

_SYSTEMS NETWORK ARCHITECTURE IN RELATIONSHIP

_WITH THE OPEN SYSTEMS INTERCONNECTION REFERENCE MODEL

P. DEBACKER

CER IBM

LA GAUDE - 06610 - FRANCE

ABSTRACT

This paper presents IBM Systems Network Architecture (SNA) by reference to the Open Systems Interconnection (OSI) provisional model and discusses the use of IBM SNA networks to facilitate transportation of end user information including the upper layer Control function of the OSI reference model.

INTRODUCTION

One of the major achievement of the OSI reference model is to present a common ground of concepts and names which already allows a number of people to communicate and undoubtly it will be used for that purpose more and more in the future.

It is therefore of interest to present IBM Systems Network Architecture in reference to the OSI model and to show how underlying concepts correspond or differ, beyond jargon differences. This will be done in the first part of this paper.

Nevertheless, this would be of academic interest if we did not go a step further and investigate what may happen when an OSI Architecture (OSA) becomes a reality i.e. standards for sets of protocols covering all six layers (not counting the application layer) exist. One may dream of a scenario in which as soon as OSA emerges, complete and perfect, all prior realisations are forgotten

and an OSA-only environment exists from then on. It is more
realistic to accept the existence of prior architectures, and how
could different architectures interconnect or rather how could OSA
architecture be supported in another architecture becomes the
interesting question.
This is of practical Importance to several parties:

- users of networks, who may wonder about current Investments or
  hesitate before further investments, not knowing if they may
  become obselete all of a sudden.

- people of various origin interested in the success of OSI
  architecture, success which eventually will be measured by
  interconnectability of manufacturer products, and believe that a
  credible. i.e. a progressive migration scenario (from where we
  are) is an essential Ingredient of that success.

- manufacturers which have already architecture and products in
  operation.

This second aspect will be addressed in the last part of this paper.

BASICS OF DISTRIBUTED PROCESSING ARCHITECTURE

Structuring a problem relies almost entirely on the proper selection
of a few primitive aspects of the problem.

After many other we will venture that Process to Process
communication requires (necessary but not suficient condition) a
service which:

- transports the information to be communicated,

- keeps information sequentiality and guarantees (with a high
  probability of truth) integrity of delivery or a notification
  event. Furthermore the service guarantees sequentiality between

information and notification event to the extent that no spill over of information prior to notification will mix with information entered after notification and vice versa.

- Two other characteristics appear to be almost as essential

    - The ability to delimit beginning and termination of the service and, of course, to keep sequentiality of these events versus information transported and notification event as well. This property may sound more trivial than really is.

    - The ability to throttle down information rate to cope with free running operation of asynchronous source/sinks where is needed to limit the instantaneous desynchronisation due to delay thru the network. In addition the same mechanism may be used to restrain the use of network internal resources.

Such a service, which hopefully has been recognized as the Transport Service of the OSI model, can be achieved by the combination of an underlying service and some protocol in the Transport Layer, one complementing the other.

In practice processes are usually located in boxes (or partly in boxes when they involve a human operator) which, in a distributed environment, i.e. a network, are attached to other boxes by links. The flow of information corresponding to process communication should be observable on links in and out of boxes housing the processes.
See figure 1.

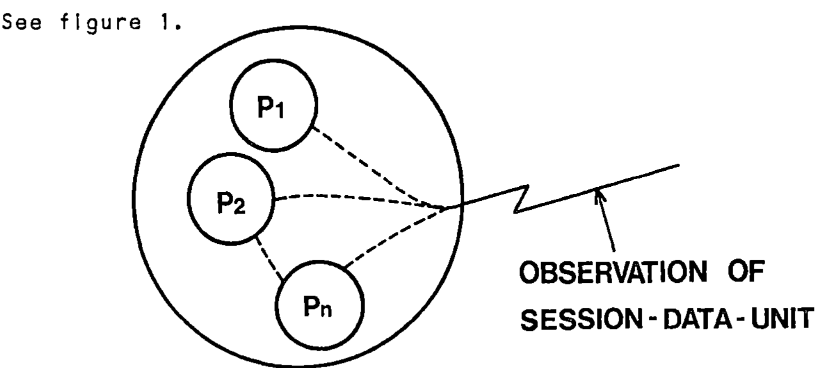

Figure 1

Results of such an hypothetical observation could lead to two types of Transport Layer.

- The <u>observed</u> information flow between two processes in session is provided by the rest of the network with the basic property of integrity, sequentiality and flow control as discussed above. This augmented, with the sequential nature of the link itself and local level notification as well as flow control mechanism can therefore result inside the box in keeping the same properties for delivery from/to process:In that case, <u>and if the rest of the network is trusted</u>, the protocol content of the Transport Layer inside the box can be minimal.

- Alternatively one or several of the following cases may happen:

    o The network is not trusted to always notify if delivery is incorrect or absent,

    o The network does not guarantee correct delivery or notification. In particular various desequencing may happen as the result of routing strategies for example. In this case detection mechanism and possibly reordering may be needed.

    o The rate of notification for misdelivery is too high. Depending on the mechanisms the notification could be only indicative of "possible" misdelivery and a better i.e. more selective detection mechanism is appropriate. Or the notification corresponds to reality and a recovery by retransmission is in order to improve the service to the using processes.

In all these cases the functional content of the Transport Layer is richer than in the other category, so that an "adequate" Tranport Service results.

In SNA, Transport Service is provided to the sessions by the Transport Layer like in OSA.

A LINK FLOW
B VIRTUAL ROUTE FLOW
C SESSION FLOW

Figure 2

A LINK FLOW
B VIRTUAL ROUTE FLOW
C SESSION FLOW

Figure 3

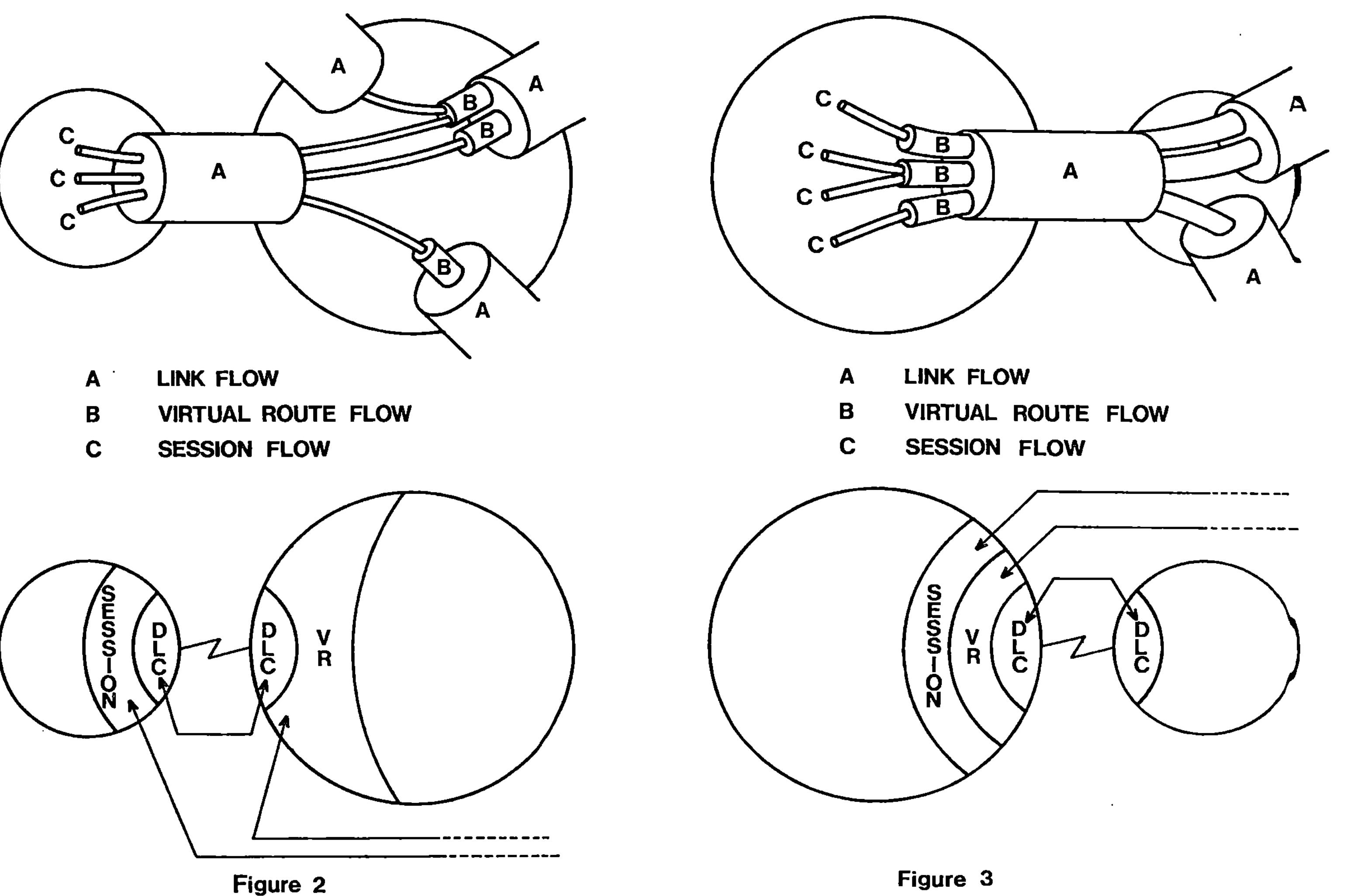

CLUSTER
CONTROLLER
HOSTS
COMMUNICATION
CONTROLLERS
TRANSPORT SERVICE
IS AVAILABLE OUTSIDE
THIS BOUNDARY

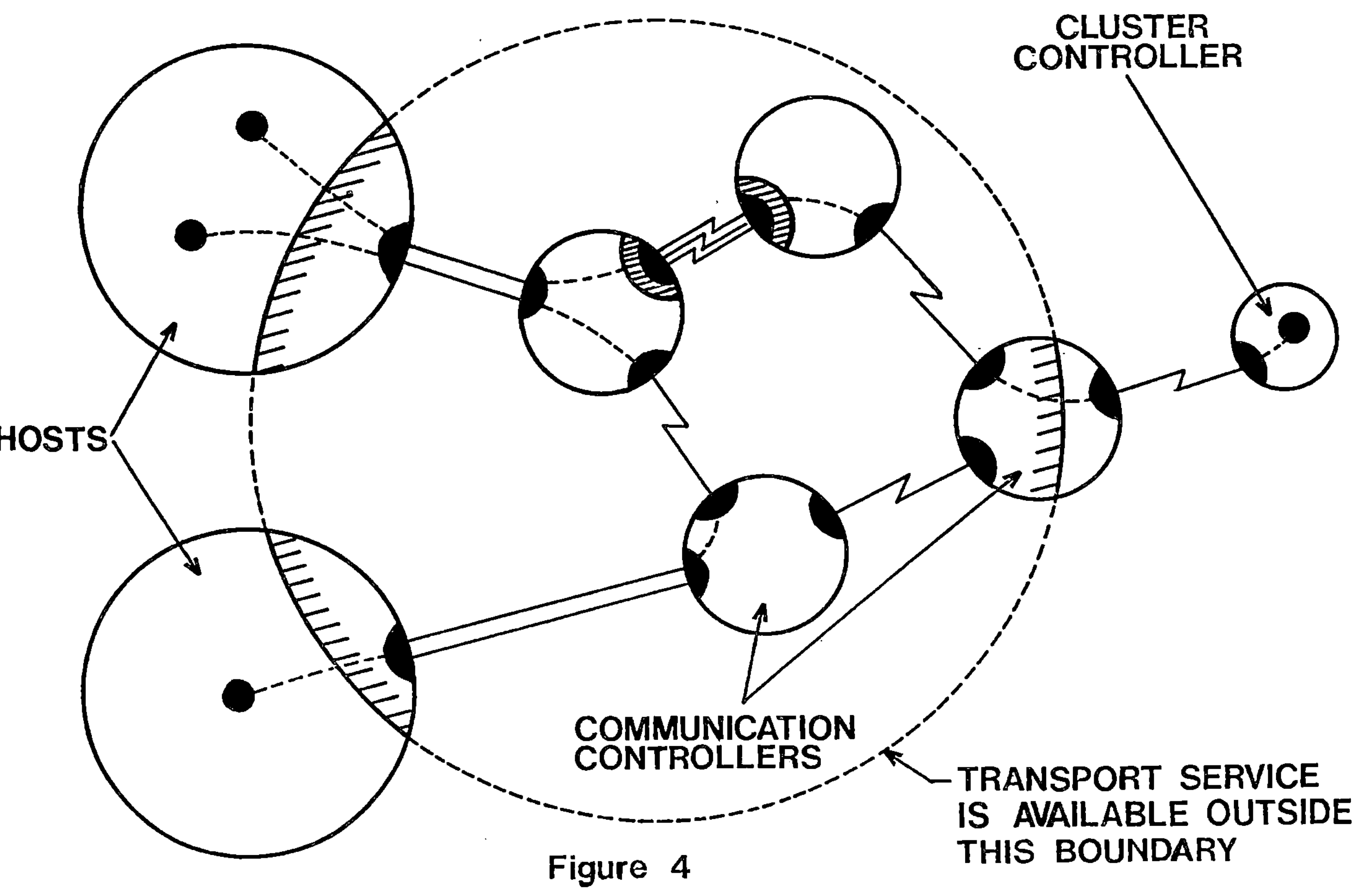

Figure 4

Depending on the type of equipment considered and the type of connection to the rest of the network of that equipment we may find either one of the two cases discussed above and therefore, either the rich functional content Transport Layer protocol which is called the Virtual Route protocol or an empty layer with a richer underneath service resulting from the concatenation of the service on the link with the service of the rest of the network.
See figure 2 and 3 which characterizes attachment of a cluster controller with an empty Transport layer and a host with a Virtual Route.

After this brief survey of Transport Layer let us move to session layer.

Processes communicate to Processes when they are in session. The service provided by the Session Layer essentially allows the using Processes to delimit various units, i.e. to initiate, terminate and (re)synchronize in protocol choice and state variable status, at various level of granularity in term of duration and/or scope of resource and context.

Some process evolution can be simple from reset state to eventually reset state and resynchronization tools may be minimal.

Other processes such as the ones associated with database transactions essentially never return to a reset state (which would correspond to an empty file) and resynchronization back to synch points require more elaborate tools, especially in the case of distributed database.

Similarly to the case of the Transport Layer content, the functional content of the Session Layer may vary, but this time as a function of the richness of services to be supplied to processes, the property of the underlying Transport Service being arbitrarily fixed, whereas in the case of the Transport Layer the different functional content was attributed essentially to different level of services of underneath layer.

Assuming some familiarity of the reader with lower layer functions and multilink protocol we are now in a position to draw an SNA network and observe on figure 4:

o   the different types of connections characteristics corresponding
     to the two categories identified above and the corresponding
     differences in functional content of the Transport Layer.

o   the pairwise matching of protocol layers which always apply even
     if different layers protocol find their counterpart in different
     boxes.

If we neglect this dimension of distribution of the basic model,
which is apparent in SNA, we can build an hypothetical model which
regroups all layers in a system and obtain the equivalence shown in
figure 5.

Figure 5   Control levels of the ISO provisional model and their SNA counterparts

ISO PROVISIONAL MODEL

#	
7	APPLICATION
6	PRESENTATION CONTROL
5	SESSION CONTROL
4	TRANSPORT END TO END CONTROL
3	NETWORK CONTROL
2	LINK CONTROL
1	PHYSICAL CONTROL

SYSTEMS NETWORK ARCHITECTURE

#	
7	END USER
6	PRESENTATION SERVICES
5	SESSION CONTROL
3,4	PATH CONTROL — VIRTUAL ROUTE CTRL / EXPLICIT ROUTING
2	LINK CONTROL
1	PHYSICAL CONTROL

After this rapid survey of SNA, leaving aside important aspects of
network management, network service and data structure models, we
are now in a position to discuss what could happen in the future
when an Open System Architecture becomes a reality in terms of
actual standards of interconnection.

THE PURPOSE OF OSI

A user would expect from an OSI Architecture to be able to
interconnect systems coming from different manufacturers. Stemming
from either a conscious multi-vendor policy or just as a result of
historical evolution the reality of the need cannot be escaped.

Let us assume an environment where a user has a network operating according to architecture A.

Let us assume some other equipment manufacturer has implemented an instance of OSI Architecture in a system B.

Let us assume that the network A is an SNA network, but the reasonning applies as well to any architecture, mutatis mutandis.

It would be sufficient in order to transport information to offer an interface within SNA boundary node which allows to map the OSA session flow onto SNA session flow and then use the SNA network to route informations wherever it is needed. Precisely OSA session could flow, multiplexed with SNA sessions in SNA VR flows, to be transported where is located the receiving partner process. This solution obviously achieves maximum use of preexisting facilities and resource-shares for transportation purpose links and intermediate nodes efficiently.(Figure 6-1).

The next step is just to assume that manufacturer of B, being in the same position, will have provided a similar solution to attach OSA equipments of manufacturer A (or C). (Figure 6-2).

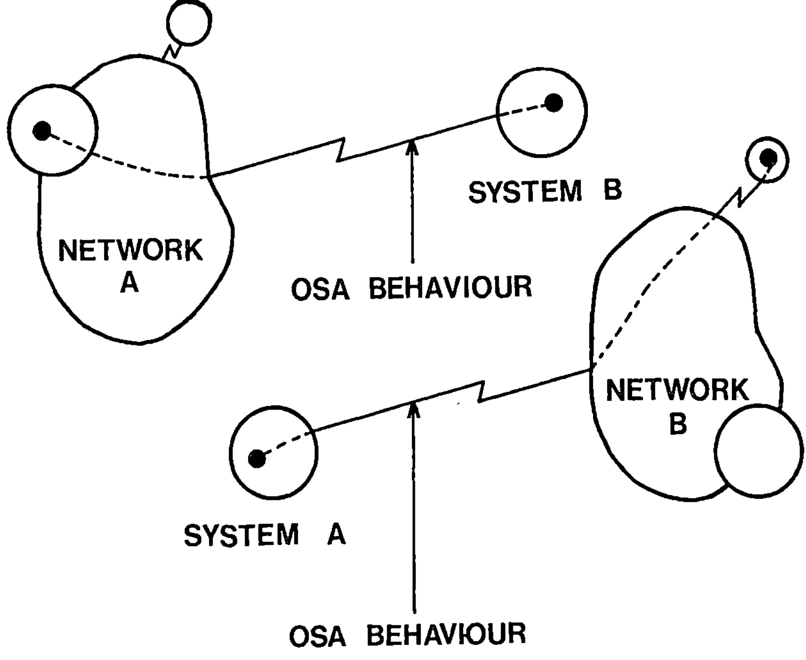

Figure   6

This leads, selecting matching peer level protocols in the session and data structure area to interconnect different manufacturer networks as well as <u>systems to networks</u>. (<u>Figure 7</u>).

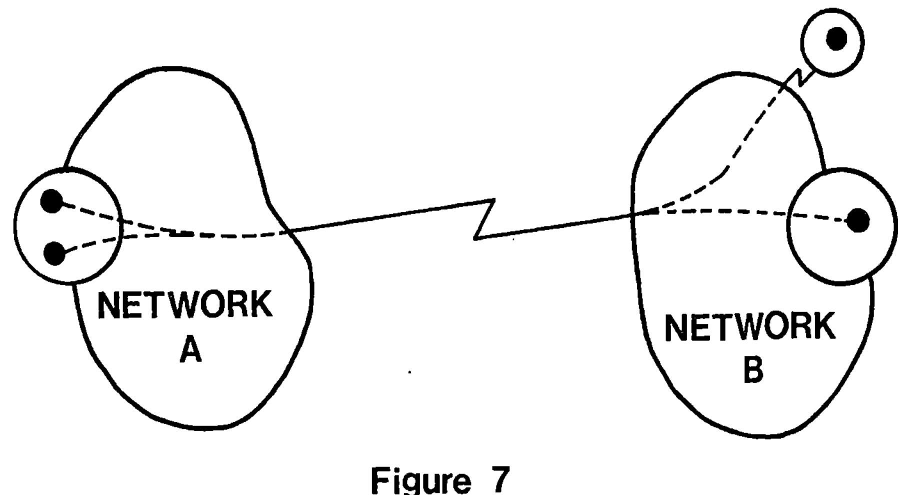

Figure 7

Clearly interconnection type 1 or 2 would be initially of practical interest for terminals whereas approach 3 would be more likely for protocol between hosts, such as File Transfer.

It is very important to realize that by stretching further our model it is possible to transit through intermediate networks of potentially different internal architecture. (Figure 8).

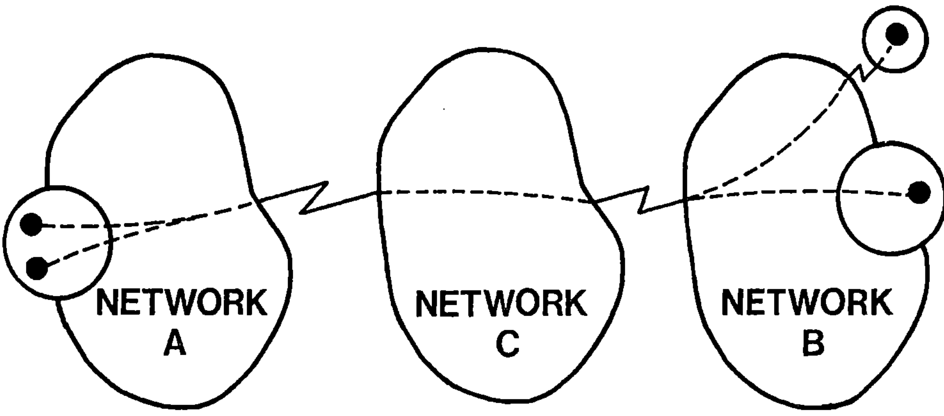

Figure 8

The outlined scenario does not realize a complete interconnectability: Preexisting SNA terminals in network A may not communicate with hosts of network B and the same applies for network B. Despite this restriction, this sort of cohabitation between OSA and non-OSA architecture is likely, not only to be the rule initially, but to continue for various reasons, if only to permit innovation.

This type of scenario implicitly __maps__ or converts essentially and only transportation-types of protocols, in order to iterate the various partial transportation functions to achieve the total process to process transportation.
This means that functional similarity of these protocols levels is needed between all the architectures involved along the path and OSA.

Higher level protocols appear different in that respect. __Mapping__ does not seem to be __needed__ because these OSA protocols could always be implemented directly in the hosting systems without reference to the corresponding protocols of the hosting architecture. Therefore the functional equivalence with the hosting architecture is not a prerequisite for those levels.

The implications of this scenario are multiple and will not be addressed here, except for the following one: The OSI architecture does not need to address internal transportation network protocols. The only definition needed relates to systems interconnected as __end-systems__, thru networks, undefined from their internal routing, flow control, management view point and defined only by the service they provide at their interface.

This aspect is important in as much as it allows OSI to achieve interconnectability without being bogged down in the specifics of internal transportation network mechanisms, where reconciliation of widely opposite technical views is not likely to happen soon.

It is necessary that such view of transportation networks, defined by the service they provide at their interface to end-systems, be extended to cover the case shown on figure 8 which would be a typical environment of two private in-house networks interconnected by a public network: The analogy to the world of telephony where

PABX's of different internal structure (e.g. time division or space division switching) can be interconnected thru a public network shows that this approach is feasible and practical by proper definition of only the interfaces.

CONCLUSION

We hope to have shed some light of SNA structure and function distribution and shown an evolutionary path to the inclusion of OSI eventual architecture in existing architectures.

This evolutive scenario should be a prime consideration in OSI and whenever applicable, be used to guide OSI architecture development.

Die Architektur des Siemens Datenfernverarbeitungs-
systems TRANSDATA im Vergleich zum ISO-Referenz-Modell

Jörg Gonschorek (Siemens AG)

1. Vorbemerkung

Inzwischen ist von dem zuständigen Komitee der Internationalen Organisation für Standardisierung (ISO)
die vierte Version des Referenz Modells für den Offenen
Rechnerverbund (ISO-Referenz-Modell) vorgelegt worden
/1/. Dieses Dokument hat den Status eines " Arbeits-
papiers", d.h. es gibt den momentanen Stand der Arbeiten in dem Komitee wieder. Das Komitee hat im
Juni 1979 dem zuständigen Entscheidungsgremium der
ISO vorgeschlagen, ein Referenz Modell für den Offenen Rechnerverbund zu normen. über diesen Vorschlag
wird im November 1979 entschieden. Die vorliegende
Version des ISO-Referenz-Modells stellt einen bedeu-
tenden Zwischenschritt auf dem Weg zu einer Norm dar.
Die endgültige Erarbeitung der Norm erfordert allerdings die Klärung weiterer wichtiger technischer Fragen, wie sie z.B. in dem vorliegenden ISO-Referenz-
Modell selbst gestellt sind. Die Arbeiten an einer
Norm für ein Referenz Modell für den Offenen Rechnerverbund werden daher zu einer Ausfüllung und Weiter-
schreibung des jetzt vorliegenden Dokumentes führen.

Das Siemens Datenfernverarbeitungssystem TRANSDATA
/2-8/ befindet sich seit mehreren Jahren bei vielen
Installationen im Einsatz. Es durchläuft dabei einen
natürlichen Evolutionsprozeß, um seinen Anwendern
neue Kommunikationsformen und Anwendungsmöglichkeiten

zu erschließen. Die TRANSDATA-Netzarchitektur (NEA)
definiert eine Zielvorstellung, an der sich Produkt-
entwicklungen und Produkterweiterungen ausrichten.

Da wie geschildert das ISO-Referenz-Modell und die
TRANSDATA-Netzarchitektur heute keine statischen Ge-
bilde sind, kann ein Vergleich zwischen ihnen nur im
Groben und nur mit einigen Vorbehalten durchgeführt
werden. Ziel soll dabei nicht sein, nachzuweisen,
daß die TRANSDATA-Netzarchitektur das ISO-Referenz-
Modell antizipiert hat. Dies ist bei genügend ober-
flächlicher Betrachtungsweise immer möglich, da natürlicherweise die auf den ersten sehr groben Blick
identifizierten Kommunikationsfunktionen in jeder
heute für ein Datenfernverarbeitungssystem entwickel-
ten Architektur feststellbar sind.

2. <u>Schichtung als Ordnungsprinzip</u>

Das ISO-Referenz-Modell setzt als Basistechnik zur
Ordnung und Strukturierung der in einem Datenfernverarbeitungssystem notwendigen vielfältigen Funktionen
das Prinzip der Funktionsschichtung ein. Dabei bauen
einzelne Funktionsschichten derart aufeinander auf,
daß jede Funktionsschicht jeweils Dienste der darunter-
liegenden Funktionsschicht in Anspruch nimmt und ihrer-
seits Dienste für die darüberliegende Funktionsschicht
erbringt. In jede Schicht sind zusammengehörige Funktionen eingeordnet. Der gesamte Funktionsumfang wird
dadurch in überschaubare Teile zerlegt, die so voneinander entkoppelt werden, daß immer nur benachbarte Funktionsschichten direkt zusammenarbeiten.

Durch die Zerlegung des Gesamtsystems in Funktionsschichten werden Teilsysteme definiert. Die Teilsysteme werden durch funktionell gleichrangige Instanzen
aufgebaut, die miteinander mittels Protokolle kooperieren. Jedes Teilsystem bietet dem darüber liegenden
Teilsystem Dienste an, die es mittels eigener Funktionen und der Dienste des darunter liegenden Teilsystems erbringt. Die Dienste eines Teilsystems beschreiben ein jeweils eigenes Abstraktionsniveau im Rahmen des
gesamten Problemkomplexes Offener Rechnerverbund.

Ein Kernpunkt bei der Anwendung des Schichtenprinzips
ist die Bestimmung der Anzahl der für ein bestimmtes
System zu verwendenden Funktionsschichten. Ist diese
Anzahl zu klein gewählt, so wird das Ordnungsziel nicht
erreicht, weil einzelne Funktionsschichten nicht zusammengehörige Funktionen enthalten. Ist die Schichtenanzahl zu groß gewählt, so wird das Ordnungsziel sicher
ebenfalls nicht erreicht. Außerdem ist zu beachten,
daß bei wachsender Schichtenanzahl die Nachteile des
Schichtenprinzips stärker in Erscheinung treten.
Nachteile sind vor allem erhöhter Speicherbedarf, erhöhter Bedarf an Rechenzeit, erhöhter Bedarf an Über-
tragungskapazität und damit letztlich insgesamt eine
Verlangsamung der Kommunikation.

Das ISO-Referenz-Modell gibt eine Reihe von Kriterien
zur Schichtenbildung an. Allerdings können diese Kriterien nur eine Richtschnur sein und erlauben keine
formale Lösung des Problems. Letzlich bleibt die
" gute" Schichtung das Werk eines guten Architekten,
das zum großen Teil aus Erfahrung und Intuition ge-
schöpft ist.

3. Vergleich der TRANSDATA-Netzarchitektur mit dem ISO-Schichtenmodell

Das ISO-Referenz-Modell führt auf den ersten Seiten
drei Elemente ein, die es für die Architektur des
Offenen Rechnerverbundes als grundlegend bezeichnet:

" (1) the application processes which exist within
the Open Systems Interconnection environment, (2)
the connections which join the application processes
and permit them to exchange information, and (3)
systems" .

Diesen Elementen entsprechen in der TRANSDATA-Netzarchitektur die Kommunikationsanwendung, die logischen Verbindungen und die Prozessorknoten. Die
Kommunikationsanwendungen repräsentieren die Benutzer
gegenüber dem Datenfernverarbeitungssystem, die logischen Verbindungen ordnen sie einander zu und ermöglichen dadurch die Kommunikation und die Prozessorknoten bezeichnen die physikalischen Einheiten, in
denen die Kommunikationsanwendungen residieren. Die
Begriffe system (deutsch: System) und Prozessorknoten
umfassen dabei einen oder mehrere Rechner mit der
zugehörigen Software, den pheripheren Geräten, Daten-
stationen, menschlichen Operateuren, usw., die in
der Lage sind, selbständig Information zu verarbeiten.
Bild 1, das aus dem ISO-Referenz-Modell entnommen ist,
stellt den Zusammenhang zwischen den drei Elementen
dar.

Bild 2 vergleicht die Funktionsschichten des ISO-
Referenz-Modells mit der Funktionsschichtung der
TRANSDATA-Netzarchitektur. Das Modell eines Daten-
fernverarbeitungssystems zerfällt bei beiden in zwei
große Teilbereiche, nämlich in den Bereich der Transportfunktionen und den Bereich der anwendungsorien-

tierten Funktionen. Beide Bereiche werden in den
beiden folgenden Abschnitten getrennt behandelt.

Im Datenfernverarbeitungssystem TRANSDATA werden so weit
vorhanden, international bzw. national genormte Protokolle verwendet und unterstützt /9/ . Für die
Funktionsbereiche, in denen keine Normen existieren,
wurden eigene Protokolle, die NEA-Protokolle, definiert. Im folgenden Vergleich werden die verwendeten
standardisierten Protokolle angegeben und die NEA-
Protokolle kurz erläutert (Bild 3).

3.1   Transportfunktionen

Das ISO-Referenz-Modell unterteilt den Transportbereich in vier Schichten während die TRANSDATA-Netzarchitektur dafür drei Schichten verwendet.

Die beiden jeweils untersten Schichten, Physical und
Link Layer bei ISO und Physical Service und Portservice bei TRANSDATA, sind hinsichtlich ihrer funktionellen Ausführung bei beiden Modellen sehr ähnlich
definiert. Der Physical Layer legt die mechanischen
und elektrischen Eigenschaften und die Signalisie-
rungsfunktionen fest, um physikalische Leitungen zwischen zwei Systemen bzw. Prozessorknoten aufzubauen,
zu betreiben und abzubauen. Der Link Layer enthält
die Funktionen zur Übertragung von Daten über eine
Leitung zwischen zwei Systemen bzw. Prozessorknoten.

Festlegungen für den Physical Layer bzw. Physical Service werden von den im CCITT zusammengeschlossenen
Postverwaltungen getroffen, bekannte Beispiele sind
die Empfehlungen V.24 und X.21. In der Bundesrepublik

Deutschland sind die zu verwendenden Protokolle und
Schnittstellen durch die Fernmeldedienste der Deutschen
Bundespost festgelegt und werden von TRANSDATA unterstützt /9/. Ein Beispiel für ein Protokoll des Data
Link Layers bzw. Portservice ist die von ISO entwickel-
ten High Level Data Link Control (HDLC) Prozedur.
Die HDLC Prozedur wird in TRANSDATA in der "balanced"
und "unbalanced" Variante verwendet. Für die Kanalkopplung wird wegen der hier vorhandenen hohen Über-
tragungssicherheit ein einfaches, eigenes Protokoll
benutzt (NEALK).

Im oberen Transportbereich unterscheidet das ISO-
Referenz-Modell zwei Funktionsschichten, nämlich
Network Layer und Transport Layer, während die TRANS-
DATA-Netzarchitektur hier nur eine Funktionsschicht,
den Transportservice vorsieht. Der Network Layer
stellt i.w. Funktionen bereit, um Daten durch ein Netz
zwischen den Endsystemen zu vermitteln, während der
Transport Layer für den zuverlässigen und kostengün-
stigen Datentransport zwischen den Endbenutzern, den
application processes, sorgt. Beide Funktionsbereiche
sind bei TRANSDATA im Transportservice zusammengefaßt.
Während das ISO-Referenz-Modell entsprechend den Regeln des allgemeinen Schichtenmodells Netzverbindungen
und Transportverbindungen unterscheidet, kennt die
TRANSDATA-Netzarchitektur im Transportservice nur den
Begriff der logischen Verbindung. Eine solche logische
Verbindung verknüpft die beiden letztlich kommunizierenden Partner, die Kommunikationsanwendungen.
Transportverbindung und logische Verbindung können
funktionell gleichgesetzt werden.

Die Definition der Dienste von Transport Layer und
Transportservice zielt in beiden Fällen darauf ab,

von den spezifischen Eigenheiten eines gegebenen Daten-
transportsystems unabhängige allgemeine Transportdienste
zur Verfügung zu stellen.

Ein Beispiel für ein Protokoll des Network Layers ist
das Protokoll der Paketebene der CCITT-Empfehlung X.25.
Für den Anschluß an öffentliche Paketvermittlungsnetze
wird diese Empfehlung im Datenfernverarbeitungssystem
TRANSDATA unterstützt. Da Normen für den Funktionsbe-
reich des Transportservice fehlen, wurden dafür eigene
NEA-Protokolle entwickelt: NEATT, NEATV, NEATD (Bild 3).
Das Protokoll NEATT dient der Vermittlung der Daten im
Netz und dem Datentransport zwischen Kommunikationsanwendungen. Das Protokoll NEATV regelt den Aufbau, Abbau und die Verwaltung von logischen Verbindungen.
Das Protokoll NEATD ermöglicht eine gezielte Datenfluß-
regelung zwischen benachbarten Prozessorknoten.

3.2 Anwendungsorientierte Funktionen

Den Bereich der anwendungsorientierten Funktionen teilt
das ISO-Referenz-Modell in drei Funktionsschichten ein.
Der Session Layer beinhaltet grundlegende Kommunikationsfunktionen. Dazu zählen z.B. der Aufbau, Abbau und die
Verwaltung von "sessions" , einfache Datenstrukturie-
rungsfunktionen und die Steuerung des Dialogs. Der zentrale Begriff des Presentation Layers ist das "presentation image". Damit verbunden ist die Erzeugung,
Veränderung und Verwaltung von virtuellen Datenstrukturen. Zusätzlich werden Datentransformationen im
Presentation Layer angesiedelt. Der Application Layer
schließlich enthält die Benutzeranwendungen und Anwendungen zur Administration des Offenen Rechnerverbundes
und der Benutzeranwendungen.

Für den Bereich der anwendungsorientierten Funktionen
sind derzeit keine ISO-Protokolle definiert. Die CCITT-
Empfehlungen X.3, X.28 und X.29 können dem Presentation
Layer zugerechnet werden.

Die TRANSDATA Netzarchitektur führt oberhalb des Bereichs der Transportfunktionen keine weitere strenge
Schichtung durch. Dies resultiert aus der Erkenntnis,
daß oberhalb des Transportbereichs funktionell durchaus
unterschiedliche Anwendungsbereiche festzustellen sind.
Die funktionelle Varianz ist dabei so groß, daß die Architektur des Bereichs der anwendungsorientierten Funktionen eine flexible Zusammenstellung von Funktionsgrup-
pen für einen spezifischen Anwendungsbereich ermöglichen
muß. Dies ist durch ein streng und formal angewendetes
Schichtenprinzip nicht erreichbar. Natürlicherweise
sind auch im Datenfernverarbeitungssystem TRANSDATA
Funktionen entsprechend Session, Presentation und Application Layer festellbar. Dabei ist auch eine gewisse
" Schichtung" zu erkennen.

Die TRANSDATA-Netzarchitektur unterteilt den Bereich der
anwendungsorientierten Funktionen in Benutzerservice-
Funktionen und eigentliche Benutzer-Funktionen. Diese
Unterteilung soll die Unterscheidung von Basisdiensten,
die vom Hersteller geliefert werden, und Funktionen, die
vom Anwender zu programmieren sind, ermöglichen. Die
Grenze zwischen diesen Bereichen ist produktspezifisch
und Änderungen im Zuge der Erweiterung der Systemdienste
unterworfen. Sie ist daher in Bild 1 gestrichelt ein-
gezeichnet.

Der Begriff der Kommunikationsanwendung in der TRANSDATA-
Netzarchitektur wurde bereits eingeführt. Eine Kommunikationsanwendung repräsentiert gegenüber dem Datenfern-

verarbeitungssystem den Endbenutzer, also z.B. ein Benutzer- oder Systemprogramm oder auch einen Datenstationsbenutzer. Die Kommunikationsanwendungen kommunizieren miteinander mittels logischer Verbindungen, die vom Transport Service aufgebaut, verwaltet und abgebaut werden. Kommunikationsanwendungen sind Prozessorknoten zugeordnet. Die Prozessorknoten stellen Instanzen des Transportsystems dar. Jede Kommunikationsanwendung ist durch ihren Anwendungsnamen im Namensraum eines Prozessorknotens eindeutig identifiziert (Bild 4).

Kommunikationsanwendungen können vordefiniert und weitgehend vorgefertigt sein, wie z.B. die Kommunikationsanwendungen TIAM und UTM als Teilnehmer- bzw. Transaktionssystem im BS2000 oder vom Anwender unter Verwendung der Programmschnittstelle IDCAM selbst definiert werden. Bild 5 zeigt am Beispiel der BS2000 Kommunikationsanwendungen als Benutzer des Transportservice.

Wie geschildert führt die TRANSDATA-Netzarchitektur im Bereich der anwendungsorientierten Funktionen eine anwendungsbezogene Strukturierung durch. Dies darf nicht zu einem Wildwuchs von Benutzerservice-Protokollen führen. Es muß daher von vornherein eine sinnvolle Strukturierung der Benutzerservice-Protokolle durchgeführt werden. So können z.B. Funktionen, die von vielen Kommunikationsanwendungen benötigt werden in einem einheitlichen Protokoll zur Verfügung gestellt werden. Die Abhandlung dieses Protokolls kann auch durch Systemsoftware unterstützt werden. Dies führt nicht zwangsläufig zu einer strengen Schichtung wie im ISO-Referenz-Modell vorgesehen.

Der Benutzerservice der TRANSDATA-Netzarchitektur verwendet die NEA-Protokolle NEABV, NEABT, NEABR und

RSPOOL2 (Bild 3). NEAVB ermöglicht den Kommunikationsanwendungen abzusprechen, welches Benutzerservice-Pro-
tokoll in ihrer Kommunikation verwendet werden soll
und ihre eigenen Charakteristika auszutauschen. Die
Protokollelemente von NEAVB werden 'huckepack' mit Pro-
tokollelementen von NEATV transportiert. NEAVB muß
zwangsläufig bei jedem Aufbau einer logischen Verbindung
verwendet werden. Die übrigen Benutzerservice-Protokolle
dienen der Abwicklung der Kooperation zwischen den Kommunikationsanwendungen. NEABT beinhaltet Funktionen zur
Dialogsteuerung und zum Betrieb von Dialog-Datenstationen
und wird von TIAM, DCAM- und UTM-Kommunikationsanwendun-
gen verwendet. NEABR wird nur von der Kommunikationsanwendung RBAM zum Betrieb von Stapel-Datenstationen verwendet. RSPOOL2 ist ein Protokoll zur Übertragung von
Dateien und wird hauptsächlich vom Betriebssystem BS1000
und zur Kopplung der Betriebssysteme BS1000, BS2000 und
BS300 eingesetzt. Weitere Benutzerservice-Protokolle
sind in der Entwicklung.

4.   Zusammenfassung und Bewertung

Die Architektur des Transportsystems ist bei der TRANS-
DATA-Netzarchitektur und im ISO-Referenz-Modell sehr
ähnlich. Beide verwenden das Schichtenprinzip zur Ordnung der Funktionen und Protokolle. Das ISO-Referenz-
Modell schichtet im oberen Bereich das Transportsystem
feiner, indem es Network und Transport Layer unterscheidet. Diese Unterscheidung wird in der TRANSDATA-
Netzarchitektur heute nicht durchgeführt.

Die Unterschiede in der Architektur der anwendungsorientierten Funktionen erscheinen wesentlicher. Während das
ISO-Referenz-Modell auch hier eine Schichtung in Session,

Presentation und Application Layer vornimmt, faßt die
TRANSDATA-Netzarchitektur die Funktionen des Session
Layers, Presentation Layers und auch teilweise des
Application Layers in einer Protokollschicht, dem
Benutzerservice, zusammen. In dieser Schicht können
unterschiedliche funktionsorientierte Protokolle ab-
laufen, welche die für die ISO-Schichten vorgesehenen
Funktionen abdecken.

In der TRANSDATA-Netzarchitektur existiert oberhalb des
Transportsystems nur noch eine Schicht gleichrangiger
kommunizierender Instanzen. In diesen Instanzen kann
eine Funktionsgruppierung ähnlich zum ISO-Referenz-
Modell festgestellt werden (Bild 6). Die weitere Aus-
arbeitung des ISO-Referenz-Modells wird ein besseres
Verständnis der Bedeutung und des Zusammenhangs der anwendungsorientierten Funktionsschichten ergeben.

Insgesamt gesehen ist zwischen TRANSDATA-Netzarchitektur
und ISO-Referenz-Modell, im Rahmen der vorliegenden Definitionen der beiden Architekturen, eine gute struktu-
relle Kompatibilität festzustellen.

Literatur

/1/   Reference Model of Open Systems Inter-
        connection, ISO/TC97/SC16/N227,
        Juni 1979

/2/   TRANSDATA Datenfernverarbeitung, Rechner-
        netze Einführung, SIEMENS AG,
        Bestell-Nr. D12/2105-01

/3/   Datenfernverarbeitung mit TRANSDATA -
        Eine Übersicht, SIEMENS AG
        Bestell-Nr. D12/2104-01

/4/   TRANSDATA Datenfernverarbeitung, Daten-
        übertragungszugriffs-System DCM, Kurz-
        beschreibung, SIEMENS AG
        Bestell-Nr. D12/3206-01

/5/   TRANSDATA Datenfernverarbeitung mit BS2000,
        Allgemeine Beschreibung, SIEMENS AG
        Bestell-Nr. D12/2095-01

/6/   TRANSDATA - einheitliches DFV-System bis
        zum Rechnernetz, J. Feldmann, P. Jilek,
        und R. Nowak, Online-adl-nachrichten,
        10/77, S.794-800.

/7/   Datenfernverarbeitung mit TRANSDATA,
        R. Nowak; telecom report 1/1978, S.9-14.

/8/   Die sieben Häute eines Netzwerkes, R. Nowak,
        Computer Magazin, 3/79, S.74-76 u. 4/79
        S.76-77.

/9/   Einbau öffentlicher Fernmeldedienste in
        TRANSDATA-Kommunikationssysteme, W. v. Pattay,
        telecom report 2/1979, S.166-173.

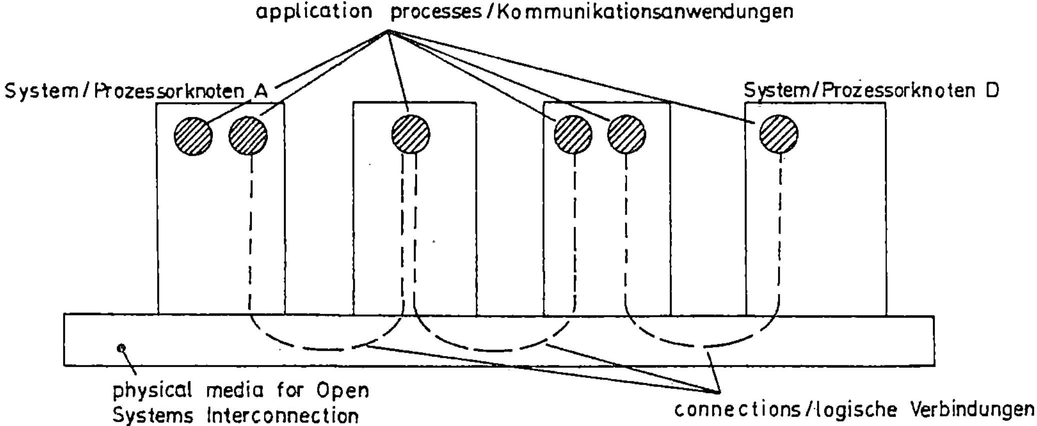

Bild 1: Die drei Basiselemente des offenen Rechnerverbundes

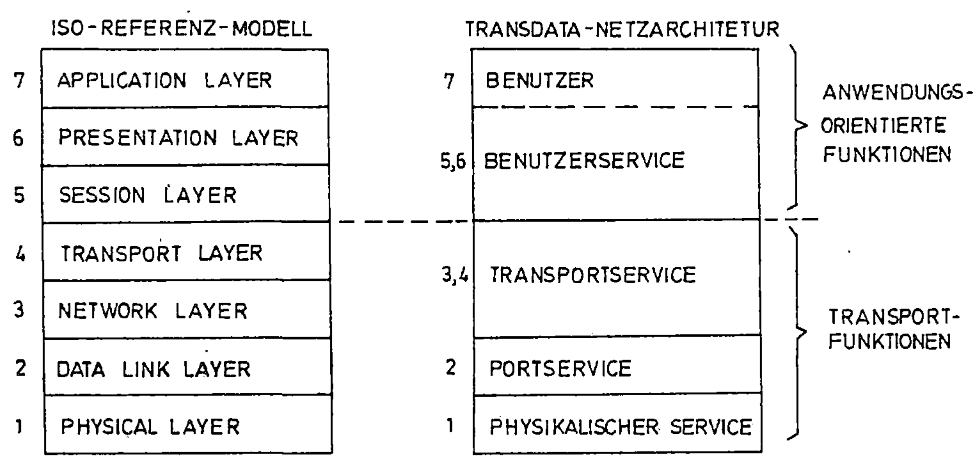

Bild 2: Funktionenschichtung des ISO-Referenz-Modells
und der TRANSDATA-Netzarchitektur

BENUTZERSERVICE:

NEABV   : NEA-Benutzerdienst-Verbindungsprotokoll
NEABT   : TIAM-Benutzerdienstprotokoll
NEABR   : RBAM-Benutzerdienstprotokoll
RSPOOL2: RSPOOL2-Benutzerdienstprotokoll

TRANSPORTSERVICE:

NEATT   : NEA-Transportprotokoll
NEATV   : NEA-Verbindungsprotokoll
NEATD   : NEA-Datenflußsteuerungsprotokoll

PORTSERVICE:

NEALK   : NEA-Linkprotokoll für Kanalkopplung
HDLC   : High Level Data Link Control
          Procedure, Balanced und Unbalanced,
          gemäß ISO-Standards

PHYSIKALISCHER SERVICE:

V- und X-Schnittstellen gemäß entsprechenden
CCITT-Empfehlungen, z.B. V.24, X.21

Bemerkung: Die CCITT-Empfehlungen X.25 und X.29
           werden für den Anschluß an Paketver-
           mittlungsnetze unterstützt.

Bild 3:   Im Datenfernverarbeitungssystem TRANSDATA
           verwendete wichtige Protokolle und Schnitt-
           stellen.

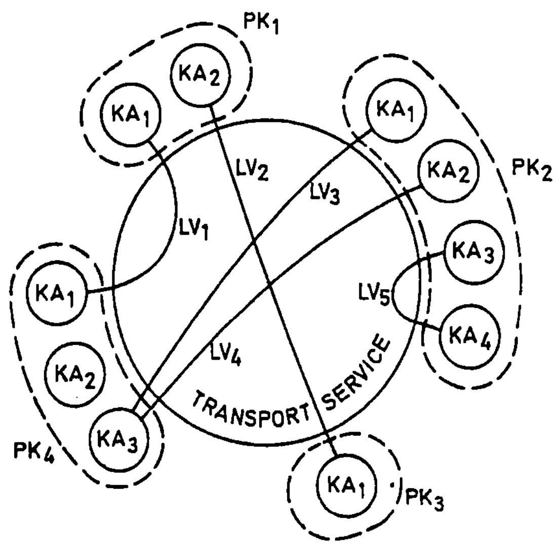

PK: Prozessorknoten

KA: Kommunikationsanwendung

LV: Logische Verbindung

Bild 4:   Das Kommunikationsmodell an der Transportschnittstelle

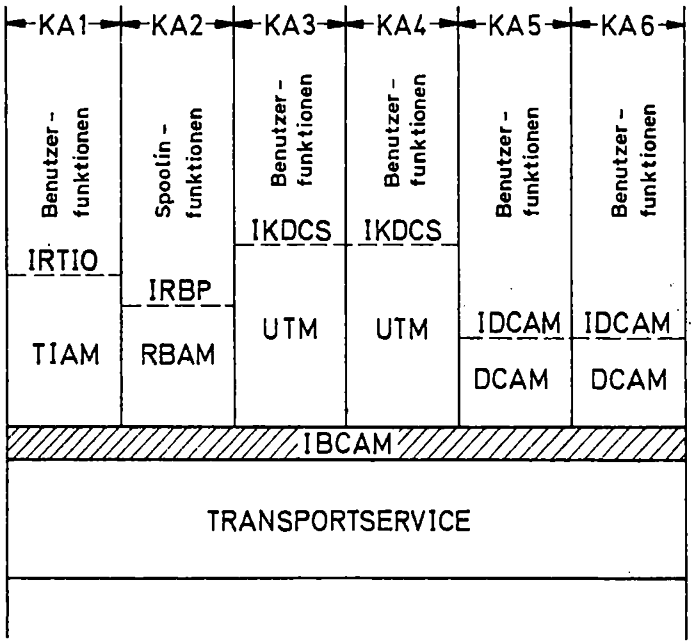

TIAM (Terminal Interactive Access Method): Zugriffsmethode für
den Teilnehmerbetrieb mit der Teilnehmerschnittstelle IRTIO.

RBAM (Remote Batch Access Method): Zugriffsmethode für den
Fernstapelbetrieb mit der Benutzerschnittstelle IRBP.

UTM (Universeller Transaktionsmonitor): Zugriffsmethode für den
Transaktionsbetrieb mit der Transaktionsschnittstelle IKDCS
(Interface kompatible Schnittstelle für Datenkommunikations-
systeme).

DCAM (Data Communication Access Method): Zugriffsmethode für den
Teilhaberbetrieb mit der Teilhaberschnittstelle IDCAM.

IBCAM (Interface Basic Communication Access Method):
Transportschnittstelle des BS 2000

KA: Kommunikationsanwendung

Bild 5: Kommunikationsanwendungen als Benutzer des
Transportservice im BS 2000

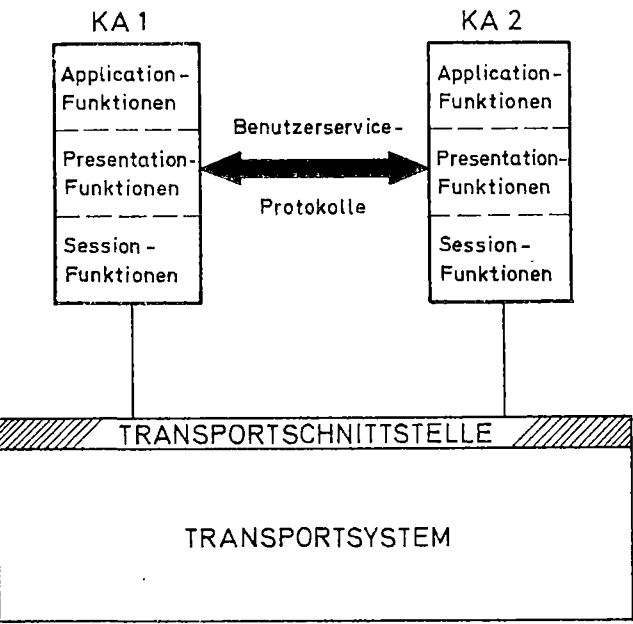

KA: Kommunikationsanwendung.

Bild 6: Darstellung der Struktur der anwendungs-
orientierten Funktionen der TRANSDATA-
Netzarchitektur unter Verwendung der
Schichtenbegriffe des ISO-Referenz-Modells

Öffnung homogener geschlossener Herstellernetze im Sinne des ISO-Referenzmodells, am
Beispiel von SNATCH, einem Funktionsverbund zwischen Siemens- TRANSDATA- und IBM-SNA-
Rechnernetzen

Gerhard Glas, DFVLR Rechenzentrum
Dr. Dietrich Lode, Siemens AG, z. Z. DFVLR

1. Einführung

Für die Kopplung von Systemen verschiedener Hersteller in einem heterogenen Netz gibt
es bis heute noch keine Standardlösung. Wesentliche nationale und internationale Normen stehen noch aus (Protokolle oberhalb von Level 3 des ISO-Referenzmodells für offene Systeme), während bereits bestehende Normen von den Herstellern noch nicht implementiert oder so in die eigenen Systeme integriert wurden, daß die Kommunikation mit
Fremdsystemen nicht möglich ist.

Für homogene Netze gibt es herstellerspezifische De-Facto-Normen, die alle Protokolle
einschließlich des Levels 7 des ISO-Referenzmodells umfassen. Die normierende Wirkung
dieser Protokolle ist aber zunächst auf den Verbund von Systemen eines Herstellers beschränkt. Sie führen damit zu geschlossenen Netzen. Ein wichtiger Aspekt beim Aufbau
von heterogenen Rechnernetzen ist deshalb die Öffnung der homogenen geschlossenen Herstellernetze im Sinne des ISO-Referenzmodells.

Eine Annäherung der verschiedenen Netzarchitekturen und damit eine Öffnung der Netze
ist langfristig nur auf der Basis von Normen zu erwarten. Für die nähere Zukunft kann
der Anwender daher nur von den derzeit durch die Hersteller angebotenen Produkten ausgehen. Änderungen dieser Produkte mit dem Ziel, Inkompatibilitäten aufzuheben, erscheinen nicht sinnvoll, solange genormte Schnittstellen für offene Systeme fehlen. Es muß
daher untersucht werden, ob die Öffnung der homogenen Netze auch dann möglich ist,
wenn die Produkte der Hersteller unverändert eingesetzt werden.

Das im Rahmen dieses Vortrags vorgestellte Projekt löst diese Aufgabe für zwei wichtige Hersteller-Netzarchitekturen, nämlich für Systems Network Architecture (SNA) von
IBM und für TRANSDATA von Siemens.

2. Das Projekt SNA and TRANSDATA Coupling of Hosts (SNATCH)

2.1 Zielsetzung

Das Rechenzentrum der DFVLR betreibt zur Zeit in den fünf DFVLR-Forschungszentren die folgenden DV-Systeme:

Braunschweig:	Siemens 7760 mit BS 2000
Göttingen:	IBM/370 Modell 158 mit MVS Release 3.7
Köln:	Siemens 7760 mit BS 2000
Oberpfaffenhofen:	Amdahl 470 V/6 mit MVS Release 3.7
	IBM/3032 mit MVS Release 3.7
Stuttgart:	Siemens 7760 mit BS 2000

Es ist beabsichtigt, diese Systeme zu einem heterogenen Rechnernetz zu verbinden. Damit soll in jedem der Forschungszentren das Leistungsspektrum aller Systeme verfügbar gemacht werden.

Unter einem Rechnernetz wird hier ein benutzergesteuerter Funktionsverbund im folgenden Sinne verstanden:

- wahlweiser Zugriff auf verschiedene Host-Systeme im Dialogbetrieb;
- wahlweiser Zugriff auf verschiedene Host-Systeme im RJE-Betrieb;
- Bereitstellung einer allgemeinen - allerdings jeweils herstellerspezifischen - Schnittstelle für die Kommunikation zwischen Programmen im gleichen oder in verschiedenen Host-Systemen. Bei diesen Programmen kann es sich auch um vom Hersteller gelieferte Subsysteme (z.B. TP-Monitore) handeln.

Damit können sowohl Geräte mit ihren Bedienern als auch Programme und Subsysteme als Endbenutzer des Netzes auftreten.

Dieser Funktionsverbund ist einerseits ein Geräteverbund. Damit ist gemeint, daß der Anwender an seinem Terminal im Dialog- und im Stapelbetrieb zu verschiedenen Verarbeitungssystemen und deren Anwendungen zugreifen kann. Andererseits erlaubt das Netz auch die Kommunikation zwischen Endteilnehmern in den Hosts und damit die Dezentralisierung von Funktionen und Daten.

Im einzelnen soll das heterogene DFVLR-Rechnernetz die folgenden Leistungen erbringen:

(1) Programm-Programm-Kommunikation über die VTAM- und DCAM-Benutzer-Schnittstellen;
(2) Dialogverkehr von ausgewählten Siemens-Terminals mit den IBM-Subsystemen TSO und IMS;

(3) Dialogverkehr von ausgewählten IBM-Terminals mit dem Siemens-Subsystem TIAM;

(4) RJE-Betrieb von ausgewählten Siemens-Stapelstationen mit dem IBM-Subsystem JES2;

(5) RJE-Betrieb von ausgewählten IBM-Stapelstationen mit dem Siemens-Subsystem RBAM;

(6) Weiterleitung von Jobs, die durch das IBM-Subsystem JES2/NJE gespoolt werden, an das Siemens-Subsystem RBAM.

Unter ausgewählten Geräten sind hier bestimmte Gerätetypen zu verstehen.

Eine Projektgruppe aus DFVLR- und Siemens-Mitarbeitern erarbeitete bis Mitte 1979 ein Konzept für die Realisierung des heterogenen DFVLR-Rechnernetzes. Da dieses Konzept von den Netzwerkarchitekturen der beiden am Netz beteiligten Hersteller - SNA bei IBM und TRANSDATA bei Siemens - ausgeht, erhielt das Projekt den Namen "SNA and TRANSDATA Coupling of Hosts" (SNATCH).

2.2 Das Lösungskonzept

Die Hersteller der am DFVLR-Netz beteiligten DV-Systeme, IBM und Siemens, bieten Hard- und Software an, mit der ihre eigenen Produkte zu homogenen geschlossenen Netzen verbunden werden können. Diese homogenen Netze erlauben einen benutzergesteuerten Funktionsverbund im Sinne von 2.1.

Ziel des DFVLR-Projekts ist es, den Funktionsverbund für die homogenen Netze auf ein heterogenes Netz zu erweitern.

Dazu werden die Systeme beider Hersteller jeweils zu einem homogenen herstellerspezifischen Teilnetz zusammengeschlossen, d. h. die IBM-Systeme zu einem SNA-Netz und die Siemens-Systeme zu einem TRANSDATA-Netz. Die beiden Teilnetze werden über ein Abbildungssystem gleichberechtigt miteinander zu einem Gesamtnetz verbunden (Bild 1). Dieses Abbildungssystem besitzt die Funktion eines Gateways und bildet damit einen Kanal zwischen den beiden geschlossenen Herstellernetzen.

Jedes Teilnetz sieht das Abbildungssystem und das andere Teilnetz als Fortsetzung des jeweiligen herstellerspezifischen homogenen Netzes. D. h. konkret:

- Das TRANSDATA-Teilnetz wird als weiteres SNA-Teilnetz mit Domains, Subareas und Logical Units betrachtet. Der Abbildungsprozessor wird über eine Cross Domain-Leitung angeschlossen und steht damit an Stelle eines Communication Controllers 3705.
- Das SNA-Teilnetz wird als weiteres TRANSDATA-Teilnetz mit Regionen, Prozessoren und Stationen aufgefaßt. Als Nachbarknoten wird im fremden Teilnetz ein Kommunikationsrechner TRANSDATA 96xx erwartet.

Nur die Software im Gateway hat Kenntnis davon, daß auf der einen Seite ein TRANSDATA-Netz und auf der anderen Seite ein SNA-Netz angeschlossen sind.

Das Abbildungssystem muß die Protokolle des einen Netzes in die Protokolle des anderen Netzes in beiden Richtungen umsetzen.

Wesentliche Schritte sind dabei:

- Die Umsetzung der Protokolle der Transportsysteme (ISO-Referenzmodell bis einschließlich Level 4) in beiden Richtungen und darauf aufbauend
- die Umsetzung der Protokolle der höheren, verarbeitungsorientierten Schichten, die - zum Teil außerhalb der Architekturen - von Geräten und Software-Subsystemen benutzt werden. (Nach dem Verbindungsaufbau verwendet der Terminalbediener für den Abruf von Leistungen allerdings die Sprache des Zielsystems; d. h., daß z. B. die Job Control Language nicht umgesetzt wird).

Die folgenden Überlegungen führten zu dem Lösungsansatz, die homogenen Netze über eine Abbildungsfunktion miteinander zu verbinden:

<u>Symmetrie des Verbundes</u>

Der Verbund soll symmetrisch sein, d. h. ohne Einschränkung der jeweiligen Netzarchitektur sollen alle am Verbund teilnehmenden Rechner (Hosts), Benutzerstationen (Terminals) und Subsysteme (Applications) gleichberechtigt am Verbund teilnehmen können.

Mit dem häufig verwendeten Verfahren der Nachbildung von Geräteschnittstellen anderer Hersteller können fremde Host-Rechner immer nur als Geräte oder Geräte-Cluster angesprochen werden. Damit ist diese Schnittstelle weder für den <u>wechselseitigen</u> Zugriff von Geräten auf Host-Systeme noch für die Kommunikation zwischen Anwenderprogrammen in den Hosts geeignet. Das Verfahren scheidet deshalb aus.

<u>Keine Systemänderungen</u>

Die Betriebssysteme der Hosts und die Systeme der Kommunikationsrechner (Front-End-Rechner und Netzknotenrechner), insbesondere die Zugriffsmethoden für die Datenfernübertragung, sollen nicht geändert werden. Erst dadurch wird das Software-Maintenance-Problem für das heterogene Netz langfristig lösbar.

Eine Alternative zu der Gateway-Lösung, die scheinbar die gleiche Forderung erfüllt, wäre der Einsatz von Relaisprogrammen in den Hosts. Solche Relaisprogramme können untereinander kommunizieren, indem sie oberhalb der Herstellerarchitekturen (auf dem

Application Level) eigene herstellerunabhängige Protokolle verwenden. Ein Nachteil der Methode ist der große Overhead, der aus zwei Gründen entsteht:

- Die Kommunikation zwischen einem Terminal und einer Anwendung muß über das Relais-programm des Hosts laufen, der das Terminal verwaltet.
- Oberhalb der Herstellerprotokolle werden nochmals eigene Protokolle eingesetzt, die die ISO-Level 3 bis 7 umfassen.

Schwerer wiegt jedoch, daß in der Regel geeignete Schnittstellen für die Kommunikation mit den Herstellersubsystemen fehlen, deren sich die Relaisprogramme bedienen könnten (man denke an TSO und JES bei IBM oder an RBAM bei Siemens), und daß es Anpassungs-schwierigkeiten an der Transportschnittstelle zum Netz gibt. Beides muß zwangsläufig zu Änderungen in der Software des Herstellers führen. Auch dieses Verfahren scheidet deshalb aus.

Konzentration der Anpassungssoftware

Die Software für die Kopplung der homogenen Netze kann in einem Siemens-TRANSDATA-Rechner implementiert werden. Sie kann dort unter Verwendung von Anwenderschnittstel-len in ein sonst unmodifiziertes System DNSP (Datenübertragungs- und Netzsteuerpro-gramm) eingebettet werden. Systemänderungen sind deshalb nicht erforderlich. Außerdem wird der bei der Methode der Relaisprogramme notwendige Umweg über die Hosts vermie-den.

Einsatz bei anderen Anwendern

Das Gesamtnetz einschließlich des Gateway muß durch Generierung konfigurierbar sein. Damit ist die Abbildungssoftware auf andere gleichartige Anwendungsfälle direkt über-tragbar.

Erweiterbarkeit

Die herstellerspezifischen Protokolle können über neutrale Schnittstellen umgesetzt werden. Als Basis zur Beschreibung und zur Realisierung solcher Schnittstellen wird das PIX-Modell dienen. Damit wird die Lösung erweiterbar:

- Die Abbildungssoftware kann auf zwei Prozessoren verteilt werden. Damit kann zwischen den homogenen Netzen als Transportsystem ein Paketvermittlungsnetz (X.25) eingesetzt werden.
- Der Anschluß weiterer Hersteller ist möglich.

2.3 Design des Gateway

Im Gateway zwischen dem SNA- und dem TRANSDATA-Teilnetz gibt es zwei Umsetzungsfunktionen (Bild 2):

- Das SNA-Anpassungs-Subsystem (SAS) für die Umsetzung zwischen SNA-Protokollen und neutralen Protokollen und
- das TRANSDATA-Anpassungs-Subsystem (TAS) für die Umsetzung zwischen TRANSDATA-Protokollen und neutralen Protokollen.

Die Einbettung dieser Umsetzungsfunktionen in das DNSP eines TRANSDATA-Rechners ist bei ausschließlicher Verwendung von Anwenderschnittstellen auf folgende Weise möglich:

- Das DNSP und damit die Transportsteuerung des DNSP erhält durch Generierung Kenntnis von allen Prozessoren in den beiden Teilnetzen. Die Prozessoren im SNA-Teilnetz werden dabei so behandelt, als seien sie Prozessoren in einem TRANSDATA-Netz.
- Die Umsetzungsfunktionen SAS und TAS werden als APS-Stationen implementiert (APS= Anwendungsorientierte Programmiersprache).
- Das SNA-Teilnetz wird über einen SDLC-Port an den Gateway angeschlossen.
- Der SDLC-Port erzeugt für alle vom SNA-Teilnetz eingehenden Nachrichten einen TRANSDATA-Transportheader, mit dem die APS-Station SAS adressiert wird. Umgekehrt entfernt der SDLC-Port bei allen auszugebenden Nachrichten den TRANSDATA-Transportheader. Damit ist gewährleistet, daß SNA-Nachrichten (Basic Transmission Units) innerhalb des Gateways transportierbar sind, und daß alle Nachrichten, die vom SNA-Teilnetz eingehen, an die APS-Station SAS ausgeliefert werden.
- Der Gateway ist, da er ein unmodifiziertes DNSP enthält, Teil des TRANSDATA-Netzes. Es ist deshalb möglich, über beliebige Ports (HDLC-Port oder ZE-Port) mit Hilfe der Transportsteuerung Nachrichten mit dem TRANSDATA-Teilnetz auszutauschen.
- Für alle Prozessoren, die zum SNA-Teilnetz gehören, wird eine empfängerprozessorspezifische (oder auch empfängerregionsspezifische) Nachrichtenbehandlungssequenz definiert, die die APS-Station TAS enthält. Damit erhält TAS alle Nachrichten, die vom TRANSDATA-Teilnetz eingehen und für Empfänger im SNA-Teilnetz bestimmt sind.
- Die APS-Stationen SAS und TAS tauschen Nachrichten über die Transportsteuerung des DNSP aus.

3. Überlegungen zur Umsetzbarkeit der Protokolle

Die Netzkonzepte beider Hersteller - SNA bei IBM und TRANSDATA bei Siemens - definieren, ähnlich wie das derzeitige ISO-Referenzmodell für offene Systeme, verschiedene logische Schichten und Protokolle zwischen Schichten gleicher Höhe. Beide Architekturen unterscheiden zwischen übertragungsorientierten und verarbeitungsorientierten

Schichten. Große Teile der Protokolle zwischen den verarbeitungsorientierten Schichten
werden jedoch von den Netzarchitekturen nicht definiert (Level 7, Subsystemprotokol-
le). Die Umsetzung der Nachrichten im Gateway muß aber auch diese Protokolle mit ein-
beziehen.

Eine ausführliche vergleichende Darstellung von SNA und TRANSDATA ist im Rahmen dieses
Vortrags nicht möglich. Hierzu sei auf die im Anhang angegebene Literatur verwiesen.
Die beiden Konzepte sollen jedoch wenigstens in sehr vereinfachter Form unter Bezug
auf das ISO-Referenzmodell einander gegenübergestellt werden (Bild 3). Im Vergleich
wird außerdem noch das PIX-Modell berücksichtigt, das bei der Umsetzung der Protokolle
die Basis für die neutralen Schnittstellen liefern soll.

Bild 3 zeigt, daß ein Teil der Funktionsschichten der hier betrachteten Architektu-
ren nicht eindeutig den 7 Layers des ISO-Referenzmodells entsprechen. Einerseits sind
Funktionen, die im ISO-Referenzmodell zu verschiedenen Layers gehören, bei PIX und
TRANSDATA in einer Funktionsschicht zusammengefaßt. Auf der anderen Seite sind bei
SNA und TRANSDATA Funktionen, die zum gleichen Layer des ISO-Referenzmodells gehören,
auf verschiedene Funktionsschichten verteilt.

Beispiele für die Zusammenfassung mehrerer ISO-Layers in einer gemeinsamen Funktionsschicht sind die TRANSDATA-Transportsteuerung (Layer 3 und 4) und der PIX-Message
Link Terminator (Layer 4 und 5).

Umgekehrt verteilen SNA und TRANSDATA die Funktionen des ISO-Sessions-Layers auf verschiedene Funktionsschichten. So wird der Session Administration Service bei SNA von
der Session Control (Teil der Transmission Control) und bei TRANSDATA vom Verbindungs-
Benutzerdienst (Protokoll NEABV) zusammen mit der Verbindungssteuerung (Teil der
Transportsteuerung, Protokoll NEATV) erbracht. Der Session Dialog Service wird jedoch
bei SNA von der Data Flow Control und bei TRANSDATA von anwendungsspezifischen Benut-
zerdiensten wahrgenommen.

Bild 3 gibt keine Auskunft über die zahlreichen im ISO-Referenzmodell vorgesehenen
Funktionen, die in den Herstellerarchitekturen fehlen. Hierfür seien zwei Beispiele
angeführt:

- Bei SNA fehlen z. Z. die Services für Network Flow Control (Layer 3). Sie werden
  erst ab SNA 4.2 (angekündigt für 1981) zur Verfügung stehen.
- Bei TRANSDATA gibt es dagegen z. Z. keine verbindungsspezifische Datenflußkontrolle (Flow Control in Layer 4) und keine Segmentierungs- und Blockungs-Funktionen
  (Layer 3).

Die Unterschiede in den Netzwerkarchitekturen und insbesondere in den Protokollen
des Application Layers machen es unmöglich, die SNA- und TRANSDATA-Protokolle ohne
Einschränkung ineinander umzusetzen. Daran ändert auch die vorgesehene Verwendung
neutraler Schnittstellen nichts. Besondere Schwierigkeiten sind immer dann zu erwarten, wenn Funktionen, die einer der Hersteller implementiert hat, bei dem anderen
Hersteller ganz oder teilweise fehlen. Ein typisches Beispiel sind die Protokolle der
Data Flow Control von SNA, für die es bei TRANSDATA keine entsprechenden Sprachmittel
gibt.

Außerdem gibt es noch ein generelles Problem. Alle Protokolle oberhalb Level 3 sind
End-to-End-Protokolle und damit eigentlich nicht kettbar. Das ist jedoch die Problematik jeder Gateway-Lösung, die höhere Protokolle einschließt. Die Umsetzung kann
deshalb nur gelingen, wenn die Abbildungssoftware, soweit erforderlich, in die Rolle
des Endbenutzers eintreten kann. Das ist nur dann möglich, wenn die Subsysteme und
die Geräte die Protokolle in vorhersehbarer Weise benutzen.

Das Lösungskonzept der DFVLR führt zum Ziel, weil sich der Verbund auf ganz bestimmte
Anwendungsfälle, d. h. auf ganz bestimmte Geräte und Subsysteme als Endbenutzer beschränkt. Ein Blick auf die unter 2.1 aufgeführten Leistungen zeigt jedoch, daß alle
für ein Rechnernetz wichtigen Funktionen erfaßt werden.

Zusammenfassung

Das Verbundkonzept der DFVLR geht zunächst davon aus, die geschlossenen Systeme zweier
Hersteller durch einen Kanal miteinander zu verbinden und damit zu öffnen.

Die vorgesehene Gateway-Lösung erlaubt es, die in der Einführung gestellte Forderung
zu erfüllen, nämlich die von IBM und Siemens für homogene Netze angebotenen Produkte
unverändert einzusetzen.

Die wechselseitige Öffnung des SNA- und TRANSDATA-Netzes kann auf weitere Anwendungen
und auf weitere Hersteller erweitert werden und führt damit folgerichtig zu einem
offenen System.

Literatur

[1] Reference Model of Open Systems Architecture (Version 4 as of June 1979)

[2] Nowak, R.
TRANSDATA von Siemens
Die sieben Häute eines Netzwerkes
Computer Magazin März und April 1979

[3] Datenfernverarbeitung mit BS 2000
Allgemeine Beschreibung
Siemens AG Bestell-Nr. D12/2095-01

[4] Datenfernverarbeitung Datenübertragungszugriffssystem DCM
Kurzbeschreibung
Siemens AG Bestell-Nr. D12/2106-01

[5] Henne, A.
Systems Network Architecture
Rahmen für IBM's Produktpolitik
Computer Magazin Februar 1979

[6] Cypser, R.J.
Communications Architecture for Distributed Systems
The Systems Programming Library, Addison-Wesley-Publishing Company, Reading
Massachusetts 1978

[7] Systems Network Architecture General Information
IBM Order No GA27-3102

[8] Systems Network Architecture Format and Protocol Reference Manual:
Architecture Logic
IBM Order No SC30-3112

[9] Kommunikationssysteme unter SNA mit Advanced Communication Function
(ACF Release 3).
IBM Order No GE12-1515

[10] ACF Release 3 Funktionsüberblick
IBM Order No GC12-1428

[11] Systems Network Architekture-
Types of Logical Unit to Logical Unit Sessions
IBM Order No GC20-1869

[12] Corr, F.P. and Neal, D.H.
SNA and emerging international standards
IBM Systems Journal Vol 18, No 2 1979

[13] Glas, G.
Siemens-TRANSDATA und IBM-SNA Gemeinsamkeiten und Unterschiede
Vortrag auf der WASCO-Tagung am 27.04.79 in München
(erscheint im WASCO-Tagungsband)

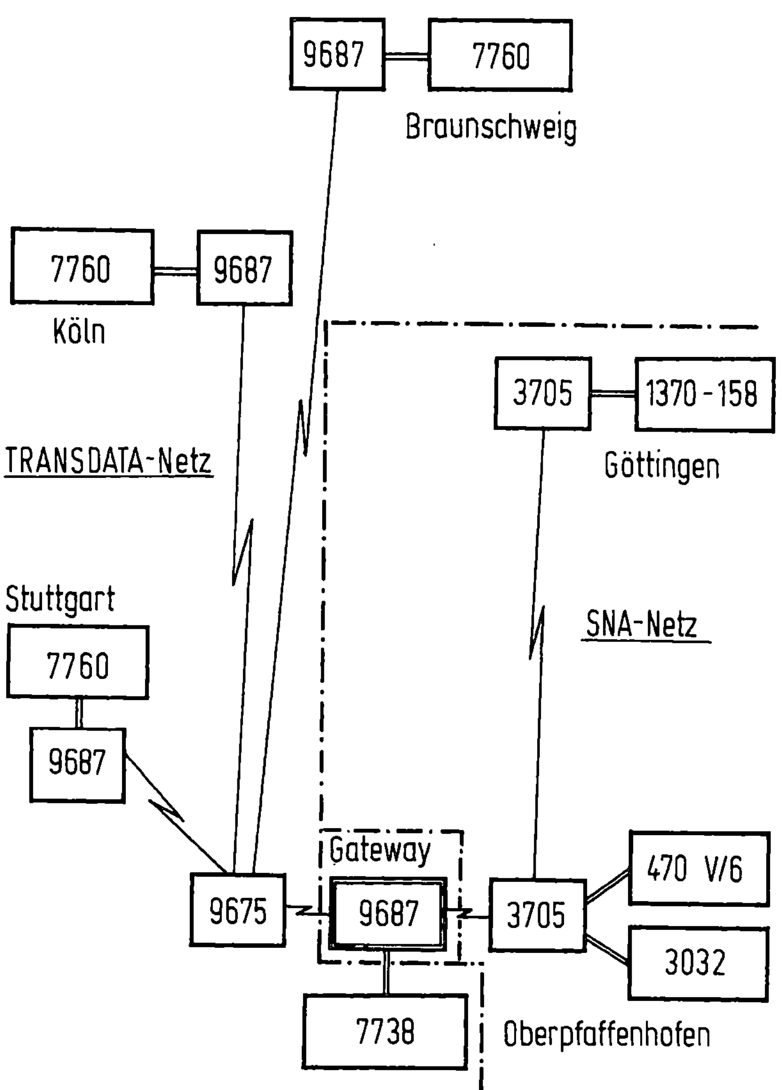

Bild 1 DFVLR-Rechnernetz

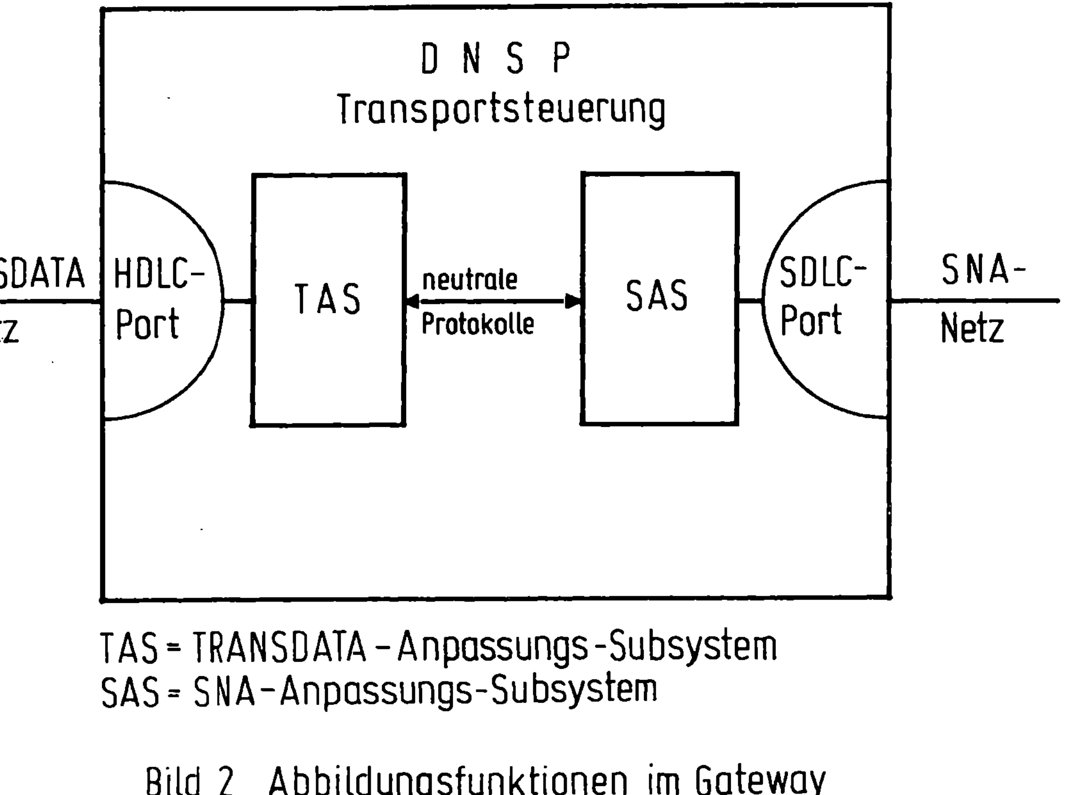

TAS = TRANSDATA - Anpassungs - Subsystem
SAS = SNA - Anpassungs - Subsystem

Bild 2   Abbildungsfunktionen im Gateway

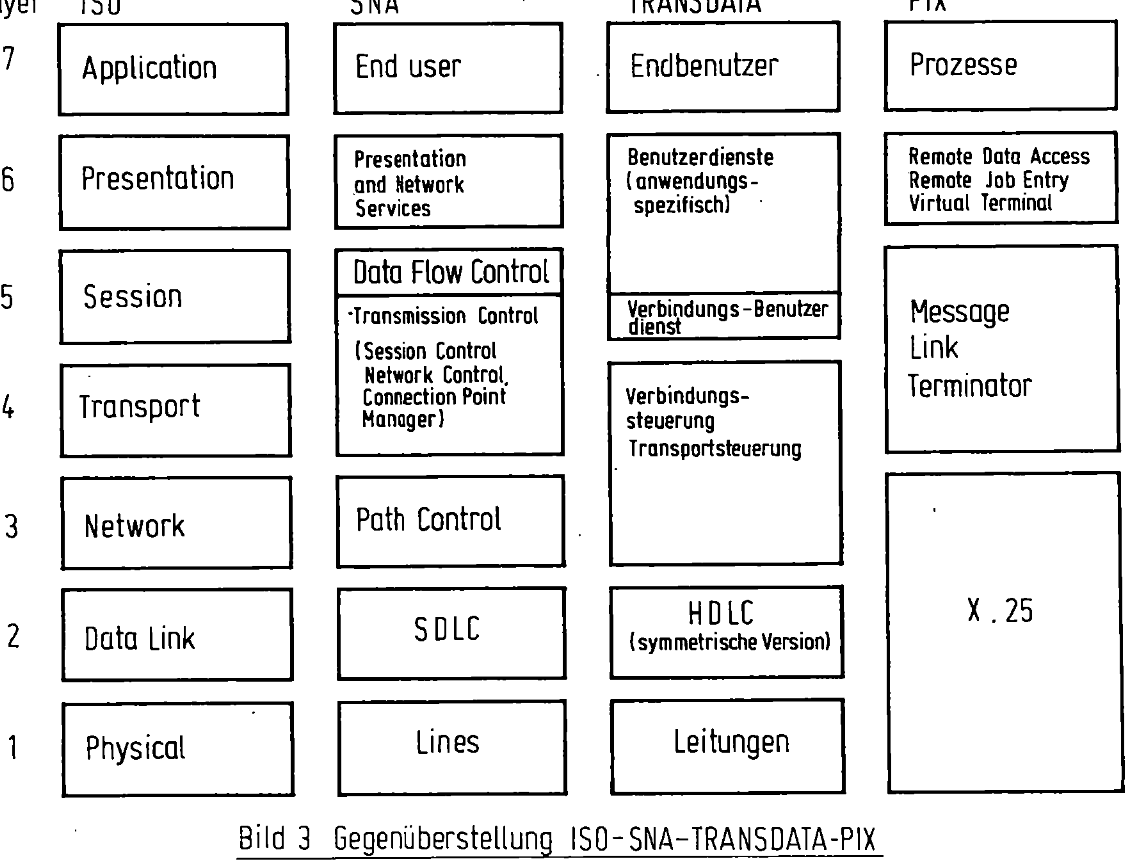

Bild 3 Gegenüberstellung ISO-SNA-TRANSDATA-PIX

Vergleich der Struktur des CDAEG-Netzes mit
dem ISO-Referenzmodell

Vortrag:
GI — Workshop
Kommunikation in verteilten Datenverarbeitungssystemen
3. — 4. Dezember 1979

Autoren:
Dr. Ing. Hans-Peter Boell, EDV-Beratung
Dipl. Ing. Georg Ebert, AEG—TELEFUNKEN

1   Einführung

1.1   Derzeitiger Einsatz des Netzes

Derzeit ist das CDAEG-Netz bei dem Leibniz-Rechenzentrum (LRZ) in München im Einsatz.
Einen Überblick über den momentanen Aufbau des Netzes gibt Bild 1.

1.2   Aufgabenstellung

Das CDAEG-Netz erlaubt den Anschluß interaktiver sowie batch-orientierter Peripherie an
CYBER-Anlagen, die zur Zeit unter dem Betriebssystem NOS Release 4 (Network Operating
System) betrieben werden. Das NOS R.4 unterstützt einen zur Zeit zweistufigen hierarchischen
Aufbau des Kommunikationsnetzes (siehe Bild 3). Die Steuerung und Überwachung des Netzes
erfolgen zentral in einer CYBER-Anlage.

Die Aufgabe des CDAEG-Netzes besteht darin, geographisch verteilt liegenden Benutzern den
Zugang zu einem oder mehreren Zentralrechnern zu ermöglichen. Der Zugang ist verfügbar für:

—   Batch-Benutzer mittels Lochkarteneingabe sowie Ausgabe über Zeilendrucker, Kartenstanzer
     und Plotter;

—   Time-Sharing-Benutzer mittels alphanumerischen sowie graphischen Sichtgeräten und Loch-
     streifenperipherie.

Dem Betreiber des CDAEG-Netzes werden in dem Remote Concentrator (RC) zusätzlich wichtige Hilfsmittel zum Betreiben des Netzes zur Verfügung gestellt, z.B.:

—   Führen von Day-file, Error-file, Dump-file und Statistic-file
     (genannt Rechenzentrumsdateien)

—   File Transmission Facility (FTF) zum Transport der Rechenzentrumsdateien an die CYBER

—   Fernladen eines RC

—   Fernbedienung des RC durch eine ausgezeichnete Konsole im Netz

—   Übertragen eines Reservebetriebssystems von der CYBER an den RC.

1.3   Netzwerkelemente, Verbindungsstrukturen und Protokolle

Es werden zwei Verbindungsarten im Netz unterschieden (siehe auch Bild 5) :

—   Service-Kanäle ohne Flußkontrolle zur Steuerung des Netzes und der Netzwerkelemente
     (Geräte, Knoten, Verbindungsleitungen, Applikationen) sowie

— Logische Verbindungen (Connections = CN's) mit Datenflußkontrolle zur Steuerung und Datenübermittlung zwischen Anwendern (Applikationen) in CYBER-Anlagen und einzelnen Geräten im Netz.

Weiterhin unterscheiden wir in einem Netzwerk physikalische und logische Elemente, die gesteuert und überwacht werden müssen.

Diese Netzsteuerung und -überwachung wird im CDAEG-Netz zentral durch die CYBER ausgeführt und besteht aus den Teilen Network Supervisor NS und Communication Supervisor CS.

1.3.1 Die Aufgaben des Network und Communication Supervisor

Der Network Supervisor ist für alle netzwerkinternen Elemente zuständig, d.h. für Elemente der 1. und 2. Netzstufe gemäß Bild 3. Dazu zählen:

1. Physikalische Elemente, z.B.

    — Front-End FE

    — Remote Concentrator RC

    — Datenübertragungsabschnitte zwischen FE und RC (genannt Trunk) sowie zwischen Host und FE (genannt Coupler)

2. Logische Elemente, z.B.

    Logical Link LL als Datenkanal zwischen einer CYBER-Anlage und einem RC, wobei ein FE als Vermittlungsknoten zwischengeschaltet ist.

Eine Steuerung von NS erfolgt durch den Netzwerk-Operateur (NOP).

Der Communication Supervisor ist für alle realen oder pseudomäßig realisierten Geräteanschlüsse an das CDAEG-Netz verantwortlich sowie für die über das Netz zugänglichen Applikationen in den Hosts. Damit werden folgende Elemente kontrolliert:

1. Physikalische Elemente, z.B.

    — Verbindung reales Gerät mit dem RC (genannt Line). Als Verbindungsart wird der Einzel- und Gruppenanschluß (Cluster) unterstützt.

    — Reales oder pseudomäßiges Gerät

2. Logische Elemente, z.B.

    — Applikationen in CYBER-Anlagen

    — Logische Verbindungen zwischen Applikation und Gerät

Eine Steuerung von CS erfolgt durch den "lokalen" Operateur (LOP) an einer CYBER-Host.

1.3.2 Bedeutung der Verbindungsarten

Zum Austausch von Steuerdaten benutzen NS und CS die Service-Kanäle, die implicit mit dem Aktivieren von Trunks existieren und benutzt werden können.

Der Logical Link (LL) als Datenkanal zwischen einer CYBER-Host und Geräteanschlüssen am RC faßt max. 256 logische Verbindungen (CN's) zu einem Kommunikationspfad zusammen. CN's werden temporär von CS eingerichtet. Zu einem RC können mehrere LL's über unterschiedliche FE's laufen. Diese Möglichkeit wird zur Zeit nur für den BACK-UP-Fall (Ausfall eines Front-End) benutzt.

Die CN's bestehen immer zwischen dem NAM (Network Access Method) in der CYBER und einem Terminal im RC. Zwischen der Applikation, mit der ein Terminal verbunden ist, und NAM existiert eine Application Connection (ACN), die in NAM auf die CN abgebildet wird.

1.3.3 Protokollschichten

Entsprechend der beiden Verbindungsarten existieren zwei unterschiedliche Protokollschichtungen (siehe Bild 4), denen die Trunk-Protokollschicht (zwischen FE—RC) sowie die Coupler-Protokollschicht (zwischen FE—Host) gemeinsam ist.

Protokolle über den Service-Kanal sind zweistufig und bestehen aus:

— Trunk- und Coupler-Protokoll

— netzwerkelementspezifischen Protokollen zur Steuerung und Überwachung von Logical Link, Line und Terminal

Protokolle über den Logical Link sind dagegen dreistufig, bestehend aus:

— Trunk-/Coupler-Protokoll

— Blockprotokoll über Logical Link

— virtuellen gerätespezifischen Protokollen über eine logische Verbindung, die einem Logical Link zugeordnet ist.

Auf der Anwendungsebene wird unterschieden in:

— lokales Anwendungsprotokoll, mit dem ein Gerätebenutzer Steuerfunktionen bezüglich seines Geräts ausführen kann (lokale Kommandos) sowie

— globales Anwendungsprotokoll zur Applikation in der Host (CYBER-spezifisches oder anwenderspezifisches Kommando).

1.4 Datenaustausch, Adressierung und Flußregulierung

1.4.1 Datenformate

In Bild 6 ist das Datenformat im CDAEG-Netz dargestellt.

Nachrichten werden in einer Folge von BLK-Blöcken (max. Größe 2047 Bytes), abgeschlossen mit einem MSG-Block, übertragen.

Für Multiplexzwecke auf Trunk-Ebene wird ein Block in Pakete (Subblöcke) von zur Zeit 120 Bytes unterteilt. Ein Subblock erhält einen Subblock-Header von 2 Bytes mit Angaben über seine Länge und Kennungen bezüglich Übertragungspriorität (high oder low) sowie Blockabschluß (Last Subblock eines Blocks).

Die Übertragungspriorität gibt die Bedienungshäufigkeit auf Trunks an, d.h. Blöcke mit der Priorität 'high' werden bevorzugt übertragen. Im CDAEG-Netz ist zur Zeit die Priorität 'high' den interaktiven Geräten zugeordnet, die Priorität 'low' den Batch-Geräten.

Der Datenverkehr auf dem Service-Kanal wird immer mit den Blocktypen CMD oder ACTL (siehe Bild 8) abgewickelt. Zusätzlich wird bei ACTL-Nachrichten eine Subtypenkennung geführt (siehe Bild 9), bei CMD-Nachrichten ein Primary- sowie Secondary-Function-Code zur weiteren Spezifizierung des Kommandos.

ACTL-Nachrichten beziehen sich nur auf die Verbindung zwischen RC und FE (Trunk) und zwischen Host und RC (Logical Link).

1.4.2 Adressierung

Jeder Block, der im Netzwerk transportiert wird, besitzt einen Blockkopf mit einer 3 Bytes umfassenden logischen Adresse, bestehend aus:

— Kennung für den Empfänger (Destination Node = DN)
— Kennung für den Absender (Source Node = SN)
— logischer Verbindungsnummer (CN).

Empfänger- bzw. Absender im Netz — mit entsprechenden Kennungen (ID's) versehen — können sein:

— jeder RC oder FE
— jeder Coupler, d.h. jede CYBER-Host
— der Network Supervisor (NS) sowie
— der Communication Supervisor (CS).

NS besitzt immer die Node-Adresse 0, CS immer die Node-Adresse 1. Bei dem Service-Kanal zwischen einem RC und der Netzsteuerung wird immer CN = 0 benutzt.

Ein Logical Link ist gemäß Bild 5 daher immer durch die RC—ID als Empfänger/Absender und die Coupler-ID als Empfänger/Absender gekennzeichnet.

Ein Trunk entsprechend durch die FE—ID und die RC—ID.

Weitere Informationen im Blockkopf sind:

— Kennung des Blocktyps (siehe Bild 8)
— Laufnummer (Block-Serial-Number = BSN), die zyklisch modulo 7 gezählt wird (nur bei Blöcken, die über einen Datenkanal des Logical Link geführt werden)
— Kennung für die Übertragungspriorität.

1.4.4 Flußkontrolle

Das CDAEG-Netz besitzt eine mehrschichtige Flußkontrolle (siehe Bild 11), bestehend aus:

1. Trunk-Regulierung gemäß HDLC-Norm (Asynchronous-Response-Mode) mit einer Fenstergröße von 8 zwischen FE und RC (siehe: [3]).

2. Blockflußregulierung auf einer CN durch Asynchronous-Response-Mode (Elemente BLK, MSG, BACK). Die Fenstergröße ist in einer Netzbeschreibungsdatei für jedes Terminal festgelegt und kann dynamisch nicht verändert werden. Ein BACK-Block quittiert immer nur einen Block und gibt damit das Senden für nur einen Block wieder frei, d.h. die Blockübertragung wird durch das Eintreffen von BACK's gesteuert.

3. Der RC kann in Empfangsrichtung zusätzlich den Datenstrom auf einer CN abbrechen oder temporär unterbrechen.

4. Regulierung des Datenflusses aller CN-bezogenen Datenströme in Empfangsrichtung auf dem Logical Link.

Bei einem Neustart des CDAEG-Netzes werden alle Netzwerkelemente (Trunk, LL, Lines, Terminals) von der zentralen Netzwerksteuerung konfiguriert. Die Beschreibung des Netzwerkes wird auf derjenigen CYBER, die die Netzsteuerung ausführt, in einer Datei gespeichert.

Die Terminals im Netzwerk werden mit einer Network Validation Facility als Applikation verbunden, damit automatisch (bei Batch-Geräten) oder benutzergesteuert ein LOGIN erfolgen kann.
Bei einem Time-out wird das entsprechende Terminal mit dem Communication Supervisor verbunden (= Rekonfiguration) und kann mittels einer beliebigen Eingabe wieder "aktiviert" werden.

2 Vergleich CDAEG-Architektur mit ISO-Referenzmodell

2.1 Erläuterung ISO-Referenzmodell

Als Beitrag zur gegenwärtigen Diskussion über eine Standardisierung hinsichtlich der Kommunikationsarchitektur hat die ISO ein 7-Ebenen-Modell (ISO-Referenzmodell) entwickelt (siehe Bild 7 und [4]).

Das ISO-Modell zeigt zwei verschiedene Protokollarten:

— End-to-End-Protokolle mit einer Bedeutung zwischen Endteilnehmern

— Transportprotokolle mit einer Bedeutung auf einem Übermittlungsabschnitt.

Entsprechend übernehmen die von ISO definierten Schichten spezifische Aufgaben, u.a.:

— Level-7-Protokolle für system- sowie anwendungsspezifische Applikationen,

— Level-6-Protokolle zur Transformation der ausgetauschten Informationen mit dem Ziel, eine Unabhängigkeit der Applikationen von realen Geräten zu erzielen,

— Level-5-Protokolle zur Steuerung der logischen Verbindung zwischen zwei Applikationen.

Der Transportdienst übernimmt den fehlerfreien Austausch von Daten auf einer logischen Verbindung, wobei der Level 4 eine vom Netzwerk unabhängige Schnittstelle anbietet.

Der Netzzugang (Level 1 — 3) hat nur eine lokale Bedeutung, d.h. nur für den Übermittlungsabschnitt zwischen DTE und DCE.

Verbindliche Normvorschläge liegen zur Zeit nur für die Level 1 — 3 vor.

2.2 Erläuterung der CDAEG-Architektur

Entsprechend dem erläuterten Nachrichtenformat (siehe Bild 6) werden Blöcke zwischen der Host und dem RC ausgetauscht. Ein dreistufiges Netzzugangskonzept existiert daher nicht.

Der Transportdienst zu einem RC hat in Sende- und Empfangsrichtung aus Durchsatzgründen (Vermeiden von Umspeichervorgängen, Warten auf Blockende) keine einheitliche Schnittstelle zu den End-to-End-Protokollebenen. In Empfangsrichtung findet kein Blockassembly statt, d.h. Subblöcke werden sofort nach ihrem Eintreffen an die höhere Ebene weitergereicht. In Senderichtung werden Blöcke an den Transportdienst zur Übertragung gegeben, wobei das Disassembly (= Aufteilung eines Blockes in Subblöcke) vom Transportdienst durchgeführt wird.

Die höheren Schichten Terminalsteuerung und Netzwerkmanagement benutzen ohne Ausnahme den Transportdienst mit der oben beschriebenen Schnittstelle.

Die Terminalsteuerung übernimmt:

— die Abwicklung eines virtuellen Terminals für batch-orientierte sowie interaktive Geräte in
Form von Verwaltungsprozessen.

— nach Umwandlung eines virtuellen Nachrichtenformats die reale Gerätesteuerung in sogenannte
Geräteprozesse.

Zur Zeit existieren Verwaltungsprozesse für:

— Interaktive Ein-Ausgabe (Interaktive Virtual Terminal IVT)

— Batch-Ausgabegeräte (gemeinsam für Zeilendrucker, Kartenstanzer und Plotter)

— Batch-Eingabegeräte (Lochkartenleser)

— Pseudogeräte Ein-Ausgabe (File Transmission Facility FTE)

Für die Batch-Geräte wird ein Batch Virtual Terminal (BVT) betrieben.

Geräte können auch direkt von der Host unter Umgehung der virtuellen Terminalsteuerung betrieben werden.

Die Gesamtheit der Batch-Geräte bildet für die CYBER-Host ein HASP-Terminal, wobei aber alle
Geräte direkt an den RC angeschlossen sind (siehe Bild 3).

Das Netzwerkmanagement (NWMAN) übernimmt zentral im RC die notwendigen Steuerungs- und
Überwachungsfunktionen für die angeschlossenen Verbindungen. Speziell für das Netzwerkmanagement wurde eine Reassembly-Funktion realisiert. Diese Reassembly-Funktion ist erforderlich, da
Nachrichten über den Service-Kanal nur eine Verarbeitung als "ganzes" zulassen. In Senderichtung
werden zusätzlich Nachrichten, die mittels zyklischer Wiederholung vor Verlust geschützt werden,
zentral abgehandelt.

Die Steuerungsfunktion gliedert sich in:

— Netzwerksteuerung, bezogen auf die Verbindung RC zu einer Host, d.h. zum FE und über
den LL zur CYBER-Host.

— Verbindungssteuerung, bezogen auf die an einem RC angeschlossenen Terminal.

— Zusatzfunktionen bezüglich Nachrichtenaustausch zwischen Netzwerkoperateur und Terminals,
zwischen Knotenoperateuren sowie Senden von Statistikdaten.

Die Überwachungsfunktion im Netzwerk bezieht sich auf die Elemente des Netzwerkes sowie der
angeschlossenen Terminals und wird "schrittweise" aktiviert. Aufgrund des verwendeten Trunk-
Protokolls (HDLC Unbalanced Mode) kann sowohl der RC als auch der FE seine Senderichtung

(als Primary) initialisieren. Nach erfolgreichem Verbindungsaufbau auf der Trunk-Ebene wird ein LINIT-Blockaustausch vorgenommen, der — falls erfolgreich ausgeführt — zum Start der Trunk-Überwachung führt. Dazu werden in Zeiten ohne Datenverkehr Dummy-Blöcke (LIDLE) zwischen FE und RC ausgetauscht und mit Hilfe eines Timers überwacht.

Mittels einer "NPU Initialized" Nachricht über den betriebsbereiten Trunk informiert der RC den NS über seine Bereitschaft, eine Konfiguration seiner Elemente durchführen zu können. Ein Logical Link wird jetzt von NS durch Konfigurierungsmeldungen an beide Enden desselben (siehe dazu Bild 5) aufgebaut. Zwischen FE und RC wird jetzt ein Protokoll abgewickelt, um die Betriebsbereitschaft des Logical Link herzustellen und die Logical Link Regulierung zu aktivieren.

Ein betriebsbereiter Logical Link kann von CS zum Aufbau logischer Verbindungen (CN's) benutzt werden. Damit tritt CN-spezifisch die Blockprotokollüberwachung in Kraft, die Bestandteil der Terminalsteuerung ist.

Zu der Schichtung der Regulierungsmechanismen siehe auch Bild 11.

2.3   Vergleich CDAEG-Architektur mit ISO-Referenzmodell

Bei einem Vergleich ist zu beachten, daß der Netzwerkzugang asymetrisch gestaltet ist (siehe Bild 12). Deshalb wird bezüglich des Netzzugangs nur der Übermittlungsabschnitt zwischen RC u. FE betrachtet.

Der Netzzugang (Level 1 — 3 gemäß ISO) benutzt im CDAEG-Netz die HDLC-Prozedur zum Austausch von Frames (siehe Bild 14). Subblöcke (siehe Bild 13) werden in einem Frame gemultiplext und im RC sowie im Front-End zu Blöcken "zusammengesetzt". Subblöcke werden entsprechend ihrer Übertragungspriorität übertragen, wobei Subblöcke mit der Priorität 'high' die Übertragung von Subblöcken mit der Priorität 'low' unterbrechen. Eine Unterbrechung findet immer an einer Subblockgrenze statt. Somit ist die Übertragungspriorität eine notwendige Größe für das "Zusammensetzen" der Blöcke, da im Subblockkopf keine Angabe über die logische Verbindung enthalten ist. Diese Angabe ist aber erforderlich, will man auf der Ebene der Subblöcke (= Pakete beim ISO-Modell) ein Netzzugangsprotokoll, wie z.B. beim X.25-Vorschlag für den Zugang zu Paketvermittlungsnetzen (siehe dazu [2]), für jede logische Verbindung abwickeln.

Daher fehlt im CDAEG-Netz ein solches Netzzugangsprotokoll (siehe Bild 14) oder der Level 3 gemäß ISO-Modell.

Elemente des Blockprotokolls (auf einem Logical Link) zur Kontrolle und Steuerung des Datenaustauschs zwischen einem RC und einer CYBER-Host sind gemäß ISO-Modell dem Level 4 (Transport-End-to-End-Protokoll) zuzuordnen. Zu diesen Elementen gehören diejenigen des Datenaustauschs auf einer CN und der Flußkontrolle auf CN (siehe Bild 8).

Eine Vollständigkeitsprüfung eines Blocks kann nicht erfolgen, da entsprechende Angaben im Block fehlen.

Dieser Nachteil wird durch Prüfungsmöglichkeiten auf der Ebene des virtuellen Terminalprotokolls und der damit verbundenen strengen Vorschriften über den Datenaufbau hierfür ausgeglichen.

Wegen der Zweistufigkeit des Netzes und seines hierarchischen Aufbaus ist aufgrund der Erfahrung eine Vollständigkeitskontrolle nicht erforderlich. Ebenso läßt sich die Vollständigkeit einer Nachricht, bestehend aus mehreren Blöcken, nicht überwachen. Dieser Nachteil ist aber gravierend und wird später noch diskutiert.

Aus dem vorher Gesagten läßt sich erkennen, daß ein Front-End als "Vermittlungsknoten" keine dedizierten Mittel zur Flußkontrolle besitzt. Tritt ein Puffermangel auf, so wird ganz global eine Regulierung über die Mechanismen des Level 2 (HDLC) vorgenommen. Das heißt, ein FE geht immer davon aus, daß empfangene Blöcke auch über den Coupler an die Host abfließen können.

Für die Ebenen gemäß ISO-Modell mit End-to-End-Charakter existiert zur Zeit nur ein Funktionskatalog (siehe: [4]). Man kann aber feststellen, daß die Ebenen 4 — 7 des ISO-Modells — wie im folgenden gezeigt — ein Analogon im CDAEG-Netz besitzen.

Die Sessionsteuerung des ISO-Modells (Level 5) wird auf der CDAEG-Seite in einer analogen Struktur (siehe Bild 5) dargestellt. Der Ablauf der Überwachung wurde in Kapitel 2.2 ausführlich dargestellt.

Mit Hilfe von speziellen Blocktypen kann im CDAEG-Netz (siehe Bild 8) die Darstellungskontrolle (Bild 16) abgewickelt werden, bestehend aus:

1. Steuerungsprotokoll, für das die Blocktypen zur Flußkontrolle auf einer CN sowie der CMD-Block benutzt werden können,

2. virtuellem Nachrichtenformat mit:
    — Gerätesteuerzeichen
    — Datenkompression.

Insbesondere kann der Benutzer eines Terminals dynamisch gewisse Terminalparameter ändern, z.B. die Größe seines Bildschirms (Page) oder die Zeilengröße eines Zeilendruckers. Die Darstellungssteuerung entspricht voll dem Umfang des ISO-Referenzmodells.

Auf RC-Seite bilden die Geräteprozesse die Applikationen im Sinne des ISO-Modells.

3   Diskussion von Problemen

Wie gezeigt wurde, besteht eine weitgehende Übereinstimmung zwischen der Schichtung im CDAEG-Netz und dem ISO-Referenzmodell.

Die Übereinstimmung fehlt in funktioneller Hinsicht auf dem Level 3 (keine Paketvermittlung). Weiterhin wurden die Ebenen 4 und 6 durch Implementierungsgesichtspunkte und Durchsatzforderungen an Schnittstellen zwischen den Schichten berührt.

Die bisherige Erfahrung sowie eine funktionelle Erweiterung der interaktiven Geräteschnittstelle haben zwischenzeitlich gezeigt, daß die Zentralisierung der Ebene 4 gemäß ISO-Referenzmodell sinnvoll ist. Die bisherige asymetrische Datenschnittstelle zum Transportsystem hat sich als geeignet erwiesen, da dadurch die Effizienz wesentlich gesteigert wurde (weniger Umspeichervorgänge, kein Warten auf vollständigen Block).

Besondere Probleme traten in Zusammenhang mit der Blockflußkontrolle, d.h. der Flußkontrolle auf dem Level 4 auf. Jede CN erlaubt unabhängig von anderen CN's innerhalb einer festgelegten Fenstergröße den Empfang von Blöcken. Bei Geräten an einen Gruppenanschluß ist daher eine Regulierung, die alle Geräte des Gruppenanschlusses berücksichtigt, nicht möglich. Es wäre daher · — auch bei anderen Netzen mit hierarchischem Aufbau — empfehlenswert, Regulierungsmechanismen an Netzelementen zu orientieren, die einen "Flaschenhals" im Datenfluß bilden. Dies wäre bei Gruppenanschlüssen in erster Hinsicht die gemeinsame Leitung zwischen RC und den Geräten. Für Sternnetze ist ein solcher Mechanismus leicht realisierbar.

Dieser Vorschlag ist aber bei einem Netz mit mehreren Hosts, an die sich Geräte "anschließen" können, nicht ohne großen Aufwand implementierbar, so daß sich hier andere Alternativen anbieten, z.B.:

1.   Ausreichender Kernspeicherausbau am RC mit einem Gruppenanschluß, d.h. Speicher für alle Blöcke der einzelnen Fenster,

2.   Regulierungsmechanismus auf einem tieferen Level, z.B. auf dem Level 3.

Generell einsetzbar wäre ein Mechanismus, bei dem dynamisch das Übertragungsfenster für den Empfang verändert werden könnte (siehe z.B. [7]).

Der Vorteil einer Regulierung auf einen Level unterhalb des Blockformats, d.h. auf der Paketebene gemäß [2], [5] oder der Subblockebene im CDAEG-Netz, liegt in dem Kontrollieren kleinerer Dateneinheiten, die erst auf einem höheren Level zu größeren Einheiten zusammengesetzt werden.

Die globale Regulierung auf dem Logical Link konnte nicht in vollem Umfang in der Praxis eingesetzt werden, da die Zeiten zum Wirksamwerden der Regulierung zu groß waren.

Auf die Regulierungsprobleme in Netzen ist an anderen Stelle schon ausführlich eingegangen worden, z.B. [5].

Im CDAEG-Netz konnte der clusterbezogene Durchsatz erst nach einem Abweichen von dem Protokollvorschlag nach DIN 66019, entsprechenden Hardware-Änderungen sowie einer Erhöhung der Abflußgeschwindigkeit zu Sichtgeräten auf 9600 Baud zufriedenstellend erreicht werden, d.h. nach einer wesentlichen Beschleunigung der Abflußgeschwindigkeit zu den über einen Gruppenanschluß angeschlossenen Geräten.

Es ist zu erwarten, daß bei einer Weiterentwicklung des CDAEG-Netzes das Problem der Flußregulierung durch zusätzliche Mechanismen gemindert wird.

Ein weiteres Problem liegt im CDAEG-Netz in der Vollständigkeitskontrolle einer Nachricht, die sich zusammensetzt aus:

1. Vollständigkeitskontrolle eines Blocks
2. Vollständigkeits- und Reihenfolgekontrolle einer Nachricht.

Diese Probleme sind im ISO-Referenzmodell auf dem Level 4 zu behandeln.

Im CDAEG-Netz sind unterhalb des Level 4 (siehe Bild 14) keine Kontrollmöglichkeiten auf Konsistenz der Daten mehr gegeben. Die Vollständigkeitskontrolle eines Blocks, d.h. die Überprüfung auf Subblockverlust, kann nur implicit aufgrund der Blockformate für virtuelle Terminals auf höheren Ebenen durchgeführt werden. Werden Terminals 'direkt' von der Host gesteuert, d.h. die Daten 'transparent' übertragen, entfällt diese Kontrollmöglichkeit.

Eine Vollständigkeitsprüfung einer Nachricht, z.B. einer Druckausgabe ist nicht gegeben, da entsprechende Laufnummern fehlen. Im Blockkopf ist zwar eine sogenannte 'Block-Serial-Nummer' (BSN) enthalten, die bei der Übertragung Host-RC zyklisch vergeben wird, doch ist die Zählweise zur Zeit nicht so, daß eine Vollständigkeitsprüfung damit durchgeführt werden könnte, insbesondere nicht bei einer temporären Unterbrechung des empfangenen Datenstroms (z.B. bei Stoptaste).

Eine solche Vollständigkeitsprüfung einer Nachricht ist aber selbst bei zweistufigen hierarchischen Netzen erforderlich.

4 Zusammenfassung

Das CDAEG-Netz zeigt, daß eine Anwendung des ISO-Referenzmodells unter Beachtung netzspezifischer Gegebenheiten möglich ist.

Die Erfahrung bei diesen Projekten hat zudem erwiesen, daß auch Prozeßrechner mit relativ geringem Kernspeicherausbau in der Lage ist, als Netzknoten eingesetzt zu werden. Das CDAEG-Netz selbst ist heute als allgemeingültiger Netzzugang an CYBER-Anlagen anzusehen.

Die bisherigen Ergebnisse des CDAEG-Netzes zeigen in Richtung ISO-Modell, daß eine Standardisierung des Level 4 dringend erscheint. Ob der Level 5 — 7 jemals standardisiert werden kann, wird die Zukunft erweisen.

5   Literaturhinweise

[1]   CDC: CCP External Reference Specifications
DCS – S 1962

[2]   CCITT: Provisional Recommendations X.3, X.25, X.28 and X.29 on packet-switched data
transmission services
Geneva 1978

[3]   ISO 4335: Data Communication – high Level Data Link Control Procedures –
Elements of Procedures

[4]   ISO: Reference Model of open systems architecture
(Version 3 as of Nov. 1978)
ISO / TC 97 / SC 16 N

[5]   BARTH, I.: Struktur der Kommunikationsprotokolle im GMD-Netz
Informatik-Fachberichte Nr. 3, S. 111 – 118

[6]   Des JARDINS, R. u.a.: ANSI Reference Model for Distributed Systems
Proceedings Comp. Com. Networks (COMPCON)
5. – 8. Sept. 1978, S. 144 – 149

[7]   ZIMMERMANN, H.: The Cyclades End to End Protocol
4th ACM/IEEE Data Communication Symposion, Quebec (Oct. 1975)

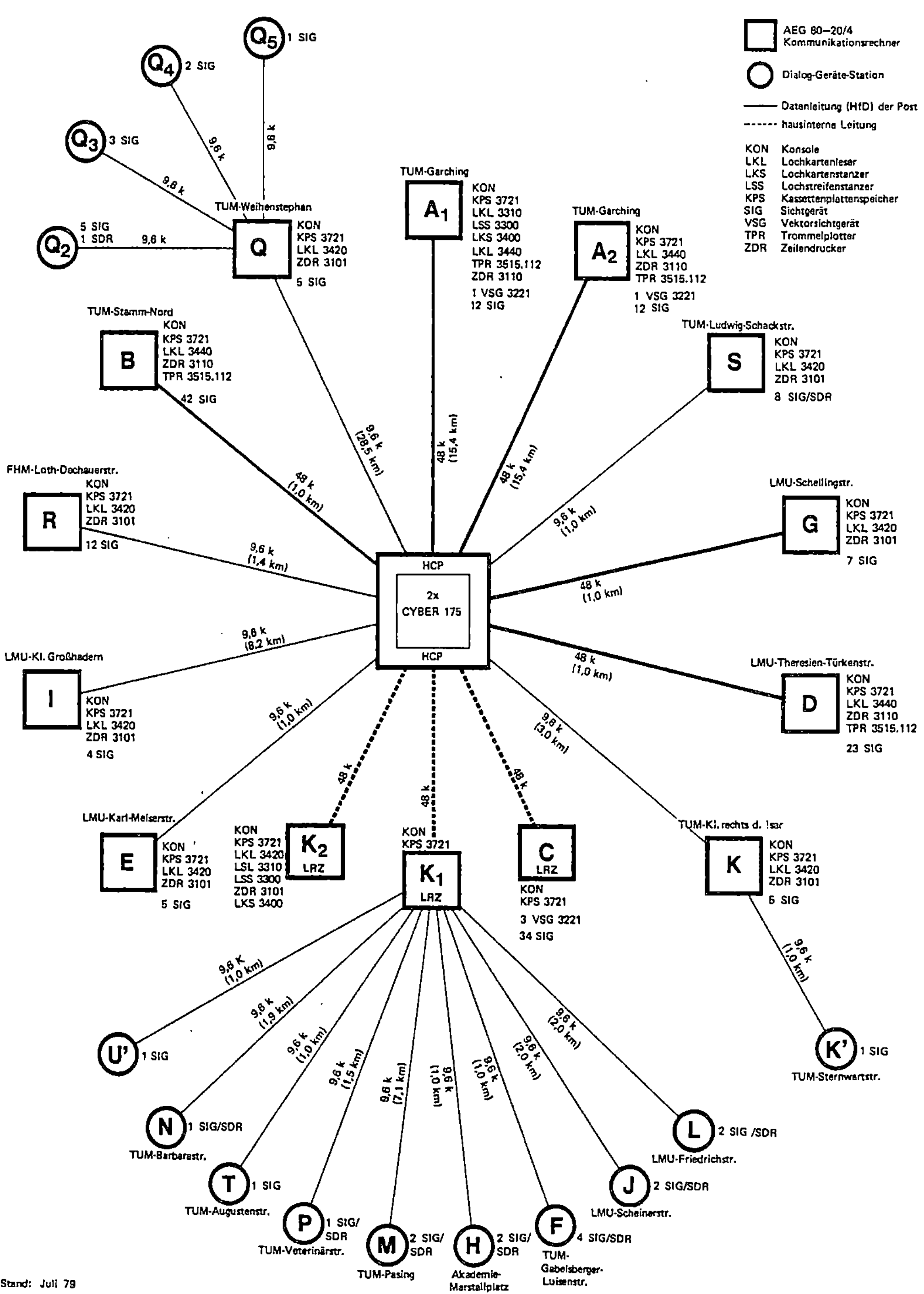

Bild 1   Datenfernübertragungs-Netz für das Leibniz-Rechenzentrum, München

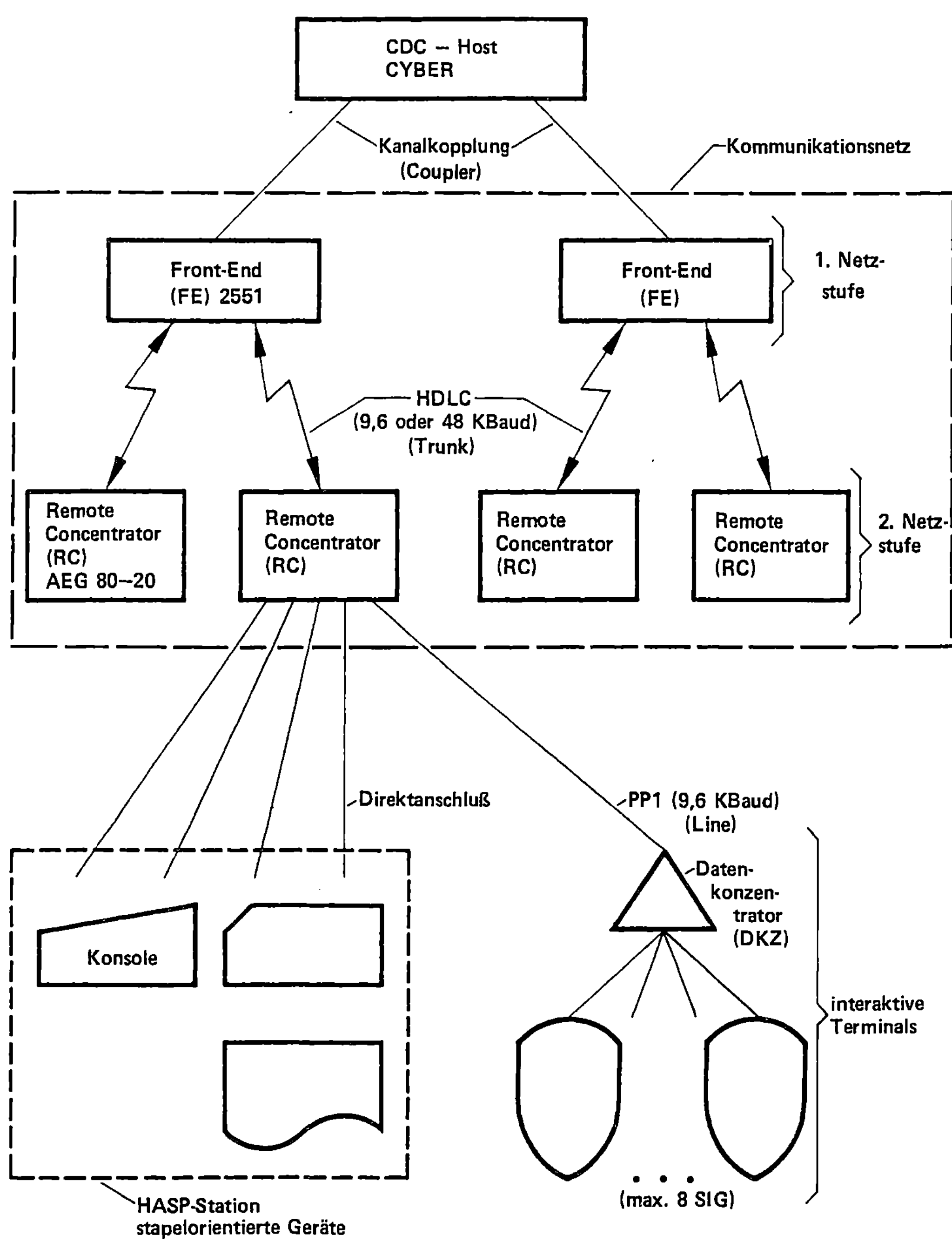

Bild 3   Netzstruktur CDAEG-Netz

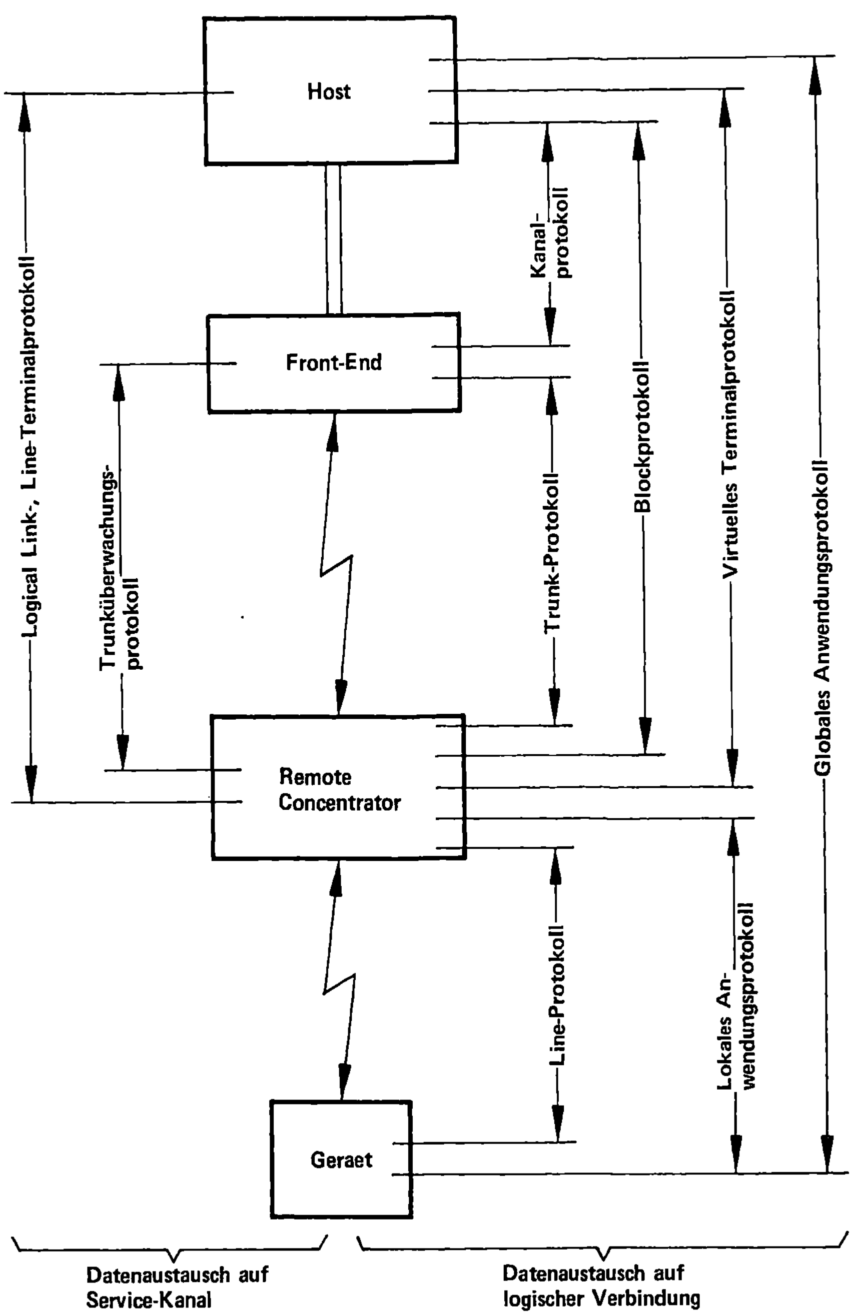

Bild 4   Protokollhierarchie im CDAEG-Netz

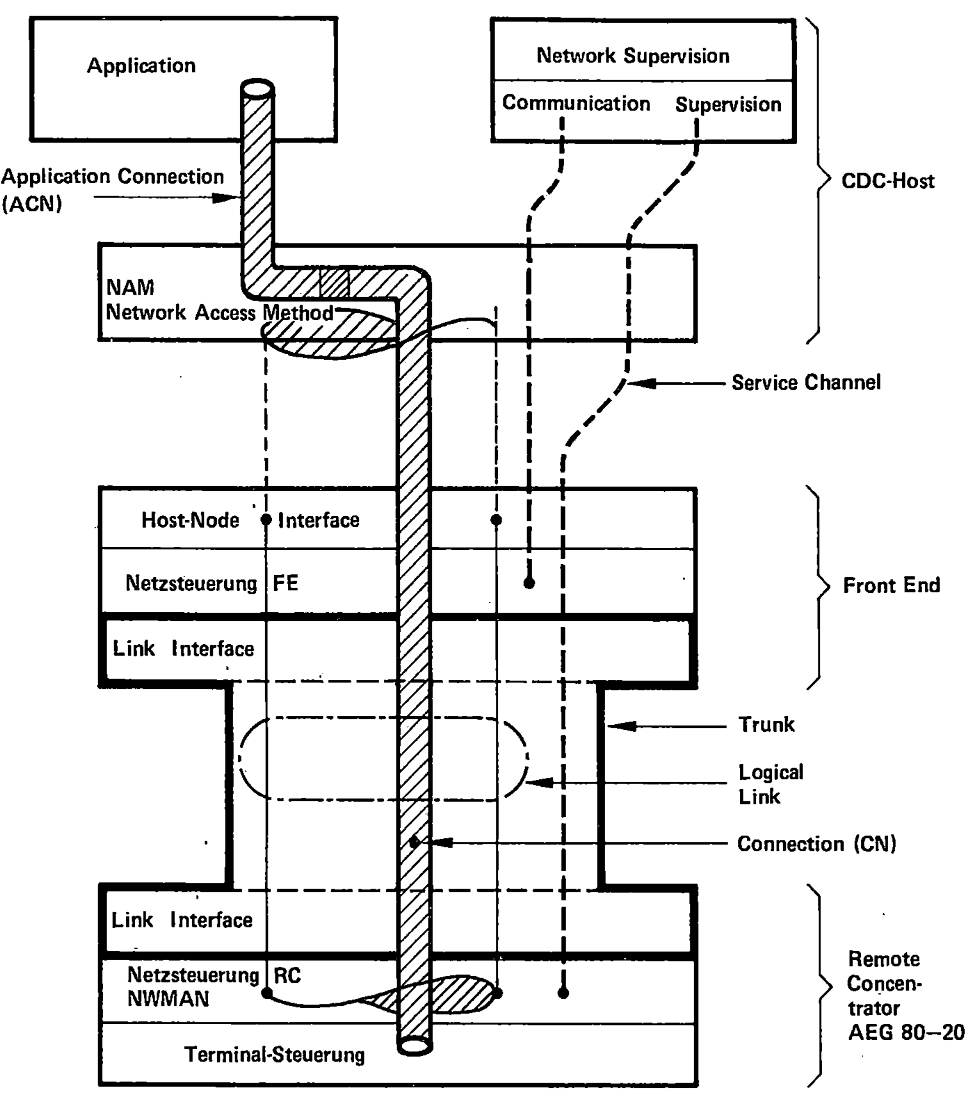

Bild 5   Logische Verbindungsstruktur des CDAEG-Netz

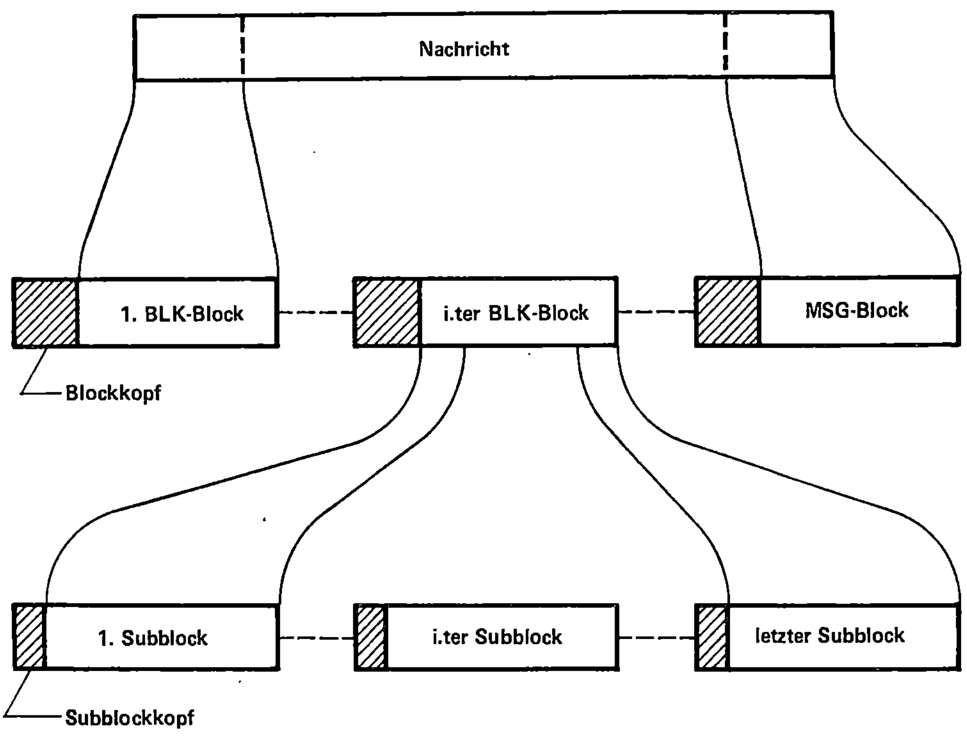

Nachricht	=	Beliebige Anzahl von Zeichen
Block	=	Einheit zum Austausch auf CN
Subblock	=	Einheit zum Austausch auf Trunk (Multiplexen)
Blockkopf	=	Netzadressen und Blocktyp
Subblockkopf	=	Längenangabe, Priorität für Transport

Bild 6   Datenformate im CDAEG-Netz

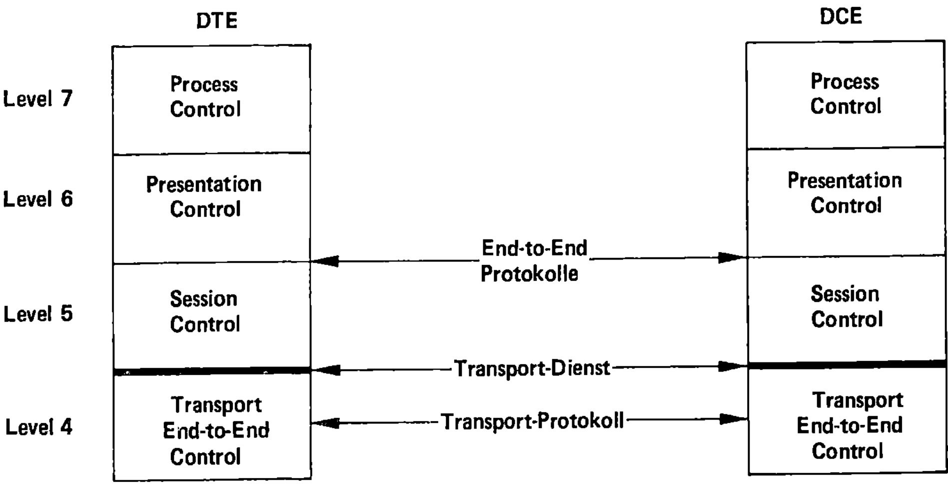

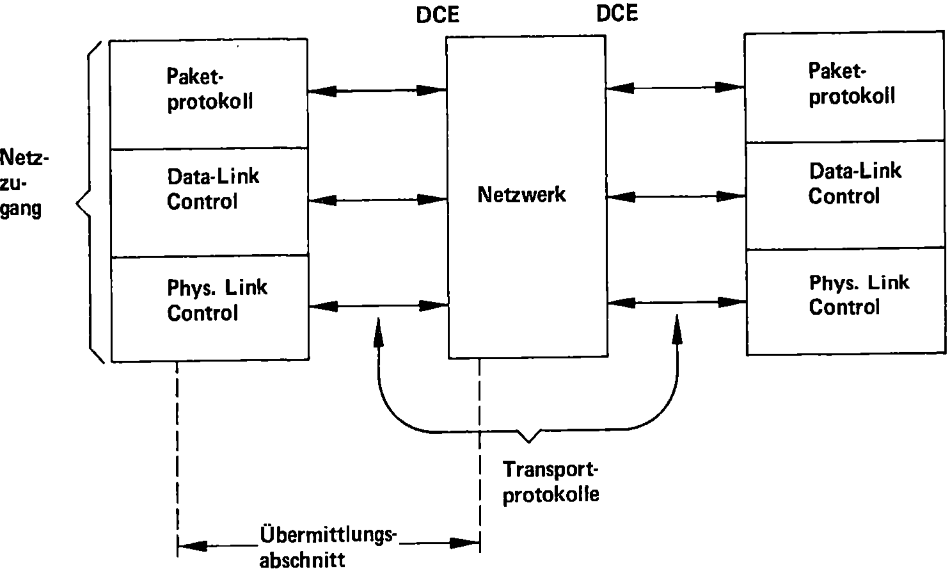

Bild 7   ISO-Referenzmodell (Übersicht)

Ver- bin- dung	Anwendung	Block- typ	Bedeutung
Logical Link	Datenaustausch auf CN	BLK	Datenblock einer Nachricht, dem weitere folgen (More-Data-Indication)
		MSG	Letzter oder einziger Datenblock einer Nachricht
	Steuer- protokoll für Gerät	CMD	Kommando an/von Gerätesteuerung
	Flußkontrolle auf CN	BACK	Block-Quittung mit Anforderung des nächsten Blocks
		BRK	Abbruch des Datenstroms in Empfangsrichtung
		STP	Temporäre Unterbrechung des Daten-stroms in Empfangsrichtung
		STRT	Wiederaufsetzen eines temporär unter-brochenen Datenstromes
		RST	Bestätigung des BRK
		INIT	Initialisierung einer CN
Service- Kanal	Service- Nachricht	CMD	Datenaustausch auf Service-Kanal
	Logical Link RC	ACTL	Kontrolle des Logical Link und des Trunk

Bild 8 Blocktypen im CDAEG-Netz

Anwendung	Subtyp	Bedeutung
Steuerung des Logical Link	CLR	Normierung des Logical Link nach Konfigurierung (FE → RC)
	PRST	Quittung auf CLR (RC → FE)
	REGL	Regulierungsnachricht (RC ↔ FE)
Trunk-Überwachung	LINIT	Bestätigung des RC über Trunk-Aufbau
	LIDLE	Kontrollnachricht (IDLE)

Bild 9   Subtyp-Kennung für Netzsteuerungsblöcke

Anwendung	PFC	Bedeutung
Laden RC	1	Neuladen (Force Load) Initialisierungsnachricht des RC
Logical Link	2	Auf-Abbau eines LL
Line Terminal	3	Auf-Abbau einer Linie Konfigurieren/Reconf./Delete eines Terminals
Status	6	Statusmeldungen LL, Line, Terminal
Statistik	7	Statistikmeldungen über Trunk, Line, Terminal
Trunk/Line	8	aktivieren / deaktivieren
NOP	10	Nachricht an NOP von RC
Boradcast	12	Nachrichtenaustausch zwischen NOP/LOP und Terminals Ändern der Terminal-Parameter

PFC = Primary Function Code

Bild 10   Service-Nachrichten im CDAEG-Netz (Übersicht)

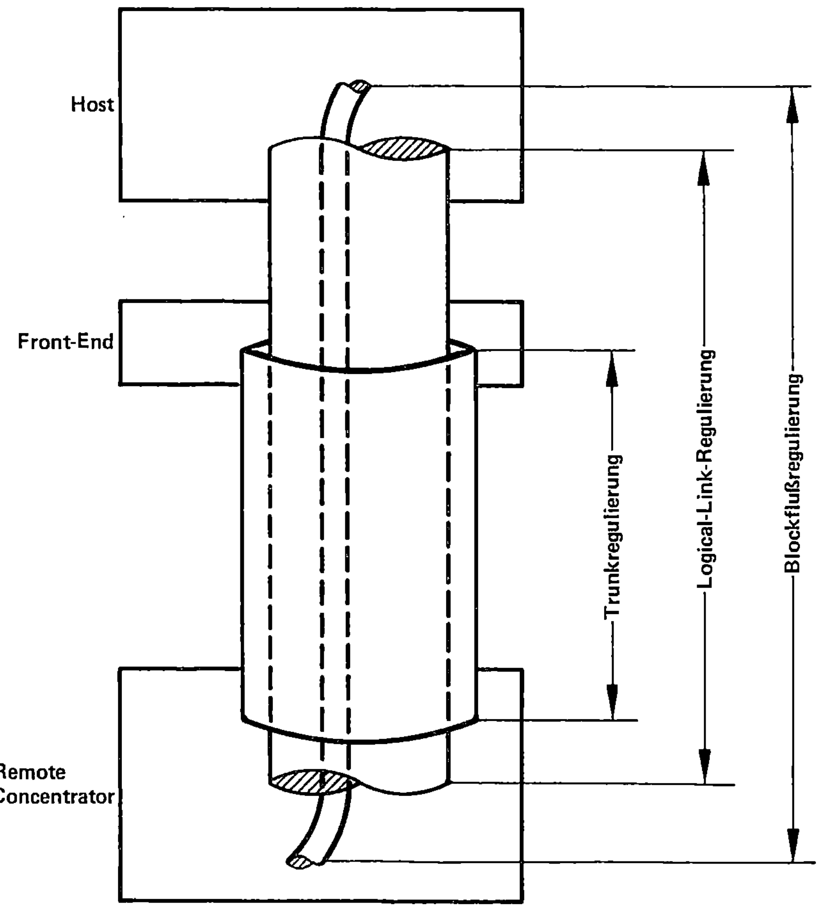

Bild 11   Regulierungsmechanismen im CDAEG-Netz

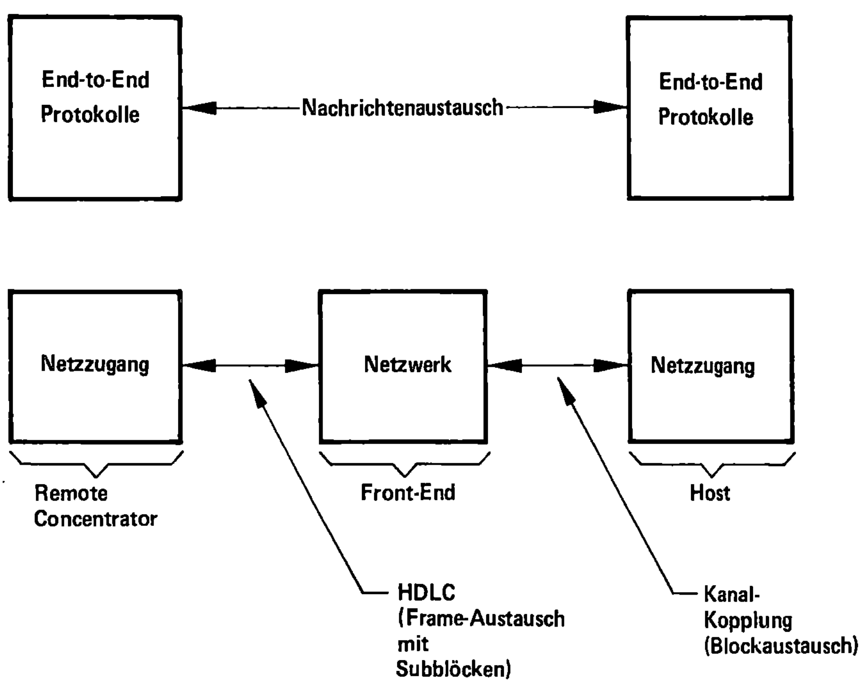

Bild 12   Vergleich CDAEG — ISO   (generelle Einordnung)

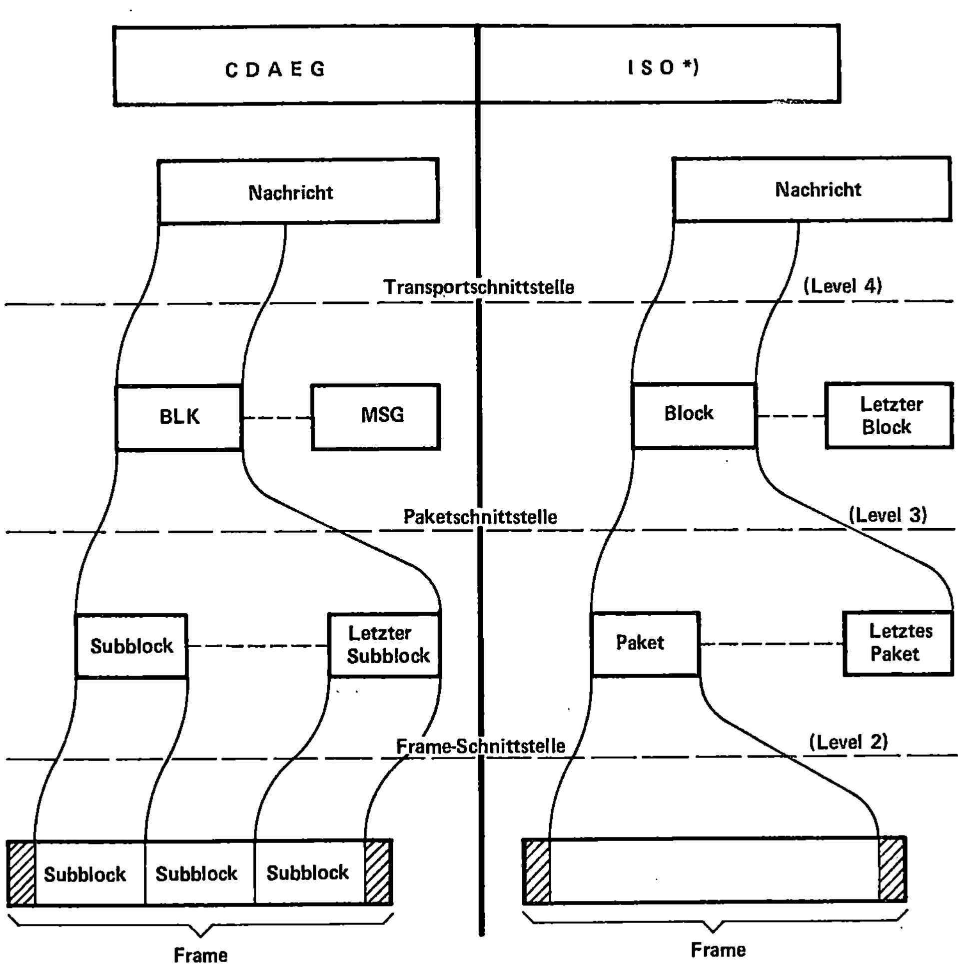

*) Annahme über Level 4 — 7
bezüglich Nachricht vorausgesetzt

Bild 13   Vergleich CDAEG — ISO (Nachrichtenformat)

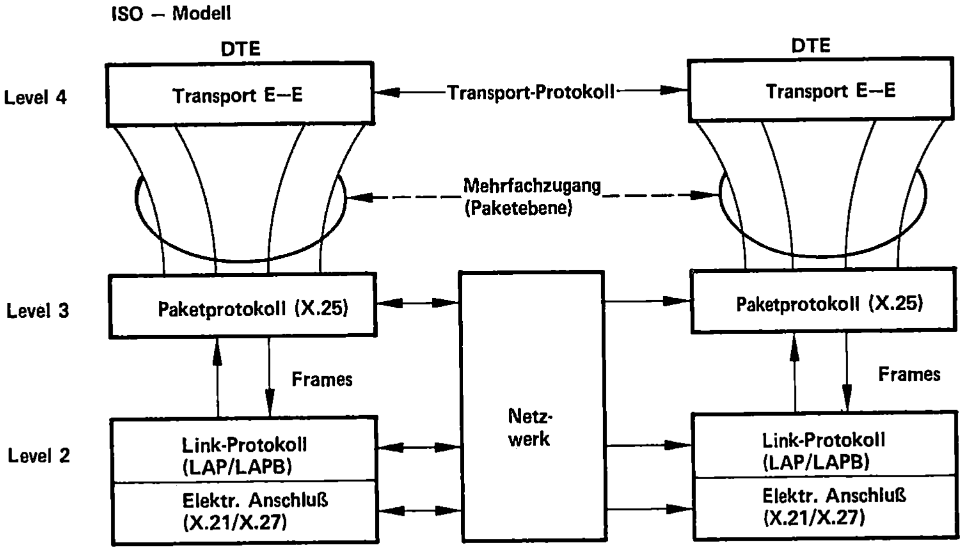

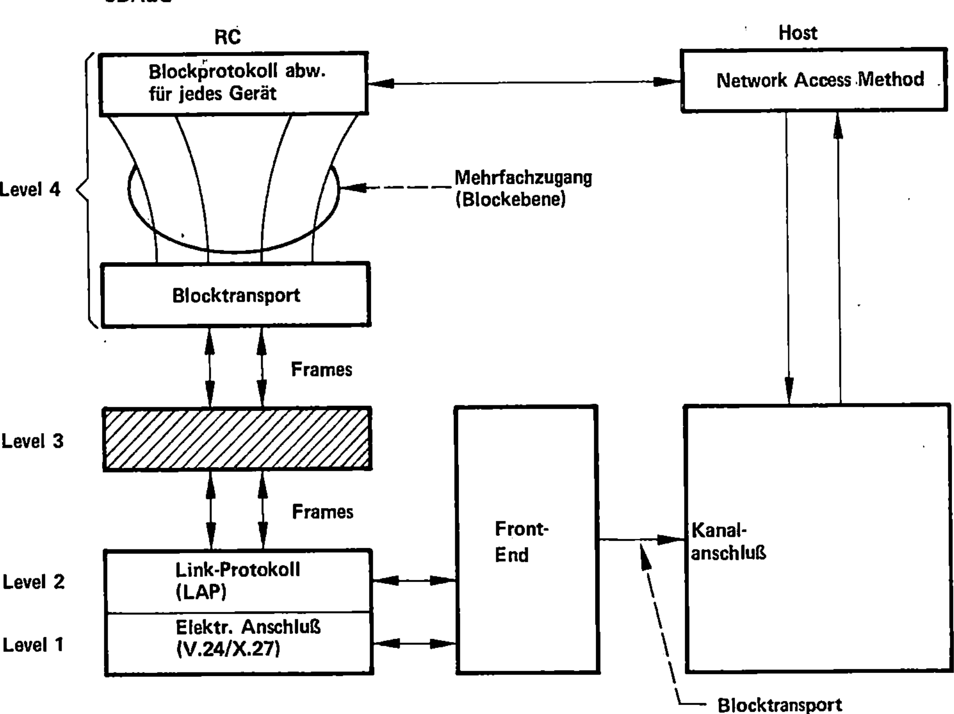

Bild 14   Vergleich CDAEG — ISO (Transportsystem)

ISO—Modell

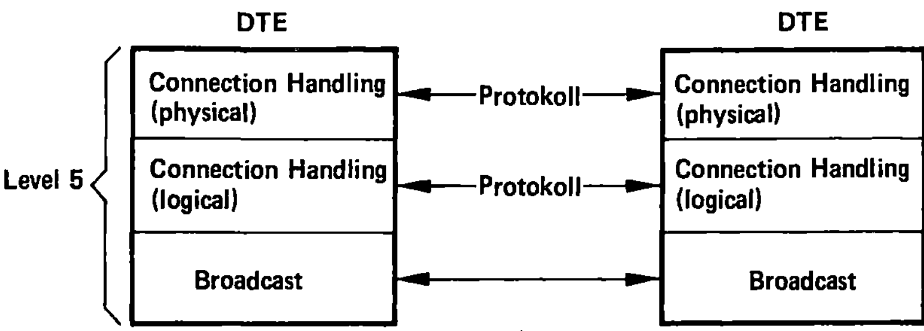

CDAEG

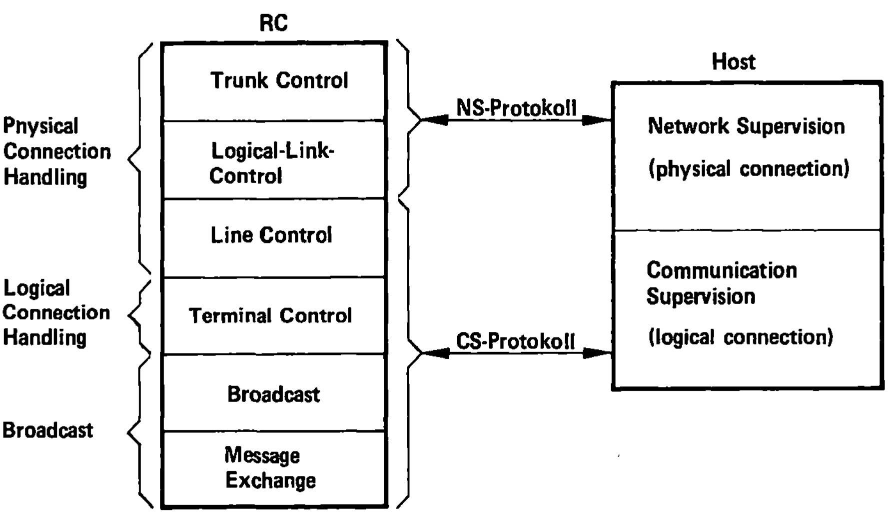

Bild 15   Vergleich CDAEG — ISO (Sessionssteuerung)

ISO – Modell

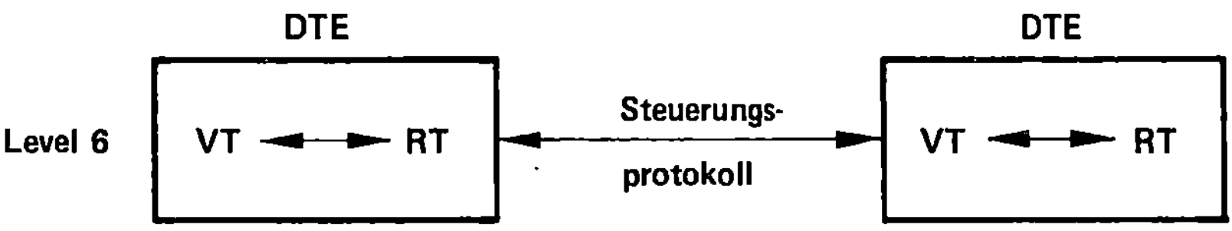

VT = virtuelles Terminal

RT = reales Terminal

CDAEG

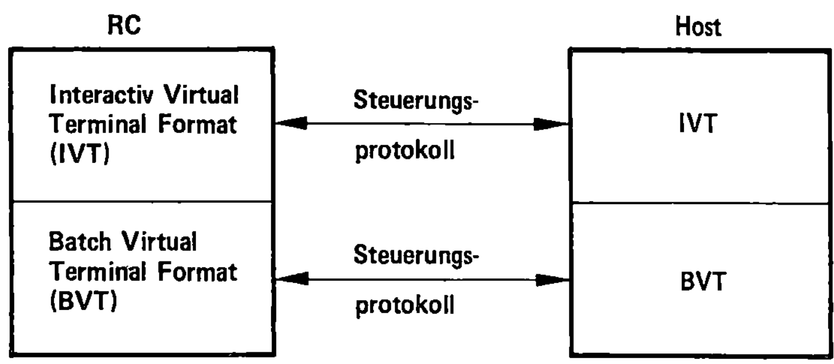

Bild 16   Vergleich CDAEG – ISO (Darstellungskontrolle)

Process Communication Structures for Distributed Systems

Klaus Böhme
Gerhard Peter
Institut für Informatik
University of Stuttgart
Azenbergstrasse 12
D-7000 Stuttgart 1
Fed. Rep. of Germany

Abstract:

In this paper problems of process interactions in a distributed system are discussed. Some basic process structures are analyzed and it is shown which communication and synchronization elements are necessary to realize a certain structure. These basic structures can be used to build any complex distributed process system.

The Distributed Data Base Management System POREL is taken as an example to show how to use the proposed model in a rather complex system with distributed control.

This work has been supported by ERO Grant No. DAERO-79-G-0008 and by DFG No. 210/3.

1. Introduction

In the area of computer communications two aspects get more and
more relevant:
- the number of networks is rapidly increasing
- the architecture of modern computers supports a
  lot of parallel processes.

New applications may use these properties for building large
process systems. But implementing such systems one notices
that corresponding software tools are missing /LA78/. Up to
now it is very difficult to write a piece of reliable software for a system where lots of parallel and asynchronous
events may occur and it is nearly impossible to prove its
correctness.

Brinch Hansen /BR78/ thinks that "what we do understand is deterministic message passing in which a receiving process performs
a completely predictable transformation of its input to its output". But for the nondeterministic message passing case he ex-
pects "a formal understanding not before the year 2000". Nondeterministic message passing means that a process does not
know which message it will receive next. If we design a system
where every process can accept every message at any time, then
this surely leads to an overspecification and a lot of unnecessary code. For the two-process case P. Zafiropulo /ZA78/ has
presented a solution. He has introduced design rules which lead
to logically complete and not overspecified protocols.

Another problem in such complex communication structures are
the different time delays which make the message flow between
processes dependent on their physical distances. This may
lead to logical inconsistences of the overall system behaviour. For a special class of systems, G. Bochmann /BO78/
has shown that their logical behaviour is independent of the
communication delays. Such systems are obtained by observing
certain regularity constraints during the system design.

Some problems in this area are already solved in the field
of operating systems. But we think that even if the basic concepts could be transferred to distributed systems, the specific

problems have to be regarded carefully. In our opinion, the
main differences we have to look for are:
- In operating systems a distinguished process exists coordi-
  nating the synchronization of all other processes.
- In networks the processes have to synchronize themselves,
  algorithms have to be found for the case of completely
  distributed control.
- In our concept <u>each</u> process may control another process,
  provided that they have agreed upon their exchange of control information.

These introductory remarks show, that there is a need for new
communication techniques and a need for the formal understanding of complex communication structures.

This paper analyzes some elementary process structures, shows
which communication and synchronization elements are necessary
for certain structures and shows furthermore in which of the
processes these elements have to reside. Our model, introduced
in chapter 3, which consists of five structures, allows the building of any complex process structure. We were confirmed in this
opinion by applying the model to our current work: the implementation of the Distributed Data Base Management System POREL.
As examples we take some characteristic parts of POREL and show
in chapter 4 how to use the model.

2. Assumptions and Definitions

A system as we want it to analyze consists of processes which
are distributed over several sites of a computer network and
which can interact with each other by means of a communication
system (CS). Interaction means that data and control information flows between the processes. To reduce the communication
overhead we observe one principle:
- all data information shall flow directly from the
  producer to the consumer process,
- however, all control information has to flow through
  the hierarchy of the controlling processes to its
  destination.

The CS is assumed to consist of a message exchange facility as
e.g. the PIX ML-protocol /PI78a/, /PI78b/, /PI77/, further
a file transfer facility /PO78/ and a data conversion service
/PO78/ which copes with the data representation of different
computer systems. Processes use this CS for connections to processes located at the same site (local) as well as to processes
located at remote sites.

Obviously the communication strategies for local connections
differ from those for remote connections. E.g. there are different time delays, different buffering, transportation, and
recovery techniques. A local file transfer e.g. can be done by
transferring only the file-identification and the authoriza-
tion rights. In the remote case of course also the data has to
be transported.

Further it is assumed that processes have not to care about the
life of their communication partners (a scheduler service will
start referenced processes if required and supervise their life).

Having characterized the underlying communication facility we
now look at the system's static and dynamic structure.

A distributed system consists of a set of __modules__ which are
implemented on some sites of a network. A subset of these modules however is implemented on each site. Several modules may
be linked to greater functional units called __process types__.
The set of process types represents the static system structure.
Occurrences of process types are called __processes__ and build the
dynamic structure. Processes of one type may exist simultaneously
on one node as well as on different nodes. Returning to the
static structure, one can say that process types need not know
the whole system but only their environment. The __environment__ of
a process type consists of all types it has to interact with
(dynamically all local and remote processes with which it wants
to communicate). The environment consists of predecessor and
successor types. Predecessors send requests to their successors
and control them. Therefore any process only has one predecessor.

3. The Process Structures

The general problem which we want to analyze is:
- A user request is to be executed by a system of
  interacting processes PO, P1, ..., Pn, where
  every process only executes part of the request.

We distinguish three cases:

1. Deterministic, only PO knows the path:
   - PO delivers parts of the request to P1, ..., Pn and
     gets parts of the result from P1, ..., Pn.

2. Deterministic, all the Pi know the path:
   - PO delivers the request and the process vector
     (PO, ..., Pn) to P1, P1 works, sends (part of) the
     results to PO and delivers (the rest of) the request
     to P2 with the same process vector, ...

3. Dynamic determination of Pi:
   - PO delivers the request to P1, P1 determines P2 as
     its successor, P2 gets (the rest of) the request,
     determines P3, ...

In POREL e.g. only case 3 occurs. There, it is even possible
that the same user request issued at different times implies
different process sequences. (If e.g. the distribution of data
of the database has changed, different nodes and therefore
different processes will carry out the request.)

All three cases have in common, that some process Pi sends a
request to another process Pj. Pj has to know
- where to send control information
- from where it gets input data
- where to send the results.
Therefore a communication element "request" is needed having
the following parameters:

```
request <rname> to <pname>
                    control on <mln> to <pname>
                    input from <pname-list>
                    results on <mln-list> to <pname-list>
```

where   rname   is a request identification

        pname   is a process name

        mln   is a message link name (a sort of a connect-ion identifier - see /PI77/ for the exact definition)

        pname-list   is a list of process names

        mln-list   is a list of message link names, with each mln of the mln-list corresponding to a process of the pname-list

3.1 Structure 1

The simplest communication structure is obtained if a process, say P0, delivers a request R1 to P1 and P1 gets all input data from P0 and sends all results to P0:

```
P0:    request  R1 to P1
                control on MLN1 to P0
                input from P0
                results on MLN2 to P0
```

Figure 1 illustrates the static structure of P0 and P1.

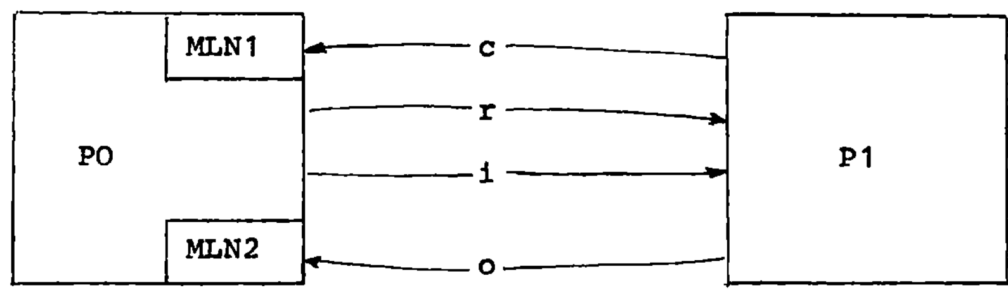


```
P0 ..... process 0
P1 ..... process 1
MLN1 ... message link 1
MLN2 ... message link 2
c    ..... control-connection
r    ..... request-connection
i    ..... input-connection
o    ..... output(results)-connection
```

Figure 1: Static Structure, all data from/to P0

To keep one's eye on communication problems only, the behaviour
of a process shall be simplified, so that there is an input phase
at the beginning and an output phase at the end of a request's
execution, i.e. these phases do not overlap.

After getting a request, P1 has to announce to the controlling
process PO when it is ready for input (begin-message), thereby
sending its exact identification (PID) and its MLN where expecting input. Further the output phase has to be announced (finished-
message) and also the end of the execution. Such a model of a
process then needs the following communication- and synchroni-
zation-code:

```
P1:    wait   (request)
       send   (begin, PID, MLN)
       wait   (input)

         .
         .       execution
         .

       send   (finished)
       send   (results)
       send   (end or error)
```

"Send" and "wait" are primitives of the CS.

"Send" transmits one protocol-unit, perhaps consisting of one
or more messages or files which are considered as one unit.
"Wait" waits for one protocol-unit thereby stopping the process until the expected protocol-unit is arrived. In the following the word "message" is used instead of "protocol-unit".

Looking now at PO, its corresponding code is:

```
PO:    send   (request R ... )
       wait   (begin, ...)
       send   (input)
       wait   (finished)
       wait   (results)
       wait   (end or error)
```

The relation between the actions of PO and P1 and the corresponding process states are shown in figure 2:

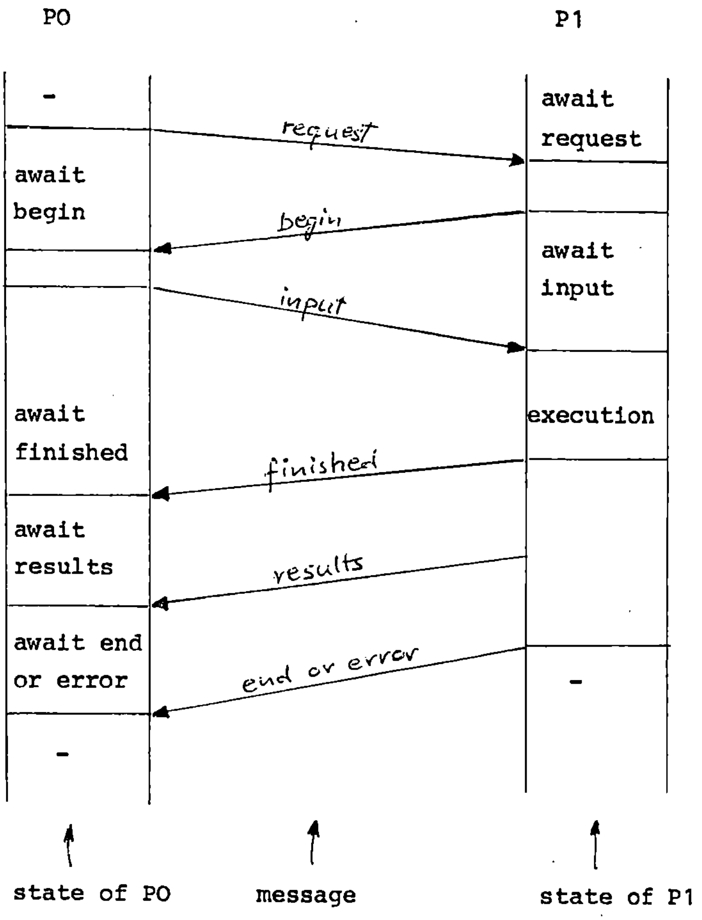

(Note: "await xy" is a process' state, "wait (xy)" is
a synchronization primitive of the CS)

Figure 2: Dynamics of PO and P1

Already in this relatively simple structure there is the problem that the controlling process does not know whether it
will receive an "end" or an "error" as last message. This problem is solved by extending the "wait" element:

wait (message 1) or (message 2) or ...

The wait-condition is satisfied if one (and only one) of the
messages has been received.

Another extension of "wait" is necessary when expecting protocol errors, i.e. if another message but the expected one is received then an error routine shall be executed:

$$\text{wait (message), err}$$

3.2 Structure 2

A more complex structure is obtained if input data arrives
from several processes:

```
PO:   request  R1 to P1
               control on MLN1 to PO
               input from P2, P3
               results on MLN2 to PO
```

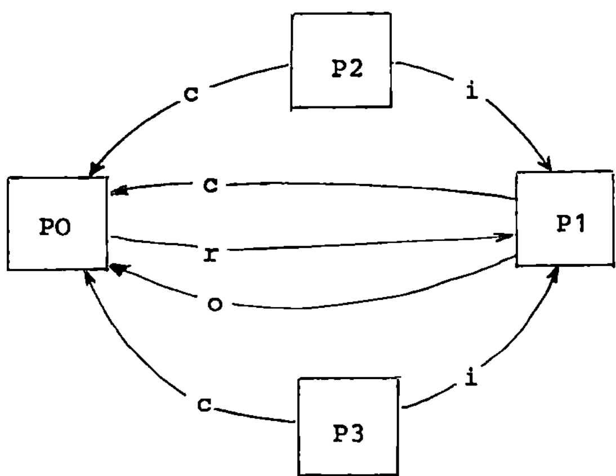

Figure 3: Static structure, input from other
processes

In this structure, the processes P2 and P3 have to know the
receiver of their data (PID and MLN of P1) and the time, when
P1 awaits input data (the CS should not maintain a large pool
of sended but not received messages). Control messages needed
for that shall come from PO (PO only duplicates P1's begin-
message and sends it to P2 and P3).

```
PO:  send  (request R1) to P1
     wait  (begin, ...)
     send  (begin P1, ...) to P2
     send  (begin P1, ...) to P3
     wait  (finished)
     wait  (results)
     wait  (end) or (error)


P1:  wait  (request)
     send  (begin) to PO
     wait  (input) from P2
     wait  (input) from P3
       .   (analogous to structure 1)
       .
       .
       .



P2, P3:
           .

           .
           .
           .

     wait  (begin P1, ...) from PO
     send  (input) to P1
       .
       .
       .
```

The processes P2 and P3 send input data to P1 after having received the "begin P1" message. Now it turned out that the
"wait" element cannot solve the problem whether P1 shall wait
first for P2's or for P3's data. Therefore other communication
elements are necessary:

```
P1:  wait   (request)
     send   (begin) to PO
     parallel
     pwait  (input) from P2
     pwait  (input) from P3
     endparallel
```

The two elements "parallel" and "endparallel" enclose a sequence
of pwait's. The meaning is, that all pwait-conditions have to be

satisfied (in any sequence) before the parallel/ endparallel
block can be left.

To intercept a nonexpected message (protocol or programming
error), "endparallel" can be extended by an error label:

       parallel

          .

          .

          .

       endparallel err

Structure 2 can easily be expanded to the more general case,
where several processes (rather than 2) send input data to P1.
PO only has to broadcast the "begin P1" message to those processes which have input for P1. P1 needs some more pwait (input)
instructions.

3.3 Structure 3

In structure 3 two requests are executed in parallel. This is a
composition of two structure 1 elements (see figure 4).

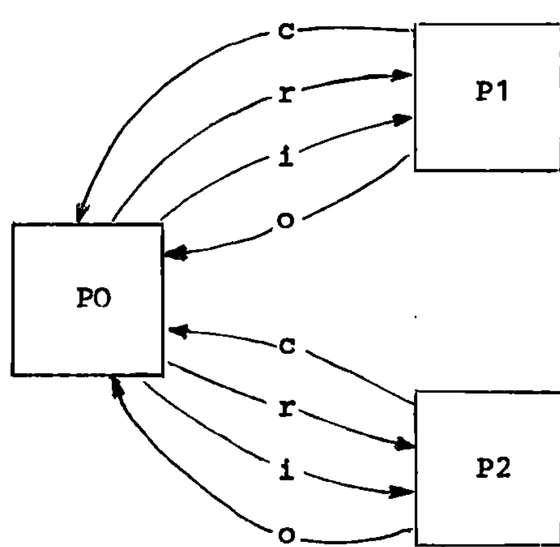

Figure 4: Parallel processes

Problems for PO arise by not knowing which one of the processes
P1 and P2 is first awaiting input or sending results or in other
words which shall be the next expected message. But with pwait's
and wait's this problem can be solved:

```
PO:  send   (request R1) to P1
     send   (request R2) to P2
     parallel
     pwait (begin) from P1

             send   (input)   to P1
             wait   (finished)   from P1
             wait   (results)   from P1
             wait   (end) or (error) from P1

     pwait (begin) from P2

             send   (input)   to P2
             wait   (finished)   from P2
             wait   (results)   from P2
             wait   (end) or (error) from P2


     endparallel
```

This structure is new as wait's are used between pwait's.
If e.g. P1 announces "begin", then "send input" is executed
and "results" are awaited from P1. In this state P2 may announce
its "begin". Therefore the CS first has to remember
       - which messages have to be sent before the "parallel"/
        "end parallel" block will be finished (pwait)
and second has to remember
       - which messages are expected and where the process
        is to be continued after receiving an expected
        message.

In a multiprocessor system the "parts" of a parallel/endparallel
block may simultaneously run on determined processors. The CS,
however, has to simulate several statement-counters in a one-
processor system to obtain the same effect.

The more general case is obtained when having several processes
executing PO's request in parallel. PO's structure is hardly
getting more complex because of the modularity of the pwait-
blocks.

3.4 Structure 4

In structure 4 PO delivers a request to P1. P1 can only carry it
out in part and therefore sends a request to P2. Results of P1
and P2 shall be received by PO.

```
PO:  request  R1 to P1
              control on MLN1 to PO
              input          from PO
              results on MLN2 to PO


P1:  request  R2 to P2
              control on MLN3 to P1
              input          from P1
              results on MLN2 to PO
```

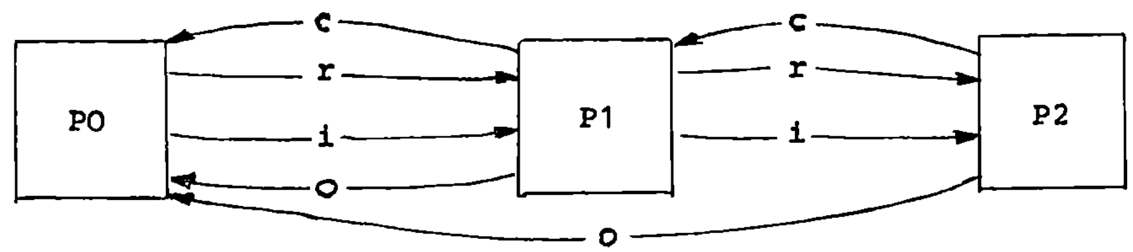

Figure 5: Two consecutive requests

In this structure, PO first has to wait for results of P1,
second for results of P2 and not for end of P1. This implies
that there is a need for another control message:

"wait for results from P2"

which flows from P1 to PO.

Figure 6 shows the dynamic relation between PO, P1 and P2 and their states.

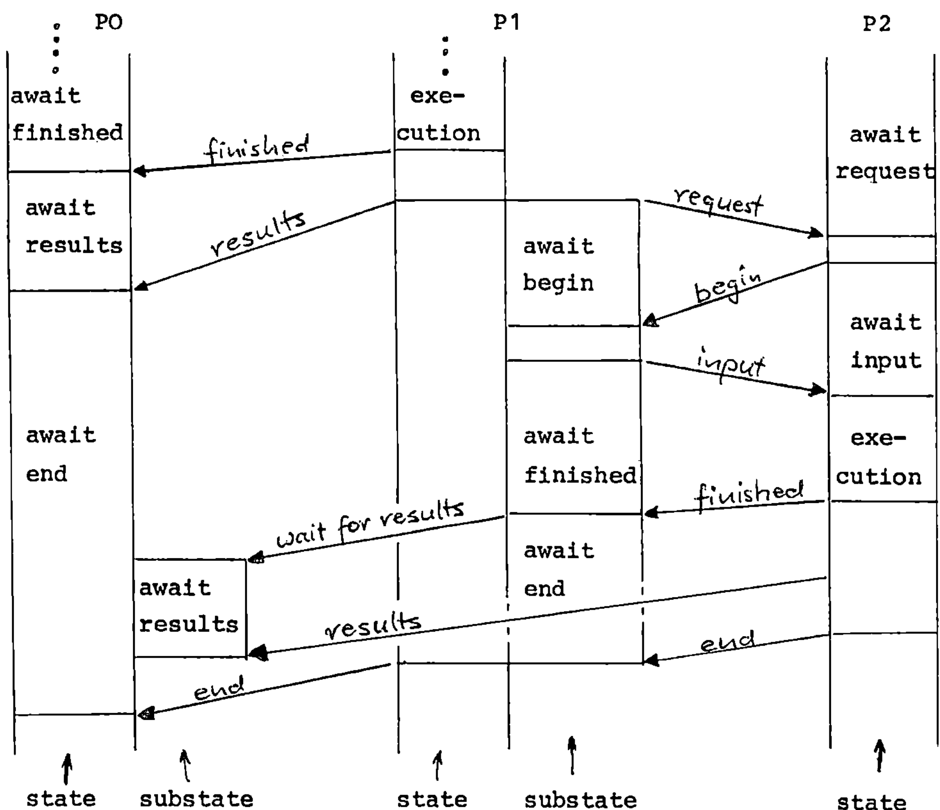

Figure 6: Two consecutive requests

As for the previous structures there exists an extention to n processes PO, ..., Pn, which then build a strictly hierarchical process system.

3.5 Structure 5

Structure 5 is the same as structure 4 except that PO controls P2. Therefore P1 may "die" before P2.

Looking at structure 4 one notices that after sending input to
P2, P1 only waits for some control messages. If this task can
be done by PO, P1 can reach its end earlier. For this P1 has to
transmit the paramters of "request" to PO and according to
structure 2, PO has to inform P1 about P2's begin (Figure 7).

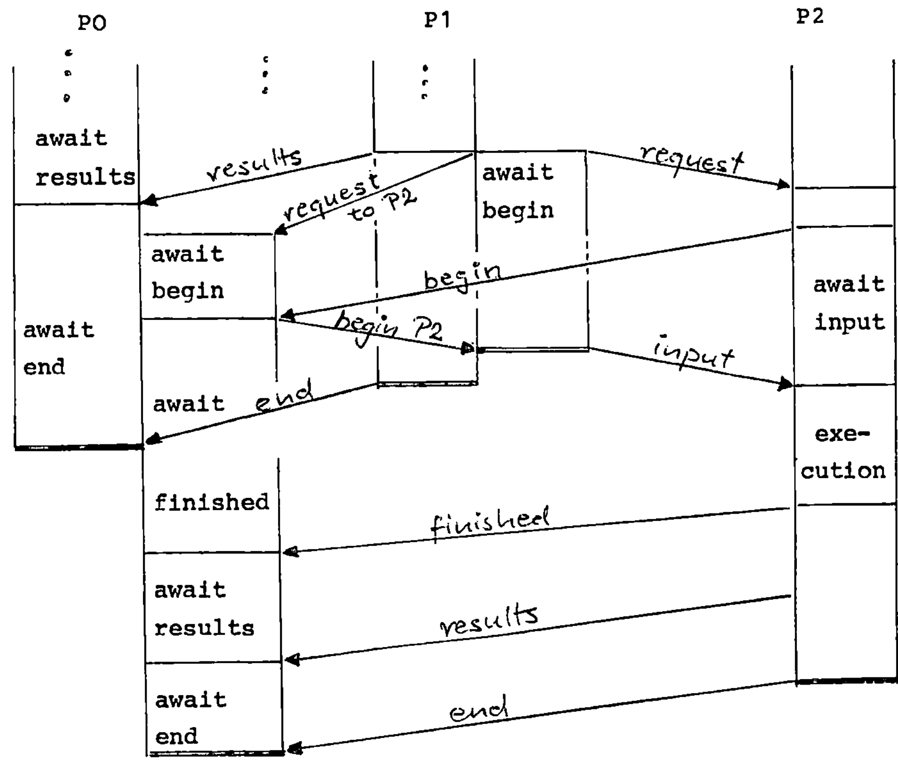

Figure 7: PO controls P2

This structure may be expanded to the n-process case as well.

3.6 Summary of chapter 3

The 5 structures presented above have shown how to realize a
certain structure with the aid of an adequate request-state-
ment. Further the necessary synchronization- and communica-
tion-code for each process was pointed out. For a given request-
statement it is possible to automatically generate this code.

In POREL this facility is used to generate all the wait and
send statements which are necessary for synchronizing the
execution of the parts of a DDBMS-user's request. Those parts
may simultaneously run on several sites of the network (ref.
ch. 4, example 2).

The rules stated in this chapter are:

(1) There is only one process controlling a request. But con-
    trol can be transferred to the process' own controller.

(2) If the controlling process (C) and the requesting process
    (R) are not identical, then process R has to send all re-
    quest parameters to C.

(3) When beginning to carry out the request, the executing pro-
    cess E has to identify itself (PID) and to specify its MLN
    where awaiting input.

(4) C has to send the "begin"-information (PID, MLN) to all
    processes which will send input to E.

(5) Analogous to (4) C has to send a "wait for results" message
    to all processes which will get some results.

4. Application in the DDBMS POREL

In this chapter we will discuss the process-communication model as we use it in POREL. We do not think that it is necessary
to show the whole POREL DDBMS with all communication possibilities but some relevant parts. First we give a short overview
of POREL as far as we need it in this paper. For further information see e.g. /PO78/, /NB77/.

POREL is a strongly layered system which can be regarded as two
sets of process types. The first set contains an I/O-support
modul which is interacting with a user guiding him to formulate
his transactions in a nonprocedural data base language. This
language is compiled to an internal form by two other moduls
called Network Independent Analysis (NUA) and Network Oriented

Analysis (NOA) respectively. At compilation time, these processes are executed sequentially. The first example deals with this set. The second set is described in the second example. Different snapshots of the system are shown below; the static structures at the time a, b, and c characterize the dynamics of the compilation phase:

a)

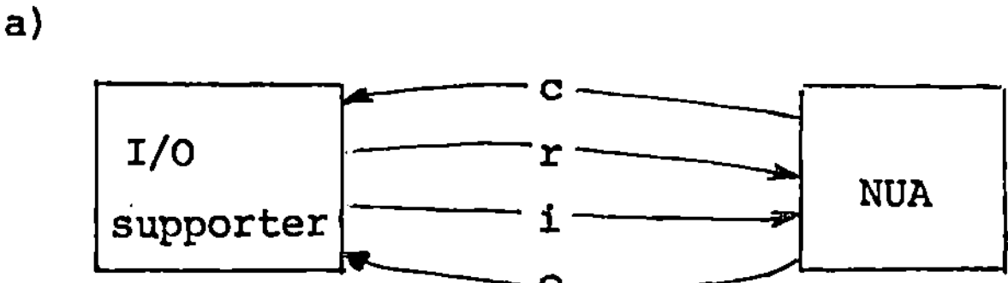

The I/O supporter controls the NUA during the whole time it is active.

b)

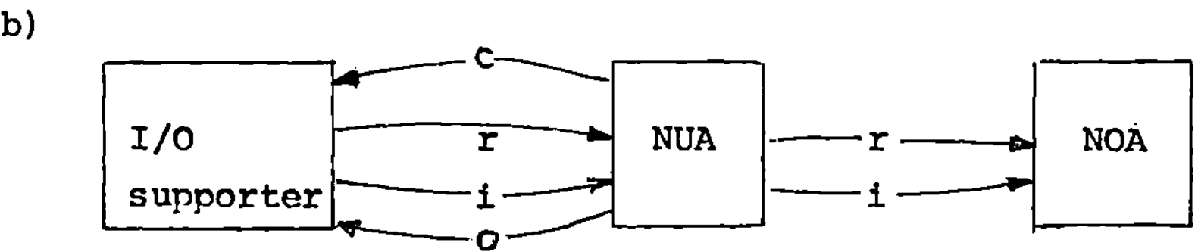

The NUA stops its own execution and starts the NOA.

c)

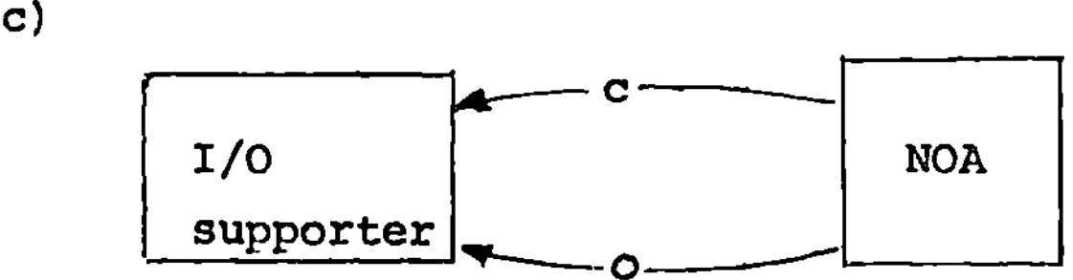

The NOA is working now and controlled by the I/O supporter.

Figure 8: Example 1

The communication and synchronization code which have to be
generated is (according to structure 5 in chapter 2):

```
I/O:   send   (request R1 to NUA
                control     to I/O
                input     from I/O
                results     to I/O)


NUA:   wait   (request)   from I/O
       send   (begin)     to I/O
       wait   (input)     from I/O

         .

         .

       execution

         .

         .

       send   (finished)  to I/O
       send   (results)   to I/O
       send   (request R2 to NOA
                control     to I/O
                input     from NUA
                results     to I/O)   to NOA
       send   (request R2 to NOA ... ) to I/O
       wait   (begin of NOA) from I/O   (I/O is controlling
                                            the NOA)

       send   (input) to NOA
       send   (end) to I/O
```

For the second example we need the second set of process types.
This set consists of Monitors and Base Machines (BM) which are
responsible for the execution of a user's database request
(transaction). Since the data is distributed, the request may
be broken into parts which are later executed by BMs at
different sites due to a time graph (parallely or sequentially).
The evaluation of the time graph, e.g. the execution of previously generated wait-statements, is done on every site by a
Monitor. These wait-statements are a means for synchronizing
the Monitors and the BMs. The latter are the only processes
which really access the data of the database.

In the example below a transaction has been started at node 1
of the network. Parts of the transaction are executed on
node 1, 2 and 3. On node 1 two BM are used in parallel.
Results from node 1 and node 3 are used on node 2, the user-
result is given directly from the BM on node 2 to the user
on node 1. The monitor 2 is not directly connected with monitor 3.

The static structure is:

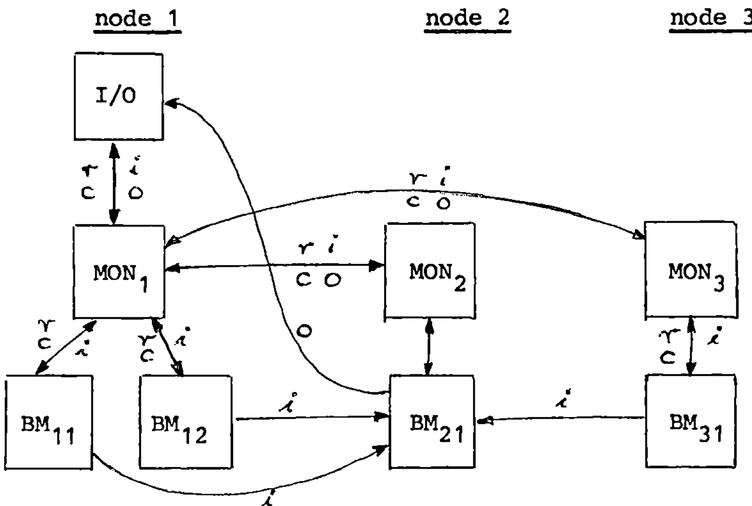

Figure 9: Example 2

In this example we have the different structures introduced
in chapter 3.

Structure 1:

PO	P1
I/O support	MON1

Structure 2:

PO	P1	P2	P3	...
MON2	BM_{21}	BM_{11}	BM_{12}	BM_{31}

Structure 3:

PO	P1	P2
MON1	BM_{11}	BM_{12}
MON1	MON2	MON3

Extended Structure 4:

PO	P1	P1	P2
I/O	MON1	MON2	BM_{21}

5. Conclusion

The introduced process communication- and synchronization
model is a suggestion towards a solution of concurrent programming in a network of computers. We think that this model
helps for the correct understanding of control- and data flow
in a complex system, as discussed by Brinch Hansen /BR78/.
Therefore it facilitates the development of reliable software.

For further studies we think that there is a great field of
interest in the understanding of the semantic of the data exchanged between the processes. We do not know how much information about the received data one process needs to interpret them in the correct matter.

Acknowledgement

We would like to thank the members of the POREL team for many
discussions during the preparation of this paper.

<u>Literature</u>

/BO78/   Gregor v. Bochmann: Synchronization in Distributed
          System Modules. 3rd Berkeley Workshop, August 1978

/BR78/   Per Brinch Hansen: A Keynote Address on Concurrent Pro-
          gramming. COMPSAC 1978

/LA78/   Christopher Layton: Computer Network Protocols, Their
          Place in European Strategy for Computer Communica-
          tions. Computer Network Protocols, Liege 1978

/NB77/   Erich J. Neuhold; Horst Biller: POREL: A Distributed
          Data Base on an Inhomogeneous Computer Network.
          3rd International Conference on Very Large Data
          Bases, Tokyo, October 1977

/PI78a/ G.V. Bochman; F.H. Vogt: Message Link Protocol,
          Functional Specification, PIX/HLP/TAG/78/02,
          1978

/PI78b/ F. Hertweck; E. Raubold; F. Vogt: The ML-Protocol
          Description, PIX/HLP/TEK/78/01, 1978

/PI77/   F. Hertweck; E. Raubold; F. Vogt: X.25 Based Pro-
          cess-Process Communication-Concepts and Facilities,
          PIX/HLP/TEK/77/01, 1977

/PO78/   Reports of the POREL Research Group, Reports No.
          78/4 through 78/13 of the Institut für Informatik,
          University of Stuttgart (in German), 1978

/ZA78/   Pitro Zafiropulo: Design Rules for Producing Logically
          Complete Two-Process Interactions and Communication
          Protocols. COMPSAC 1978

Zur Programmierung verteilter Systeme

Harald Kemen

Fachbereich Informatik
Universität Hamburg
Schlüterstr. 70
D-2000 Hamburg 13

ABSTRACT

A concept for programming distributed systems is presented, called the
virtual network machine. This approach conceives the entire distributed
hardware configuration as a single virtual machine which is capable of
executing a system of cooperating processes formulated in a suitable
high level language, in this case CONCURRENT PASCAL. All processes communicate by means of MONITORs regardless wether they reside on the same
node computer or on different ones. The current status of our ongoing
implementation is reported and the relation to the ISO-Reference-Model
of Open Systems Architecture is discussed.

1. Einleitung

Das ISO-Referenz-Modell [6] zur Standardisierung der Kommunikationsarchitektur verteilter Systeme basiert auf dem Konzept kooperierender An-
wendungsaktivitäten (application processes, sessions). Die Kooperation
von Anwendungsprozessen in einer 'session' wird als unabhängig davon
angesehen, ob die beteiligten Prozesse auf einem Knotenrechner (system)
eines verteilten Systems oder auf verschiedenen alloziert sind, gegebenenfalls wird unsichtbar für die Anwendungsprozesse der Dienst eines
Kommunikationssystems ('transport service') in Anspruch genommen.

Auch das hier vorgestellte Konzept zur Programmierung von Mehrrechner-
systemen geht von der Vorstellung aus, daß die Aktivitäten eines verteilten Systems am besten von einem System kooperierender Prozesse modelliert werden. Es wird zur Zeit am FB Informatik Hamburg implementiert
und soll seine Anwendung in der Steuerung einer umfangreichen Spezialperipherie zur Bildverarbeitung und in der Bildvorverarbeitung finden.

2. Das Konzept der Netzwerkmaschine

2.1 Charakterisierung des Konzeptes

Die (virtuelle) Netzwerkmaschine [3b,8] ist die logische Sicht eines
Mehrrechnersystems durch den Anwender. Folgende Eigenschaften charak-
terisieren sie:

1. Die Gemeinschaft der Knoten eines Mehrrechnersystems bildet eine logische Einheit.

2. Zugriffe auf Objekte (Zustandsvariable von Prozessen, gemeinsame Daten, Betriebsmittel) lassen sich ohne Rücksicht auf ihre physische Realisation spezifizieren.

3. Es existiert eine einheitliche Benutzerschnittstelle, d.h. der Benutzer kann seine Problemlösung in einem einzigen Programm für das gesamte Mehrrechnersystem formulieren, unabhängig von der aktuellen Konfiguration. Wir nennen ein solches Programm Netzwerkprogramm.

4. Ein Kommunikationssystem ermöglicht es, Nachrichten zwischen allen
beteiligten Knotenrechnern auszutauschen. Über die Natur dieses Systems
werden jedoch keine weiteren Annahmen gemacht. Das Konzept der Netzwerkmaschine modelliert die im ISO-Modell mit 'data-processing oriented
function' bezeichnete Schicht oberhalb des 'transport service'. In welcher Beziehung die Schichten 'application-, presentation- und session-
layer' zum Konzept der Netzwerkmaschine stehen, wird diskutiert.

2.2 Sprachliche Formulierung der Kommunikation von Prozessen

Zur Formulierung eines Programms für die Netzwerkmaschine ist zunächst,
gegebenenfalls erst nach entsprechenden Erweiterungen, jede höhere Programmiersprache geeignet.
Wir wollen jedoch nur solche Sprachen ansprechen, die schon Konstrukte
enthalten, die die Formulierung paralleler Aktivitäten gestatten.
Wichtigstes Unterscheidungsmerkmal ist hier die in den Sprachen benutzte
Technik der Interprozesskommunikation. Wir können zwei grundlegende

Techniken unterscheiden, die Kommunikation von Prozessen sprachlich auszudrücken [10]:

- als expliziten Austausch von Nachrichten (message - oriented system)

- als (prozeduralen) Zugriff auf gemeinsame Datenbereiche (procedure -
  oriented system)

Eine nachrichtenorientierte Kommunikation scheint auf den ersten Blick
die adäquate Technik für verteilte Systeme zu sein, ist doch das wich-
tigste Betriebsmittel des 'transport service' die Nachricht.
Aus der Sicht des Programmierers kann es jedoch vorteilhafter sein, die
Interprozeßkommunikation in Form von Prozeduraufrufen zu formulieren
und nicht als expliziten Nachrichtenaustausch. Die Semantik der Interprozeßkommunikation vereinfacht sich nämlich dadurch, die Programmierung
gewinnt an Sicherheit.

(1) Als ein Beispiel für blockorientierte Sprachen soll hier PEARL erwähnt werden.
Aktivitäten paralleler Prozesse werden mittels des 'task'-Konzeptes ausgedrückt. Die Interaktion von Prozessen (tasks) geschieht durch Zugriff
auf gemeinsame Variable, die globalen Variablen. Als Synchronisations-
werkzeug stehen SEMAPHOR-Variable zur Verfügung. Der Programmierer kann(!)
mit ihrer Hilfe die Sperrsynchronisation globaler Variable formulieren.
Der Vorteil liegt in der großen Flexibilität der Programmierung von Syn-
chronisationschemata, hierin liegt aber auch eine Gefahr. Die Zugriffsrechte auf Variable ergeben sich aus den algol-ähnlichen Sichtbarkeitsregeln.

(2) Auch in CONCURRENT PASCAL [1] wird die Kommunikation zwischen Prozessen als Zugriff auf gemeinsame Daten realisiert. Allerdings sind
diese Daten Variable eines Monitors. Alle Zugriffe auf die gemeinsamen
Daten sind nur im wechselseitigen Ausschluß durch Aufruf der öffentlichen
Prozeduren des Monitors möglich, ein Beitrag zur Sicherheit der Programmierung. Es sollen hier nicht die Vor- und Nachteile des Monitorkonzeptes
diskutiert werden, CONCURRENT PASCAL steht hier als eine der Sprachen,
die ein bestimmtes Konzept des gesicherten Zugriffs auf gemeinsame Daten
realisiert haben, diese Sicherung also nicht dem Programmierer überlassen.
Die Sichtbarkeitsregeln für Variable von Programmkomponenten (PROCESS,
CLASS, MONITOR) folgen sowohl dem Prinzip der Isolation der Komponenten
gegeneinander als auch dem der sicheren Voreinstellung. Alle Variable
sind nämlich nur innerhalb einer Programmkomponente bekannt, es sei denn,

sie werden explizit nach außen bekannt gemacht (Schlüsselwort ENTRY)
und importiert durch Aufführen des Objektes in der Liste der Zugriffsrechte im Kopf der Programmkomponente. (s. hierzu auch [13])

(3) In [4] wird PASCAL - PLITS vorgestellt, eine u.a. zur Programmierung
verteilter Systeme entwickelte Sprache. 'MODULE' und 'MESSAGE' sind ihre
Grundstrukturen. Ein 'MODULE' ist eine Programmkomponente, die der
SIMULA-CLASS ähnelt. Eine Kommunikation zwischen 'MODULEs' ist nur durch
Nachrichtenaustausch mittels der Standardprozeduren 'SEND MESSAGE (va-
riable) TO (module)' bzw. 'RECEIVE (variable) FROM (module)' möglich.

(4) Ebenfalls ein Derivat von PASCAL ist die Sprache PLATON [11].
Auch diese Sprache realisiert das Prozeßkonzept. Die Kommunikation von
Prozessen geschieht durch Zugriff auf sog. 'SHARED VARIABLEs'. Jedoch
hat nur der Prozeß das exklusive Zugriffsrecht auf solche Kommunika-
tionsvariable, der dieses vorher angefordert hat. Mit Hilfe der Standardprozeduren SIGNAL und WAIT tauschen kommunizierende Prozesse Zugriffsrechte auf SHARED VARIABLEs aus. Die Sprache ist nachrichtenorien-
tiert, weil diese Zugriffsrechte (Adressen der Variablen) als Nachrichten
versendet werden. Durch die Versendung der Zugriffsrechte wird das Ko-
pieren der Daten umgangen, wie es z.B. in CONCURRENT PASCAL notwendig
ist. Hier müssen ja Daten zunächst Variablen eines Monitors zugewiesen
werden, bevor ein anderer Prozeß diese lesen kann.

Auf der Basis dieser Sprachen sind Konzepte zur Programmierung verteilter Systeme entwickelt worden bzw. werden noch entwickelt. In [12] wird
z.B. ein System diskutiert, das auf der Sprache PEARL beruht. Die Zugriffe auf netz-globale Variable werden dadurch möglich, daß die physische Adresse der Variable so erwertert wird, daß sie im Netz eindeutig
bleibt.

3. Die Realisation einer Netzwerkmaschine auf der Basis von CONCURRENT
PASCAL [3,8]

Das Typenkonzept und das der abstrakten Datentypen - PROCESS, CLASS,
MONITOR - macht die Sprache besonders attraktiv für die Verwendung als
Programmiersprache eines verteilten Systems, sind doch Prozeß und Monitor
als Werkzeug zur Kommunikation Elemente der Sprachdefinition. Ferner ist
wegen der Festlegung der Zugriffsrechte im Quelltext und aufgrund der

Sichtbarkeitsregeln von Variablen der Übersetzer in der Lage, die korrekte Anwendung dieser Zugriffe zur Übersetzungszeit zu überprüfen. Dadurch wird die Wahrscheinlichkeit des Auftretens von Laufzeitfehlern beträchtlich reduziert. In einer Umgebung, wo die echte parallele Ausführung von Prozessen die Reproduzierbarkeit von Abläufen zur Fehlersuche erschwert, ist solch eine frühzeitige Überprüfung ein wertvoller Beitrag zur Reduktion des Erstellungsaufwandes von Programmen. Die von der Sprache auferlegten Restriktionen werden als Preis für die gewonnene Sicherheit wohl gern in Kauf genommen.

3.1 Die Allokation der Programmkomponenten

CONCURRENT PASCAL (CP) ist also die Programmiersprache einer virtuellen Netzwerkmaschine, die dank ihrer Hardwarestruktur in der Lage ist, ein System paralleler Prozesse auszuführen. Diese virtuelle Maschine wird auf einem Netz von Knotenrechnern realisiert, die im einzelnen von lokalen Betriebssystemen kontrolliert werden und durch ein Kommunikationssystem miteinander so verbunden sind, daß jeder Knotenrechner Nachrichten an jeden anderen senden kann. Auf die Knotenrechner des Systems muß das in CP geschriebene Programm verteilt werden.
Diese Verteilung kann man zu verschiedenen Zeitpunkten vornehmen:

- zum Zeitpunkt der Abfassung des Programms (Übersetzungszeit)
- zum Zeitpunkt des Ladens oder Bindens (Ladezeit)
- zur Laufzeit des Netzwerkprogramms

Hier befassen wir uns nur mit solchen Netzwerkprogrammen, deren Verteilung auf die Knotenrechner (Zuweisung der Zentraleinheit) schon zur Übersetzungszeit festgelegt werden kann. Dabei ist es durchaus möglich, daß weitergehende Betriebsmittelanforderungen in verschiedenen Programmabläufen von unterschiedlichen Knotenrechnern befriedigt werden. Man denke z.B. an die Ausführung eines Druckauftrages.

Der Einfachheit halber haben wir uns in unserer Implementation entschieden, die Festlegung der Verteilung der Programmkomponenten dem Programmierer zu überlassen. Die Sprache muß also so ergänzt werden, daß er die Allokation der Komponenten seines Programms in sicherer, übersichtlicher Form formulieren und variieren kann, falls die aktuelle Konfiguration der Hardware sich ändert oder eine alternative Allokation versucht werden soll.

Man kann sich vorstellen, daß für eine gegebene Anwendung ein Übersetzer
befähigt werden kann, durch Analyse der geforderten Betriebsmittel (z.B.
Gleitkommaarithmetik etc.) diese Aufgabe zu übernehmen. Ein solches
System könnte dann auch durch Variation des Allokationsschemas versuchen,
den Anteil der Interprozeßkommunikation über Rechnergrenzen hinweg zu
minimieren.

Die Bausteine eines in CP geschriebenen Programms sind die Programmkomponenten, also Prozesse, Klassen und Monitore. Ein Prozeß (PROCESS) definiert einen sequentiellen Ablauf. Einmal initialisiert, existieren
seine Zugriffsrechte und privaten Variablen für immer. Andere Programmkomponenten haben keinen Zugriff auf diese Variablen.
Ein Monitor (MONITOR) definiert gemeinsame Daten ('shared data') und
die Zugriffsoperationen auf diese (ENTRY-PROCEDURE, ENTRY-FUNCTION - im
folgenden zusammenfassend als ENTRY-Routinen bezeichnet). Einmal initialisiert, existieren diese Daten ebenfalls für immer. Andere Programmkomponenten können, falls sie explizit dieses Recht bekommen haben, mittels
der ENTRY-Routinen auf die gemeinsamen Daten im wechselseitigen Ausschluß zugreifen.
Eine Klasse (CLASS) ist eine dem Monitor ähnliche Programmkomponente,
auf die andere Programmkomponenten allerdings n i c h t simultan zugreifen können. Eine Klasse muß als permanentes Objekt innerhalb einer
Programmkomponente deklariert werden; ein Zugriffsrecht auf sie kann nur
an andere Klassen weitergegeben werden, nicht jedoch an einen Prozeß
oder Monitor. Eine Sperrsynchronisation beim Betreten der Klasse ist daher
zur Laufzeit überflüssig.
Sie werden häufig auch dazu benutzt, 'codesharing' zu ermöglichen.
2 Prozesse können dann simultan ohne Sperrsynchronisation auf das ab-
laufinvariante Codesegment zugreifen, die Daten der Klasse werden jedoch
prozeßbezogen in den Prozeßdatenbereichen der Prozesse alloziert. Auf-
rufe von ENTRY-Routinen, die ja auf diese Daten zugreifen, sind daher
wegen der nicht benötigten Sperrsynchronisation ähnlich effizient wie
die von lokalen Prozeduren einer Programmkomponente.
Die formalen Zugriffsrechte werden bei der Typendefinition festgelegt,
die aktuellen werden erst im sog. INIT-Teil des CP-Programms vergeben
(s.u.).

Kandidaten für eine Verteilung auf verschiedene Knotenrechner sind im
Prinzip alle Programmkomponenten. Eine feinere Aufteilung ist aus praktischen Gründen und auch wegen der innerhalb von Programmkomponenten
gültigen (PASCAL-ähnlichen) Sichtbarkeitsregeln von Variablen unsinnig,

wenn nicht unmöglich; abgesehen davon, daß innerhalb einer Komponente
ein sequentieller Ablauf formuliert wird. Man könnte natürlich an eine
Allokation verschiedener, parallel ausführbarer Prozeduren einer Programmkomponente auf die Knotenrechner denken. Dieser Ansatz ist hier
jedoch ausgeschlossen.
Auch erscheint es nicht sinnvoll, Klassen unabhängig von der Programmkomponente, in der sie deklariert sind, zu allozieren. Die Klasse stellt
eher eine Substruktur einer Komponente dar und ist also nach außen nicht
sichtbar.
CP erlaubt auch die Formulierung hierarchischer Prozeß-Systeme. Es
können dazu innerhalb von Prozessen weitere Prozesse und Monitore deklariert werden. Außerhalb deklarierte Prozesse können mit diesen nur
durch auf der Ebene des äußeren Prozesses liegende Monitore kommunizieren.

Nur Prozesse und Monitore - deklariert auf der Ebene des äußersten Prozesses, des INITIAL-Prozesses, können auf verschiedene Knotenrechner
verteilt werden. Alle innerhalb dieser Komponenten deklarierten Komponenten werden dann zusammen mit ihnen alloziert.

Die Aufgabe, ein Netzwerkprogramm zu übersetzen und für u.U. typ-ver-
schiedene Rechensysteme Codedateien zu erzeugen, übernimmt ein 2-stufiges
Übersetzungssystem, bestehend aus einem Rumpfcompiler, der das CP-Programm
in den Code einer hypothetischen Zwischenmaschine [3a] übersetzt. Für
jeden der betroffenen Knotenrechner wird eine entsprechende Codedatei
erzeugt, die dann von Codegeneratoren in Maschinencode übersetzt werden
kann oder auch in den Knotenrechnern interpretiert werden könnte (s.
Abb. 1).

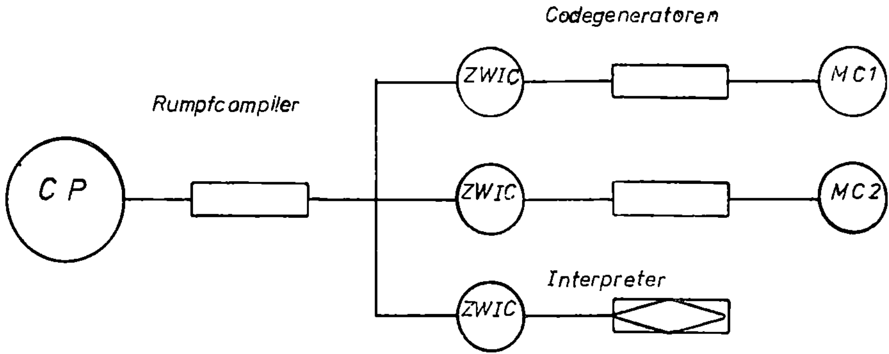

Abb. 1   Die Übersetzung eines Netzwerkprogramms

Wie kann nun der Programmierer ausdrücken, auf welchem der Knotenrechner die Programmkomponenten des CP-Programms alloziert werden sollen?
Dies kann sicher nicht so geschehen, daß etwa die Köpfe der Komponenten
so erweitert werden, daß für jede Komponente angegeben werden kann, auf
welchen Knotenrechner sie schließlich kommen soll. In diesem Fall wäre
nämlich das Gebot der leichten Rekonfigurierbarkeit des Programms in
Abhängigkeit von der aktuellen Konfiguration verletzt, müßte doch der
Programmierer Änderungen an vielen verstreuten Stellen des Programms
anbringen.

Ein CP-Programm besteht aus einem namenlosen, äußersten Prozeß, dem
INITIAL-Prozeß. Dieser ist aufgebaut aus Typendefinition, Variablenallo-
kation und einem Rumpf, dem INIT-Teil, wo die aktuellen Zugriffe definiert und die einzelnen Komponenten initialisiert werden. (s. Abb. 2)

```
< cp - programm > : --->  < block >  ---->
< block > :
        --->CONST -->......
        --->TYPE --->......
        --->VAR --->......
        --->BEGIN ---> INIT .... ---> END --->
```

Abb. 2 Auszug aus dem Syntaxdiagramm

Beim Start eines CP-Programms wird dieser Urprozeß ausgeführt, nach
Beendigung sind alle Komponenten des Systems initialisiert. Zur Initialisierung aller Komponenten eines verteilten Systems benötigen wir also
je Knotenrechner einen solchen INIT-Prozeß. Wir drücken das dadurch aus,
daß wir je Knotenrechner eine BEGIN-END Klausel (eine Blockanweisung)
mit den entsprechenden INIT-Anweisungen definieren. Die verschiedenen
Blockanweisungen können dann parallel auf den durch eine zusätzliche
START-Anweisung bezeichneten Knotenrechnern ausgeführt werden. Hier und
nur hier hat der Programmierer Änderungen vorzunehmen, wenn er sein
System in veränderter Form allozieren will.
Zur Zeit sind in diesen 'Blockanweisungen' nur einfache INIT-Anweisungen
erlaubt. Es zeigt sich jedoch, daß sowohl einfache Kontrollstrukturen
als auch strukturierte Variablen bestehend aus Programmkomponenten bei
komplexeren Systemen notwendig werden. So ist die Initialisierung einer
Anzahl gleichartiger Prozeß-Systeme für verschiedene Knotenrechner mit
Hilfe von Schleifenanweisungen denkbar oder auch die Initialisierung

eines ARRAY OF PROCESS.

Das folgende Beispiel mag unser Vorgehen erläutern:

Gegeben sei ein System bestehend aus 3 Prozessen und einem Monitor
(Abb. 3).

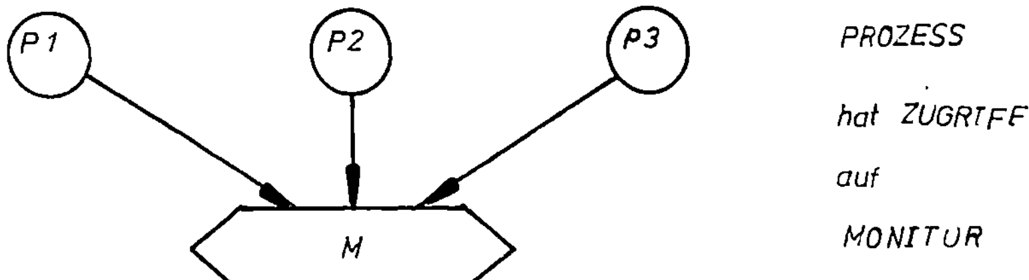

Abb. 3   Der Zugriffsgraph eines Netzwerkprogramms

Das Programm:

```
TYPE              { Typendefinition }
resource = MONITOR ;
.....
.....
reader = PROCESS( res : resource );
BEGIN....END


writer = PROCESS( res : resource );


BEGIN....END


VAR               { Inkarnationen }
m : resource ;
p1,p2 : reader ;
p3 : writer ;

                  { Initialisierung }
BEGIN
INIT m ;
INIT p1(m),p2(m),p3(m);
END .
```

Typendefinition und die Angabe, welche Objekte zu schaffen sind, sind unabhängig von der aktuellen Maschinenstruktur. Daher unterscheidet sich ein Programm für ein 2-Knotensystem (Abb. 4) nur im Initialisierungs-teil.

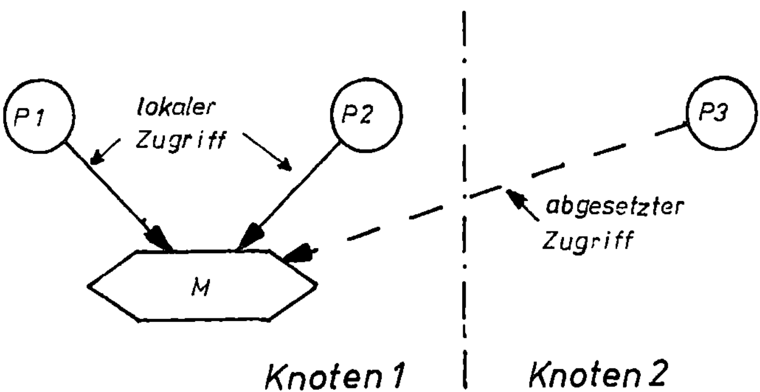

Abb. 4 Zugriffsgraph für ein 2-Knotensystem

Der erweiterte Initialisierungsteil:

```
START NODE1;
BEGIN
INIT m;
INIT p1(m),p2(m);
END;


START NODE2;
BEGIN
INIT p3(m);
END.
```

Es fällt auf, daß die Formulierung der Zugriffsrechte keine Rücksicht darauf nimmt, ob Zugriffe auf Komponenten erfolgen, die auf demselben Rechner alloziert sind oder auf einem anderen.

3.2 Realisation des Zugriffs auf abgesetzte Komponenten

Der Zugriff eines Prozesses auf einen in einem räumlich getrennten Rechner realisierten Monitor geschieht mit Hilfe eines vom Übersetzer in den Zugriffspfad eingefügten Überbrückungsmechanismus, der aus 2 Modulen besteht, einer Monitorhülle und einem Stellvertreterprozeß (Abb. 5).

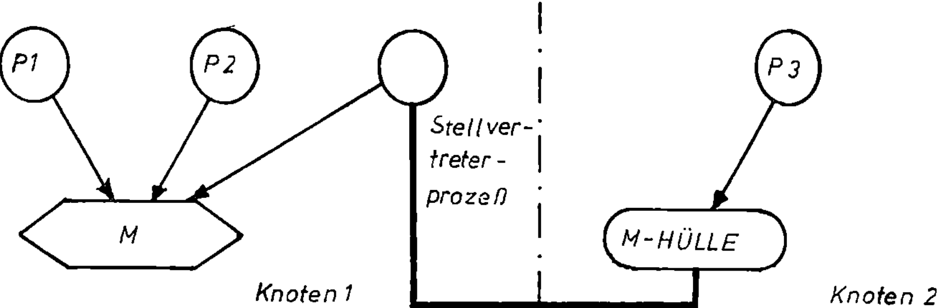

Abb. 5 Der Überbrückungsmechanismus

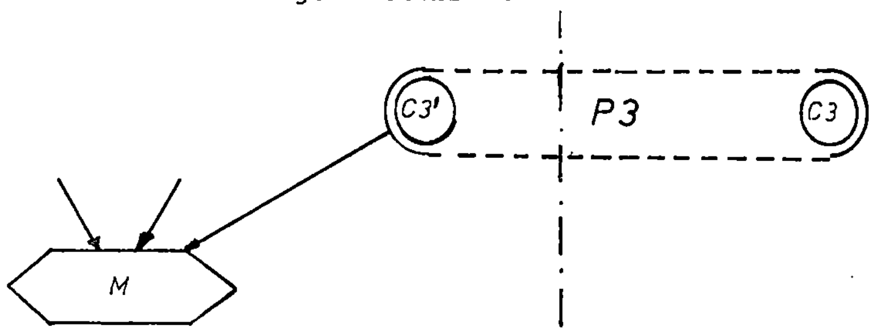

Abb. 6 Der Überbrückungsmechanismus als Koroutinenschema

Stellvertreterprozeß und Originalprozeß agieren wie Koroutinen (Abb. 6).
Bei Aufruf einer abgesetzten Monitorroutine durch den Originalprozeß
C3 wechselt die Aktivität über die Rechnergrenze hinweg zum Stellvertreterprozeß, der Koroutine C3'. Diese führt nun im Auftrage des Original-
prozesses den eigentlichen Monitorzugriff aus, in Konkurrenz mit anderen
Prozessen, die ebenfalls Zugriffsrechte auf den Monitor haben und z.B.
auf dem gleichen Knotenrechner alloziert sind. Durch dieses Verfahren
ist die Sperrsynchronisation beim Betreten des Monitors möglich. Der
Stellvertreter kann auch im Monitor verzögert werden, falls eine Bedin-
gung noch nicht eingetreten ist, da stets zu einem Stellvertreterprozeß
nur ein Originalprozeß gehört und diese als Koroutine arbeiten. Nach
Beendigung des Aufrufs wechselt die Aktivität von der Koroutine C3' zur
Koroutine C3, dem Originalprozeß.
Für jeden abgesetzten Zugriff muß solch ein Überbrückungsmechanismus
vom Übersetzer erzeugt werden, also je abgesetzten Zugriff auch eine
virtuelle Kommunikationsverbindung. Anfangs- und Endpunkt jeder Verbindung sind zur Übersetzungszeit bekannt (Abb. 7).

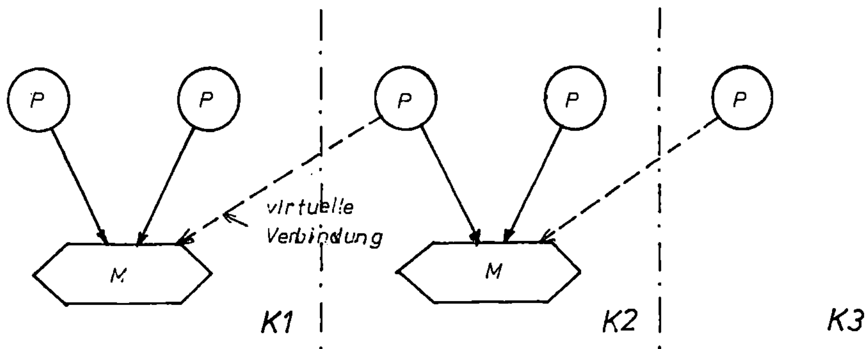

Abb. 7 Ein 3-Knotensystem mit 2 virtuellen Verbindungen

Wird bei der Programmübersetzung erkannt, daß ein abgesetzter Zugriff
vorliegt, werden für diesen Zugriffspfad Monitorhülle und Stellvertreterprozeß erzeugt. Die Monitorhülle ist ein Abbild des gerufenen Monitors. Sie besteht aus den Köpfen der ENTRY-Routinen des Monitors, zeigt
also dem Prozeß die gleiche Schnittstelle wie der Monitor. Die Aufgabe
der Hülle ist es, den Aufruf einer abgesetzten Monitorroutine in den
einer Koroutine, des Stellvertreterprozesses umzusetzen. Sie bedient
sich dabei der Dienste des Kommunikationssystems, um die folgende Nachricht zu versenden:

- Identifikation des Stellvertreterprozesses
- Name des gewünschten Monitors
- Name der gewünschten Monitor-Routine
- alle Eingabeparameter.

Ein Vermittlungsprozeß empfängt am Orte des Stellvertreterprozesses der-
artige, von den verschiedenen Knotenrechnern eintreffende Nachrichten,
genauer ihre Köpfe, d.h. die Identifikationen der gewünschten Stellver-
treterprozesse, und vermittelt dem Adressaten den Zugriff auf das Kommunikationssystem, damit dieser den Rest der Nachricht empfangen kann
[5]. (Dieses geschieht mit Hilfe eines Sprachkonstruktes, um das wir
CP erweitert haben. Mit Hilfe einer derartigen, monitorähnlichen Programmkomponente, MANAGER genannt [9], ist es möglich, optionale Zugriffsrechte (capabilities) von Programmkomponenten auf Klassen und Monitore
zur Laufzeit in reale Zugriffsrechte umzuwandeln.)
Der Stellvertreterprozeß führt nun, wie schon erwähnt, den eigentlichen
Zugriff aus.
Nach Verlassen der Monitorroutine wird vom Stellvertreterprozeß eine

Nachricht zusammengestellt, die die Identifikation der Monitorhülle
und alle Ausgabeparameter der aufgerufenen Monitorroutine enthält. Sind
keine Ergebnisse zu übertragen, besteht die Nachricht nur aus der Identifikation. Diese Nachricht wird über das Kommunikationssystem an den
Knotenrechner gesendet, in dem die zugehörige Monitorhülle alloziert
ist, vom dortigen Vermittlungsprozeß empfangen und weitergegeben. Der
Originalprozeß wird wieder aktiviert, da der abgesetzte Zugriff beendet
ist.

Unsichtbar für den Programmierer wird also durch den Überbrückungsmechanismus die (benutzerorientierte) prozedurale Technik der Interprozeß-
kommunikation (s. Abschn. 2.2) umgesetzt in eine nachrichtenorientierte,
die mehr Rücksicht auf die technischen Gegebenheiten eines Kommunikationssystems nimmt. Bis auf die Tatsache, daß ein Monitoraufruf über
Rechnergrenzen eine komplexe Operation ist und mehr Zeit in Anspruch
nimmt, existiert kein Unterschied zwischen dem Aufruf einer lokalen
Monitorroutine oder einer abgesetzten. Auch Leitungszusammenbrüche führen
nicht zu einer unsicheren Situation, da das Betreten des Testabschnittes
zur Prüfung, ob der Monitor frei ist, erst nach Übertragung der gesamten
Nachricht erfolgt.

Der Überbrückungsmechanismus wurde zunächst selbst in CP formuliert und
getestet. Inzwischen wird dieser Mechanismus vom Übersetzer automatisch
eingefügt.

Der Übersetzer erzeugt also schließlich in unserem Beispiel zwei Codesequenzen, eine für Knotenrechner NODE1 bestehend aus den Codesequenzen
zweier Prozesse, eines Monitors und eines Stellvertreterprozesses, eine
für Knoten NODE2 bestehend aus den Codesequenzen eines Prozesses und
einer Monitorhülle.

3.3 Die Schnittstellen zu lokalen und verteilten Betriebssystemdiensten

Bisher haben wir nur die Kommunikation zwischen Anwendungsprozessen betrachtet. Diese Prozesse haben jedoch i.a. auch Bedarf an anderen Betriebsmitteln, z.B. einem Dateizugriff. Auch hier muß das Prinzip gel-
ten, daß alle Zugriffe auf Objekte, also auch auf Betriebsmittel wie
Dateien, unabhängig von der aktuellen Realisation spezifiziert werden
können. Diese Aufgabe übernimmt das Netzbetriebssystem der Netzwerk-

maschine. Dieses Betriebssystem ist selbst wieder ein System kooperierender Prozesse, die teilweise über Rechnergrenzen kommunizieren müssen, um globale Steuerungsaufgaben übernehmen zu können. Daneben sind aber auch die Aufgaben einer lokalen Betriebsmittelverwaltung und Gerätesteuerung zu erfüllen. Erschwerend für die praktische Implementation kommt hinzu, daß i.a. verteilte Systeme auf vorhandenen Betriebssystemen aufbauen. So basiert z.B. unsere Implementation an der DEC10 auf dem Betriebssystem TOPS10.
Für die in CP geschriebenen Programme muß daher eine einheitliche Schnittstelle zu den Betriebssystemdiensten geschaffen werden.
CP bietet als Schnittstelle zur Laufzeitunterstützung und damit zu den Betriebssystemdiensten die Standardprozedur IO an:

IO(v,e,d)

Dabei bezeichnet v eine (mit allen Typen verträgliche) Ein-/Ausgabevariable (z.B. einen Puffer), e ist eine Datenstruktur, die genauere Steuerinformationen für das angesprochene Gerät d enthält.

Aus der Sicht des Anwendungsprogrammierers ist jedoch diese Universalschnittstelle zu wenig komfortabel und zu unsicher. Die 'natürliche' Schnittstelle zu Betriebssystemdiensten ist die ENTRY-Prozedur einer Systemkomponente. So sind die ENTRY-Routinen von Systemprozessen die Schnittstellen zwischen 'PROGRAMs' (geschrieben in PASCAL) und den Betriebssystemprozessen [2]. Unsere Anwendungsprogramme sind jedoch selbst Prozeß-Systeme. Es ist daher notwendig, Schnittstellen zwischen 2 Prozeß-Systemen zu definieren. Prozesse kommunizieren durch Aufruf geeigneter Monitorprozeduren miteinander. Folgerichtig sind diese Routinen die Schnittstellen zwischen Betriebssystem und Anwendungssystem (Abb. 8).

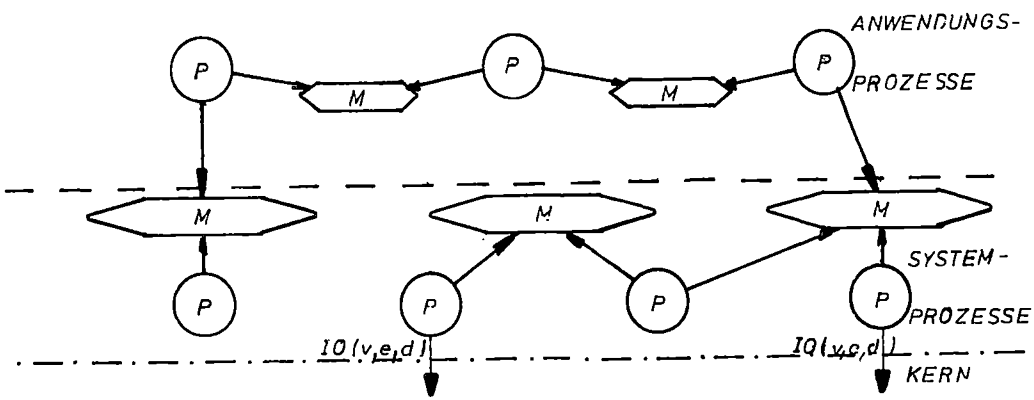

Abb. 8 Schnittstellen

Das Betriebssystem exportiert also Zugriffsrechte auf Monitore, das
Anwenderprozeß-System importiert diese. Werden die exportierten bzw.
importierten Rechte in Form von Deklarationen formuliert, kann der Übersetzer überprüfen, ob erlaubte Zugriffsrechte ausgeübt werden. Man denke z.B. an die Auflistung aller Rechte in einer USED- und einer DEFINED-
Liste in MODULA [13]. Dieses EXTERNAL-Konzept ist dem des 'programinterface' zwischen SEQUENTIAL und CONCURRENT PASCAL Programmen ver-
wandt [2]. Die praktische Realisation wird z.Z. diskutiert. Dieser Mechanismus soll einen geschichteten Aufbau von in CP geschriebenen Prozeß-Systemen aus verschiedenen getrennt übersetzten Teilen ermöglichen
(ein auch für die Programmierung von Einzelsystemen nützliches Instru-
ment).

Mit Hilfe des EXTERNAL-Konzeptes kann nun eine Schicht von Prozessen
und Monitoren geschaffen werden, deren Aufgabe es ist, die verschiedenartigen Schnittstellen zu den lokalen Betriebssystemen und dem 'transport service' in einheitliche Schnittstellen zu den Systemdiensten zu
transformieren, die unabhängig von der aktuellen Realisation sind.
Eine weitere Aufgabe dieser Schicht ist, die netzweit angebotenen Betriebsmittel zu verwalten.

3.4 Zusammenfassung

Das folgende Bild (Abb. 9) zeigt die verschiedenen Ebenen der in diesem Konzept verwirklichten Kommunikationsarchitektur, die Hierarchie
der Protokolle und die Schichten der beiden Konzepte, der Netzwerkmaschine und des ISO-Referenz-Modells.

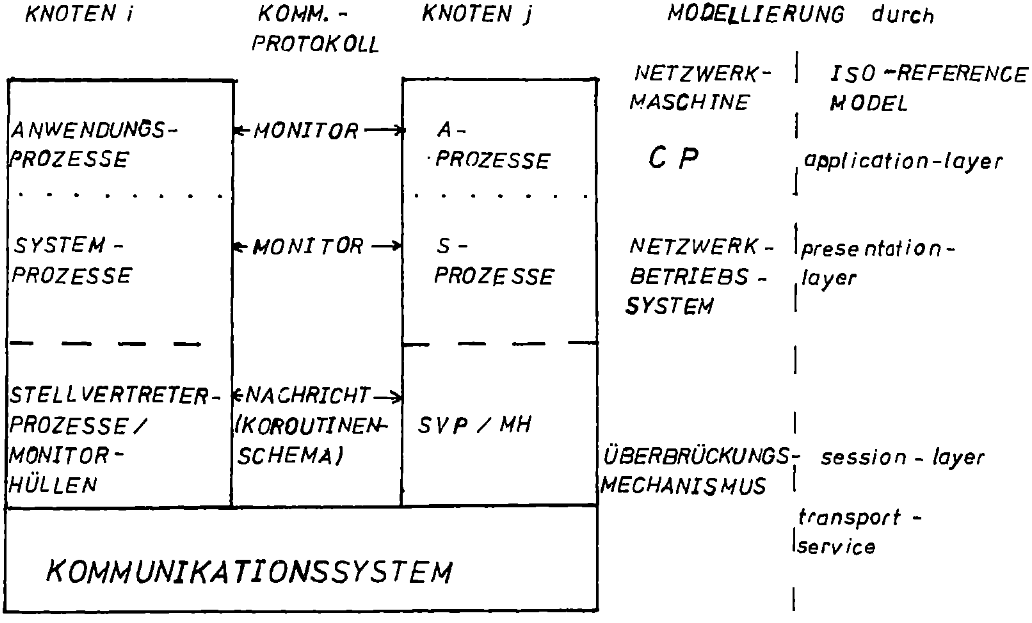

Abb. 9 Modellierung verteilter Systeme

Als Basisschicht des Modells sehen wir das Kommunikationssystem. Das
ISO-Modell gliedert diese Ebene noch feiner auf, hier soll jedoch nur
die oberste Ebene, 'transport layer' aufgeführt werden.

Die Module der nächsten Schicht (Stellvertreterprozeß und Monitorhülle)
bilden den Überbrückungsmechanismus. Sie bedienen sich dabei der Dienste
des 'transport service'. In dieser Schicht ist ebenfalls die Aufgabe
des Auf- und Abbaus von Verbindungen zwischen Monitorhüllen und Stell-
vertreterprozessen anzusiedeln. Diese Funktion wird sowohl beim Aufbau
des Netzbetriebssystems als auch zum Start und zur Beendigung von Anwenderprozessen benötigt. Die Aufgaben der 'session layer' des ISO-
Modells sind in [6] mit Unterstützung der Interaktion zwischen kooperierenden Objekten umschrieben. Zu diesem Zweck werden 2 Arten von
Diensten benötigt:
(a) Auf- und Abbau von Verbindungen
(session-administration-service)
(b) Datenaustausch und Synchronisation der kooperierenden Objekte
(session-data-transfer-service)

Die 2. Kategorie von Aufgaben dieser Ebene entspricht dem Überbrückungs-

mechanismus. Die erste Aufgabe reduziert sich in unserem Fall auf das
Laden und Starten von CP-Programmen. Die für den Überbrückungsmechanis-
mus benötigten Module sind in den Compilaten enthalten. Existiert ein
Netzbetriebssystem, so übernimmt dieses die Aufgabe, Anwenderprozeß-
Systeme zu laden und zu starten.

Die Aufgabe der 'presentation layer' des ISO-Modells ist,eine Reihe von
Diensten den Anwenderprozessen anzubieten, die es ihnen erlauben, die
Betriebsmittel des verteilten Systems zu benutzen. Beispiele sind etwa
der Dienst des 'virtual terminal service' oder des 'virtual file store'.
Auch diese Aufgabe übernimmt das Netzbetriebssystem der Netzwerkmaschine.
Die kooperierenden Systemprozesse bedienen sich dabei wieder des Über-
brückungsmechanismus. Zusätzliche Funktionen des Netzbetriebssystems
sind die lokalen Betriebssystemdienste (z.B. die Gerätebedienung). Auf
der Anwendungsebene ist dadurch schließlich eine große Flexibilität und
Unabhängigkeit von der aktuellen Konfiguration erreicht.

4. Stand der Implementation und Erfahrungen

4.1 Die Konfiguration

Die z.Z. verfügbare Konfiguration besteht aus 5 Kleinrechnern (DIETZ
Mincal 621x2 und 621/8), die teilweise die Spezialperipherie der For-
schungsgruppe betreiben (Ziel: Analyse von Fernseh-Bildfolgen). Zwei
der Kleinrechner sind über eine PDP11/20 an den Zentralrechner des Fach-
bereichs, ein   DECSystem10, gekoppelt. Das Ziel ist, Vorverarbeitungs-
algorithmen auf den Kleinrechnern z.T. parallel auszuführen, um nur
stark reduzierte Datenmengen auf dem Zentralrechner bearbeiten zu müssen.

4.2 Stand der Implementation

Für alle beteiligten Rechner stehen uns sowohl PASCAL- als auch CP-
Compiler zur Verfügung. Da das DEC10-System im Teilnehmerbetrieb betrieben wird, kann ein CP-Programm hier nur als Benutzerauftrag ausgeführt werden [3b]. Der Rumpfcompiler erzeugt Code für eine hypothetische,

byteorientierte (!) Zwischenmaschine (der DIETZ-Rechner ist ein Byterechner), so daß auf der DEC10 eine Bytemaschine simuliert werden muß. Das befreit uns jedoch von Problemen, die mit der unterschiedlichen Representation der Datentypen auf den verschiedenen Rechensystemen zusammenhängen. Da eine solche Simulation nicht gerade effizient ist, ist ein Neuentwurf auf der Basis der bisherigen Erfahrungen geplant. Insbesondere ist die jetzige Implementation wenig zur Implementation des PROGRAM-Konzeptes [2] auf der DEC10 geeignet. Das 'programinterface' zum Anschluß von SEQUENTIAL PASCAL Programmen an CP-Prozesse ist auch auf den Kleinrechnern nur sehr eingeschränkt implementiert. Die Erweiterung ist jedoch geplant.

Wir können z.Z. Netzwerkprogramme in CP formulieren, der Übersetzer erzeugt den Überbrückungsmechanismus und die notwendigen Codesequenzen automatisch.
Die Teilsysteme, die auf den verschiedenen Rechnern laufen sollen, müssen allerdings noch getrennt mit Hilfe der lokalen Betriebssysteme geladen und gestartet werden. Die oben erwähnte Aufgabe der 'session control', Verbindungen auf- und abzubauen, ist also noch nicht implementiert.

4.3 Erfahrungen im Umgang mit CONCURRENT PASCAL

Zunächst sind die CP-Compiler nur zur Entwicklung von Programmen für die Einzelsysteme benutzt worden. So wurde der Compiler, der Code für das DECSystem 10 erzeugt, für studentische Übungen eingesetzt, der Compiler für den Kleinrechner zur Entwicklung von Systemsoftware. Vorhandene in Assembler geschriebene Programme wurden in CP von Studenten neu geschrieben und ihre Leistungsfähigkeit verglichen. Ein quantitativer Vergleich ist allerdings kaum möglich, da die in der höheren Programmiersprache geschriebenen Systemprogramme wesentlich komfortablere Benutzerschnittstellen hatten, wodurch schon der Speicherplatzbedarf anstieg. Die teilweise beobachtete Laufzeitvergrößerung hatte ihre Hauptursache in der Tatsache, daß bei der Weitergabe von Daten von einem Prozeß zum anderen wegen des Monitorkonzeptes zusätzliche Kopiervorgänge nötig sind, es können ja nicht wie in den Assemblerprogrammen die Adressen etwa von Puffern weitergegeben werden. War auch Speicherplatzbedarf und Laufzeitvergrößerung teilweise beträchtlich, so zeigte sich jedoch ein Nettogewinn dadurch, daß Entwicklungs- und Implementationszeit merklich

kürzer waren. Als Hauptproblem dieser Implementation stellt sich der
Speicherplatzbedarf der CP-Programme heraus. Dieses ist jedoch ver-
ständlich, wenn man sich vor Augen führt, daß keinerlei Anstrengungen
zur Optimierung des Codes gemacht werden. In dieser Implementation
liegt das Schwergewicht auf dem Nachweis der Realisierbarkeit des Ansatzes der virtuellen Netzwerkmaschine auf der Basis von CP, so daß es
gerechtfertigt erschien, die Codeoptimierung als nachrangig zu behandeln.
Eine vernünftige Lösung könnte sein, Interpretation einer geeigneten
Zwischensprache und Erzeugung von Targetcode zu mischen, um Speicherplatzbedarf und Laufzeit zu optimieren.

Auch bei der Entwicklung der ersten verteilten Programme zeigte sich
wieder der positive Einfluß der Sprache auf den Entwicklungsaufwand.
Die prinzipielle Unabhängigkeit der Formulierung der Programme von der
aktuellen Konfiguration erlaubt es, Programme zum Beispiel auf dem
DEC10 System zu entwickeln und zu testen. Im gegebenen Augenblick wird
die Allokation umformuliert, um das Programm auf mehrere Knotenrechner
zu verteilen. Die daraus entstehenden verteilten Programme sind meistens
auf Anhieb lauffähig. Fehler, die erst in dieser Phase auftraten, waren
häufig durch Compiler- oder Codegeneratorfehler verursacht. Fehler im
Synchronisationsschema der Prozesse traten selten auf.

Auch zeigt die bisherige Erfahrung, daß CP-Programme recht schnell
auch von solchen Programmierern formuliert werden können, die nicht mit
der Sprache vertraut sind. So konnte an der Entwicklung eines Kontroll-
programms für ein graphisches Sichtgerät die "Eroberung" der Sprache
durch den Entwickler des Systems beobachtet werden. Das Kontrollprogramm
bestand anfangs nur aus einem großen Prozeß, bezeichnenderweise MAIN
genannt. Zunehmend traten zur besseren Modularisierung Klassen hinzu,
bis schließlich neue und alte Aufgaben des 'sequentiellen' CONCURRENT
PASCAL Programms durch mehrere kooperierende Prozesse formuliert wurden.
Der nächste Schritt, ein solches Mehrprozeß-System auf mehrere Knotenrechner zu verteilen, ist dann leicht getan.

4.4 Entwicklung verteilter Betriebssysteme

Bislang müssen CP-Programme ohne Unterstützung eines Netzwerkbetriebs-
systems geladen und gestartet werden. In [5] wird ein Betriebssystem
entwickelt, dessen Aufgabe es ist, mehreren Benutzern die Betriebsmittel

des Netzes zugänglich zu machen. Als Programmiersprache für dieses verteilte Betriebssystem wird das erweiterte CP benutzt.

Die Anwender werden in die Lage versetzt, ein oder mehrere sequentielle Programme zu laden und zu starten. Die sequentiellen Programme eines Benutzers können dabei über vom Netzbetriebssystem angebotene Kommunikationswege Nachrichten austauschen. Z.Z. ist es also nicht geplant, mit Hilfe dieses Betriebssystems auch Anwenderprozeß-Systeme zu laden und zu starten. Die derzeitige Lösung sieht als Benutzerschnittstelle des Betriebssystems das 'programinterface' vor. Ein nächster Schritt wird sein - nach Implementation des EXTERNAL-Konzeptes - auch Prozeß-Systeme zu laden.

4.5 Weitere Entwicklungen

Die Formulierung von Betriebssystemdiensten in CP deckt im Zusammenhang mit verteilten Systemen bestimmte Schwächen der statischen Definition eines Prozeß-Systems auf. Besonders wenn man an die Möglichkeit denkt, daß einzelne Knotenrechner des Systems zeitweise ausfallen können. Die Erweiterung der Sprache um Konzepte, die die dynamische Verwaltung von Betriebsmitteln erleichtert, ist daher geplant. Als Vorbereitung haben wir, wie schon erwähnt, das Managerkonzept [9] implementiert, das die Verwaltung von 'capabilities', optionalen Zugriffsrechten, die erst zur Laufzeit in aktuelle Rechte umgewandelt werden, gestattet.

Daneben ist daran gedacht, auf der Basis von CP eine Kommandosprache für unser Netz zu entwickeln. Diese Sprache soll es ermöglichen, von einem Terminal aus interaktiv Prozesse und Monitore zu verteilen, sie mit aktuellen Zugriffsrechten zu versehen und zu starten.

5. Literatur

[1] P. Brinch Hansen, The Programming Language
CONCURRENT PASCAL,
IEEE Trans. on Software Engineering 1 (1975), pp. 199-207

[2] P. Brinch Hansen, The Solo Operating System -
A Concurrent Pascal Program.
Software-Practice & Experience 6 (1976), pp. 141-149

[3a] B. Brügge, B. Gisch, T. Kahl, H. Linde,
Ma. Mittelstein, H. Westphal,
CONCURRENT PASCAL Compiler für Kleinrechner,
Institut für Informatik, Universität Hamburg
IfI-HH-B-30/76 (Dec. 76)

[3b] B. Brügge, B. Linde, H. Linde, Ma. Mittelstein,
P. Rubarth, C. Ruhe, H. Westphal,
COPANET - CONCURRENT PASCAL Netzwerkmaschine,
Fachbereich Informatik, Universität Hamburg,
Diplomarbeit (1978)

[4] J.A. Feldman, High Level Programming for
Distributed Computing,
CACM 22,6, pp. 353-369 (June 1979)

[5] V. Haarslev, P. Subel, A. Urbahn,
Entwurf und Implementation eines verteilten Betriebssystems,
Fachbereich Informatik,Universität Hamburg,
Diplomarbeit in Vorbereitung (1979)

[6] Reference Model of Open Systems Architecture,
ISO/TC97/SC16 Version 3 (Nov. 1978)

R. desJardin , G. White, ANSI reference model for
distributed systems;
Ch. Bachman, M. Canepa, The session control layer of an
open system interconnection,
Proc. IEEE COMPCON Fall 78, Wash. D.C., pp. 144-156 (1978)

[7] A.K. Jones, R.J. Chambler, I. Durham, P. Feiler, K. Schwans,
Software Management of Cm* - A Distributed Multiprocessor,
AFIPS Conf. Proc. NCC vol. 46 (1977), pp. 657-663

[8] H. Kemen, H.-H. Nagel, Konzept einer virtuellen
Netzwerk-Maschine auf der Basis von CONCURRENT PASCAL,
Kurzvortrag auf der Jahrestagung 1977 der Gesellschaft für
Informatik, Nürnberg, Sept. 77, p. 82
- -, Experiences with a Virtual Network Machine Concept for an
Inhomgeneous Local Computer Network, Proc. IEEE COMPCON Fall
78, Wash, D.C. pp. 280-286 (1978)

[9] R.B. Kieburtz and A. Silberschatz, Capability Managers,
IEEE Trans. Softw. Eng. SE-4, pp. 467-477 (1978)

[10] H.C. Lauer and R.M. Needham, On the Duality of
Operating Systems Structures, Proc. Second Int. Symp. on
Operating Systems,
IRIA, Oct. 1978 repr. in SIGOPS, 13, 2, pp. 3-19 (1979)

[11] J. Staunstrup, A Comparison of Monitors and Message
passing,
Comp. Sci. Dep. Aarhus University, DAIMI PB-92 (1978)

[12] H. Steusloff, Zur Programmierung von räumlich
verteilten, dezentralen Prozeßrechensystemen, Dissertation,
Fakultät für Informatik der Universität (TH) Karlsruhe,
(Feb. 1977)

[13] N. Wirth, MODULA: A Programming Language for Modular
Programming,
Software-Practice & Experience 7,1, pp. 3-35 (1977)

Lecture Notes in Computer Science